RELIGIOUS COMPETITION
IN THE GRECO-ROMAN WORLD

WRITINGS FROM THE GRECO-ROMAN WORLD
SUPPLEMENT SERIES

Clare K. Rothschild, General Editor

Number 10

RELIGIOUS COMPETITION IN THE GRECO-ROMAN WORLD

Edited by
Nathaniel P. DesRosiers and Lily C. Vuong

SBL PRESS

Atlanta

Copyright © 2016 by SBL Press

All rights reserved. No part of this work may be reproduced or transmitted in any form or by any means, electronic or mechanical, including photocopying and recording, or by means of any information storage or retrieval system, except as may be expressly permitted by the 1976 Copyright Act or in writing from the publisher. Requests for permission should be addressed in writing to the Rights and Permissions Office, SBL Press, 825 Houston Mill Road, Atlanta, GA 30329 USA.

Library of Congress Cataloging-in-Publication Data

Names: DesRosiers, Nathaniel, editor.
Title: Religious competition in the Greco-Roman world / edited by Nathaniel P. DesRosiers and Lily C. Vuong.
Description: Atlanta : SBL Press, 2016. | Series: Society of Biblical Literature. Writings from the Greco-Roman world Supplement series ; Number 10 | Includes bibliographical references and index.
Identifiers: LCCN 2016012119 (print) | LCCN 2016015874 (ebook) | ISBN 9781628371369 (pbk. : alk. paper) | ISBN 9780884141587 (hardcover : alk. paper) | ISBN 9780884141570 (e-book)
Subjects: LCSH: Christianity and other religions. | Christianity and other religions--Roman--History. | Christianity and other religions—Greek—History. | Church history—Primitive and early church, ca. 30–600 . | Rome—Religion—History. | Greece—Religion—History.
Classification: LCC BR127 .R448 2016 (print) | LCC BR127 (ebook) | DDC 200.938—dc23
LC record available at https://lccn.loc.gov/2016012119

Printed on acid-free paper.

Contents

Acknowledgments ix
Abbreviations xi

Introduction: Conflict, Cooperation, and Competition in Antiquity
    Nathaniel P. DesRosiers and Lily C. Vuong 1

Part 1: Competition and Material Culture

Introduction: Competition and Material Culture through Real
and Imagined Spaces
    Gregg E. Gardner 11

The Perils of Idolatrous Garb: Tertullian and Christian Belonging in
Roman Carthage
    Carly Daniel-Hughes 15

The Philosopher Type in Late Roman Art: Problematizing Cultural
Appropriation in Light of Cultural Competition
    Arthur P. Urbano Jr. 27

Suns, Snakes, and Altars: Competitive Imagery in Constantinian
Numismatics
    Nathaniel P. DesRosiers 41

"Built from the Plunder of Christians": Words, Places, and Competing
Powers in Milan and Callinicum
    Catherine M. Chin 63

Part 2: Competition and Neoplatonism

Introduction: Defining Competition in Neoplatonism
    Todd Krulak 79

Origen's Allegoresis of Plato's and Scripture's "Myths"
    Ilaria L. E. Ramelli 85

The Neoplatonic Transmission of Ancient Wisdom
    Gregory Shaw 107

Julian's Philosophy and His Religious Program
    Laura B. Dingeldein 119

Part 3: Religious Experts and Popular Religion

Introduction: Competition Between Experts and Nonexperts
    Daniel Ullucci 133

Why Expert versus Nonexpert Is Not Elite versus Popular Religion: The Case of the Third Century
    Stanley K. Stowers 139

Great Is the Mystery of Piety: Contested Claims to Piety in Plutarch, Philo, and 1 Timothy
    T. Christopher Hoklotubbe 155

Nuptial Imagery, Christian Devotion, and the Marriage Debate in Late Roman Society
    Karl Shuve 167

Competing for the Competitors: Jewish and Christian Responses to Spectacle
    Loren R. Spielman 179

CONTENTS

Part 4: Competition and Relics

Introduction: The Competition for Relics in Late Antiquity
   Susan Ashbrook Harvey 199

Relics? What Relics?
   Mary Joan Winn Leith and Allyson Everingham Sheckler 205

A Hair's Breadth: The Prophet Muhammad's Hair as Relic in Early Islamic Texts
   Adam Bursi 219

Promoting a Cult Site without Bodily Relics: Sacred Substances and Imagined Topography in *The Syriac Life of Symeon the Stylite*
   Dina Boero 233

From Asclepius to Simeon: Votives and Sacred Healing in Late Antiquity
   Gary Vikan 247

Bibliography 259
Contributors 293
Ancient Sources Index 299
Modern Authors Index 309
Subject Index 315

Acknowledgments

In so many ways, the contributions in this volume exemplify the goals and vision of the Religious Competition in Late Antiquity unit of the Society of Biblical Literature, from which these papers are derived. We are incredibly grateful to the contributors for their hard work in producing excellent papers and thoughtful, diverse reflections on the theme of religious competition in late antiquity. The exciting challenge of bringing together essays from such different fields of study produced new and meaningful discussions on the ancient world as the result of such interactions. This endeavor would not have been possible without the input of all those who supported the group and functioned as critical interlocutors. We are especially thankful to Michael Satlow, Ross Kraemer, Heidi Marx-Wolf, Saul Olyan, Jordan Rosenblum, Debra Ballentine, Steve Larson, Ari Finkelstein, Andrew McGowan, Karen Stern, Mira Balberg, Kevin McGinnis, Jacob Latham, and Gil Klein, who have contributed much to the discussion and framing of the volume.

Many thanks go to Ron Hock, whose careful eye read the entire work and whose expertise and insights helped to tighten arguments and improve the overall volume, and to Clare Rothschild, the current series editor, who read the final product. We are also grateful to Nicole Tilford and the staff at SBL Press, who skillfully oversaw the final production.

Finally, we thank our families and friends who continue to provide us with love, support, and, of course, patience.

Nathaniel P. DesRosiers, Massachusetts, 2016
Lily C. Vuong, Washington, 2016

Abbreviations

Primary Sources

'Abod. Zar.	Avodah Zarah
Act. Scil.	Acts of the Scillitan Martyrs
Acts John	Acts of John
Aen.	Vergil, *Aeneid*
Agr.	Tacitus, *Agricola*
Apol.	Pamphilius, *Apology*; Tertullian, *Apology*
Autol.	Theophilus, *Ad Autolycum*
b.	Babylonian Talmud
Bek.	Bekhorot
Ber.	Berakhot
Bibl.	Photius, *Bibliotheca*
C. Ap.	Josephus, *Contra Apionem*
Cels.	Origen, *Contra Celsum*
Cher.	Philo, *De cherubim*
C. Jul. op. imp.	Augustine, *Contra secundan Juliani responsionem imperfectum opus*
Comm. Alc.	Proclus, *Commentary on First Alcibiades*
Comm. Cant.	Origen, *Commentarius in Canticum*
Comm. Jo.	Origen, *Commentarii in evangelium Joannis*
Comm. Ps.	Origen, *Commentarius in Psalmos* (Pamphilus, *Apol.* 157: Origen's lost commentary on Ps 6)
Comm. Tim.	Proclus, *Commentary on the Timaeus*
Comp.	Dionysius of Halicarnassus, *De compositione verborum*
Cor.	Tertullian, *The Crown*
Corp. herm.	Corpus hermeticum
Crat.	Plato, *Cratylus*
Cult. fem.	Tertullian, *De cultu feminarum*

Decal.	Philo, *De decalogo*
Decr.	Athanasius, *De decretis*
De or.	Cicero, *De oratore*
Diatr.	Epictetus, *Diatribai (Dissertationes)*
Doct. chr.	Augustine, *De doctrina christiana*
Ecl. proph.	Eusebius, *Eclogae propheticae*
Enn.	Plotinus, *Enneades*
Ep.	*Epistula(e)*
Ep. extr. coll.	Ambrose, *Ep. extra collectionem*
Ep. Greg.	Origen, *Epistula ad Gregorium Thaumaturgum*
Epist.	Jerome, *Epistulae*
Epit.	Lactantius, *Epitome divinarum institutionum*
Fr. Gen.	Origen, *Fragmenta in Genesim*
Fug.	Lucian, *Fugitivi*
Gorg.	Plato, *Gorgias*
Haer.	Irenaeus, *Against Heries*
Hell. Ther.	Theodoret of Cyrrus, *Hellenikon Therapeutike Pathematon (Cure for Greek Maladies)*
Hist.	Tacitus, *Historiae*
Hist. Aug. Vopisc. Tac.	Historia Augusta: Vospiscus, Tacitus
Hist. eccl.	Eusebius, *Historia ecclesiastica*; Evagrius Scholasticus, *Historia ecclesiastica*; Galasius, *Historia ecclesiastica*; Socrates Scholasticus, *Historia ecclesiastica*
Hom. Ezech.	Origen, *Homiliae in Ezechielem*
Hom. Gen.	Origen, *Homiliae in Genesim*
Hom. Jer.	Origen, *Homiliae in Jeremiam*
Hom. Ps.	Origen, *Homiliae in Psalmos*
Idol.	Tertullian, *Idolatry*
Inst.	Quintilian, *Institutio oratoria*
Isaac	Ambrose, *De Isaac vel anima*
Is. Os.	Plutarch, *De Iside et Osiride*
Jov.	Jerome, *Adversus Jovinianum libri II*
L. Daniel Styl.	Life of Daniel Stylites
L. Simeon Styl. Eld.	Life of Simeon Stylites the Elder
L. Simeon Young.	Life of Simeon the Younger
Leg.	Athenagoras, *Legatio pro Christianis*
Lives	Diogenes Laertius, *De clarorum philosophorum vitis*

ABBREVIATIONS

m.	Mishnah
Mart.	Origen, *Exhortatio ad martyrium*
Mart. Perp.	Martyrdom of Perpetua
Migr.	Philo, *De migratione Abrahami*
Mir. Art.	Miracles of Artemios
Mir. Cos. Dam.	Miracles of Cosmas and Damian
Mir. Cyr. John	Sophronius, *Miracles of Cyrus and John*
Mir. Dem.	Miracles of Demetrius
Mir. Thec.	Miracles of Thecla
Mort.	Lactantius, *De mortibus persecutorum*
Mos.	Philo, *De vita Mosis*
Myst.	Iamblichus, *De mysteriis*
Nat.	Tertullian, *Ad nationes*
Nigr.	Lucian, *Nigrinus*
Ob. Theo.	Ambrose, *De obitu Theodosii*
Oct.	Minucius Felix, *Octavius*
Onir.	Artemidorus Daldianus, *Onirocritica*
Or.	Julian, *Orations*; Libanius, *Orations*
Or. Graec.	Tatian, *Oratio ad Graecos (Pros Hellēnas)*
Pall.	Tertullian, *The Pallium*
Pan.	Epiphanius, *Panarion (Adversus haereses)*
Pan.	Pliny the Younger, *Panegyricus*
Phaed.	Plato, *Phaedo*
Phaedr.	Plato, *Phaedrus*
Phaedr. Schol.	Hermias, *Scholion on Phaedrus*
Phil. hist.	Theodoret of Syria, *Historia Philothée/Historia Religiosa (History of the Monks of Syria)*
Praem.	Philo, *De praemiis et poenis*
Praep. ev.	Eusebius, *Praep. evangelica*
Princ.	Damascius, *De principiis*; Origen, *De principiis (Peri Archōn)*
Res gest.	Ammianus Marcellinus, *Res gestae*
Resp.	Plato, *Republic*
Šabb.	Shabbat
Sel. Num.	Origen, *Selecta in Numeros*
Spec.	Philo, *De specialibus legibus*
Spect.	Tertullian, *De spectaculis*
S.T.	Aelius Aristides, *Sacred Tales*
Stoic. rep.	Plutarch, *De Stoicorum repugnantiis*

Strom.	Clement of Alexandria, *Stromateis*
Superst.	Plutarch, *De superstitione*
Symp.	Plato, *Symposium*
t.	Tosefta
Theaet.	Plato, *Theaetetus*
Theatr.	John Chrysostom, *Contra ludos et theatra*
Theo. Plat.	Proclus, *Theology of Plato*
Tim.	Plato, *Timaeus*
Tranq. an.	Plutarch, *De tranquillitate animi*
Virg.	Ambrose, *De virginibus*; Tertullian, *De virginibus velandis*
Virginit.	Ambrose, *De virginitate*
Virt. prof.	Plutarch, *Quomodo quis suos in virtue sentiat profectus*
Vit. Const.	Eusebius, *Vita Constantini*
Vit. Hil.	Jerome, *Vita S. Hilarionis eremitae*
Vit. Mos.	Gregory of Nyssa, *De vita Mosis*
Vit. phil.	Diogenes Laertius, *Vitae philosophorum*
Vit. Plot.	Porphyry, *Vita Plotini*
y.	Jerusalem Talmud

Secondary Sources

AAAHP	*Acta ad archaeologiam et artium historiam pertinentia*
ABull	*The Art Bulletin*
ACW	Ancient Christian Writers
AIRF	*Acta Instituti Romani Finlandiae*
AJP	*American Journal of Philology*
ANF	*The Ante-Nicene Fathers: Translations of the Writings of the Fathers Down to A.D. 325*. Edinburgh: T&T Clark; Grand Rapids, Eerdmans, 2001.
ANost	*Auctores Nostri: Studi e testi di letteratura cristiana antica*
ANRW	*Aufstieg und Niedergang der römischen Welt: Geschichte und Kultur Roms in Spiegel der neueren Forschung*. Part 2, *Principat*. Edited by Hildegard Temporini and Wolfgang Haase. Berlin: de Gruyter, 1972–.

Aperion	*Apeiron: A Journal for Ancient Philosophy and Science*
ARIDSup	Analecta Romana Instituti Danici Supplementa
Aug	*Augustinianum*
AWL	Akademie der Wissenschaften und der Literatur
BABesch	*Bulletin antieke beschaving*
BERG	Beiträge zur Europäischen Religionsgeschichte
BETL	Bibliotheca Ephemeridum theologicarum Lovaniensium
BGA	Bibliotheca geographorum Arabicorum
BJS	Brown Judaic Studies
BSOAS	*Bulletin of the School of Oriental and African Studies*
ByzF	*Byzantinische Forschungen*
CCARB	*Corsi di Cultura sull'arte Ravannate e Bizantina*
CCSA	Corpus Christianorum, Series Aprocryphorum
CH	*Church History*
ClQ	*Classical Quarterly*
CognPsych	*Cognitive Psychology*
CRINT	Compendia Rerum Iudaicarum ad Novum Testamentum
CSCP	Cornell Studies in Classical Philology
CSEL	Corpus Scriptorum Ecclesiasticorum Latinorum
CSS	Cistercian Studies Series
CulSt	*Cultural Studies*
DChAE	*Deltion tes Christianikes Archaiologikes Hetaireias*
DOP	*Dumbarton Oaks Papers*
EC	*Early Christianity*
EccOr	*Ecclesia Orans*
ECF	Early Church Fathers
EDB	Edizioni Dehoniane Bologna
EPla	*Études platoniciennes*
EvQ	*Evangelical Quarterly*
FC	Fathers of the Church
FChr	Fontes Christiani
G&R	*Greece & Rome*
HellSS	Hellenic Studies Series
Herom	*Herom: Journal on Hellenistic and Roman Material Culture*

Historia	*Historia: Zeitschrift für Alte Geschichte*
HTR	*Harvard Theological Review*
HTS	Harvard Theological Studies
Hug	*Hugoye: Journal of Syriac Studies*
IHC	Islamic History and Civilization: Studies and Texts
IJCT	*International Journal of the Classical Tradition*
IJPT	*International Journal of the Platonic Tradition*
InvLuc	*Invigilata Lucernis*
IPS	International Plato Studies
ISACR	Interdisciplinary Studies in Ancient Culture and Religion
JAAR	*Journal of the American Academy of Religion*
JAJSup	Journal of Ancient Judaism Supplements
JAS	*Journal of Asian Studies*
JBL	*Journal of Biblical Literature*
JECH	*Journal of Early Christian History*
JECS	*Journal of Early Christian Studies*
JESHO	*Journal of Economic and Social History of the Orient*
JLA	*Journal of Late Antiquity*
JMEMS	*Journal of Medieval and Early Modern Studies*
JQR	*Jewish Quarterly Review*
JR	*Journal of Religion*
JRp	*Jahrbuch für Religionsphilosophie*
JRS	*Journal of Roman Studies*
JSAH	*Journal of the Society of Architectural Historians*
JSAI	*Jerusalem Studies in Arabic and Islam*
JTS	*Journal of Theological Studies*
KKMK	Kataloge des Kunstgewerbemuseums Köln
LCL	Loeb Classical Library
MAAR	*Memoirs of the American Academy in Rome*
MdByz	Le Monde Byzantin
MEFRM	*Mélanges de l'École française de Rome: Moyen Âge*
MJK	*Marburger Jahrbuch für Kunstwissenschaft*
MMed	The Medieval Mediterranean Peoples, Economies, and Cultures, 400–1453
MSLCA	*Miscellanea di studi di letteratur Cristiana antica*
MTSR	*Method and Theory in the Study of Religion*

MVAW	Münchner Vorlesungen zu Antiken Welten
MW	*The Muslim World*
NICNT	New International Commentary on the New Testament
NovT	*Novum Testamentum*
NPNF	A Select Library of Nicene and Post-Nicene Fathers of the Christian Church
Numen	*Numen: International Review for the History of Religions*
OrChrAn	Orientalia Christiana Analecta
OSAP	*Oxford Studies in Ancient Philosophy*
Pacifica	*Pacifica*
PACS	Philo of Alexandria Commentary Series
PBSR	*Papers of the British School at Rome*
PG	Patrologia Graeca. Edited by J.-P. Migne. 162 vols. Paris: Migne, 1857–1886.
PhA	Philosophia Antiqua
P&P	*Past and Present: A Journal of Historical Studies*
P&PSup	Past and Present Supplements
PTT	Platonic Texts and Translations Series
REAug	*Revue des études augustiniennes*
REL	*Revue des études latines*
RGRW	Religions in the Graeco-Roman World
RhM	*Rheinisches Museum für Philologie*
RIASA	*Rivista dell'Istituto Nazionale di Archeologia e Storia dell'Arte*
RIN	*Rivista italiana di numismatica e scienze affini*
SAEMO	Sancti Ambrosii Episcopi Mediolanensis Opera
SC	Sources chrétiennes
SCH	Studies in Church History
SCL	Sather Classical Lectures
SCS	Society of Classical Studies
SEMA	Studies in the Early Middle Ages
SFSHJ	South Florida Studies in the History of Judaism
SGLG	Studia Graeca et Latina Gothoburgensia
SGRR	Studies in Greek and Roman Religion
SIs	*Studia Islamica*
Spec	*Speculum*
SPhiloA	*The Studia Philonica Annual*

SSRH	Sociological Studies in Roman History
StPatr	Studia Patristica
SubHag	Subsidia Hagiographica
SVF	*Stoicorum Veterum Fragmenta*. Edited by Hans Friedrich August von Arnim. Stuttgart: Teubner, 1903; repr. Munich: Saur, 2004.
TAPA	*Transactions of the American Philological Association*
TDNT	*Theological Dictionary of the New Testament*. Edited by Kittel Gerhard and Gerhard Friedrich. Translated by Geoffrey W. Bromiley. 10 vols. Grand Rapids: Eerdmans, 1964–1976.
ThSo	*Theory and Society*
TJ	*Trinity Journal*
TPAPA	*Transactions and Proceedings of the American Philological Association*
Traditio	*Traditio*
TRE	*Theologische Realenzyklopädie*. Edited by Gerhard Krause and Gerhard Müller. 36 vols. Berlin: de Gruyter, 1976–2004.
TS	*Theological Studies*
TSAJ	Texte und Studien zum antiken Judentum
TTH	Translated Texts for Historians
TTR	*Teaching Theology and Religion*
VC	*Vigiliae Christianae*
VCS	Variorum Collected Studies Series
VSpirSup	*La Vie Spirituelle Supplement*
WBC	Word Biblical Commentary
WGRW	Writings from the Greco-Roman World
WGRWSup	Writings from the Greco-Roman World Supplement Series
WII	Word and Image Interactions
ZAC	*Zeitschrift für antikes Christentum*
ZPE	*Zeitschrift für Papyrologie und Epigraphik*

Introduction:
Conflict, Cooperation, and
Competition in Antiquity

Nathaniel P. DesRosiers and Lily C. Vuong

This volume seeks to address the ever-growing scholarly interest in religious competition and exchange in late antiquity. The primary goal of our inquiry is to interrogate ancient sources that demonstrate competitive interaction among differing socioreligious groups from the period and to explore the ways that these groups mutually influenced one other. We seek specifically to use competition as an approach to enlighten the origins, contours, and nuances of socioreligious discourses in antiquity and to put forth a general methodological framework for the study of these ancient dialogues. The intensification of interest in religious competition in recent decades has stimulated research in various case studies that often focused on one aspect of religious conflict/cooperation or specific scholarship exclusively targeting competition between two religions. Such studies tend to gloss over or simply ignore the complexities of late antique discourses. For example, many scholars discuss the writings of early church fathers, late antique rabbis, and Neoplatonic philosophers in light of later textual and historical events. In doing so, scholars often take the viewpoints presented in the writings of such elite cultural producers at face value, accepting them as accounts of normative contemporary beliefs and practices that accurately depict the religious activities of the rank and file. As a result, these texts are often read through a false lens, providing an incomplete and inaccurate view of these late antique figures and the religious movements they represent.

Alternatively, the present volume differs from the previous scholarship by examining cultural producers/elites and their particular viewpoints and agendas in an attempt to shed new light on the religious thinkers, texts, and material remains of late antiquity. Authors were encouraged to analyze or construct the intersections between parallel religious and philosophical communities of this era, including points of contact either between or among practitioners of Greco-Roman religions, Jews, Christians, and Muslims. In doing so, the contributors traced the development and influence of new religious perspectives and cultural identities in a crowded and contested sociopolitical landscape. As a result, the material contained within this volume is both comparative in nature and interdisciplinary in approach. The exploration of diverse themes, including physical matter and the body, education, rank and status, mythology, and iconography, through the lens of competition reveals enlightening dialogues and mutual influence among these groups that had a lasting impact well beyond antiquity. These religious and philosophical dialogues are not only of great interest and import in their own right, but they also can help us to understand how later cultural and religious developments unfolded.

The present volume, along with its sister volume focusing on religious competition in the third century,[1] signals the extent of interest in and the value of employing competition as a lens through which to offer more fruitful discussions on the broad socioreligious landscape of the ancient world. The papers represented in this volume were delivered at the Society of Biblical Literature's Religious Competition in Late Antiquity Unit between 2012 and 2014, and they reflect the major goal of reexamining and redescribing late antique discourses. The over thirty papers presented at the Society of Biblical Literature Annual Meeting during this period ranged in terms of social and political contexts, literary and textual traditions, and ritual practices and material discourses within the religious and philosophical realms of Judaism, Christianity, Roman religion, and early Islam. While diverse in individual research, contributors were able to bind these varied interests together through the intentional focus on competition.

Aims and Content

This collection thus seeks to explore competition between and among diverse social groups of the Mediterranean basin during late antiquity

---

1. Jordan D. Rosenblum, Lily C. Vuong, and Nathaniel P. DesRosiers, eds., *Religious Competition in the Third Century CE: Jews, Christians, and the Greco-Roman World*, JAJSup 15 (Göttingen: Vandenhoeck & Ruprecht, 2014).

through the development of broadly comparative methodologies that delineate the ways this competitive interaction reshaped cultural and religious landscapes. The papers focus on unique contexts within Judaism, Christianity, Islam, and various philosophical circles, while at the same time opening up the conversation and developing new approaches and methodologies centered on the concern for competition. We have chosen to organize the volume into four thematic sections rather than group the papers together according to religious or philosophical traditions in order to highlight the theoretical issues and novel methodological approaches developed and employed by each contributor through his or her focus on competition.

. The first part, "Competition and Material Culture," showcases a variety of theoretical frameworks for the examination of both interreligious and intrareligious competition among religious and philosophical groups in late antiquity through material culture (that is, via art, architecture, ritual objects, clothing, and so forth). The papers demonstrate the ways that material objects and the physical spaces that they occupy (whether real or rhetorical) can express competitive interactions both between and among philosophers, Romans, Jews, and Christians in this period. These dialogues of competition expressed through material objects and physical spaces concern belonging and identity (Carly Daniel-Hughes), contestations over the use and appropriation of iconography (Arthur P. Urbano), the redefinition of images by cultural producers (Nathaniel P. DesRosiers), and claims over the power of words within physical spaces (Catherine Chin). The papers in this section illustrate how the use or disuse of certain culturally significant, meaning-laden objects and images may be read as rhetorical strategies for promoting the specific religious agendas of individual cultural producers. Furthermore, the adoption and adaptation of these media represent an active competition to create new meanings and identities for material objects that in turn amplify the credibility and prominence of those who used them.

Part 2, "Competition and Neoplatonism," recognizes the importance of textual reception in the process of identity formation by showcasing how philosophers and Christians interpreted both their own "canonical" texts and the texts of other communities, including those that may have been construed and sometimes labeled as "pagan," "heretical," or "barbarian." These essays explore how competition for dominance in interpretation and the definition of "orthodoxy" became the battleground for the cultural producers of the third century and beyond. Specifically, papers in this section discuss the use of Platonic myths as a locus of competition between and among both Christians and philosophers (Ilaria L. E. Ramelli); the debate over the interpretation, treatment, and proper transmission of wisdom (Gregory Shaw); and the ways that Neoplatonic speculation on theurgy could be used to compete against Christianity (Laura B. Dingeldein). As in the previous section, these papers aim to demonstrate the ways that meaning and definition could be produced in the late antique world. Here the focus is not on the material images and objects that could have a much broader scope of competitive influence; instead, these essays show how subtle and nuanced competition could be. Producing or assigning new semantic, semiotic, or ontological meanings in late antique philosophical circles certainly represents one of the most rarified and exclusive of competitive arenas, but it is nonetheless one of the most valuable. Competition among intellectual elites was often not blunt and openly combative but ethereal and penetrating, highlighting and celebrating the exclusivity and superiority of this competitive arena and its players. For those who participated, the stakes were indeed high since a loss in the form of the refutation of ideas meant tarnishing one's reputation and credibility, while winning arguments could reveal new truths about the divine and yield personal academic immortality for the victor.

Part 3, "Religious Experts and Popular Religion," questions the reliability of ancient sources for understanding lived religion in the ancient world. Since the views of religious experts were not necessarily reflective of the views of the (now silent) majority, papers in this section debate the influence of the religious expert who sought to shape the beliefs and practices of the lay audience through competitive discourse with other members of this elite group. The essays contained in this section discuss the competitive dynamics of the relationship between the religious practices of elites and nonelites (Stanley Stowers), the delineation and claim to the concept of piety (T. Christopher Hoklotubbe), the propagation of elite ideas among rank-and-file Christian congregants (Karl Shuve), and the development of Jewish and Christian rhetorical arguments to defend their nonparticipation in Roman practices (Loren R. Spielman). Building on the previous sections, these papers illustrate how elite cultural producers have influenced our understandings of religious "meaning." Since both ancient and modern interpreters have privileged texts, our understandings and standard historical reconstructions of ancient religions, which emphasize practice over supposed normative interpretations, are skewed.

The papers included here show that the rituals, meanings, and ideologies espoused in texts generally did not reflect the actual character and form of the lived religious customs practiced by the majority. Using this as a starting point, these papers show how contestations over proper interpretations of practice and analytical value ultimately won out by creating and fostering reciprocally beneficial social structures (such as the philosophical school, church, or synagogue) that could support and maintain these complex ideas. More broadly, these essays demonstrate how competition influenced the world that we live in by forging the religious structures that we have inherited.

Our final part, "Competition and Relics," explores the role of relics in Christianity and Islam during late antiquity. Papers not only consider the competition to possess and use these items as objects of symbolic power but also examine the contexts of rivalry that made the veneration of relics more or less relevant in certain areas. Through their rigorous investigation of the objects themselves and the literature that discusses them, these authors unearth the role that these items played in intra- and extramural worship (Mary Joan Winn Leith and Allyson Everingham Sheckler), identity formation (Adam Bursi), authority and sacred geography (Dina Boero), and political propaganda (Gary Vikan). In many ways, this section brings all of the pieces of the previous sections together. These essays are important case studies both phenomenologically and socially, illustrating how competition could encompass both inter- and intrareligious competition through a very specific medium, across a variety of historical, geographical, and cultural contexts. We see how contestation over the relics themselves, their spaces, and their uses demonstrate expansion over traditional religious practices and an enhanced focus on the value of materiality. In doing so, these essays show us not only variations on a theme, but they also enrich our understandings about the religious systems and groups themselves. We see the needs, hopes, and aspirations of adherents from different religious traditions and the way that these significant objects helped to create identities and meanings. Such studies validate the multivalent nature of religious competition and how this lens can bring to light new insights into the intellectual discourses, cultural borrowings, and meaning-making that dominate religious landscapes.

While the essays in this volume cover a broad range of topics and traditions, each provides a useful exploration into the countless ways that individuals and groups of late antiquity interacted and influenced one another. The overarching goal of these essays is to provide new insights into and interpretations of old objects and texts. Understanding that our ancient cultural producers put forth primarily esoteric, exclusive works that were not representative of the religious thoughts and actions of the majority of ancient practitioners requires us to recalibrate our view of the ancient religious landscape. These elites speak for only a relatively small percentage of the population and often for themselves alone. While we have assumed that these texts and their authors speak for normative practice and belief, the reality is that they rarely, if ever, represented anything like consensus or even mainstream Mediterranean religiosity. Because of this tenuous situation, the competition between and among our subjects was both very real and necessary.

Competition as it is framed here is more than a simplistic "ours is better than yours" debate, which provides little critical insight.[2] These papers also go beyond standard scholarly presentations that generically discuss the agonistic nature of ancient Mediterranean and especially Greek societies, where individuals were striving for honor, merit, and wealth through athletic and military contestation.[3] Instead, the papers here broadly fit into more modern sociological models such as those of Pierre Bourdieu, who theorized that individuals participating in a given field sought to acquire cultural capital within their chosen symbolic economy.[4] For the philosopher, the bishop, or even the emperor, intellectual contributions and their acceptance over and against one's peers and opponents represented successful competitive interactions and gains in symbolic capital. Accordingly, these essays bear witness to moments of cultural production among

---

2. See in this volume Arthur P. Urbano, "The Philosopher Type in Late Roman Art: Problematizing Cultural Appropriation in Light of Cultural Competition."

3. The classic treatments of this topic include Arthur W. H. Adkins, *Merit and Responsibility: A Study in Greek Values* (Oxford: Clarendon, 1960); and Alvin W. Gouldner, *Enter Plato: Classical Greece and the Origin of Social Theory* (New York: Basic, 1965), 49–51, 82–87. For more recent discussion, see Douglas L. Cairns, *Aidos: The Psychology and Ethics of Honour and Shame in Ancient Greek Literature* (New York: Oxford University Press, 1993), 14–47. Such interpretive models have also been expanded to Christianity; see, for example: Bruce J. Malina, *The New Testament World: Insights from Cultural Anthropology* (Atlanta: John Knox, 1981), 35–37; Jerome H. Neyrey, *Honor and Shame in the Gospel of Matthew* (Louisville: Westminster John Knox, 1998).

4. Pierre Bourdieu, *The Field of Cultural Production: Essays on Art and Literature*, ed. Randal Johnson (New York: Columbia University Press, 1993), 82–83.

intellectual elites, which often ultimately resulted in the development of normative iconographies, orthopraxies, and theologies.

Part 1
Competition and Material Culture

Introduction: Competition and Material Culture through Real and Imagined Spaces

Gregg E. Gardner

Material culture plays an important role in religious traditions, as not everything that is meaningful or significant is necessarily expressed in words or preserved in texts. Religions incorporate and create patterns of feelings and sensations bound up with performances, objects, and spaces; they regulate bodies, generate and study images, and use architecture to construct and define sacred spaces.[1] The materiality of religion has increasingly attracted the attention of scholars of late antiquity who have begun to examine the social and cultural meanings that ancient Christians, Jews, Greeks, and Romans have attached to objects. As the papers in this section will show, attention to material culture can help us understand competition between late-antique religious groups. Through their examinations of funerary art, dress, coins, and public architecture, these studies help us understand the competitive dynamics that are embedded in the production, circulation, and consumption of objects and spaces.

The dynamics of how religious competition shapes material culture are brought to the fore in Arthur Urbano's study of Christian funerary art. In particular, he examines third-century sarcophagi from Rome featuring the "philosopher type": men dressed in Greek-style mantles, conversing in groups, often set against architectural and bucolic backgrounds. Urbano questions the common perception that these are examples of Christian appropriation and redefinition of the Roman philosopher type. He rightly notes that the appropriation model assumes that the image or material expression in question is assumed to be initially extrinsic to Christianity

---

1. Richard M. Carp, "Teaching Religion and Material Culture," *TTR* 10 (2007): 2–3; David Morgan, "Introduction: 'The Matter of Belief,'" in *Religion and Material Culture: The Matter of Belief*, ed. David Morgan (London: Routledge, 2010), 1–20.

and that its new Christian context represents an effort to shift its meaning. It also assumes a clear bifurcation between Roman and Christian identity. Instead, Urbano reads these sarcophagi as demonstrating that Christians embraced the philosopher type as a representation of *paideia*, thereby positioning the deceased among the ranks of the educated elite. Urbano notes how biblical scenes adjacent to the philosopher type provide a hermeneutic with signifiers of Christian narratives, resulting in a slight—but not seismic—shift in meaning. The new Christian meaning supplements, but does not replace, the existing understanding. Instead of appropriation, Urbano advocates a model of cultural competition: the appearance of the philosopher type (including its distinctive garments) on sarcophagi is the product of a struggle to accumulate cultural capital.

Dress was an important locus of social competition in the Roman world. It formed part of a common "semiotic language," which Webb Keane defines as the "basic assumptions about what signs are and how they function in the world."[2] Depending on their attributes (color, fabric, form, etc.), garments signified one's relative wealth and social status.[3] In her paper, Carly Daniel-Hughes examines the discourses on dress by second-third century Christian writer Tertullian. The Christians of Carthage should dress modestly by choosing the *pallium* over the toga, which Tertullian associates with idolatry. For Tertullian, idolatry was not limited to acts of idol worship. Rather, it can be found in festivities, social obligations, and civic duties—and, thus, extended to the clothing that was typically worn at such events. Against Tertullian's views, one could contrast early rabbinic approaches to accommodate to their Roman surroundings by defining pagan religiosity in a very narrow way: activities that were religious but technically noncultic were acceptable aspects of urban culture.[4] Notably, Tertullian does not deny the existence of the semiotic code of his day. Rather, he accepts it and alters it, inverting the hierarchy from toga and social prestige to *pallium* and Christian religiosity. The choice to wear a *pallium* over other possible garments, therefore, would make

---

2. Webb Keane, "Semiotics and the Social Analysis of Material Things," *Language and Communication* 23 (2003): 410.

3. For an overview, see Gregg E. Gardner, *The Origins of Organized Charity in Rabbinic Judaism* (Cambridge: Cambridge University Press, 2015), 52–53.

4. Seth Schwartz, *Imperialism and Jewish Society, 200 B.C.E. to 640 C.E* (Princeton: Princeton University Press, 2001), 164–65.

one's adherence to Christian beliefs readily apparent—a sign of conspicuous piety.

Similar to Urbano and Daniel-Hughes, Nathaniel DesRosiers argues that Christian material culture—namely, the coins of Constantine—should be read as an engagement with well-known Roman semiotics and themes. He demonstrates how the emperor chose to emphasize military and political might in keeping with long-standing traditions in imperial coinage. These messages were especially important for Constantine in the face of competition for power and his image as a usurper. Coins were particularly useful media for these purposes, because the emperor could control their appearance (and, thus, strongly influence the messages that they convey), and, as means of exchange, they reached wide audiences. DesRosiers shows how Constantine's uses of coins to broadcast Christian ideologies were less prominent than scholars have believed. Rather, for Constantine, the importance of military messages won over the signification of Christian triumphalism in the competition for space on his coins.

Whereas funerary art, dress, and coinage can be significantly shaped by an individual, other forms of material culture are defined by a broad array of stimuli and interested parties. The form of public architecture, such as synagogues, is not wholly under the discretion of the particular community that constructs and uses that space. Rather, as the case of the Callinicum (Syria) synagogue demonstrates, its physical form (here, in ruins or reconstructed) is the product of several negotiated, competing factors. Catherine Chin examines Ambrose's request in the late fourth century that the emperor Theodosius rescind his order that the bishop of Callinicum finance the reconstruction of a synagogue. What appears to be a straightforward case of restitution to Callinicum's Jews is transformed by Ambrose into a competition between Jews and Christians for imperial favor. If the synagogue were restored, then the Jews would not only triumph over the Christians. Instead, an ephemeral moment of victory would be concretized, broadcast, and memorialized by the physical presence of the synagogue. Just as the toga and other forms of prestigious Roman dress assumed contexts of idolatry for Tertullian, so too the reconstructed synagogue would mark impiety for Ambrose.

The authors in this section demonstrate how the lens of religious competition brings out insights into late-antique material culture. In contrast to models of appropriation and art historical frameworks, the context of competition helps us uncover the dynamic processes by which material religion took shape. The appearance, size, and texture of objects and features cannot be taken as presupposed inevitabilities. Rather, the form of each object that is known to us today—whether physical (archaeological) or inscribed in a text—is the product of a dynamic struggle for limited space and limited resources. Space, cost, and technology constrain the quantity and qualities of decorations on a sarcophagus; here, the philosopher type won out over numerous other possible images and motifs. Clothing, or the means to make or purchase them, is a scarce resource, and Tertullian proclaims the *pallium* as the victor over the toga for those wishing to demonstrate their piety. From a nearly limitless treasure trove of possible images and themes, those related to the military won the competition for space on Constantine's coins. For Ambrose, the site of the synagogue ought to be dedicated to the structure's ruins rather than a living Jewish sanctuary. Those surveyed here—the anonymous commissioners of funerary art, Tertullian, Constantine, and Ambrose—demonstrate their authority in cultural production and help define (or redefine) the normativity of acceptable objects, images, and the use of spaces.

The Perils of Idolatrous Garb:
Tertullian and Christian Belonging in Roman Carthage*

Carly Daniel-Hughes

"The principal crime of humanity, the greatest crime of the world, the source of judgment, is idolatry," Tertullian exclaims to members of his Christian community (*Idol.* 1.1).[1] Writing in the Roman colony of Carthage, he warns fellow Christians that *idolatria*, service to idols, has a broader definition than they might suppose. It is not just holding a priestly office or offering a sacrificial banquet; it is not limited to the confines of temples (*Idol.* 2.1–5). One can commit this sin even when "idols" are not present. *Idolatria* covers a whole range of social interactions and practices that marked life in Carthage.[2] Its threat can be found in the name of deities, festivities, civic offices, and social obligations—all of which are means for demons to pervert nature, to divert unsuspecting Christians from worship of the true God.[3] Tertullian, thus, recommends modest and simple dress as a rampart against idolatry's ever-present dangers.

---

* Thank you to Stephanie L. Cobb for her feedback on an earlier version of this paper as well as to the anonymous reviewer and the editors of this volume. Their insights helped to focus my argument and have provided some interesting suggestions for developing the analysis I undertake here.

1. Latin: *Principale crimen generis humani, summus saeculi reatus, tota causa iudicii idololatria*. Latin text is from Tertullian, *De idolatria*, ed. A. Reifferscheid and G. Wissowa, CCSL 2 (Turnhout: Brepols, 1954).

2. See Éric Rebillard, *Christians and Their Many Identities in Late Antiquity: North Africa, 200–450 CE* (Ithaca, NY: Cornell University Press, 2012), 35–31. The term is not native to Latin or Roman cults but is comprised of two Greek loanwords (*eidolon* and *latreia*). See J. C. M. Van Winden, "Idolum and Idolatria in Tertullian," *VC* 36 (1982): 108–14.

3. Guy G. Stroumsa, "Tertullian and the Limits of Tolerance," in *Tolerance and*

Tertullian's advice here depends heavily on the prevailing Roman ideal that dress, and bodily comportment more generally, were privileged indicators of virtue or its lack. Roman moral discourse conceived of virtue—defined by modesty, shame, honor, and also piety—as characteristics that could be cultivated through bodily performances and displayed by them.[4] In this, Roman writers often presented virtue as a regulatory mechanism that worked within an individual to police behavior, reinforce social hierarchies and group boundaries, and promote shared values.[5] For this reason, dress (and corporeal deportment more generally) provided elites with strategies to negotiate the agonistic arenas of imperial and civic politics.[6] Dress could also be read as "signs" of another's moral fitness, and the significance of clothing could be called upon to claim virtue for oneself and one's community.

Among Christian authors, Tertullian ranks as the earliest and most prolific author to maximize the symbolic power of dress in this regard.[7] My analysis here focuses on how Tertullian establishes links between certain looks and "idolatry" in the treatises directed to Christian insiders, notably *On Idolatry, On the Pallium, On the Military Crown,* and *On the Apparel of Women*.[8] Here he marks particular fashions—the toga, wreaths,

---

Intolerance in Early Judaism and Christianity, ed. Graham N. Stanton and Guy G. Stroumsa (Cambridge: Cambridge University Press, 1998), 177.

4. This discourse was fueled by the introduction of Greek physiognomic literature into the Latin West, which held that virtue and vice could be read on the "physical signs of the body." See Kristi Upson-Saia, *Early Christian Dress: Gender, Virtue, and Authority*, RSAH 3 (New York: Routledge, 2011), 30.

5. See Shadi Bartsch, *The Mirror of the Self: Sexuality, Self-Knowledge, and the Gaze in the Early Roman Empire* (Chicago: University of Chicago Press, 2006), 115–82, and Carlin Barton, "Being in the Eyes: Shame and Sight in Ancient Rome," in *The Roman Gaze: Vision, Power, and the Body*, ed. David Frederick (Baltimore: Johns Hopkins University Press, 2002), 226–35.

6. The classical study is Maud Gleason, *Making Men: Sophists and Self-Presentation in Ancient Rome* (Oxford: Oxford University Press, 1995), and, for Roman sources, Erik Gunderson, *Staging Masculinity: The Rhetoric of Performance in the Roman World* (Ann Arbor: University of Michigan Press, 2000).

7. For more discussion, see Carly Daniel-Hughes, *The Salvation of the Flesh in Tertullian of Carthage: Dressing for the Resurrection* (New York: Palgrave Macmillan, 2011).

8. David E. Wilhite considers the ethnic and status components of dress and his conclusions resemble some of the arguments that I make here; see *Tertullian the African: An Anthropological Reading of Tertullian's Context and Identities* (Berlin: de Gruyter, 2007).

and luxurious garb generally—as stained by idolatry and, thus, unsuitable for Christians. The looks Tertullian promotes for his Christian audience, alternatively, are not novel but simply humble garb. Avoiding idolatry in dress, for Tertullian, is less about following a dress code and more about viewing civic life as a minefield of potential conflict that might compromise a Christian's virtue. I argue that Tertullian cited the perils of idolatrous garb as part of a bigger project: to facilitate a shared sensibility of group belonging among members of his audience, one that would dominate all other allegiances and affiliations that they held.[9] However, his writings imply that such an attempt was perhaps not met with success (a point that I take up at the close of my discussion).

The Garb of Idols

Historians of dress have emphasized that clothing derives its meaning from the contexts in which it is worn or represented. They note too that clothing can communicate different messages about a person at once: status, age, ethnicity, group affiliation, profession, emotional state, and worldview. Discourse about clothing, notes Roland Barthes in *The Fashion System*, attempts to foreclose the possible meanings of particular looks.[10] At the same time, it aims to condition its audience about how to read those looks, even their own. If this point is true of dress generally, it is perhaps especially salient when considering Tertullian's discourse on idolatrous garb.

In Roman antiquity, there were no separate costumes worn during ritual or civic festivities. With the exception of certain archaic Roman priesthoods (the Flamen Dialis, the Vestal Virgins) and priests of foreign cults (Cybele or Isis),[11] ritual clothing—the garb worn during sacred rites, festivities, and initiations—was comprised of a combination of familiar elements: tunics, mantles (whether the Greek *pallium* or Roman toga), and

---

9. Here I have in view the discussion by Rogers Brubaker and Frederick Cooper, "Beyond Identity," *ThSo* 29 (2000): 1–47, esp. 19–21. Brubaker and Cooper describe "groupness" as a subjective form of belonging. It is the feeling that one belongs to a collective community, which is distinguishable from others.

10. Following the argument in Roland Barthes, *The Fashion System*, trans. Matthew Ward and Richard Howard (New York: Hill &Wang, 1983).

11. For a discussion of cultic and ritual dress in antiquity, see Carly Daniel-Hughes, "Belief," in *The Oxford Berg History of Dress*, ed. Mary Harlow (Oxford: Oxford University Press, forthcoming).

various types of headwear (veils, crowns, ribbons or *vittae*, and, of course, wreaths).[12] A related issue is that while we find variations in clothing styles among different ethnic groups,[13] such variety was often subtle, and it did not serve to distinguish easily among them. As a result clothing retained a range of semiotic possibilities, and Tertullian's sartorial discourse often thrived on this potential.

Context determined the suitability of particular items of clothing in most civic and religious festivities. Tertullian, for instance, advises Christian men to don the squared-off mantle, the *pallium*, and not the elaborate, rounded folds of the Roman toga. He notes that this garment, normally associated with Greek *paideia*, is the "equivalent" of what the public priests of Asclepius in Carthage wore (*Pall.* 1.2.1 and 4.10.3).[14] The garment was likely worn by indigenous Africans as well (Roman pictorial representations commonly present the garment as the dress of African men),[15] and, in practice, it was regularly featured in the everyday wardrobe of Roman men (along with other tunics and trousers).[16] In other words, one could not rely simply on costume to distinguish a Greek philosopher from a

---

12. Generally, clean, well-made clothing was anticipated for women and men in sacred rites and processions. See Laura Gawlinski, *The Sacred Law of Andania: A New Text and Commentary*, Sozomena 2 (Berlin: de Gruyter, 2012), 135.

13. See Alexandra T. Croom, *Roman Clothing and Fashion* (London: Tempus 2002), 125–45. For instance, while ancient Jews had some unique clothing habits related to biblical injunctions, they were not necessarily visually distinctive from other groups in the Roman world; see Dafna Shlezinger-Katsman, "Clothing," in *The Oxford Handbook of Jewish Daily Life in Roman Palestine*, ed. Catherine Hezser (Oxford: Oxford University Press, 2010), 362–81.

14. For the *pallium*'s association with Greek philosophy as it relates to Christian discourse, see Arthur Urbano, "Sizing Up the Philosopher's Cloak: Christian Verbal and Visual Representations of the *Tribōn*," in *Dressing Judeans and Christians in Antiquity*, ed. Kristi Upson-Saia, Carly Daniel-Hughes, and Alicia Batten (Surrey, UK: Ashgate, 2014), 175–94.

15. Janet Huskinson, "Elite Culture and the Identity of Empire," in *Experiencing Rome: Culture, Identity and Power in the Roman Empire*, ed. Janet Huskinson (London: Routledge, 2000), 108–9.

16. The toga was designed for stately occasions and not everyday wear; see Caroline Vout, "The Myth of the Toga: Understanding the History of Roman Dress," *G&R* 43 (1996): 211; and Mary Harlow, "Clothes Maketh the Man: Power Dressing and Elite Masculinity in the Later Roman Empire," in *Gender in the Early Medieval World*, ed. Leslie Brubaker and Julia M. H. Smith (Cambridge: Cambridge University Press, 2005), 49.

priest of Asclepius, a vacationing statesman, or a Christian. Indeed, the multivalence of the *pallium* is precisely what recommends this garb to Tertullian—its signification could be expansive. Whereas the *pallium* (a garment that was versatile) can be ascribed with positive meanings, the toga's association with Roman politics made it the source of Tertullian's ire. Roman artistic representations in the imperial period keep the image of the *romani* as Vergil's acclaimed "toga-clad race" alive (*Aen.* 1.229–296). His defense of the *pallium* represents a valorization of it that was necessary precisely because the toga was the indicator of Roman pedigree and was the rightful garb of the citizen. In *On the Pallium*, Tertullian highlights the toga's civic character, best suited for the forum and Senate house. Yet, he warns, it is a garment that perverts and corrupts its wearer—it is a fussy piece of clothing imposed on the population by grievous colonizers who show an amazing disregard for modesty (*Pall.* 4.8.1).

In *On Idolatry*, he goes further in his denunciation of the toga. To wear it demands that a Christian participate in all kinds of idolatrous acts. Can a Christian truly hold civic office and not undertake its duties: "neither sacrificing, nor lending his authority to sacrifices; not farming out victims; not assigning others the care of temples; not looking after their tributes; not giving spectacles at his own or the public charge…?" (*Idol.* 17.3).[17] But the dangers of the toga prove even more invasive, an even greater threat to true piety. In wearing the garb, a man associates himself with idolatry: "If you put on a tunic," Tertullian exclaims, "defiled in itself, it perhaps may not be defiled through you; but you, through it, will be unable to be clean" (*Idol.* 18.4).[18] We should not miss the implication here: to reject the toga, a man would also necessarily reject the manifold privileges that Roman citizenship might afford him.

Tertullian makes a similarly stark argument about crowns and wreaths, the former a regular feature of priestly costume as well as military life and imperial cult and the latter a ubiquitous indicator of "ritual and festival time."[19] In his treatise *On the Military Crown*, he considers

---

17. Latin: *neque sacrificet neque sacrificiis auctoritatem suam accommodet, non hostias locet, non curas templorum deleget, non uectigalia eorum procuret, non spectacula edat de suo aut de public…?* All translations with some modifications from vols. 3–4 of the *Ante-Nicene Fathers*.

18. Latin: *Tunicam si induas inquinatam per se, poterit forsitan illa non inquinari per te, sed tu per illam mundus esse non poteris.*

19. Gawlinski, *Sacred Law of Andania*, 110.

whether wearing festive crowns can be justified, which ultimately leads him to conclude that Christians cannot be soldiers. Tertullian reminds his audience that decorating their heads and lintels with these objects is no innocent affair: "Nothing must be given to an idol, and so nothing taken from one," he exhorts. "If it is inconsistent with faith to recline in an idol temple, what is it to appear in an idol dress?" (*Cor.* 10.5). The opening of this treatise, however, provides us some indication that to avoid crowns—and in this way, identify oneself as "Christian"—was a display of piety whose stakes were high. Tertullian opens the treatise with the case of an accused Christian soldier who, on the eve of an imperial birthday, refused to wear a laurel crown gifted to him. The soldier, Tertullian notes, was imprisoned and then killed. Where Tertullian presents his actions as an admirable display of piety, he indicates that others who likewise took the name "Christian" interpreted the act as ignorant and even dangerous (*Cor.* 1.4).[20]

Tertullian's arguments about dress in *On the Pallium*, *On the Military Crown*, and *On Idolatry*, we should note, are targeted at men. They reveal how displays of masculinity were entangled in Roman imperial politics.[21] The suggestion that Christian men eschew togas and various crowns—and in doing so, retain their status as virtuous men—unsettles the link between *romanitas* and *virtus* forged in Roman imperial propaganda and on display in Roman political oratory. Tertullian's remarks in these treatises have been read as "anti-Roman," but such an ascription misses how Tertullian's rhetoric relies on Roman ethnocentric logic. These treatises wrest normative Roman conceptions of virtue and masculinity from Roman statesman, figuring them instead as the characteristics of Christian men.[22]

Tertullian can apply the charge of idolatry to women's adornment as well. Tertullian warns in *On the Apparel of Women* that when women wear the latest fashions—make-up, jewelry, and luxurious fabrics—they make their own bodies into idols. They become a veritable "gateway" to the

---

20. Rebillard, *Christians and Their Many Identities*, 19–20.

21. See, for instance, Mathew Kuefler, *The Manly Eunuch: Masculinity, Gender Ambiguity, and Christian Ideology in Late Antiquity* (Chicago: University of Chicago Press, 2001), esp. 19–69. Also in view of dress, see Glenys Davies, "What Made the Roman Toga *Virilis*?" in *The Clothed Body in the Ancient World*, ed. Liza Cleland, Mary Harlow, and Lloyd Llewellyn-Jones (Oxford: Oxbow, 2005), 121–30.

22. For discussion of Tertullian's construction of masculinity with other studies of early Christian materials, see Daniel-Hughes, *Salvation of the Flesh*, 45–61.

demonic (*Cult. fem.* 1.1.2). Tertullian again relies on the tactics of shame and fear: he charges that a woman attempts to exalt herself over God when she ought to cultivate humility (*Cult. fem.* 2.3.2). Since she is not trying to impress with the latest styles, she should have no cause to attend temples, games, or other festive occasions but instead should spend her time caring for the sick and visiting prisons—activities that call only for humble attire (*Cult. fem.* 2.11.1–3).

Here, too, Tertullian's comments depend on Roman political discourse, based on what Maria Wyke calls "a conceptual pattern in which the regimen of the body is thought to parallel the regimen of the state, excessive care for the body is treated as symptomatic of the softening of the state's moral fibre."[23] A woman's dress, then, not only indicated her moral character, it also represented the character of the group to which she belonged. But for Tertullian to call on this conceptual pattern was precisely a means to suggest that women attending Christian assemblies should understand themselves as members of a "group." By insisting on humble dress, Tertullian trades on Roman moralizing discourse to enforce uniformity and obscure distinctions among women. We know from a variety of sources (particularly artistic and archaeological remains) that ornamentation was a marker of beauty, status, and power for noble women. Station was advertised through grooming and raiment. Thus, a matron's pearls were compared to the public honors and glories that men obtained in their political and military feats. By not wearing jewelry or luxurious clothing, a woman would, in effect, mute or hide a potentially large set of indicators that implied belonging to groups beyond the Christian community, such as martial and maternal status as well as material and familial ties.[24]

Outfitting Christians

It is interesting to note that Tertullian's approved fashions—the *pallium* instead of the toga for Christian men and simple tunics and head-covering mantles for women—were hardly innovative looks. As we have seen, the

---

23. Maria Wyke, "Woman in the Mirror: The Rhetoric of Adornment in the Roman World," in *Women in Ancient Societies: An Illusion of Night*, ed. Léonie J. Archer, Susan Fischler, and Maria Wyke (London: Routledge, 1994), 141.

24. For a longer discussion, see Daniel-Hughes, *Salvation of the Flesh*, 83–91. On Christian women and the display of wealth and status through dress, see also Alicia Batten, "Carthaginian Critiques of Adornment," *JECH* 1 (2011): 3–21.

pallium was associated with Greek philosophers, worn by priests of Asclepius, and indigenous Africans. It figured into the everyday garb of Roman men as well. In a similar way, Tertullian's fashion advice to women in his community could not claim novelty. The modest look was recommended by various Roman writers[25] and was also a regular sartorial requirement for religious solemnities.[26]

But Tertullian does not assert uniqueness for the looks he espouses. He argues instead that Christians alone demonstrate virtue in their dress. When Tertullian calls attention to the dress of religious adherents of Carthaginian cults, we might anticipate that he would highlight the idolatrous character of their garb. Instead, he uses these references to shame and cajole his Christian audience to follow his sartorial advice. Having advised Christian men to reject the laurel crown in *On the Military Crown*, Tertullian ends the treatise by pointing out that even the initiates of Mithras cast off the laurel wreath, a demonic trick where they "mimic" that which belongs to the true God.[27]

On other occasions, Tertullian derides the clothing of religious initiates and officials as inauthentic displays of piety. In *On the Pallium*, Tertullian notes how commonly dress can be deceptive: brothel owners dress as matrons; freeman wear the insignia of equestrians. He points out that the followers of Ceres, Bellona, and Saturn profess piety when, in reality, they increase their numbers because of their "novel fashions [*novitatis vestitu*]" (*Pall.* 4.10.1–2). White tunics, *vittae* (ribbons), and *galeri* (caps) were the signature garb of Ceres's devotees in Carthage, but the followers of the goddess, Bellona, wore the opposite—dark clothing. The most spectacular clerical garb, however, belonged to the priests of Saturn whose tunics were of a particular hue of red known as "Galatian scarlet [*Galatici ruboris*]" (see Tertullian, *Apol.* 9.2–4).

---

25. See Kelly Olson, "Matrona and Whore: Clothing and Definition in Roman Antiquity," in *Prostitutes and Courtesans in the Ancient World*, ed. Christopher A. Faraone and Laura K. McClure (Madison: University of Wisconsin Press, 2006), 186–204.

26. See Harrianne Mills, "Greek Clothing Regulations: Sacred and Profane?" *ZPE* 55 (1984): 255–65.

27. Tertullian's comments seem to reflect some knowledge of Mithraic initiation; see Laura Gawlinski, "'Fashioning' Initiates: Dress at the Mysteries," in *Reading a Dynamic Canvas: Adornment in the Ancient Mediterranean World*, ed. Cynthia S. Colburn and Maura K. Heyn (Newcastle, UK: Cambridge Scholars), 153.

It is not inconsequential that Tertullian's rhetoric contrasts these two groups. The cults of Saturn and Bellona were a common part of Christian invective against Roman cults: Saturn, due to its association with child sacrifice (see Tertullian, *Apol.* 9:2–4; Minucius Felix, *Oct.* 30.5; Lactantius, *Epit.* 18.2), and Bellona because her initiates reportedly engaged in self-mutilation (see Tertullian, *Apol.* 9.10).[28] Tertullian additionally selected Saturn and Ceres as examples of ostentatious piety, because devotion to both deities is well attested in North Africa. The cult of Saturn, in particular, is one of the most ancient cults in the region; evidence for it is vast.[29]

Pointing to these counterexamples, Tertullian aims to convince his audience to participate in the agnostic politic landscape of Roman Carthage, vying together to authenticate their superior virtue. He makes this point most explicitly when advocating simple dress for women: "It is not enough for Christian modesty to seem to be true, it is to be seen to be true," he explains (*Cult. fem.* 2.13.3).[30] To cite another example, Tertullian claims that the Christian wearing a *pallium* makes vice itself turn red with shame (*improbi mores ... erubescunt*) (*Pall.* 6.1.3).

The Fluidity of Belonging in Roman Carthage

Throughout the treatises I have considered here, Tertullian calls members of his audience to avoid "idolatrous" dress. He asks them to attend to the significance of dress—to what it may communicate and to the ways it might shape their moral disposition. He seizes on the semiotic potential of dress, establishing the link between the sweeping definition of "idolatry" and signature pieces of clothing (toga, wreaths, jewelry) as a disciplinary tactic. He works to instill a hermeneutic in his audience in which they would search out the subtle perversions of idolatry at every turn. In

---

28. See Tertullian, *De Pallio: Translation with Commentary*, ed. and trans. Vincent Hunink (Amsterdam: Gieben, 2005), 238.

29. James B. Rives, *Religion and Authority in Roman Carthage from Augustus to Constantine* (Oxford: Clarendon, 1995), 142–51. The popularity of both cults in Carthage is also evident from the Martyrdom of Perpetua. When entering the gates of the arena, Perpetua and her company are handed costumes: "the men were forced to put on the robes of priests of Saturn, the women the dress of the priestesses of Ceres. But the noble Perpetua strenuously resisted this to the end" (Mart. Perp. 18.4). Translation from Herbert Musurillo, *The Acts of the Christian Martyrs*, OECT (Oxford: Clarendon, 1972), 126–27.

30. Latin: *Pudicitiae Christianae satis non est esse, verum et videri.*

so doing, Tertullian calls his audience together as a viable and distinctive group, as "Christians." To follow Tertullian's advice, a person would find a whole set of daily rituals and civic engagements sites of conflict but also opportunity to assert Christian difference and to exhibit moral virtue.

Rather than treating Tertullian's comments as evidence that those in Christian assemblies routinely abstained from participation in the civic and social life of their colony or that idolatry was a regular source of concern for them, we might, alternatively, investigate the comments for the opposite conclusion. In fact, Tertullian's rhetoric provides evidence that people attending Christian gatherings also attended sacrifices, hung laurel wreaths on their doors and lit lamps, enjoyed political offices and went on imperial military campaigns, sponsored or attended games, visited the theater and circuses, exchanged gifts and blessings with neighbors, cared for household deities, attended naming ceremonies, married non-Christians, and marked imperial cult holidays.[31] We might conclude that they interpreted these actions as civic exercises, which were demanded as a matter of course for life in a Roman colony but held little relevance for their affiliation with a Christian *ecclesia*. As Éric Rebillard argues in his study, *Christians and Their Many Identities in Late Antiquity*, for people in Roman Carthage, Christian allegiance "was only one of the multiple identities that mattered in their everyday life, and we should not assume that the degree of groupness associated with the Christian category was as high, stable, and consistent as Tertullian claims it should be."[32]

If we look beyond Tertullian's writings, in fact, we discover that in his lifetime, we have no epigraphic or archaeological data for "Christians," which calls into question whether those who affiliated with this group identified themselves as part of a separate community.[33] Indeed, we do not even have evidence for a dedicated area exclusively used for Christian burial.[34] When Christian groups gathered for worship (daily in the

---

31. I draw on Rebillard's analysis who employs Gabriel Spiegel's notion of "social logic" of texts to draw out the traces of the "extra-textual pressures at work with texts," a reading strategy that is well suited for Tertullian's pastoral writings directed to Christian audiences; see *Christians and Their Many Identities*, 5–6.

32. Ibid., 9.

33. See J. Patout Burns Jr. and Robin M. Jensen, *Christianity in Roman Africa: The Development of Its Practices and Beliefs* (Grand Rapids: Eerdmans, 2014), 87–88.

34. Christians in North Africa routinely were buried in mixed cemeteries; see Rebillard, *Christians and Their Many Identities*, 69.

THE PERILS OF IDOLATROUS GARB   25

morning and weekly, in the evening, for a meal, as Tertullian indicates that they did, *Apol.* 29.16–19), they occupied buildings that were apparently indistinguishable from the meeting places of other associations, likely domestic dwellings.[35] Those attending Christian meetings were not distinguished by unique names[36] or by the language they spoke (Tertullian himself wrote in both Latin and Greek).[37] They occupied different social and economic positions.[38]

The Roman province of *Africa Proconsularis*, in which Tertullian lived and wrote, boasted wealthy cites (like Carthage), a rich countryside, and diverse populations of Africans (Libyans), Phoenicians, Greeks, Judeans, and, of course, Romans.[39] Carthage played a critical role in imperial administration, as the seat of the Roman provincial governor.[40] Life in Roman Carthage was defined by civic and imperial politics and was populated with an ethnically diverse population. Those who attended Christian meetings lived alongside and were drawn from the many peoples who inhabited this Roman territory.[41] In this Roman colony, communal belong-

---

35. Ibid., 14–15, citing L. Michael White, *The Social Origins of Christian Architecture*, 2 vols. HTS 42–43 (Valley Forge, PA: Trinity Press International, 1996), 2:54–62.

36. Rebillard, *Christians and Their Many Identities*, 67.

37. At the outset of *On the Veiling of Virgins*, Tertullian mentions that he had already argued in Greek for the virgins to veil (*Virg.* 1.1). None of his Greek writings are preserved.

38. Tertullian himself speaks on numerous occasions about slaves, indicating that he was himself a slave-holder; see J. Albert Harrill, "The Domestic Enemy: A Moral Polarity of Household Slaves in Early Christian Apologies and Martyrdoms," in *Early Christian Families in Context: An Interdisciplinary Dialogue*, ed. David L. Balch and Carolyn Osiek (Grand Rapids: Eerdsmans, 2003), 231–54. Felicitas and her companion Revocatus are named as slaves in the Martyrdom of Perpetua (2.1).

39. See Rives, *Religion and Authority*, 17–28; Fergus Millar, "Local Cultures in the Roman Empire: Libyan, Punic, and Latin in Roman Africa," *JRS* 58 (1968): 126–34; Wilhite, *Tertullian the African*, 27–31; and Leslie Dossey, *Peasant and Empire in Christian North Africa* (Berkeley: University of California Press, 2010), esp. 11–16.

40. According to Rives, the seat of the provincial governor and administrative center of Africa Proconsularis became "one of the largest and wealthiest" cities "in the Roman World" (*Religion and Authority*, 27). On the Augustan founding of Carthage, see Allen Brent, *Cyprian and Roman Carthage* (Cambridge: Cambridge University Press, 2010), 29–31.

41. See Wilhite, *Tertullian the African*, 29–30; Dossey, *Peasant and Empire*, 12–13. Our earliest source for Christians in this region, the Acts of the Scillitan Martyrs, features martyrs with Latinized Punic names; see *Act. Scil.* 14 and 16.

ing necessarily took porous and fluid forms. Here provincial elite variously ascribed to themselves a degree of "Roman-ness," even as they maintained overlapping (sometimes even conflicting) affiliations with indigenous and pre-Roman languages, customs, and cultic practices (Afro-Libyan, Greek, Punic, Judean).

We should imagine that affiliation with Christian assemblies was likewise marked by ambiguity and contingency. Tertullian seems keenly aware of these facts. Thus, he undertakes a rhetorical campaign to enable social interaction and practices that might cultivate a feeling of difference—an internalized sensibility of belonging, of "groupness"—to adhere in the members of Christian assemblies.[42] The warning against idolatrous dress suggested itself as one powerful strategy for doing so.

---

42. On "groupness," see Brubaker and Cooper, "Beyond Identity," 20, and the discussion of Brubaker in Rebillard, *Christians and Their Many Identities*, 2–3.

The Philosopher Type in Late Roman Art: Problematizing Cultural Appropriation in Light of Cultural Competition

Arthur P. Urbano Jr.

The funerary complex known as the Hypogeum of the Aurelii was discovered in 1919 in Rome. Dated to the third century CE, it has been the subject of much speculation and analysis.[1] In addition to various narrative scenes, the walls of the two-tiered mausoleum are literally plastered with images of men dressed as philosophers in a variety of sizes, styles, and contexts—conversing and gesticulating in groups, gathered in stylized architectural settings, seated in a bucolic backdrop. None of these figures seems to be portraits of historical philosophers. Instead, they are stylized representations of the learned and virtuous wise man. Some may, in fact, be portraits of the deceased. While scholarly debate has swirled around the religious identities of the monument's patrons, one thing is clear: no matter the "identity" of the patrons or deceased, the site's decoration is emblematic of how pervasive the culture of *paideia* was in third-century Rome.

Early interpreters of the site, including Joseph Wilpert, Goffredo Bendinelli, and Jérôme Carcopino, grappled with the ambiguous nature of its iconography. The juxtaposition of what appeared to be biblical and Homeric scenes with the presence of philosopher figures—including a bearded one assumed to be Christ—led to interpretations of the site as

---

1. For recent analysis, see Fabrizio Bisconti, ed., *L'ipogeo degli Aureli in viale Manzoni: Restauri, tutela, valorizzazione e aggiornamenti interpretativi* (Vatican City: Pontificia Commissione di Archeologia Sacra, 2011); and Alison Crystal Poe, "The Third-Century Mausoleum ('Hypogaeum') of the Aurelii in Rome: Pagan or Mixed-Religion Collegium Tomb" (PhD diss., Rutgers University, 2007).

"heretical," "syncretistic," and "gnostic."[2] A more recent interpretation has identified the patrons as a pagan *familia* that "had departed from the traditional state religion."[3] Another reads it as an example of the "private syncrisis" of a Christian *familia*.[4] Still another understands the patrons as a *collegium* of freedmen with mixed pagan and Christian membership.[5] That one can read the decorative program in all of these ways reveals something about the landscapes of religion and intellectual culture in the third-century Roman Empire. It also exposes presuppositions surrounding the interpretation of iconography and raises important methodological questions about how scholars have conceptualized cultural processes.

In this essay I will use the "philosopher type," like those decorating the Hypogeum of the Aurelii, as a springboard to problematize the concept of "appropriation" when discussing art produced for and by Christians in the third century. Coming to the subject not as an art historian, but as a scholar of religion, I adopt an interdisciplinary approach that brings art-historical perspectives into conversation with cultural and social theory. When treating themes in early Christian art that coincide with Greek and Roman artistic traditions, scholars at different times have applied models of cultural spoliation, adaptation, or continuity. While my position tends towards the latter, I attempt here to account for such continuity without a vague appeal to cultural context as a kind of osmosis. By analyzing examples of the "philosopher type" in third-century Roman art, I focus on one dimension of broader cultural processes. I contend that the appearance of the type in early Christian art attests to how the dynamic contours of third-century *paideia* contributed to the coding and proliferation of the philosopher type as a multivalent cultural sign. After a general description of the philosopher type, I present several theories of cultural appropriation that are tested against four third-century examples of sarcophagi from the city of Rome that prominently feature the philosopher type.

---

2. For an overview of scholarly interpretations, see Agnese Pergola, "Il quadrante delle interpretazioni," in Bisconti, *Ipogeo degli Aureli in viale Manzoni*, 81–124.

3. Nikolaus Himmelmann, *Das Hypogäum der Aurelier am Viale Manzoni: Ikonographische Beobachtungen*, AWL 7 (Wiesbaden: Steiner, 1975), 7–26.

4. Fabrizio Bisconti, "L'ipogeo degli Aureli in viale Manzoni: Un esempio di sincresi privata," *Aug* 25 (1985): 889–903. Recently Bisconti has suggested that the site may not be Christian at all. See Bisconti, "Il sogno e la quiete: L'altro mondo degli Aureli," in Bisconti, *Ipogeo degli Aureli in viale Manzoni*, 11–20.

5. Poe, "Third-Century Mausoleum."

I propose "cultural competition" as a superior model to appropriation when considering this particular type. By cultural competition, I do not mean a simplistic "ours is better than yours" model, which itself is rather vacuous. Instead, following Pierre Bourdieu, I understand competition as a struggle to accumulate cultural capital in a symbolic economy so as to take positions within a field of cultural production.[6] This struggle required knowing the logic of the practices inculcated through *paideia* and, in certain cases, strategies to redefine the capital considered to be of value. If we imagine a subset of the cultured and educated class of late antiquity—and those who aspired to be part of it—as claiming and displaying in funerary contexts visual symbols associated with *paideia*, such as the philosopher type, alongside visual symbols indicative of a Christian identification, we see part of a process whereby the identity of the *pepaideumenos* and the terms for claiming that identity are defined and negotiated.

The Philosopher Type

By the "philosopher type," I mean the stylized portraiture of the intellectual in ancient Greece and Rome. The overwhelming majority of these are male, though there are some female examples.[7] While the type was somewhat variable, some standard elements were retained from classical Greece through the late Roman period. These elements contributed to a vestimentary code whereby clothing, accessories, and other aspects of appearance served as signifiers of gender, social location, profession, and moral constitution.[8] The broad scope of meanings ascribed to dress and appearance were delimited by transforming the garment into words through oral and written descriptions and into images through visual representations. While scholarly attention has most often focused on hair and beard styles, the most consistent and, in my opinion, the most iden-

---

6. Pierre Bourdieu, *The Field of Cultural Production: Essays on Art and Literature*, ed. Randal Johnson (New York: Columbia University Press, 1993), 75, 82–84.

7. For example, the sarcophagus of Crispina in the Pio Cristiano collection of the Vatican Museums (inv. 31552). See also Stine Birk, "Man or Woman? Cross-Gendering and Individuality on Third Century Roman Sarcophagi," in *Life, Death and Representation: Some New Work on Roman Sarcophagi*, ed. Jaś Elsner and Janet Huskinson (New York: de Gruyter, 2010), 229–60.

8. Roland Barthes, *The Fashion System*, trans. Matthew Ward and Richard Howard (New York: Hill & Wang, 1983), 98.

tifying element is the Greek-style mantle. Rectangular in shape, it was wrapped around the waist and draped over the left shoulder, usually leaving the right shoulder and torso bare. Sometimes a tunic was worn underneath. Accessories were also fairly consistent: a scroll or codex in one hand or sometimes a staff, indicating pedagogical *auctoritas* or itinerancy. Gestures of acclamation or declamation indicated teaching or public oratory. Setting is also significant: the subject might be seated, reading from a scroll in a bucolic or architectural setting; the subject might be alone or accompanied by a Muse or other intellectuals; or the subject may be standing in the act of speaking. Though largely associated with Cynics in the early empire, the philosopher's look also was donned by adherents of other philosophical schools.[9]

References to the "philosopher's look" or appearance in both Greek and Roman literature further inform us of its broad social and cultural significations. First, the look signified the profession and lifestyle of a philosopher, as Lucian's description of the Platonist Nigrinus demonstrates (Lucian, *Nigr.* 2). It was also an ethnic marker signaling Greekness in the Roman world. Tertullian contrasted the *romanitas* of the toga with the Greekness of the *pallium*, the Latin term for the philosopher's robe (Tertullian, *Pall.* 3.7.2). To an ancient viewer, the garment indicated that its wearer was an intellectual, but more information was needed to determine his affiliation and allegiances. High and late imperial authors (including the emperor Julian) complained about the floods of bawdy men who had no right to assume the philosopher's look (Julian, *Or.* 9). To delimit and define the signification of the philosopher's look, many intellectuals engaged in a tailoring rhetoric that transformed the material garment into words.[10] With intellectuals of all stripes asserting the superiority of their system, the garment served as a locus of competition as cultural producers, those who "mediate the relationship between culture and class," negotiated its proper custody and the practices to be performed in and by it.[11]

---

9. Arthur P. Urbano, "Sizing up the Philosopher's Cloak: Christian Verbal and Visual Representations of the *Tribōn*," in *Dressing Judeans and Christians in Antiquity*, ed. Kristi Upson-Saia, Carly Daniel-Hughes, and Alicia J. Batten (Surrey, UK: Ashgate, 2014), 178–79.

10. Barthes, *Fashion System*, 235–36.

11. David Swartz, *Culture and Power: The Sociology of Pierre Bourdieu* (Chicago: University of Chicago Press, 1997), 93–94. See also Bourdieu, *Field of Cultural Production*, 41–42.

By the third century, the philosopher's look had become a cultural asset and requirement for those seeking to climb social and political ladders. Roman funerary monuments habitually incorporated the physical and vestimentary traits of the educated, cultured, and moral man. If *paideia* was the social and cultural glue of the Roman aristocracy, the intellectual look was its visible symbol.[12] For the lower classes and freed slaves, the display of learning could indicate social advancement and cultural respectability. In addition, "amateur intellectuals" sought to create an "impression of learning" through a display of cultural goods and signs that could continue to yield honor and prestige even in death.[13] Thus, portraits in the style of the philosopher type could transform the memory of the deceased into a second order "myth"—a signifier of cultural, educational, and moral values.[14] The portraits of the Hypogeum of the Aurelii become imbued with social and cultural meaning that goes beyond the individual Aurelii but is still bound to their memory, elevating their souls and their status.

Henri Irénée Marrou's 1938 study, *Mousikos anēr*, offers a catalog of sarcophagi and monuments with scenes of "the intellectual life," evidence for a milieu he calls a "cult of learning."[15] Building upon Marrou's work, Paul Zanker's masterful *The Mask of Socrates* studies the development of the portraiture of the intellectual from classical Greece to imperial Rome, giving attention to cultural and social contexts. While these studies offer an excellent review of the development of the image of the philosopher in antiquity, they do not adequately account for the cultural and social processes (not just contexts) that saw the entrance of Christians into the ancient intellectual field.

Theorizing Appropriation

The idea that early Christians borrowed and stole from the surrounding culture may have originated among Christians. Origen of Alexandria

---

12. Peter Brown, *Power and Persuasion in Late Antiquity: Towards a Christian Empire* (Madison: University of Wisconsin Press, 1992).

13. Paul Zanker, *The Mask of Socrates: The Image of the Intellectual in Antiquity*, SCL 59 (Berkeley: University of California Press, 1995), 279.

14. Roland Barthes, *Mythologies*, trans. Annette Lavers (New York: Hill & Wang, 1972), 111–17.

15. Henri Irénée Marrou, *Mousikos anēr: Étude sur les scènes de la vie intellectuelle figurant sur les monuments funéraires romains* (Grenoble: Didier & Richard, 1938).

developed a theory of cultural interaction through allegorical exegesis of the "spoliation of the Egyptians" (Exod 12:35–36). Christians could identify and extract certain elements of Greek philosophy and literature as "useful" for understanding the Christian scriptures (Origen, *Ep. Greg.* 2–3). This idea persisted in the thought of later authors (see Gregory of Nyssa, *Vit. Mos.* 115; Augustine, *Doctr. chr.* 2.42). Interestingly, this theory often coexisted with the so-called "dependency theory." First developed among Jews in the Hellenistic period, this theory claimed that the earliest Greek philosophers plagiarized the more ancient ideas of Moses.[16] Together these two ancient forms of cultural theory attempted to explain commonalities in the face of differing identities. Each assumes an idea or practice "belongs" to one group and is taken by another.

In modern scholarship, the notion that Christians "borrowed," particularly in the realm of material culture, has been used to argue for the corruption, or corrupting force, of Christianity. Adolf von Harnack regarded Christian engagement with Greek philosophy and the appearance of Christian art as a corrupting Hellenization of pure Christianity.[17] In contrast, Edward Gibbon and Friedrich Nietzsche saw Christianity as the debasement of classical purity with Christian art emerging as a cultural parasite.[18] These models failed to appreciate the broader semantic system of Roman art, which gradually and organically developed as a dynamic visual language across the various strata of Roman society.[19] These models also presume (perhaps unwittingly) that Christians were a community of strangers to the art, literature, and ideas of the world around them while (wittingly) assuming that these were antithetical to Christianity.

In recent years, scholars have applied more sophisticated analytical lenses that have softened, even blurred the boundaries between "Christian" and "Roman" identities. Robin Jensen notes that "the trend now is to perceive more continuities than discontinuities in the visual culture of

---

16. Daniel Ridings, *The Attic Moses: The Dependency Theme in Some Early Christian Writers* (Göteborg: Acta Universitatis Gothoburgensis, 1995).

17. Paul Corby Finney, *The Invisible God: The Earliest Christians on Art* (New York: Oxford University Press, 1994), 8.

18. See Averil Cameron, *Christianity and the Rhetoric of Empire: The Development of Christian Discourse* (Berkeley: University of California Press, 1991), 120–21.

19. Tonio Hölscher, *The Language of Images in Roman Art* (Cambridge: Cambridge University Press, 2004), 2.

the various religious groups" of Roman antiquity.[20] Taking issue with Jaś Elsner inasmuch as he casts early Christian art as a religious subcategory of Greco-Roman art, Jensen sees not a simple use or transformation of earlier models but a rejection of these models and the creation of new ones.

In the theoretical discourse of cultural analysis, scholars often characterize the Christian participation in ancient culture, especially art, as "appropriation."[21] In *Orientalism*, Edward Said defined "appropriation" as a hegemonic apparatus of representation in an imperial context, a "relationship between cultural unequals."[22] The art historian Robert Nelson has theorized "appropriation" as an active and motivated "adoption of preexisting elements." Rejecting the terms "borrowing" and "influence," he relies on the work of Roland Barthes, who understands "appropriation" as a distorting myth-making through signs. This kind of appropriation "maintains but shifts the former connotations to create the new sign and accomplishes all this covertly." [23] Nelson's examples expose the individual motivations of postmodern artists who consciously appropriate by relocating and reinterpreting objects and images in critique or resistance. However, Nelson also considers appropriation through a postcolonial lens, which views appropriation as an apparatus of power: dominated peoples have little or no control over their own representation.

Mary Louise Pratt speaks of "transculturation" to describe ways that "subordinated or marginalized groups select and invent from materials transmitted to them by a dominant or metropolitan culture." Transculturation occurs within "contact zones," defined as "social spaces where disparate cultures meet, clash, and grapple with each other, often in highly asymmetrical relations of domination and subordination." Transculturation pertains to peoples geographically and historically separated. In colonial contexts, dominated groups do not control what emanates to them from the dominant culture, but "they do determine to varying extents what they absorb into their own, how they use it, and what they make it

---

20. Robin M. Jensen, "Compiling Narratives: The Visual Strategies of Early Christian Visual Art," *JECS* 23 (2015): 1–26.

21. Cameron, *Christianity and the Rhetoric of Empire*, 120–23.

22. Discussed in Kathleen M. Ashley and Véronique Plesch, "The Cultural Processes of 'Appropriation,'" *JMEMS* 32 (2002): 1–15.

23. Robert S. Nelson, "Appropriation," in *Critical Terms for Art History*, ed. Robert S. Nelson and Richard Schiff, 2nd ed. (Chicago: University of Chicago Press, 2010), 162–64.

mean."²⁴ In some cases, colonized subjects represent themselves in ways that engage the colonizers' terms and communicate to their own community. In this regard, Kathleen Ashley and Véronique Plesch have described "appropriation" as a "two-way process" in which exchange and creative response take place.²⁵

Memorialized in Stone

Having reviewed these models and contexts, I turn now to examine four examples of the philosopher type on third-century sarcophagi from the city of Rome.

An Accomplished Young Man

A strigilated sarcophagus housed in the Palazzo dei Conservatori (inv. MC 821/S) depicts a young man in two types of dress (fig. 1). On the left, he wears what Björn Ewald described as an "unusual traditional costume," while on the right, he is depicted in a mantle, without a tunic, barefoot, and with a bundle of scrolls at his feet.²⁶ Multiple portraits in different costumes was not unusual in this period. The emperor Tacitus (275–276) was depicted in a palace fresco in a number of different costumes, including as *palliatus* (Hist. Aug. Vopisc. Tac. 16.2). On the "Brothers Sarcophagus" in the National Archaeological Museum in Naples, the deceased is portrayed in several different styles of dress, including the philosopher's look, a display of the roles and values with which he wished to memorialize himself.²⁷ The young man on the Conservatori sarcophagus remains memorialized by costume representing his place of origin and moral and intellectual character.

Roman Power in Greek Clothing

The third-century sarcophagus of L. Pullius Peregrinus (Museo Torlonia 424) memorialized the deceased, a centurion, in the garb and pose of a

---

24. Mary Louise Pratt, *Imperial Eyes: Travel Writing and Transculturation* (London: Routledge, 1992), 7.
25. Ashley and Plesch, "Cultural Processes of 'Appropriation,'" 6.
26. Björn Christian Ewald, *Der Philosoph als Leitbild: Ikonographische Untersuchungen an römischen Sarkophagreliefs* (Mainz: von Zabern, 1999), 192 (F18).
27. Zanker, *Mask of Socrates*, 279–80.

Figure 1. Strigilate sarcophagus with two portraits of the deceased, one in "traditional costume" (left), the other in philosopher's mantle (right). Third century CE. © Roma: Sovrintendenza Capitolina ai Beni Culturali-Musei Capitolini, inv. 821/S. Photo: Lorenzo De Masi.

man of study rather than a toga or military uniform (fig. 2).[28] Surrounding him and a female figure in the style of a Muse (presumably his wife) are six figures dressed in the Greek mantle, torso exposed, sporting long unkempt hair and beards, and engaged in discussion and contemplation. While Ewald identified these figures as "stylized Cynics," this need not be the case.[29] Since adherents of most schools adopted this look, they could be any brand of philosopher. There is a striking visual contrast between Peregrinus and his learned companions. The Greekness of their long hair, beards, and bare torso emphasize the Romanness of Peregrinus's cropped hair, shaved face, and tunic. He is a Roman robed and surrounded by the cultural capital of Greekness. While the scene gives a nod to Greek cultural superiority, it also evokes Roman colonization. The Greek "other" acts as ornamentation. Peregrinus has appropriated his dress.

A Learned Christian

A sarcophagus dated to the last quarter of the third century is one of the earliest examples of the philosopher type juxtaposed with emerging

---

28. Ibid., 272–75.
29. Ewald, *Philosoph als Leitbild*, 66.

Figure 2. Sarcophagus of L. Pullius Peregrinus depicting the centurion dressed in the philosopher's mantle and reading from a scroll, while surrounded by other philosopher figures and the Muses. 240–260 CE. Rome: Museo Torlonia, inv. 424. DAI (Negative D-DAI-ROM-31.958) Photo: C. Faraglia.

Christian iconography (fig. 3).[30] Discovered in excavations in the church of Santa Maria Antiqua in the Roman Forum, the sarcophagus was moved there from an unknown location. The general scheme bears some similarity to the Peregrinus sarcophagus in its incorporation of the seated philosopher type. In the center are figures of a man and a woman (as *orans*), both with unfinished faces. Dressed in a Greek mantle, the man sits in profile beneath a tree, reading from an open scroll. Instead of being surrounded by Greeks and Muses, the man and woman are flanked by a shepherd, a scene of the baptism of Jesus, and episodes from the story of Jonah. These latter two identify the piece as a Christian commission.

The Philosopher Jesus

Two relief slabs with residual paint, known as the "polychrome fragments," are likely fragments of a late third-century sarcophagus.[31] Engraved with scenes from the New Testament, the fragments present one of the earliest

---

30. Friedrich Wilhelm Deichmann, Giuseppe Bovini, and Hugo Brandenburg, *Rom und Ostia*, vol. 1 of *Repertorium der christlich-antiken Sarkophage* (Wiesbaden: Steiner, 1967), 306–7.

31. Deichmann, Bovini, and Brandenburg, *Rom und Ostia*, 320–22 (fig. 773 a and b).

Figure 3. Christian sarcophagus with male figure seated at center dressed in the philosopher's mantle and reading from a scroll. Circa 260–270 CE. Rome: Santa Maria Antiqua. Photo: Robin Margaret Jensen, used with permission.

extant examples of Jesus in the philosopher's look. While most are healing scenes, an image right of center in the lower register shows Jesus seated frontally on a hill, with curly hair and beard, wearing a mantle with his shoulder and torso exposed (fig. 4). His right hand is extended in an oratorical gesture, and he holds a scroll in the left. The dress, hair, and posture of Christ emphasize ethnic otherness and pedagogic authority. Most art historical readings have focused on Jesus's hair and beard; cursory attention has been paid to his clothing.[32]

Unlike the other examples, there is no portrait of the deceased. Christ, depicted as an eastern wise man, is the focus. Early Christian sources attest to the existence of statuettes of Jesus worshipped alongside images of "the philosophers of the world," including Plato and Pythagoras, by the sect of the Carpocratians (see Irenaeus, *Haer.* 1.25.6). Moreover, as early as the second century, philosophically-trained Christians, like Clement of Alexandria, spoke of Christ as *the* cosmological *paidogogos*. The polychrome Christ is not an appropriation of an extrinsic visual sign but an example of the crafting of a visual mythology that ascribes a new layer of signification to the philosopher type, while affirming the cultural value and social prestige it affords.

---

32. Zanker, *Mask of Socrates*, 300–301.

Figure 4. Detail of polychrome fragments depicting Christ dressed in the philosopher's mantle, holding a scroll, and displaying an oratorical gesture. Circa 290–310 CE. Rome: National Roman Museum-Palazzo Massimo alle Terme. Photo: Arthur P. Urbano, used with permission of the Ministry of Cultural Heritage, Activities, and Tourism-Soprintendenza Speciale per il Colosseo, il Museo Nazionale Romano e l'Area archeologica di Roma.

Evaluating Appropriation

Three incompatibilities present themselves when considering the appearance of the philosopher type in Christian art through the lens of the models of appropriation described above. First, many of these models presume a shift in a symbol's "original" meaning after it has been appropriated—in this case, that it signifies *paideia* in non-Christian contexts but not in Christian contexts. Second, in most, but not all cases, appropriation is understood as occurring from a position of power. Clearly, Christians were not in a position of political power in the third century. Third, while from a postcolonial perspective, appropriation has a transcultural dynamic, in the context of the third-century Roman Empire, permeated as it was by the institutions of Greek learning, Christians experienced cultural, intellectual, and social formation through the same processes as other Romans—most even before they were Christian.

Are the Santa Maria Antiqua sarcophagus and polychrome fragments examples of Christian "appropriation"? The models outlined above offer some helpful directions for answering this question, but none adequately addresses the contexts of *paideia*. Moreover, since ancient sarcophagi were not simply works of art in the modern sense, the input of both consumer and sculpting workshop must be considered with the possibility that the consumer was Christian while the sculptors were not.[33] What really makes the philosopher type of the Christian examples different from the sarcophagi of Peregrinus and the accomplished young man? The type is not really "out of place" on the Christian examples unless we presume that the values represented by the philosopher type were extrinsic to third-century Christian culture and practice. Clearly, the commissioner of the Santa Maria Antiqua sarcophagus invested in the cultural and social prestige of a "sign" that belonged to a visual vocabulary of self-representation signaling metaphysical and cultural elevation. These Christian examples are not wholesale attempts to redefine the type. Instead, they embrace the value of literate education and assert a claim to a position among the ranks of the educated elite. The framing biblical scenes provide a hermeneutic to the contested philosopher type with signifiers of Christian narratives that result in "a shift in the visual rhetoric of Christian iconography."[34] However, this shift was not seismic. These Christian examples demonstrate that the broad cultural signification of the philosopher type was not extrinsic to the lives and values of their Christian commissioners. Rather, it received an additional set of visual hermeneutics that supplemented an already existing cultural code of understanding.

Nelson's postcolonial construction of "appropriation" as an "apparatus of power" is helpful for understanding the ornamental Hellenes on the Peregrinus sarcophagus and, possibly, the two Christian examples, depending on the identity of the commissioners. The images of eastern provincials add a bit of "mystique" to Peregrinus's sarcophagus as cultural capital and serve as reminders of Rome's territorial and cultural appropriation of Greece. On the Santa Maria Antiqua sarcophagus, John the Baptist is depicted as an eastern intellectual and also ornaments the piece. Here the eastern mystique could serve as an evocation of the superior and more ancient origins of Hebrew wisdom for a Roman Christian. However, if the commissioner were of *eastern* origin, that is, a Greek-speaking Christian resident in Rome, the philosopher type could serve as a *reclaiming* of the garb and an assertion of the east's cultural and spiritual superiority over Rome, through the manifestation of Christian wisdom, itself

---

33. Ben Russell, "The Roman Sarcophagus Industry: A Reconsideration," in *Life, Death and Representation: Some New Work on Roman Sarcophagi*, ed. Jaś Elsner and Janet Huskinson (New York: de Gruyter, 2010), 137–38.

34. Jensen, "Compiling Narratives," 15.

considered a purified form of Greek wisdom that did not preclude the study of Greek philosophers.

Pratt's approach to cultural appropriation by "transculturation" is intriguing but would necessitate that something called Christianity be a "disparate culture," separated geographically and historically from Roman culture. Obviously this was not the case. Nevertheless, we can glimpse *intracultural*, rather than intercultural, "contact zones" in the arenas of *paideia*, where Christians participated and introduced new terms of engagement. While Christians living in the Roman Empire (especially those in the east) did not simply have a culture of *paideia* suddenly thrust upon them, since *paideia* itself was a product of the eastern Mediterranean world; they did "to varying extents" absorb some elements of it and reject others at points in the course of their educational formation.

My intention in this paper has not been to offer a general theory on the development of early Christian art or on the relationship between Roman and Christian art. Other models may be more appropriate in later eras of Christian history and cultural production, especially following the Constantinian and Theodosian periods.[35] Instead, focusing on a specific example in a specific period, I have argued that cultural competition, rather than appropriation, provides a model that better takes account of the processes that help us understand the appearance of the philosopher type in third-century Christian art. Within the matrix of this discourse and the expansion of Christian visual vocabulary, the philosopher's look acquired a new direction of signification. This, in turn, became part of the language of competition among the nexus of practices in which the educated elite of Roman Christian communities struggled with each other and with outsiders to enter or remain in the arenas where philosophical ideas, authority, and image were contested.

---

35. See Cameron, *Christianity and the Rhetoric of Empire*, 120–54; and most recently Lee M. Jefferson and Robin Margaret Jensen, eds., *The Art of Empire: Christian Art in Its Imperial Context* (Minneapolis: Fortress, 2015).

Suns, Snakes, and Altars: Competitive Imagery in Constantinian Numismatics

Nathaniel P. DesRosiers

The coinage of Constantine (306–337 CE) presents a variety of interpretive issues, many of which are unique to the period. Since this age saw both junior and senior emperors as well as many claimants and usurpers, a significant array of types and legends exist. In addition, careless numismatic readings and attributions have further complicated issues. For example, many coins *depicting* Constantine were not minted by the emperor but rather were produced by his father, coemperors, and rivals. Similarly, many coins were minted by his sons for years after his death, often representing Christian themes that are not found on Constantine's original types. This means that motifs and religious iconography often did not necessarily represent the actual numismatic program under Constantine. Generally, this has resulted in overly-Christianized and triumphal interpretations of Constantine and his numismatic record, which ignore the historical and political realities of the period. Using this as a starting point, my goals in this essay are two-fold. First, through an examination Constantine's coins dating from his acclamation as Caesar in 306 CE to his defeat of Licinius in 324 CE, which left him as sole ruler of the empire, I will show that coinage represents a powerful medium for tracing and interpreting competition among elites. In doing so, I will show that the numismatic enterprise was a competitive field designed to do much more than just broadcast imperial propaganda. Second, I will demonstrate that the presumed Christianization of his motifs is not only overstated; it misses the entire purpose of issuing coins in this period. Through a careful rereading of Constantine's bronze issues in concert with the historical record, I will show that the coins paint the picture of a shrewd and pragmatic leader whose goal was political and military success in unprecedented times and not a preoccupation with publicly promoting the triumph of Christianity.

Coins, Producers, and Viewers

Among the most consistent problems with the study of ancient numismatics is determining the author and intended viewer. Specifically, who designed and authorized imperial issues? Did emperors or their officials design or approve iconographic motifs? While it is not possible to fully address these issues here, a few general observations are necessary. Numismatists agree that it is unlikely that the emperor himself designed coin types. In fact, types were so consistent in their use of stock images and legends over decades (if not centuries) that it seems that officials at the mints made the initial choices. Only then were styles approved by higher officials and, perhaps, by the emperor himself.[1] While this may be the case, one should not undervalue the importance of coins and their messages for Roman emperors. Certainly the portraiture, motifs, and messages were intended to relate very specific ideas and messages about the emperor, but who was the intended audience?

This leads to another major point of contention among scholars: did coins act as a means of propaganda for disseminating imperial policies and influencing public opinions? One on-going question is whether illiterate individuals understood the legends on their coins and could associate such images with imperial ideologies.[2] It has been suggested that different types were produced for specific audiences or even different social classes.[3] For example, in speaking of the coins of Constantine, Patrick Bruun argued

---

1. For example, see Barbara Levick, "Propaganda and the Imperial Coinage," *Antichthon* 16 (1982): 107–8; M. H. Crawford, "Roman Imperial Coin Types and the Formation of Public Opinion," in *Studies in Numismatic Method: Presented to Philip Grierson*, ed. C. N. L. Brooke, B. H. I. H. Stewart, J. G. Pollard, and T. R. Volk (Cambridge: Cambridge University Press, 1983), 47–64; Carol Humphrey Vivian Sutherland, *Coinage in Roman Imperial Policy: 31 B.C.–A.D. 68* (London: Methuen, 1951), 131.

2. A. H. M. Jones, "Numismatics and History," in *Essays in Roman Coinage Presented to Harold Mattingly*, ed. Carol Humphrey Vivian Sutherland and Robert A. G. Carson (Oxford: Oxford University Press, 1956), 13; Andrew Wallace-Hadrill, "The Emperor and His Virtues," *Historia* 30 (1981): 307–8; Levick, "Propaganda and the Imperial Coinage," 104–16.

3. At minimum, several argue that the legends on coins were directed to liter-

that the bronze *folles* coins were probably minted for the armies and that these related general aspects of imperial rule. Alternatively, the gold issues gave an account of specific historical events, and these may have been meant for the upper classes.[4] Furthermore, a handful of examples from antiquity indicate that there was a general awareness of whose image was depicted on coins.[5] In other words, the achievements of emperors could live on beyond their reign in both their monuments and their coins.[6] So, while the primary goal in designing coin imagery may have been to show the emperor as he wanted to be seen, there was "a high degree of sensitivity" in the selection of images that would best reach their target.[7]

While scholars are far from reaching consensus on these points, most generally agree that coins did present a tangible form of "publicity" that served to illustrate the power and prestige of those who minted them.[8] Accordingly, two tentative conclusions may be put forth that are relevant to this essay. First, following Barbara Levick, coins should be understood as more than public propaganda. Instead, they served as "composite portraits" that mirrored how the emperors saw themselves.[9] As such, emperors and their mint masters could emphasize any number of themes that illustrated past achievements, religious and political continuity, and, above all, the unmistakable iconography of power. Second, ancients were used to complex amalgamations of visual images and especially those of their emperors. Therefore, as William Metcalf has argued, coins would serve to remind the masses of the past achievements of the emperor and

---

ate upper classes. For discussion, see Wallace-Hadrill, "Emperor and His Virtues," 298–323.

4. Patrick M. Bruun, *Constantine and Licinus A.D. 307–337*, vol. 7 of *The Roman Imperial Coinage* (London: Spink & Son, 1966), 1–23; see also Paul Stephenson, *Constantine: Roman Emperor Christian Victor* (New York: Overlook, 2010), 70.

5. E.g., Matt 22:21; Mark 12:17; Luke 20:24; Epictetus, *Diatr.* 3.3.3; 4.5.15–17; Cassius Dio, *Roman History* 78.16.5.

6. Andrew Meadows and Jonathan Williams, "Moneta and the Monuments: Coinage and Politics in Republican Rome," *JRS* 91 (2001): 27–49.

7. William E. Metcalf, "Whose *Liberalitas*? Propaganda and the Audience in the Early Roman Empire," *RIN* 95 (1993): 343–46.

8. Generally, scholarship has tried to avoid the term "propaganda" in recent years, suggesting that it is a loaded and misleading term. Coins did not try to present misinformation or secret agendas. For discussion, see Levick, "Propaganda and the Imperial Coinage," 104–7.

9. Ibid., 108.

the continued promise of present and future beneficence.[10] Accordingly, Bruun has argued that the reverses of the coins of Constantine represent a commentary on the affairs of the state.[11] This is not to say that Roman emperors needed to issue coins to sway public favor towards their programs and ideologies. As autocratic rulers, emperors did not rely on public consensus for their policies. Rather, coins and their content could have promoted a certain form of loyalty to the sovereign by reminding them of their duty to repay imperial favors. From the perspective of the emperor, coins were one of the many (if not minor) ways of paving the way for a less turbulent principate.

While coins and the images contained on them may have had many possible functions, I would like to suggest that cultural competition among elites is also an appropriate model for interpreting imperial numismatic iconography. Thus, following Pierre Bourdieu's theory on symbolic capital, I am suggesting that emperors could use coins to demonstrate their own qualifications for rule by touting religious, political, and military achievements.[12] Understanding Roman coins in this way is valuable to the current study, because it can help us to understand how emperors competed with other elites—including one another—through this medium. In the coins of Constantine, one can trace how competition between himself and both past and contemporary coemperors evolved and adapted.

Competitive Space

Perhaps most daunting is the figure of Constantine himself whose giant shadow and unquestioned importance to Christianity have made him a particularly difficult subject of study. Readers often see the edicts of Constantine and his contemporaries as signs of tolerance and, following Eusebius, many view nearly any religious activity as a statement of Constantine's true faith, no matter how ambiguous the evidence. For example,

---

10. Metcalf, "Whose *Liberatitas*," 346.
11. Bruun, *Constantine and Licinius*, 64–74.
12. Naturally, emperors had the financial capital as well as symbolic capital necessary to acquire the throne. For discussion of symbolic capital, see Pierre Bourdieu, *The Field of Cultural Production: Essays on Art and Literature*, ed. Randal Johnson (New York: Columbia University Press, 1993), 82–84; and, in this volume, Arthur Urbano, "The Philosopher Type in Late Roman Art: Problematizing Cultural Appropriation in Light of Cultural Competition."

Hal A. Drake describes Constantine's clemency towards those of varying religious devotions as acts of tolerance, although he also characterizes them as "minimal and grudging" actions that are tilted towards his own preference for Christianity. Drake continues by asserting that Constantine wanted to create a "neutral public space" that allowed for, but did not promote, other views.[13]

Although Drake's work is commendable in most respects, his claims about Contantine's motivations suffer from the same methodological inconsistencies that plague many works on Constantine. First, as Steve Larson has rightly argued, tolerance is an anachronistic term that really does not apply to the ancient world. "Toleration" means to "allow to exist" or "to be done or practiced without authoritative interference or molestation." After all, inclusiveness in a crowded polytheistic system is not the same thing as tolerance.[14] Moreover, in the Roman world it was generally understood that the emperor outlined proper religious practices for his subjects.[15] The historical evidence demonstrates that under Constantine the imperial system remained consistent in this regard. Therefore, again following Larson, we might imagine that the religious edicts of the age represent a decrease in control for the sake of other motives, not an abandonment of religious ideology and control altogether.

Linked to the discussion of tolerance is the issue of space and the competition to control it. As Larson has persuasively argued, "neutral" or more properly "neutral space" did not exist in the ancient world.[16] Whether one is discussing sacred space, the texts developed by cultural producers, or material artifacts including official coins issued by monarchs, competition is always present with each group vying to present its message and its superiority concretely. In fact, all of these examples, and especially the minting of coins, represent a very specific form of competition: that which

---

13. Hal A. Drake, "Constantine and Consensus," *CH* 64 (1995): 1–15.

14. Steven J. Larson, "The Trouble with Religious Tolerance in Roman Antiquity," in *Religious Competition in the Third Century CE: Jews, Christians, and the Greco-Roman World*, ed. Jordan D. Rosenblum, Lily C. Vuong, and Nathaniel P. DesRosiers (Göttingen: Vandenhoeck & Ruprecht, 2014), 50. See also A. D. Lee, "Traditional Religions," in *The Cambridge Companion to the Age of Constantine*, ed. Noel Lenski (New York: Cambridge University Press, 2006), 164–67.

15. Larson, "Trouble with Religious Tolerance," 58.

16. For discussion and examples, see ibid., 50–59; Steven Larson, "What Temples Stood For: Constantine, Eusebius, and Roman Imperial Practice" (PhD diss., Brown University, 2008).

is conducted between the most elite members of ancient society in the context of political power and what Stanley Stowers calls the religion of the literate cultural producer. In this specific mode of religion, the cultural producer, including the emperor himself, seeks to defend, define, and change understandings of religious practice and meaning.[17] Thus, this mode sees the emperor himself competing with others in the process of meaning making, with the goal of promoting civic interests.[18] Certainly one could argue that some motifs used by Constantine in his coins appear "unaligned" or "unbiased" religiously, since only a small percentage of types display anything that could be interpreted as Christian and many of his coins lack depictions of traditional deities. However, I contend that this should not be counted as tolerance or neutrality. Instead, this is a very deliberate attempt to refine and/or defend certain events, ideas, slogans, and images in the name of promoting a very specific civic interest: that which aligns directly with how the emperor saw himself. Thus, I will argue that even these seemingly innocuous or "unaligned" images actually relay very potent statements of Constantine's intentions and religious policies that are just as powerful as anything his more traditional predecessors minted on their own coins.

While Constantine himself may have held very particular religious beliefs, recent history would have taught him that both persecution and the promotion of novel gods usually had disastrous results. Accordingly, Constantine described his own rule as mild and full of clemency, while those of his predecessors and opponents are often cast as cruel, tyrannical, and even uncivilized. Constantine's own words—which seem to reflect on

---

17. Stanley K. Stowers has theorized that there are four analytical modes of religiosity in the ancient world. These are: (1) those practicing the religion of everyday social exchange, (2) the religion of the literate cultural producer, (3) civic religion, and (4) the religion of the literate cultural producer and political power. See Stowers, "The Religion of Plant and Animal Offerings versus the Religion of Meanings, Essences, and Textual Mysteries," in *Ancient Mediterranean Sacrifice*, ed. Jennifer Wright Knust and Zsuzsanna Várhelyi (New York: Oxford University Press, 2011), 35–56; and Stowers's article in this volume, "Why Expert versus Non-expert Is Not Elite versus Popular Religion: The Case of the Third Century."

18. Stowers, "Religion of Plant and Animal Offerings," 53–54. While Stowers specifically has ritual practices in mind when discussing these modes, I am extending his model to include the practice of claiming space and producing iconographic forms including those on coins, as these are very clear examples of literate experts using their political power to refine and define practice and opinion.

his many years of successful rule—will help to demonstrate this point. In his letter to Alexander of Alexandria and Arius (October 324), Constantine says that he aims to unite the inclinations of all people on divine matters through the "mind's eye into a single sustaining habit."[19] His second stated goal was to bring the empire back together through military might. Although this later goal is often read as a reference to the uniformity of Christianity, or even tolerance, I would argue that Constantine's message was much more transparent: he is making an imperial commitment to restore the empire and bring about sustainable peace, as he himself says. Downplaying or nuancing the religious motivation of his message also fits more readily with the second part of the statement: that he wanted to reunite the empire through might.[20]

Though Drake finds the style of Constantine's language to be "maddeningly elliptical,"[21] I believe that such "political" language is intentional. Even when Constantine appears to lean more in favor of Christianity during his later reign, he is generally pragmatic and uses open-ended language and iconography to avoid excluding either Christians or practitioners of traditional religions. In fact, his numismatic output is very traditional in most ways, indicating that the program was meant to demonstrate continuity not novelty. Most important, given Constantine's complicated rise to power and his history of civil war, the coinage represents deliberate efforts not to alienate anyone, especially members of his army, which undoubtedly had many practitioners of traditional religions among its members. Thus, Constantine's use of elliptical language (whether in speech or on coins) and his mix of symbols could "contain a number of ambiguous and even contradictory meanings that can be manipulated according to the speaker's purposes."[22]

---

19. The letter is attested in multiple sources, including Eusebius, *Vit. Const.* 2.64–72; Socrates, *Hist. eccl.* 1.7; Gelasius, *Hist. eccl.* 2.4. For discussion, see Stuart G. Hall, "Some Constantinian Documents in the *Vita Constantini*," in *Constantine: History and Historiography*, ed. Samuel N. C. Lieu and Dominic Montserrat (New York: Routledge, 1998), 86–104.

20. In fact, Constantine articulates a similar view in his "Letter to the Eastern Provincials" (ca. 324). Here he emphasizes the "advantages of peace and quiet," and he orders, "let no one disturb another" in religious matters (*Vit. Const.* 2.48–60, esp. 2.56.1).

21. Drake, "Constantine and Consensus," 12.

22. Ibid.

Rereading Constantine's Numismatic Output

Guided by the assumption that Constantine was drawing on a variety of traditional themes as well as "elliptical" or devotionally "indefinite" images, I will demonstrate that the use (or disuse) of certain images and legends is intentional, and such selective iconography was designed to help Constantine realize his goals of promoting peace and putting the common cause of empire first. In this way, Constantine's official coins do not demonstrate "tolerance" or "neutrality" but rather represent a conspicuous form of competition, promoting the carefully choreographed and controlled religious, military, and political policies of a thoughtful and skilled leader.

Early Coins: Constantine the Usurper

In 306 CE at the death of his father Constantius, Constantine was proclaimed Augustus by his father's army, even though under the Tetrarchy's rules of succession Constantine had no claim to the throne. Several recent scholars have emphasized that Constantine's rise to power gave him the appearance of a usurper.[23] Since his ascension was problematic, if not illegal, Constantine worked to fashion himself as a legitimate claimant, and the competing images on the coinage of this period demonstrate the controversy. Accordingly, many of Constantine's earliest coins were not of his own design, due in part to the haste of his elevation. During the imperial period, it was also common for successors to retain coin types and legends as a means of maintaining continuity with those who preceded them. Given the joint rule of the Tetrarchy, emperors often copied one another's types and minted coins of each other as a way of demonstrating unity. Furthermore, in Tetrarchic art, it is difficult if not impossible to tell the difference between figures, thus emphasizing the office of the ruler instead of a particular individual (see fig. 1).[24] Accordingly, early types depicting

---

23. See Mark Humphries, "From Usurper to Emperor: The Politics of Legitimation in the Age of Constantine," *JLA* 1 (2008): 82–100, 84–87; Raymond Van Dam, *The Roman Revolution of Constantine* (New York: Cambridge University Press, 2007), 36; Robert Frakes, "The Dynasty of Constantine Down to 363," in *The Cambridge Companion to the Age of Constantine*, ed. Noel Lenski (New York: Cambridge University Press, 2006), 100–103; against this view, see Timothy D. Barnes, *Constantine and Eusebius* (Cambridge: Harvard University Press, 2006), 38.

24. Cf. Jaś Elsner, "Perspectives in Art," in Lenski, *Cambridge Companion to the*

Constantine were minted by other tetrarchs in their usual style, including issues from 307 CE by Maxentius depicting Constantine as a junior Caesar and Galerius calling him "Filius Augustus" (son of Augustus).²⁵ In that same year, perhaps in an effort to improve his image as a legitimate ruler, Constantine also minted coins of his coemperors for circulation in his own territory.²⁶

Although many of Constantine's earliest coins show continuity with Tetrachic types, it would not be long before he issued new forms, which favored his own particular and more distinctive iconography. Among his earliest issues from 307 to 312 CE were coins with new style portraits that broke away from Tetrarchic convention, including a clean-shaven, Augustan-looking likeness of the emperor carrying the self-appointed title of Augustus (figs. 2 and 3). On the reverse of these coins is a prince with a spear and the legend "in honor of the prince of youth."²⁷ While this revival of Augustan iconography and language is interesting

Figure 1. Constantine I, Ticinum Mint, 306–307 CE. Obverse: CONSTANTINVS NOB CAES ("Constantine our Caesar"). Courtesy of the American Numismatic Society.

Age of Constantine, 255–77, 260–64. Lactantius, *Mort.* 25.1–2, suggests that Constantine sent his own official portraits to Galerius, perhaps demonstrating that from the beginning Constantine sought to legitimate and differentiate both his power and his imagery from that of the Tetrarchs.

25. In 312 CE, types begin to appear depicting Constantine on the obverse with Hercules on the reverse with the legend "to Hercules the victor." This is an example of a coin that was common in the Tetrarchy, since the Western emperors Maximian and Constantius (Constantine's father) aligned themselves with Hercules. While this coin is often identified as proof that Constantine was committed to the traditions of the past, evidence suggests that he never minted this coin. It was issued by either Galerius or Licinius since the type was minted in Nicomedia, a region Constantine did not control in 312 CE.

26. Patrick Bruun, *Studies in Constantinian Numismatics: Papers from 1954 to 1988*, AIRF 12 (Rome: Institutum Romanun Finlandiae, 1991), 133.

27. For discussion, see Stephenson, *Constantine*, 117.

in and of itself, it is likely that certain historical events gave rise to the minting of these types. For example, the very ancient title "prince of youth" perhaps represents the precarious state that Constantine found himself in during these early years. Galerius the Augustus in the east had only accorded Constantine the title of Caesar before 310 CE, but in his own territory, Constantine functioned as, and held the title of, Augustus.[28] To emphasize his right to this title while also separating himself from his rivals, Constantine restored Augustan motifs, modeling himself in the Julio-Claudian style of eternal youth. Reviving such a type would not only represent a powerful statement of legitimacy and continuity with traditional *imperium* but presumably to reignite the optimism for new beginnings emphasized in the Augustan program.

Figure 2 (left). Constantine I Gold Solidus. Treveri Mint. 310–313 CE. Obverse: Bust of Constantine I. CONSTANTINUS PF AUG ("Constantine pious and fortunate Augustus"). Courtesy of the American Numismatic Society. Figure 3 (right). Constantine I Gold Solidus. Treveri Mint. 310–313 CE. Reverse: Prince with a spear. PRINCIPI IVVENTUTIS ("in honor of the prince of youth"). Courtesy of the American Numismatic Society.

In addition, the coins of 307 to 312 CE relate the competitive rivalry between Constantine and Maxentius that was continuing to deepen. Like Constantine, Maxentius was himself a usurper, and his coins depict his portrait in Tetrarchic type with very traditional reverses representing dei-

---

28. Humphries, "From Usurper to Emperor," 92.

ties such as Roma and Romulus and Remus with the She-Wolf (figs. 4 and 5). Accordingly, Constantine began to develop a military numismatic theme that would last throughout his reign. Though military motifs were hardly novel—they were among the most popular of types throughout Roman history—the choice to emphasize these types points to how Constantine understood himself. In particular, Constantine issued coins announcing himself as Augustus on the obverse with reverses depicting Mars Conservatori (Mars the protector) and Mars Parti Propugnatori (defender of the father) (fig. 6). Numerous types of these coins exist, and they were minted up until 315 CE. While Mars is clearly a traditional god and one featured on many Roman coins in the third and early fourth centuries, the choice of these images probably is less reflective of personal conviction and more in keeping with the military theme that is the most frequently recurring topic on his coins. Instead

Figure 4 (top). Maxentius. Rome Mint. 308–310 CE. Reverse: Roma Temple. Courtesy the American Numismatic Society. Figure 5 (left). Maxentius. Ostia Mint. 309–312 CE. Reverse: Romulus and Remus with the She-Wolf. Courtesy the American Numismatic Society. Figure 6 (right). Constantine I. Trier Mint. 307-308 CE. Reverse: MARTI PARTI PROPUGNATORI ("Mars defender of the fatherland"). Personal collection of Nathaniel R. DesRosiers. Photograph by author.

of appearing as the usurper, these images styled Constantine as a legitimate, traditional, and moderate ruler, who presented a clear alternative to his rash, cruel, and tyrannical counterpart.

The next significant event that is reflected in the coinage occurs in 310 CE, when Maximian had fallen out with his son and, in a desperate grab for power, tried to seize Constantine's holdings. After this failed coup, Constantine forced him to commit suicide.[29] To commemorate these events a new type appeared featuring a reverse depicting Constantine on horseback with the legend "Adventus Augustus" (fig. 7). This coin was minted in London, and it has been suggested that it was struck in preparation for an imperial visit that never happened. However, I would argue that this coin was minted as a statement: the old Augustus was gone, and a new one had risen. Much like the "prince of youth" legends, these coins demonstrated the optimism of a new reign, giving more authenticity to Constantine's claim to the title Augustus. These events also resulted in other new types, including issues promulgating the concord of the army and perpetual peace. These are the first signs of the new program that would mark Constantine's rule: the praise of the army for its steadfastness and the goal of establishing lasting peace through this army.

Figure 7. Constantine I. London. 310–312 CE. Reverse: Constantine on horseback. ADVENTVS AVGG ("arrival of Augustus"). Copyright of the Trustees of the British Museum

Aside from the fact that Constantine was breaking with Tetrarchic style, there is little that is unusual about Constantine's coins up to the year 315 CE. In fact, as Steven Hijmans describes it, these issues were "typical in every respect."[30] While this may be true as far as innovative images and legends are concerned, this statement overlooks the real value of minting such coins. It was not in the best interest of an emperor—and especially a

---

29. Timothy D. Barnes, *The New Empire of Diocletian and Constantine* (Cambridge: Harvard University Press, 1982), 70.

30. Steven E. Hijmans, "Sol: The Sun in the Art and Religions of Rome" (PhD diss., University of Groningen, 2009), 612.

new one without a clear path to the throne—to develop unfamiliar, erratic, or confrontational types. This emperor not only wanted to appear traditional to maintain the support of his subjects (and especially the army), he also wanted to see himself in this way. Moreover, selecting certain types of coins represented a carefully choreographed competition between those vying for control of territories and those living in it.

The Rise of Sol

Numerous significant events occurred between 310 and 313 CE, and these served as catalysts for important changes in Constantine's coinage. In addition to the defeat of Maximian, 310 CE is the year that Constantine had his famous vision near the temple of Apollo, perhaps near Grand, Vosges in Gaul. From this point onward, Constantine "began trumpeting the idea that he had special connections to Apollo or to an even more popular sun god among previous emperors, Sol."[31] Accordingly, the god Sol would become one of the most enduring images on Constantine's coins. Sol was of course a very important deity, appearing on coins in the first and second centuries CE, with increased frequency from Septimius Severus onward. Most important, Sol served as the patron god of several third-century emperors from Aurelian down to Constantine.[32] The elevation of Sol among later Roman emperors is often read as innovative and an expression of henotheism since Sol's veneration comes to dominate imperial ideology. However, I would suggest that the focus on this god, like so many other images on Constantine's types, is better understood as a revival of traditional religious policy, reflecting Roman religious conservatism. Constantine's father favored Sol, and both were related to Aurelian as well. As an emperor who was competing for power against others,

---

31. For discussion, see Noel Lenski, "The Reign of Constantine," in Lenski, *Cambridge Companion to the Age of Constantine*, 66–70; Barnes, *Constantine and Eusebius*, 36.

32. Aurelian elevated this cult, making its priests *pontifices* and not just *sacerdotes* as had been the case. All priests in this cult were also members of the senatorial elite, suggesting that emphasizing this cult would be a means of galvanizing the support of other elites. See Hijmans, "Sol," 504–5; Stephenson, *Constantine*, 78. For a specific discussion of coins depicting Sol, see John F. White, *Restorer of the World: The Roman Emperor Aurelian* (Stonehouse, UK: Spellmount, 2007), 135–36; George C. Brauer Jr., *The Age of the Soldier Emperors: Imperial Rome, A.D. 244–284* (Park Ridge, NJ: Noyes, 1975), 229–32.

emphasizing the family bonds in this way would be critical for demonstrating legitimacy.

Interestingly, the earliest Sol types minted by Constantine are unusual since the god is depicted as rather stout, unlike any previous portrait (fig. 8). This early trend has led some to speculate whether the intent was to make Sol look more like Constantine or a family grouping.[33] Also, emperors who connected themselves to Sol or any deity were demonstrating their own personal relationships to that divinity, indicating both a personal piety and a reinforced statement about their positions of power.[34] On his Sol coins, Constantine also employed the somewhat unusual epithet of "unconquerable," usually associated with Jupiter, Mars, and Hercules.[35] Likewise, the god also is described as the emperor's "companion," further linking the "family" together. What is also often overlooked is the fact that Sol was among the most appropriate of gods for consolidating power. Sol was one of the *sacra gentilicia*, making him one of the oldest traditional gods of the city,[36] and as stated above, aristocrats populated the god's priesthoods. Perhaps most important, the Sol cult was popular among the military, and there can be little doubt that the soldier emperors intentionally linked their successes to those gods favored by their armies. Taking all of this together, Constantine's multivalent connections to Sol helped him to strengthen his cultural capital, making his regnal powers all the more powerful both figuratively and literally. At the same time, he was able

---

33. This is also a common feature in traditional imperial iconography, with emperors as early as Augustus seeking to resemble gods such as Apollo, Hermes, Hercules, and Jupiter. See Paul Zanker, *The Power of Images in the Age of Augustus* (Ann Arbor: University of Michigan Press, 1998), 33–77.

34. This is reminiscent of Augustus's religious program after his own civil war. When Augustus was seeking to prove his own qualifications as the next leader of Rome, he needed to link himself to Caesar's Venus Genetrix. See Zanker, *Power of Images*, 53–65.

35. Hijmans, "Sol," 18.

36. While Sol was an early god, it appears that his cult had waned by the early second century CE. It was revived in the third century under Aurelian, and some argue that it was a completely different cult from its Republican origins. For discussion, see Steven E. Hijmans, "The Sun Which Did Not Rise in the East: The Cult of Sol Invictus in the Light of Non-literary Evidence," *BABesch* 71 (1996): 115–50. However, I would suggest that it is irrelevant to Constantine's purposes whether the cult was continuous or not. What would be valuable is the appeal to both family and traditional Roman history.

to use these connections to compete more effectively against other emperors and imperial claimants.

New Uses for Traditional Types

By 313 CE, Constantine's so-called edicts of toleration coauthored with Licinius had gone into effect. Constantine also had conquered Maxentius at the Milvian Bridge, leaving him as sole ruler of the west. Such events had major effects on Constantine and his rule, which are reflected in the coinage. Having strengthened his power base and demonstrated his clemency to his subjects, Constantine could commemorate these events and celebrate his fortune.

Figure 8. Constantine I. Treveri Mint. 310 CE. Reverse: Bust of Sol. SOLI INVICTO COMITI ("Sol, the unconquered companion"). Courtesy of the American Numismatic Society.

That said, one does not suddenly see a proliferation of Christian images in Constantinian iconography. In fact, it is difficult to prove historically that Constantine harbored any definitive monotheistic Christian sentiments this early, unless one relies on the apologetic accounts of Eusebius (*Vit. Const.* 27–32) and Lactantius (*Mort.* 44.5). However, even if one does accept that Constantine was a Christian at this point, one should not expect to see overt professions of faith as part of his official numismatic program. As an astute emperor and general who was championing peace and clemency while at the same time trying to maintain an army that probably was still practicing traditional religion, Constantine could not afford to abandon tradition all at once.

Evidence for Constantine's calculated response is apparent in the coins of Sol minted after 312 CE. Images of the god not only persist, they still dominate many types until the year 325 CE (fig. 9). The significant difference is that more traditional portraits of a standing and slender Sol replace the more corpulent images. Although the reasons for this change are not entirely clear, it certainly does open up speculation. Was Constantine distancing himself somehow by making the images of himself and the god more distinct? Did individual mints continue the type without Constantine's direct consent? Whatever the case may be, it is clear that the continued use of this image was important for demonstrating imperial continuity and an affinity with soldiers and aristocrats. However, unique variations begin to appear slowly, and between 316 and 317 CE, an issue from the Ticinum mint depicts Sol with a cross in the field to Sol's right (fig. 10). While we have no way of knowing whether this cross was an overt Christian symbol at this point or anything more than a local variation, I would suggest that this represents at the very least the kind of mixed religious iconography that encapsulates Constantine's policy of peace. Such mixed image coins become too common in the coming years to imagine that they are just chance. Perhaps again this is the type of "elliptical language" that "contain[s] a number of ambiguous and even contradictory meanings that can be manipulated according to the speaker's purposes."[37] In short, as an elite cultural producer in political power, the emperor is able to refine those images that are important for his civic purposes. In this case, mixing images casts the broadest possible audience: elites/nonelites, Christians/non-Christians, and soldiers/civilians.

By 318 CE, a variation on another very old traditional type appears. The obverse depicts Constantine in armor with a reverse showing two

Figure 9 (left). Constantine I. Arles Mint. 312–318 CE. Reverse: Sol standing. SOL INVICTI COMITI ("Sol, the unconquered companion"). Personal collection of Nathaniel R. DesRosiers. Photograph by author. Figure 10 (right). Constantine I. Ticinum Mint. 316–317 CE. Reverse: Sol with cross in field. SOL INVICTI COMITI ("Sol, the unconquered companion"). Personal collection of Nathaniel R. DesRosiers. Photograph by author.

---

37. Drake, "Constantine and Consensus," 12.

victories holding a shield with the inscription "VOT P R" (vows of the Roman people) and the legend VICTORIAE LAETAE PRINC PERP "Joyous Victory to the Eternal Prince." Once again, the perspective of the viewer will create great variation in the interpretation of these symbols. On the one hand, this coin is very traditional; it uses the ancient iconographic themes of two victories, the *vota*, or vows of the people conducted since the time of Augustus,[38] a traditional altar for sacrifice, and Constantine (or perhaps Sol?) as the eternal prince. Yet, all of these may be read as Christian symbols. Instead of victories, there are angels, a church altar, and Jesus (though not pictured) is the eternal prince.[39] Subtle differences in the types, including what looks like a cross on the front of the altar also fuels debate (fig. 11). While the symbol could be a Christian cross, the coins of decidedly non-Christian emperors such as Vespasian and Valerian also have similar cross shapes on altars when they minted victory/wreath/altar types. Furthermore, one could question whether the average practitioner of traditional religions would notice such a subtle change. On the other hand, such variation could be significant to a small percentage of the Christian population and the emperor himself who might be aiming to refine the meaning of the cross shape through such scenes.

Images of Altars

As indicated above, altars are very commonly represented on Roman coins. The iconographic meaning also seems to be clear: traditional devotion to the gods results in continued blessing for Rome and her leaders. However, if Constantine was indeed Christian by this period, the appearance of these altars is potentially problematic. Surprisingly, scholars have largely overlooked the coins of Constantine bearing the inscription *beata tranquillitas* (blessed peace) on the altar itself (fig. 12). First, it should be noted that these are of a completely unique design; this particular type was issued only by Constantine and minted between 320 and 325 CE.[40] The

---

38. Tacitus, *Agr.* 21; *Hist.* 1.76; Pliny, *Ep.* 10.35–36, 101–102. This type of vow is derived from the practice of ancient consuls who would make vows to the gods for the well-being of the state. Livy, *Ad Urbe Condita* 22.10; see Mary Beard, John North, and Simon Price, *A History*, vol. 1 of *The Religions of Rome* (New York: Cambridge University Press, 1998), 32–35, 320.

39. See Bruun, *Studies in Constantinian Numismatics*, 54–56.

40. Constantine himself is not the only figure depicted on the obverse of these

Figure 11. Constantine I. London Mint. 320 CE. Obverse: cuirassed bust of Constantine I. Reverse: two victories holding a votive shield over an altar. VICTORIAE LAETAE PRINC PERP ("joyous victory to the eternal prince"). Copyright of the Trustees of the British Museum.

altars are Roman style and not Christian, since Christian altars apparently were traditional tables made of wood until the sixth century CE (Augustine, *Ep.* 185.27). Furthermore, already by Constantine's time, many Christian authors had described traditional non-Christian altars as abhorrent places of sin.[41] That said, some observations should be made that can push us in the direction of fruitful interpretation. First, altars are an established symbol, and this should be read as another example of Constantine's appreciation for continuity with Rome's traditional strengths, including religious devotion. Second, the altars depicted are of the votive type, like those found dedicated by soldiers in places like Maryport and Housesteads in England.[42] Thus, these coins show yet a further connection between the emperor and his armies. Third, the coin's legend of "blessed peace" again

---

coins. He also minted coins depicting his sons Crispus, Constantine, Constantius, and Constans who were recently elevated as Caesars. This could potentially be understood as competition of a different type; he is signaling who the next rulers are to any potential claimants and denying any possibility of returning to Tertrachic rules of succession.

41. For example, see 1 Cor. 10:21 where Paul calls altars "tables of demons." In Acts John 42, the apostle destroys an altar of Artemis. Cf. Tertullian, *Nat.*10; Minucius Felix, *Oct.*10; Origen, *Cels.* 8.17–20; Cyprian, *Ep.* 55.14.1, 59.12.2, 65.1.

42. See Martin Henig, *Religion in Roman Britain* (New York: Routledge, 2003), 74.

captures the stated goal of Constantine's reign. In sum, the message is that through piety (and perhaps not at the exclusion of traditional cult at this point) the empire will be unified.

The Final Stage

Between 323 and 325 CE, there was an abrupt discontinuation of many of the most popular coin types from the early years of Constantine's reign. Images of Sol and both sacrificial and votive altars disappear and are replaced by completely new styles. It is perhaps no coincidence that in 323 CE the Council of Nicaea was held with Constantine himself overseeing the proceedings. It also seems that Constantine no longer offered sacrifices at Rome as Pontifex Maximus during this time, indicating that at this point his personal religious convictions had fully shifted.[43] However, this should not be understood as the only motivation. Relations between Constantine and his coemperor Licinius were in constant tension for nearly ten years. After Constantine defeated him in 324 CE, there were no longer any direct threats from rival claimants to his throne nor were there any real blockades to limit the scope of his policies. As a result, several new types develop representing the new goals and achievements of the now aged emperor.

Figure 12. Constantine I. London Mint. 323–324 CE. Reverse: altar with globe. BEATA TRANQUILLITAS ("blessed peace"). Copyright of the Trustees of the British Museum.

Perhaps the most compelling coin issue that followed the defeat of Licinius is the SPES PUBLIC (hope of the people) type depicting a snake on the obverse speared by an imperial standard crowned with a Chi Rho emblem (fig. 13). Constantine minted this coin between the years 327

---

43. While there is some evidence that Constantine refused to perform blood sacrifices in Rome, he did maintain the title of Pontifex Maximus throughout his life. The date of Constantine's refusal to sacrifice is often apologetically dated to 312–313 CE, more recent scholarship has suggested that either 315 or even 325 CE is a more likely date. In either case, the sources are perhaps deliberately unclear on this point. See Zosimus, *Historia Nova* 4.36.4. For discussion, see Lee, "Traditional Religions," 171.

and 328 CE as one of the first types produced in the soon to be capital of Constantinople. This is the only Constantinian coin that has clear Christian competitive symbolism, and it is interesting that his defeat of Licinius seems to be equated with a victory over the devil himself. This is made even more striking when one considers the subject matter of many of Licinius's late coins, which usually depicted Jupiter as the emperor's personal companion and protector (fig. 14).[44] Furthermore, it is remarkable that Constantine ceases production of his altar coins, perhaps indicating yet another shift in attitude. Although it is easy to read such Christian ideas onto these coins, I again would suggest caution. While one could imagine that certain Christian viewers would understand the meaning of such an image, there is no reason to assume that a non-Christian in the middle of the fourth century would ever pick up the same highly theological meaning. To be sure, the image would be unusual, but there is little reason to assume that non-Christians would read this as Christian victory over Satan and traditional Roman cults rather than Constantine's conquest over Licinius and his armies.

Figure 13 (above). Constantine I. Constantinople Mint. 327 CE. Obverse: Bust of Constantine I. Reverse: Chi Rho on imperial standard piercing a snake. Copyright the Trustees of the British Museum. Figure 14 (left). Licinius. Arles Mint. 317–318 CE. Reverse: Jupiter with thunderbolt and scepter. IOVI CONSERVATORI ("Jupiter Protector"). Courtesy of the American Numismatic Society.

---

44. See Bruun, *Studies in Constantinian Numismatics*, 61–63. Also, it should be noted that Cyprian connected chthonian deities depicted on altars with snakes and describes these creatures as images of the devil himself (*Ep.* 55.14.1).

Conclusion

Although Constantine is in many ways a mysterious and seemingly ambiguous figure, this reinterpretation of Constantinian numismatics has demonstrated that there is continuity and a sophisticated program behind his coin issues. This, in turn, can inform us about the man himself and his policies. Instead of focusing on perceived contradiction in these media, one should embrace the crafty and skillful general and statesman that could produce and maintain such images. Although Constantine's rule may be viewed as a turbulent period in Roman history, his goals of unity and peace through both conquest and clemency are consistently represented in both his actions and his coins. Images and legends on coins were carefully selected, adapted, and refined to produce a pointed depiction of the emperor as he understood himself and his role. In doing so, Constantine could breathe new life into standard scenes while at the same time inserting newer themes, which often blended seamlessly creating novel and varied meanings in order to appeal to a wider audience. Coins represent one of the comparatively few instances where we can see Constantine's programs and policies at work without first refracting them through the lens of pious biographers.

Most of all, I have hoped to demonstrate how numismatic evidence provides one of the clearest examples of religious competition in action. Coins were publicity that could articulate how the emperor saw himself and his policies, signaling a call to appropriate forms of civic devotion to those who possessed their currency. Above all, the words and images on coins made a statement that could reach and influence a much wider audience than any literary text. As such, one can see how Constantine was competing with his rivals for political and military supremacy, without attributing Christian religious motivations as the primary catalyst for his actions.

"Built from the Plunder of Christians": Words, Places, and Competing Powers in Milan and Callinicum

Catherine M. Chin

Ambrose of Milan believed that he was a rational immortal soul inhabiting a perishable human body. He also believed that the world was full of invisible beings, including angels and demons who might appear in a variety of bodies. He further believed that the power of particular offices, such as that of bishop or emperor, could manifest itself in the material emblems of those offices, such as statues or banners, or in the physical places that such officials frequented, such as church buildings or palaces. Lastly, he believed that words could transform, summon, compete with, or manipulate the powers of souls, angels, and demons. This is the beginning of what Ambrose believed about buildings and about the words that come from them.[1]

What Ambrose believed about words, souls, powers, and invisible beings is important to what he believed about buildings, because the buildings that Ambrose built, occupied, and worked in were also bodies that

---

1. Two of the most recent and useful explorations of Ambrose's beliefs in invisible beings and in the power of places are Dayna S. Kalleres, *City of Demons: Violence, Ritual and Christian Power in Late Antiquity* (Berkeley: University of California Press, 2015), 199–237; and Christine C. Shepardson, *Controlling Contested Places: Late Antique Antioch and the Spatial Politics of Religious Controversy* (Berkeley: University of California Press, 2014), 213–26. Shepardson provides an extremely helpful overview of the ways that considering religious conflict through the lens of cultural geography can illuminate aspects of late fourth-century urban strife (see *Controlling Contested Places*, 1–10). The most influential recent work on Ambrose's career overall remains Neil B. McLynn, *Ambrose of Milan: Church and Court in a Christian Capital* (Berkeley: University of California Press, 1994).

such forces could inhabit. Like a human body in complex interaction with the rational soul that animates it, Ambrose's buildings each had its own difficult and complicated life. Some buildings lived longer than others; some were consumed by the buildings around them; some decayed and sent parts of themselves into buildings far away from them. Their vitality was inevitably entangled in the many other forces and beings that surrounded each structure. Thus trees, brick, and stone, with their different rates of growth or wear, were the earthly materials from which the buildings were made. In turn, the actions of builders, users, inhabitants, neighbors, and passersby all wore down buildings but were at the same time shaped by what the buildings would let them do; the same was true of traffic flowing into cities and away from them. Seasonal or daily moods of weather worked their own changes on materials, traffic, and people all at once.[2] Ambrose's world was, materially, enmeshed in forces that worked well beyond what we today would consider natural human boundaries. One of the places where such forces became both perceptible and, to some extent, usable, was in language.[3] Language was, of course, magic and persuasion,

---

2. For a theoretical overview of the issues at stake in the notions of entanglement and vitality, see especially Ian Hodder, *Entangled: An Archaeology of the Relationships between Humans and Things* (Malden, MA: Wiley-Blackwell, 2012); and Tim Ingold, *Being Alive: Essays on Movement, Knowledge and Description* (London: Routledge, 2011). On the life of buildings, see especially Annabel Wharton, "The Tribune Tower: Spolia as Despoliation," in *Reuse Value: Spolia and Appropriation in Art and Architecture from Constantine to Sherrie Levine*, ed. Richard Brilliant and Dale Kinney (Burlington, VT: Ashgate, 2011), 195. On the residence of spirits in places, see David Frankfurter, "Where the Spirits Dwell: Possession, Christianization, and Saints' Shrines in Late Antiquity," *HTR* 103 (2010): 27–46.

3. The literature on ideologies of language in late antiquity is far too vast to survey here. One excellent point of entry is Jeremy M. Schott, "Language," in *Late Ancient Knowing: Explorations in Intellectual History*, ed. Catherine M. Chin and Moulie Vidas (Berkeley: University of California Press, 2015), 58–79. To a certain extent, of course, the discussion in the current essay is indebted to the seminal work of J. L. Austin (*How to Do Things with Words* [Cambridge: Harvard University Press, 1962]) and to the many studies of speech acts that it engendered, particularly the work of Judith Butler (*Excitable Speech: A Politics of the Performative* [London: Routledge, 1997]. In general, these works assume a clear connection between linguistic force and fundamentally human forces as well as a kind of uniqueness to linguistic action. I suggest here that Ambrose's understanding of linguistic force is predicated on the existence, indeed dominance, of invisible nonhuman forces that manifest in many beings and places, language being only one of them.

law and liturgy. But words were also located in urban space, and physical places provided the points of origin for certain kinds of efficacious speech: nonhuman force could be transferred from buildings to words, or vice versa, in the same way that a demon could move from body to body and back again. So buildings, too, did things with words, and words did things in, and with, buildings. Buildings and words served simultaneously as actors and as vessels (if at times unruly or fragile vessels) for nonhuman or superhuman forces. In Ambrose's world, we can see the forces that inhabited buildings using the conventions of language that originated in those buildings to balance against, or to compete with, other forces, located in other buildings, all in larger-than-human ways. Words were, of course, not the only vessels for the forces that nonhuman beings used in this world, but they are some of the remnants of these forces that are now most easily accessible to us, and so words-from-places will be my focus here, as an example of the many forces Ambrose believed he was navigating in the empire of the later fourth century.

Late in the year 388 or early in 389 CE, Ambrose publicly approved a mob action that had occurred in the Syrian city of Callinicum: at the urging of their bishop, Christians in the town had burned down a synagogue. The emperor Theodosius, who was at that time in Milan, had ordered the bishop of Callinicum to pay for the synagogue's restoration on receiving a report of the incident. Ambrose objected. Some of the rationales for his objection are laid out in his letter 74 (or *Ep. extr. coll.* 1a).[4] In this letter,

---

4. I use here the Latin text of Michaela Zelzer (Ambrose, *Epistularum liber decimum: Epistulae extra collectionem; Gesta Concilii Aquileiensis*, part 3 of *Epistulae et acta*, vol. 10 of *Sancti Ambrosii Opera*, ed. Michaela Zelzer, CSEL 82.3 [Vienna: Hoelder-Pichler-Tempsky, 1982]). Except where modifications are noted, the English translation of J. H. W. G. Liebeschuetz (Ambrose, *Political Letters and Speeches*, ed. J. H. W. G. Liebeschuetz, TTH 43 [Liverpool: Liverpool University Press, 2005]) is used below. The bibliography on the Callinicum riot is extensive, but surprisingly little attention has been paid to the role of language in letter 74. McLynn (*Ambrose of Milan*, 301) is not untypical when he describes the main arguments of the letter as "only loosely related to [Ambrose's] major theme" and "contrived." The best recent studies of the Callinicum incident are H. A. Drake, "Intolerance, Religious Violence, and Political Legitimacy in Late Antiquity," *JAAR* 79 (2011): 193–235; and Ulrich Gotter, "Zwischen Christentum und Staatsraison: Römisches Imperium und religiöse Gewalt," in *Spätantiker Staat und religiöser Konflikt: Imperiale und lokale Verwaltung und die Gewalt gegen Heiligtümer*, ed. Johannes Hahn (Berlin: de Gruyter, 2011), 133–58. Both Drake and Gotter review trends in scholarship on the controversy, although

Ambrose describes three points of origin for the efficacious words that are at the heart of the controversy over the destroyed synagogue. These points of origin are: the palace (*regia*), the church (*ecclesia*), and the synagogue (*synagoga*). These places are not abstract categories nor are they reducible to the Roman Empire, Christianity, or Judaism. It is important to Ambrose's understanding of the conflict that they are specific physical structures located in specific cities, in this case Milan and Callinicum. In Ambrose's view, these places are inhabited by three different camps of effective words that exist in balance with each other. When this balance is disrupted, the verbal camps surge against each other, form uneasy alliances, and threaten those around them. In this essay, I read Ambrose's letter 74 as a document describing the actions and alliances of words from different places in different cities, words that make those cities their home.

Built from the Plunder of Christians: Words from Palace and Synagogue

Ambrose's narrative about the Callinicum synagogue in letter 74 does not begin with the destruction of the building. He views mob action as one of the occupational hazards of city life and asks Theodosius, "Why are you so angry? Is it because some public building or other has been burnt or because it was a synagogue? If you are moved to anger by the burning of even the most worthless buildings ... do you not remember, emperor, how many mansions of prefects have been burnt at Rome without anyone exacting punishment?" (74.13).[5] Riots here are simply a fact of urban existence; they do not require an imperial response. The urban landscape is fundamentally fluid in terms of human presence and action and in terms of the configuration of buildings that make up that landscape. Buildings serve as physical homes for political forces (as in the *Romae domus praefectorum*) and as points of physical attack. This fact is, for Ambrose, both obvious and unremarkable: if a building were to be, so to speak, "avenged," the most likely candidate would be the house of a prefect in the city of Rome, not a synagogue in Syria. Ambrose identifies the problem instead as

---

both (as is common in the literature overall) focus primarily on the political nature of the events.

5. *Quid tamen movet, utrum quia quodcumque aedificium publicum exustum est an quia synagogae locus? Si aedificio incenso moveris vilissimo ... non recordaris, imperator, quantorum Romae domus praefectorum incensae sint et nemo vindicavit?*

misdirected imperial words: "It was reported by the count of the East that a synagogue was burnt, at the instigation of the bishop. You ordered the other participants to be punished, and the synagogue to be rebuilt by that bishop" (74.6, modified).[6] Ambrose notes that this order was given before the bishop of Callinicum's statement arrived in Milan (74.6) and without the consultation of other bishops (74.27). He also indicates, later in the letter, that Theodosius has sworn an oath to punish the people responsible (74.31). In other words, the problem is that efficacious words have gone out from the Milanese palace in the direction of Syria, without Theodosius considering that speech from the church, either in Callinicum or in Milan, might act as a contrary force.[7] Whereas ordering the rebuilding of a prefect's house in Rome would align words from the *regia* in Milan appropriately with the forces in that house and city, ordering the rebuilding of a synagogue in Syria sends the wrong sort of words to the wrong sort of structure in an utterly inappropriate place.

Ambrose spends much of letter 74 arguing that the meeting of this initial set of words from the *regia* in Milan with words from the synagogue in Callinicum will have disastrous consequences. By joining with words from the synagogue, the force of words from the *regia* will create dangerous new ways for the synagogue to act in the city overall. Ambrose defines a synagogue fundamentally as a place of contrary speaking, "a place where Christ is denied [*locus in quo Christus negaretur*]" (74.8). This definition of a synagogue as a house of negating speech allows Ambrose to call it simply "a site of perfidy, a house of impiety, a refuge of madness [*perfidiae locus, impietatis domus, amentiae receptaculum*]" (74.14). Both the physical place and the words spoken there are thus homes and bodies for contrary forces: *perfidia, impietas, amentia*. A "refuge of madness" buttressed by imperial words, however, is extremely threatening, and the threat will become visible in the words and building of the new synagogue. Thus Ambrose presents his audience with the troubling possibility that the rebuilt synagogue will include a triumphal inscription: "We read of idol temples founded long ago from the plunder of the Cimbri and from the spoils of other enemies. The Jews will write this inscription on the façade of their synagogue: 'The temple of impiety, built from the plunder of Christians'" (74.10, my

---

6. *Relatum est a comite orientis … incensam esse synagogam idque auctore factum episcopo. Iussisti vindicari in ceteros, synagogam ab ipso exaedificari episcopo.*

7. In *Ep. extr. coll.* 1.1, Ambrose tells his sister that he was in Aquileia, not in Milan, when the order occurred: *iussum erat me Aquileiae posito.*

translation).⁸ Ambrose imagines the transformation of the synagogue into a monument of physical triumph. The classicizing reference takes on additional weight if we recall the importance of spoliation and material reuse in late ancient building more generally.⁹ Reuse of earlier building materials, both structural and decorative, was widespread enough in the fourth century that multiple laws attempted to regulate it. For example, *Theodosian Code* 15.1.19, of 376 CE, says the following about building in the city of Rome: "If any person should wish to undertake any new building in the City, he must complete it with his own money and labor, without bringing together old buildings, without digging up the foundations of noble buildings, without obtaining renovated stones from the public, without tearing away pieces of marble by the mutilation of despoiled buildings" (15.1.19).¹⁰ The Basilica Portiana in Milan, over which Ambrose had confronted Valentinian II and Justina in 386 CE, had been built partly with reused materials from a demolished amphitheater, likely with imperial support for both the demolition and the subsequent building projects.¹¹ The imperial order to rebuild the Callinicum synagogue turns the synagogue into a double of the Milanese basilica. Thus, the danger of synagogue words joined to imperial words is fantastically embodied in the public inscription of the imagined new building, which proclaims that this word-home can threaten other homes and records that it has already physically consumed material from the church.

Words from the synagogue also consume the human population of Callinicum, as Ambrose continues: "What other slanders will they not zealously take up, these people who have defamed Christ himself with false evidence?... Whom will they not inform against ... so that they can

---

8. *Legimus templa idolis antiquitus condita de manubiis Cimbrorum, de spoliis reliquorum hostium. Hunc titulum Iudaei in fronte synagogae suae scribent: "Templum impietatis factum de manubiis Christianorum.*

9. For an overview, see Dale Kinney, "Spolia: *Damnatio* and *Renovatio Memoriae*," *MAAR* 42 (1997): 117–48; at greater length, Maria Fabricius Hansen, *The Eloquence of Appropriation: Prolegomena to an Understanding of Spolia in Early Christian Rome*, ARIDSup 33 (Rome: L'Erma di Bretschneider, 2003); and Beat Brenk, "Spolia from Constantine to Charlemagne: Aesthetics versus Ideology," *DOP* 41 (1987): 103–9.

10. Clyde Pharr, trans., *The Theodosian Code and Novels, and the Sirmondian Constitutions* (Princeton: Princeton University Press, 1952), 425.

11. Richard Krautheimer, *Three Christian Capitals: Topography and Politics* (Berkeley: University of California Press, 1982), 88; Dale Kinney, "The Evidence for the Dating of S. Lorenzo in Milan," *JSAH* 31 (1972): 92–107.

witness innumerable files of chained members of the Christian people ... so that the servants of God are buried in darkness, smitten with axes, delivered to the flames or sent to the mines...?" (74.19, modified).[12] As with the imagined inscription, Ambrose here imagines a verbal attack that violates the Christian community. He adds that this attack will be repeated in synagogue speech annually: "The Jewish people will enter this feast-day into their calendar and will assuredly rank it with the days on which they triumphed over the Amorites, or over the Canaanites, or over Pharaoh the king of Egypt.... They will now add this festival, signifying that they have celebrated a triumph over the people of Christ" (74.20).[13] The ritualized triumph of the synagogue over the lines of chained members of the Christian community recalls the stereotypical Roman triumphal arch, which Ambrose here verbally re-creates for the Callinicum synagogue. Perhaps more specifically, however, it recalls the location of Ambrose's Basilica Romana (also called the Basilica Apostolorum), built in the first half of the 380s, just outside Milan on the colonnaded Via Romana that connected Milan to Rome, along the route that served as the triumphal entry point to the city. A few hundred meters away from this basilica, on the same road, was a four-sided triumphal arch from the late third century.[14] The four-sided arch was echoed in the cruciform plan of the Basilica Romana, with its central altar. The dedicatory inscription, written some time in the 390s, would insist that the cruciform shape of the building itself was a "holy triumphal sign" that "seals the place" (*sacra triumphalis signat imago locum*).[15] In other words, a few years before imagining an imperial Jewish triumph over Christians in Syria, Ambrose had built a church along an explicitly triumphal imperial route in Milan. Then, a few years after he imagined a ritualized triumph being inscribed on a synagogue and becoming part of a Jewish liturgy, Ambrose's church

---

12. *In quas praeterea non prosiliant calumnias qui etiam Christo falsis testimoniis calumniati sunt?... Quos non appetent ... ut catenatorum ordines innumeros spectent de Christiano populo ... ut condantur in tenebras dei servuli, ut feriantur securibus, dentur ignibus, tradantur metallis ...?*

13. *Referet Iudaeorum populus hanc sollemnitatem in dies festos suos et inter illos profectos numerabit, quibus aut de Amorreis aut de Chananeis triumphavit aut de Pharao rege Aegypti.... Addet hanc celebritatem significans se de Christi populo triumphum egisse.*

14. Suzanne Lewis, "Function and Symbolic Form in the Basilica Apostolorum at Milan," *JSAH* 28 (1969): 90–91.

15. See discussion in ibid., 86 n. 6.

received its own inscription, claiming that its physical form, with its central liturgical focus, transformed the location into a site of sacred triumph.

Ambrose sees the alliance of palace and synagogue words as a combined force that will change the urban landscape of Callinicum, creating a weird mirror version of both the original riot and the tropes of Roman urban order writ large. More specifically, they will create an inversion of the urban landscape of late fourth-century Milan, a landscape that Ambrose himself had only recently mastered and whose church structures worked in tandem with imperial structures to align the forces of *regia* and *ecclesia*. Without considering the physical origins for the words that Ambrose describes as acting in the world, it would be tempting to read Ambrose's concerns as baselessly hyperbolic. Returned to the physical setting of fourth-century Milan, they are a mildly exaggerated account of what Ambrose himself had recently accomplished. The new alliance of words from palace and synagogue is a fundamental disruption of the recently-established balance of verbal powers between *regia* and *ecclesia*. Ambrose is clearly at pains to emphasize the ways in which imperial words cannot align with words from the synagogue. As he claims, "Although they deny that they are bound by the laws of the Romans to the point that they think the laws criminal, they now think that they have a right to be avenged … on the basis of Roman laws" (74.21).[16] Ambrose's description of the situation in Callinicum creates a picture of an illegal assembly hall that transforms it, much as Ambrose's Nicene Christian buildings in Milan had recently done, into an imperially-sponsored triumphal structure through an alliance with the force of imperial words. As a response, the rest of Ambrose's argument in letter 74 attempts to recover what he claims is the appropriate alliance of palace words with words from the church.

Lest It Be Necessary for You to Hear Me in Church: Speech from Palace and Church

Ambrose opens letter 74 with a reminder of the close ties between palace and church: "So I beg you to listen patiently to what I have to say. For if I am unworthy to be heard by you, I am also unworthy to offer sacrifice for you, to be trusted with your vows and your prayers" (74.1).[17] Here

---

16. *Et cum ipsi Romanis legibus teneri se negent ita ut crimina leges putent, nunc velut Romanis legibus se vindicandos putent.*

17. *Itaque peto ut patienter sermonem meum audias; nam si indignus sum qui*

Ambrose connects the spaces of imperial and ecclesial speech in Milan. The balance of verbal forces on which Ambrose depends is one in which there is both sympathy and physical proximity between palace and church. With Theodosius resident in Milan, the likelihood that Ambrose would in fact interact with him on this question in either a court or church setting, or both, was always high. Indeed, we know from *Ep. extr. coll.* 1 that such interaction occurred. This physical closeness, however, is also what facilitates Ambrose's ability to take up Theodosius's words in church and for Theodosius, in turn, to take up Ambrose's words in the palace. Physical closeness is a calque for verbal closeness. It is important, then, that Ambrose establishes his own physical proximity to the emperor before describing the Callinicum incident as stemming from a report from the *comes Orientis*: words that have come from far away, that have escaped the contrary words of the bishop of Callinicum, whose report was slower to arrive (74.6). The implication is that the physical closeness between the *comes Orientis* and the bishop of Callinicum might have solved the problem, although the closeness between Theodosius and the bishop of Milan is now able to do so. H. A. Drake reminds us that the entire episode must be understood in light of the immense difficulties the emperor faced in imposing control over faraway places;[18] in such a world, nonhuman forces resident in words and places work best in proximity to each other.

To challenge the verbal disorder that words from far away have created, Ambrose proposes a realignment of forces, which will neutralize the force of the palace words that have gone on their way from Milan to Callinicum. First, Ambrose suggests that the bishop of Callinicum, on meeting these words, might prefer to be martyred rather than rebuild the synagogue and, in fact, that the bishop might lie in order to gain martyrdom: "I think that the bishop will say that he himself raised the fire, assembled the crowds, and led the people, so as not to lose the opportunity for martyrdom.... O blessed falsehood, by which a man wins acquittal for others and grace for himself!" (74.8).[19] The imagined lie is a reconfiguration of

---

a te audiar, indignus sum qui pro te offeram, cui tua vota, cui tuas committas preces. Drake ("Intolerance," 216) astutely notes the innovation in the fourth-century situation: "for the first time emperors had to share the privilege of access to the divine with a class that had established its own, independent lines of communication with that very potent source."

18. Ibid., 210–11.

19. *Puto dicturum episcopum quod ipse ignes sparserit, turbas compulerit, populos*

remoteness and proximity. On the one hand, it is a reminder that the absence of Theodosius from Callinicum renders him helpless in the face of a faraway untruth; on the other, it locates the bishop as primary actor at the heart of the physical events, close to the synagogue. Ambrose next dramatically appropriates this lie: "I declare that I burnt the synagogue, or at any rate that I instructed them that there should be no building where Christ was denied" (74.8).[20] The threat of asking to be martyred consists partly in the act of public verbal defiance of imperial speech, but it also relocates Ambrose to Callinicum and aligns his lie with the lies that he claims the Jews there will tell, "so that the servants of God are ... smitten with axes" (74.19).[21] In this scenario, lies from the church and lies from the synagogue come together to manipulate imperial forces from Milan. Ambrose's explicit introduction of this blessed falsehood, which brings the bishops to the synagogue and underlines their distance from the *regia*, creates new martyrs. These martyrs would of course be housed in buildings. The scenario that Ambrose imagines thus relies on Ambrose's own contribution to martyr cults in Milan. He had, in 386 CE, very publicly discovered the bodies of local martyrs Gervasius and Protasius, whom he had buried in the Basilica Ambrosiana, declaring his own desire to be buried with them. The Basilica Romana, the triumphal church, was also known as the Basilica Apostolorum for its housing of apostolic relics, possibly including those of the quintessential Roman martyrs Peter and Paul.[22] Ambrose's appeal to the possibility of new martyrdoms simultaneously reveals the attenuated force of words from the *regia* that must travel over long distances, the force of words from church and synagogue, if spoken in the same place and to the same end, and the power of the bodies currently housed in the church buildings in Milan.

---

conduxerit, ne amittat occasionem martyrii.... O beatum mendacium, quo acquiritur sibi aliorum absolutio, sui gratia.

20. *Proclamo quod ego synagogam incenderim, certe quod ego illis mandaverim, ne esset locus in quo Christus negaretur.*

21. For the Latin text, see n. 11. Michael Gaddis, *There Is No Crime for Those Who Have Christ: Religious Violence in the Christian Roman Empire* (Berkeley: University of California Press, 2005), misconstrues Ambrose's use of the language of martyrdom here, claiming that "'martyrdom' now encompasses aggressive and provocative violence against non-Christians" (196). But the force of Ambrose's argument is precisely that Theodosius can be compelled by both Jewish and Christian lies to use violence against Christians.

22. McLynn, *Ambrose of Milan*, 230–32.

Ambrose's goal, of course, is the reunion of ecclesial and imperial words in Milan itself. This is offered at the end of letter 74, in which Ambrose proposes himself as intercessor to assure Theodosius that he can change his order to rebuild the synagogue without violating an oath: "I pledge myself on your behalf to our God on this point. And you are not to be afraid because of your oath" (74.31).[23] Ambrose's pledge marks the realignment of imperial and ecclesial speech, bringing words from *ecclesia* and words from *regia* together in the person of Ambrose. It also echoes Ambrose's earlier willingness to take the place of the bishop of Callinicum.[24] As he had claimed to do at the beginning of letter 74, Ambrose again offers to stand in Theodosius's place before God and take responsibility for imperial vows at the end of the letter. Ambrose's well-known letter 1 outside the collection, a sequel to letter 74, in which Ambrose describes preaching to Theodosius in person and persuading him to rescind his order, reveals his further use of sermon and liturgy to complete the reunion of ecclesial and imperial speech in this incident. Indeed, Ambrose emphasizes the force of episcopal homiletic speech in his later editorial addition to letter 74, whose revised version ends: "I, for my part, have done all I could ... to get you to hear me in the palace, so that it might not become necessary for you to hear me in church" (74.33).[25] As we know from Ambrose's letter 1 outside the collection, Theodosius did hear Ambrose in church and, according to this letter, Ambrose's words from this place were instrumental in stopping Theodosius's order from going forward. The dialogue of bishop and emperor, physically located in the church, thus resolved the tension between ecclesial and imperial words.[26] In Ambrose's telling, the resolution of the synagogue controversy at Callinicum occurred in the convergence of palace and church in Milan.

---

23. *In hoc me ego deo nostro pro te obligo nec verearis sacramentum.*

24. On Ambrose's notion of episcopal inhabitation of other persons, see Catherine M. Chin, "The Bishop's Two Bodies: Ambrose and the Basilicas of Milan," *CH* 79 (2010): 531–55.

25. *Ego certe quod honorificentius fieri potuit feci, ut me magis audires in regia, ne si necesse esset audires in ecclesia.*

26. The dialogue between emperor and bishop at *Ep. extr. coll.* 1.28 enacts this resolution: *Aio illi, ago fide tua, et repetivi, ago fide tua. Age, inquit.* This striking alliteration (*aio... ago... ago... age*) is unlike any other passage in either letter and brings emperor and bishop into verbal accord.

Conclusion

Ambrose's letter 74 on the Callinicum synagogue presupposes a world in which urban space is infused with an unstable mix of forces that occupy both language and the physical structures in which language originates. These forces can easily become unbalanced and slip out of control, creating new and dystopian urban landscapes. The tenuous nature of their balance is revealed in the counterfactual anxieties that drive Ambrose's argument: the imagined all-consuming triumphal inscription or the lies leading to unconsummated martyrdom. Although the fantasies that Ambrose describes are unreal, we should assume he believed that the forces that might bring them about were really present. Ambrose lived in a world in which magic might work and miracles might happen. These forces are not part of our contemporary repertoire of historical explanation, but that is perhaps all the more reason to try to understand how they might have motivated those actors for whom they were indeed real. Ambrose was thoroughly enmeshed in the competitive human politics of the Milanese court, but there is no reason to believe that he did not also consider those politics to be shot through with nonhuman or superhuman powers, which also competed with each other. By attending to the common late antique belief in the efficacy of language, especially language that originated in certain heavily ritualized material contexts, we can in fact see an additional dimension to Ambrose's political dexterity, one that manipulates the possibilities of the superhuman as well as the merely human.

The competitive forces that filled this world were not exclusively bounded by religion. The importance of words from the *regia* in this episode makes clear that greater-than-human forces existed in spheres beyond those that we would normally define as either "religious" or "magical." If Ambrose is to be seen as a skillful politician, as indeed he was, Theodosius in turn must retain his own status as a sacral figure, managing and exercising the more-than-human forces that imperial structures and emblems provided. By the time of Theodosius, the Roman emperor had been a sacred figure for centuries, considered so both during and after his lifetime.[27] The rise of Christianity redefined, but did not eliminate, the emperor's more-than-human power. Ambrose's funeral oration on Theo-

---

27. See especially the classic study of Simon R. F. Price, *Rituals and Power: The Roman Imperial Cult in Asia Minor* (Cambridge: Cambridge University Press, 1984), esp. 234–48.

dosius, written only a few years after the events in Callinicum unfolded, attests to Ambrose's belief that Theodosius held special status with God and treats Theodosius's body as if it were itself a set of holy relics (*Ob. Theo.* 54–55). The competitive superhuman forces at work in this episode are thus not just those aligned with Christians and Jews but are between those tied to all figures and places in whom, or in which, ritual and speech could summon great power. For this reason, neither should the prospect of an imperial synagogue seem out of place in this balance of forces, although it did not in fact come to pass. The idea that the forces of language from the *regia* and forces of language from the *synagoga* could align to overcome the words from the *ecclesia* would be no more surprising, in this historical world, than the fact that forces from *regia* and *ecclesia* had already been seen to align, with demonstrable physical results in the city of Milan and ultimately in the city of Callinicum as well. The tensions and alliances between late antique forces were at times unpredictable and, as all the parties in this conflict knew, were impossible to control entirely. In this complex world in which politics and theology played out in both human and superhuman arenas, Ambrose's political maneuvering worked both with and within all of these invisible forces, as they shaped the perishable cities in which all of the actors lived.

Part 2
Competition and Neoplatonism

Introduction:
Defining Competition in Neoplatonism

Todd Krulak

Late antique Platonists viewed the universe as layered and complex. The general embrace of the Aristotelian/Ptolemaic model of concentric spheres demonstrates this in the physical cosmos. Articulations of layering in abstract categories as seen in the so-called "Neoplatonic virtues" and in increasingly elaborate ontologies, culminating in the stratified metaphysics of Proclus, indicate that this complexity permeated the Platonism of this period. Layers of these sorts are, from the human perspective, "greater than"; that is, our viewpoint is one that looks up to the heights of the physical heavens or to the deities occupying strata beyond the visible realm. The papers in this section remind us that other layers existed for the Platonists that may initially appear to a modern reader to be comparatively mundane, but, when peeled back by the philosopher, they reveal rich meanings that facilitated understanding of and/or nearness to divinity. With the stakes so high, it was important for the philosopher to reach proper conclusions about the meaning and importance of these layers and to defend these interpretations against those who sought to undermine or repudiate them. Thus, definition, that is, the designation of "meaning," a term that refers to truths about the soul, the universe, and/or the divine, was a competitive game in which there were winners and losers. To win meant that the contribution made by the successful definition, no matter how small, was a moment of cultural production or, depending on how one views philosophy in the context of ancient society, of subcultural production; to lose ensured that the interpretation withered or, at the very least, was relegated to the footnotes.

It must be emphasized that for the philosopher, winning the game of definition was not merely about burnishing the *curriculum vitae*, producing culture, or even the enhancement of legacy, but was an effort at finding deeper meaning by revealing subcutaneous truths that led to knowledge and experience of the Divine. Every victory, therefore, was a step towards an understanding and knowledge of the transcendent. In order to access the deeper truths available in a source, however, it was necessary first to agree that the potential repository of wisdom was an actual one. If a text or rite was deemed by one party to make no contribution to the articulation of meaning, then the other party needed to establish the prospective source's bona fides before contesting the meaning held within. Successes in the excavation of meaning were hard won when the debate was confined to students of the Academy, the Lyceum, or the Stoa, who, if not always embracing the cultic environment in which they found themselves, did not revile it and all for which it stood. With the emergence of a Christian literati in the second and third centuries CE, a second front opened that controversially marshaled the tools historically utilized by philosophers to uncover meaning and truths about Divinity that were employed in the service of defining the Christian God and worldview.

This is illustrated nicely in Ilaria Ramelli's essay. Ramelli uses Porphyry's famous, or infamous, depiction of the Christian Origen as one who lived like a Christian but "played the Greek" by figuratively reading "foreign tales" (ὀθνεῖοι μῦθοι; a reference to the Judaic scriptures) as a means to illustrate common practices, interpretations, and sources used by the Neoplatonist Origen and the Christian Origen, who she deems one and the same (apud Eusebius, Hist. eccl. 6.19). The issue for Porphyry was not the source material per se; the Hebrew Bible was a viable source from which ancient wisdom could be mined.[1] In this aspect, the two philosophers were in accord. Though Porphyry decried Origen's eisegetical approach to the Hebrew Bible in which he supposedly found Greek ideas in the scriptural narrative, even this does not stand out as being at odds with the manner in which most philosophers read textual repositories of ancient wisdom. Instead, Porphyry's disdain for Origen resulted from his perception that the Christian used Greek interpretive methods to elevate a particular "barbarian" text above all others, "barbarian" or Greek.[2] Jeremy Schott reads Porphyry's statement as an expression of frustration that Origen was unwilling to accept Greek cultural hege-

---

[1]. For a full discussion, see Jeremy M. Schott, *Christianity, Empire, and the Making of Religion in Late Antiquity* (Philadelphia: University of Pennsylvania Press, 2008), 69–74.

[2]. Ibid., 73–74.

INTRODUCTION: DEFINING COMPETITION IN NEOPLATONISM 81

mony and the "carefully constructed, hierarchical dichotomy between Greeks and others."[3] This was a macrolevel concern for Porphyry, but the more immediate issue was the articulation of meaning and, more to the point, which textual source(s) was (were) to be viewed as its arbiter(s) and whether the Hebrew Bible allowed for meaningful figurative reading which exposed deeper truths. Porphyry critiqued biblical texts such as Hosea (in which the prophet is made to marry a prostitute) and Jonah (in the belly of the fish) as being so crude as to not merit philosophical consideration. Origen, of course, had no such reservations and, as Ramelli notes, read the biblical materials both literally and allegorically, save for Genesis and the Apocalypse of John which, in keeping with the example of Plato who also mythologized "ἀρχή and τέλος accounts," merited only figurative readings. Indeed, for Origen, Job was a prized book whose subject was thought to be "earlier than Moses himself" (*Cels.* 6.43 [Chadwick]), who in turn was even earlier than Homer (*Cels.* 4.22). The antiquity of the Hebrew Bible served to justify its claim to wisdom, a point agreed upon by both Porphyry and Origen. But for the Christian, it was a work rooted in the past that looked towards and, in fact, prophesied about the coming Christ, the divine *logos*, which further confirmed the unique quality of this particular text of ancient wisdom (*Cels.* 1.49–60). If any text was worthy of figurative reading and led to the excavation of deep meaning, it surely was the Judaic Scriptures. For Porphyry, meaning was not the province of any single cultural collection of texts and to elevate one text above all others would ensure that the deep meaning he thought to be available only through the collation of wisdom from an array of cultures, Greek and "barbarian" alike, would be lost.

Ancient wisdom is at the heart of Gregory Shaw's essay. In reference to wisdom, *ancient* did not denote something chronologically prior but "*ontologically* prior" that "opened the soul to an awareness that *precedes* discursive activity." Necessarily, however, this wisdom was accessed in a material cosmos, in spite of limitations placed upon the soul by its embodiment. Once more, Porphyry is at the center of another dispute over meaning and the medium in which it is thought to reside, this time in his debate with his erstwhile pupil, Iamblichus of Chalcis. Textual matters are not in focus this time, but rather it is Porphyry's question in his *Letter to Anebo* about the import of *onomata barbara*, the divine names of

---

3. Ibid., 73.

the gods invoked aloud in theurgic prayer, that have no discernible meaning. Why, he wondered, did theurgists not use language understandable to both speaker and audience? There was nothing inherent to a name that connected it with a deity; language was the product of convention. So why not simply invoke a deity by its Greek name? This was a continuation of a debate as old as Plato's *Cratylus* and found also in Origen's *Contra Celsum* in which the Christian, unsurprisingly, adopted a position antithetical to that of Porphyry (and Celsus, too, his interlocutor) and argued for the efficacy of names in their original language (*Cels.* 1.24–25; 5.45). In *On the Mysteries*, Iamblichus took a similar stance and insisted that there was a real and powerful link between the name of the deity and the deity to whom it referred. These names were theurgic tokens of the gods or, as Shaw phrases it, "the names of gods *are* the gods in audible form, properly received and vocalized." When uttered, the theurgist became unified with the deity and embodied it.

In his letter, Porphyry appears to have been troubled by one who heartily embraced a "reading" of a "text," albeit one that was vocalized, that landed too squarely outside of appropriate Greek parameters, but Iamblichus rejected the very suggestion that all things Greek were superior to all things non-Greek. He claimed that the names and prayers were "endlessly altered according to the inventiveness and illegality of the Hellenes … and they preserve nothing which they have received from anyone else, but even this they promptly abandon and change it all according to their unreliable linguistic innovation." The effects of this were seen in the present circumstances in which "both the names and places" have "lost their power" (*Myst.* 7.5.259).[4] Iamblichus's point is clear: the decline of divine activity at sacred shrines and oracular sites was attributable, in part, to those with a thoroughly Greek filter who, by insisting that language was a matter of convention and that meaning was transferable, had neutered the power of the rites and limited the power of the gods. The *onomata barbara* did have meaning and was a legitimate source for its communication; true, the meaning was inaccessible to humans, but this was not the intended audience. The gods understood the meanings behind the invocations, responded to them, and, in the process, enabled unification between humanity and divinity.[5]

---

4. Text and translation from Iamblichus, *On the Mysteries*, ed. and trans. Emma C. Clarke, John M. Dillon, and Jackson P. Hershbell, WGRW 4 (Atlanta: Society of Biblical Literature, 2003).

5. One must be wary about reading passages such as this as a repudiation of all

INTRODUCTION: DEFINING COMPETITION IN NEOPLATONISM

In the final essay of this section, the focus remains on ritual. Laura Dingeldein considers the emperor Julian's reading of the practices surrounding the springtime celebration of the Magna Mater elucidated in the *Hymn to the Mother of the Gods*. She argues for a middle way between two scholarly poles that debate the degree to which the emperor's own personal piety, influenced heavily by the theurgic tradition associated with Iamblichus, impacted his public religious program and the reinvigoration of the cults. In his position as emperor, Julian was what Dingeldein, borrowing from Stanley Stowers's theoretical model of different categories of religious activity in the ancient Mediterranean, describes as a "literate specialist with political power." As such, he had the tools, intellectual and educational, to articulate a coherent position or worldview and the authority and audience to advance it on a wide scale. In the *Hymn to the Mother of the Gods* (*Or.* 5), part of Julian's project was to interpret aspects of Metroac myth that unnamed others found objectionable, so that Attis became the substance of demiurgic Mind and the Mother the "source of the intellectual and creative gods" and the "cause of all generation" (*Or.* 5.166A–B).[6] In focus, too, was the dietary component of the rites, which, against general philosophical opinions on matters of purity, advocated the consumption of certain meats and forbade the ingestion of grains and fruits. Julian associated plants whose roots reached into the soil and animals like pigs and fish that swam in the depths of the sea with terrestrial or chthonic realms that hindered the soul's ability to assimilate to divinity. When followed assiduously, the sacred rites contributed to an existential state in which the individual was prepared for illumination by divine light (*Or.* 5.178B). Though in a different context, the hymn provides yet another example of something already possessing a level of sanctity being imbued with a different and deeper meaning. As a possessor of political power, Julian knew that his reforms would be enacted and those who wished to

---

things Greek. Iamblichus was a Greek-speaking philosopher raised in the Greek philosophical tradition who, for the purposes of this response to Porphyry, adopted the guise of an Egyptian priest. Determining the balance between what is merely Iamblichus's attempt at role-playing and what represents his true conviction is difficult. Ilinca Tanaseanu-Döbler (*Theurgy in Late Antiquity: The Invention of a Ritual Tradition*, BERG 1 [Göttingen: Vandenhoeck & Ruprecht, 2013], 95–135) demonstrates that Iamblichus should not be defined solely by the theurgic *On the Mysteries* but that he was quite adept in more traditional philosophical argumentation.

6. Text and translation from Julian, *The Works*, trans. Wilmer C. Wright, 3 vols., LCL 13, 29, 157 (Cambridge: Harvard University Press, 1913–1923).

practice the ancestral traditions would do so with or without philosophical justification. At the same time, however, the emperor recognized that many were skeptical of the reforms he put into place. Therefore, he sought to provide justification for his embrace of traditions that ran afoul of the dominant philosophical opinion, on the ingestion of meat in this case, by indicating that such practices signified a deeper meaning, which promised benefits for the soul.[7]

For the late Platonists, the layered nature of the universe made for a complex world that invited investigation. Observation alone led to many advances in knowledge of the natural world, but truths about the nature of the soul or the gods were inaccessible to observation alone. It was the savvy philosopher who saw in sacred myths and texts, inarticulate ritual utterances, and cathartic dietary practices signifiers of deeper meaning that was available to those with the right interpretive skill set.[8] The essays in this section remind the reader that not only was the meaning of an interpretation a matter of debate, but the sources themselves were probed to determine their hermeneutical fecundity, and this, too, was an area ripe for contestation. Was the Hebrew Bible simply one of many ancient texts in which wisdom was deposited, or was it *the* ancient text above all others? Did the names and language by which the gods were addressed in prayer matter, or would they respond similarly to any form of address? Did Metroac dietary praxes in which the consumption of meat was advocated have cathartic and anagogic value, or were they residue from an antiquated complex of rites that offered little to the sophisticated fourth-century philosopher? Establishing the viability of the sources enabled the cultivation of meaning, which, in turn, helped to determine the hermeneutical and performative trajectories of late antique religio-philosophical traditions.

---

7. Julian was not the sole member of his court engaged in the making of meaning. Sallustius, too, in his primer of late Platonism, *On the Gods and the Cosmos*, described the benefits of sacrifice and suggested how the cultic forms of the gods indicated something of their qualities. For a discussion of sacrifice in Sallustius, see Todd Krulak, "Θυσία and Theurgy: Sacrificial Theory in Fourth- and Fifth-Century Platonism," *ClQ* 64 (2014): 353–82. Even Ammianus Marcellinus, who was sympathetic to Julian's aims, found cause to criticize the emperor for his excessive devotion (*Res gest.* 22.12.6; 25.4.17).

8. For a detailed discussion of this issue, see Peter T. Struck, *Birth of the Symbol: Ancient Readers at the Limits of Their Texts* (Princeton: Princeton University Press, 2004).

Origen's Allegoresis of Plato's and Scripture's "Myths"

Ilaria L. E. Ramelli

Neoplatonism and the Allegorical and Salvific Meaning of Plato's Dialogues and Myths

Jay Kennedy claimed that musical structures are embedded in Plato's genuine dialogues.[1] Raymond Barfield highlighted Plato's criticism of poetry and its replacement with a new type of poetry: the Platonic dialogue.[2] The symbolism inherent in poetry is transposed to Plato's dialogues. In *Resp.* 10, after stating that poetry failed in presenting ethical values, Plato used poetic patterns to describe the world of becoming—in order to help the readers' senses support the intellect in its ascent to the Forms.[3] Although there is no evidence that Neoplatonists perceived a musical structure in Plato's dialogues, Neopythagoreans and Neoplatonists believed that these

---

1. J. B. Kennedy, "Plato's Forms, Pythagorean Mathematics, and Stichometry," *Apeiron* 43 (2010): 1–32; Kennedy, *The Musical Structure of Plato's Dialogues* (repr., New York: Routledge, 2014). Harold Tarrant, review of *The Musical Structure of Plato's Dialogues*, by J. B. Kennedy, *IJPT* 7 (2013): 244–45, suspends judgment.

2. Raymond Barfield, *The Ancient Quarrel between Philosophy and Poetry* (repr., Cambridge: Cambridge University Press, 2014), 10–31.

3. Zacharoula A. Petraki, *The Poetics of Philosophical Language: Plato, Poets and Presocratics in the Republic* (Berlin: de Gruyter, 2011); see also Fabio Massimo Giuliano, *Platone e la Poesia: Teoria della composizione e prassi della ricezione*, IPS 22 (Sankt Augustin: Academia, 2005); Pierre Destrée and Fritz-Gregor Herrmann, eds., *Plato and the Poets* (Leiden: Brill, 2011); Walter G. Leszl, "Plato's Attitude to Poetry and the Fine Arts, and the Origins of Aesthetics Part 1," *EPla* 1 (2004): 113–97; 2 (2006): 285–351; 3 (2006): 245–336.

were allegorical. Some, such as the Athenian Neoplatonist Hermias (410–450 ca. CE), even insisted that their symbolic meaning was salvific.

In a lost *Life of Pythagoras*, Plato is presented as the ninth successor of Pythagoras and a disciple of Archytas; Plato learned "theoretical philosophy and physics from Italian Pythagoreans" (Photius, *Bibl.* 249).[4] Hierocles the Neoplatonist, an admirer of Ammonius, Origen's and Plotinus's teacher, provides a good example of the allegorical interpretation of Plato's dialogues. In *On Providence and Fate and the Accord between What Depends on Us and Divine Sovereignty* (Photius *Bibl.* 214, 251), where Hierocles endeavors to harmonize Plato's and Aristotle's doctrines, he offers a symbolic reading of Plato's *Republic*; for example, he interprets youngsters as sense-perception and their educators as the intellect (*Bibl.* 251.464b).[5] The reading of symbolism in Plato's dialogues is in line with Hierocles's idea that Plato's doctrines were also expressed by poets such as Homer and Orpheus (*Bibl.* 214.173a). Hierocles interpreted Plato's Demiurge as the God who created "all visible and invisible entities" without "any preexistent substratum," because "his will sufficed to the coming into existence of all beings" (214.172a). This is not Plato's doctrine but that of Pantaenus, Ammonius, and Origen, all Christian Platonists.[6] Indeed, in *On Providence* 6, Hierocles reviewed all Platonists up to Ammonius, praising those who regarded Plato's and Aristotle's ideas as convergent; and in book 7 he praised Ammonius, Origen, Plotinus, Porphyry, and Iamblichus as divine thinkers "in agreement with Plato's purified philosophy" (214.173a). All these Platonists, including Origen, as I shall show, deemed Plato's dialogues allegorical.

---

4. Unless otherwise stated, all translations of Greek and Latin materials are my own.

5. I suppose Eusebius knew that Origen interpreted Plato's *Republic* allegorically. Based on Porphyry and Iamblichus, Jeremy Schott ("Founding Platonopolis: The Platonic *Politeia* in Eusebius, Porphyry, and Iamblichus," *JECS* 11 [2003]: 501–32), argues that Neoplatonists were interested in classical political philosophy, and Eusebius's comparison of Moses's legislation with Plato's *Laws* and *Republic* in *Praep. ev.* 12 must be read in the context of Neoplatonic political thought. I add: also in the context of Origen's reflection on Plato's political thought and his interpretation of Plato's *Republic*. All the more so since, as Schott acknowledges (523), Eusebius's citations indicate access to a complete Platonic corpus—from Origen's library. But also Origen's interpretations of Plato, not only his texts, were available to Eusebius.

6. See Ilaria Ramelli, "Origen, Patristic Philosophy, and Christian Platonism: Rethinking the Christianization of Hellenism," *VC* 63 (2009): 217–63.

Hermias, like Ammonius and Olympiodorus, taught Aristotle propaedeutically first and then Plato's dialogues arranged in series, from ethics, logic, and mathematics to physics and theology. Hermias claimed that perceiving the symbolic meaning of Plato's dialogues, particularly those of Plato's myths,[7] was even salvific (*Phaedr. Schol.* 241E8). Two possible remarks followed a myth by Plato: "And so the myth has been saved, and *it will save us*, too, if we follow it," as Plato says at the end of the myth of Er;[8] or, "And so the myth was lost." The latter, according to Hermias, is the case if we follow "the appearance of the myth," that is, its literal interpretation. In this way, "we shall be lost as appearances are lost." But "if we follow the *hidden vision*," that is, the symbolic meaning, "which the myth indicates in a mystical way, *we shall be saved*, because we are elevated to the thought of the inventor of the myth, not simply to the myth itself" (*Phaedr. Schol.* 241E).

According to Carlos Fraenkel, Plato's myths are symbolic "images and parables" of his true doctrine, "likenesses which provide non-philosophers with an understanding (albeit imperfect in comparison to the philosopher's knowledge) of the metaphysical foundation of the natural and political order."[9] However, Plato may also have expressed mythically what he felt impossible to convey theoretically/scientifically—as he states in the case of the *Timaeus* myth—positing an intrinsic gnoseological limit.

Origen the Neoplatonist: Interpreting Plato's Dialogues Allegorically

Origen was a Christian Middle/Neoplatonist, probably identifiable with the homonymous Neoplatonist, a disciple of Ammonius, of whom Porphyry (in his biography of Plotinus), Hierocles, and Proclus speak.[10] He is

---

7. On which, see Catherine Collobert, Pierre Destrée, and Francisco J. González, eds., *Plato and Myth: Studies on the Use and Status of Platonic Myths* (Leiden: Brill, 2012); Daniel S. Werner, *Myth and Philosophy in Plato's Phaedrus* (Cambridge: Cambridge University Press, 2012).

8. Vishwa Adluri argues that the notion of salvation in the *Republic* reworks the Homeric *nostos* of Odysseus into Parmenidean ontology, conceiving salvation as a vertical ascent to the transcendent world; "Plato's Saving *Mūthos*: The Language of Salvation in the *Republic*," *IJPT* 8 (2014): 3–32.

9. Carlos Fraenkel, *Philosophical Religions from Plato to Spinoza: Reason, Religion, and Autonomy* (Cambridge: Cambridge University Press, 2012), 67, 80.

10. Ramelli, "Origen, Patristic Philosophy, and Christian Platonism"; Ramelli,

reported to have expounded Ammonius's ideas in *On Spirits* and *The King is the Only Creator.*[11] In the latter writing, Origen may have confronted Numenius, whose works were among Origen's favorite readings according to Porphyry. Indeed, Numenius distinguished precisely the King from the Creator, identifying the former with the first God, who creates nothing and the latter with the second: "The First God is the King. He does not occupy himself with any works. But God the Creator is the leader. He makes his rounds through the heavens" and animates the world (frag. 12).[12]

Moreover, Origen was profoundly conversant with imperial Neopythagoreans, as Porphyry attests (*apud* Eusebius, *Hist. eccl.* 6.19.8), listing Origen's favorite readings in philosophy: "He was always with Plato and was in conversation with the treatises of Numenius, Cronius, Apollophanes, Longinus, Moderatus, Nicomachus, and the most illustrious Pythagoreans; he also used the books by the Stoic Chaeremon and Cornutus, from whom he learned the allegorical method that was typical of the mysteries of the Greeks and applied it to the Jewish scriptures." Origen's interest in Neopythagoreanism is tellingly mentioned immediately before his interest in allegory, which Porphyry connects with Origen's readings of Neostoic allegorists. Porphyry claims that Origen applied Stoic *allegoresis* or allegorical exegesis to Scripture, without mentioning that Scripture was already extensively allegorized by Philo and Clement. Numenius's heritage was claimed by both Origen and Porphyry. Porphyry based his allegoresis of the Nymphs's cave on Numenius, whom he names several times. It is Porphyry who attests that Origen was familiar with Numenius in the passage quoted. Indeed, Origen esteemed Numenius and cited him four times (*Cels.* 1.5; 4.51; 5.38; 5.57). Numenius inspired Origen in both exegesis and theology. Numenius's allegorical reading of Scripture parallels his exegesis of Plato, where, among other points, he associated the myth of Er with Homer's representation of the underworld in the *Odyssey*. Due to his

---

"Origen the Christian Middle/Neoplatonist," *JECH* 1 (2011): 98–130; Ramelli, *Origen of Alexandria Philosopher and Theologian* (Cambridge: Cambridge University Press, forthcoming).

11. Besides the arguments adduced in Ramelli ("Origen, Patristic Philosophy, and Christian Platonism" and "Origen the Christian Middle/Neoplatonist"), I add the full correspondence with Origen's *Selecta in Psalmos* (cat.) PG 12:1560,42: Ἡ μὲν δημιουργικὴ αὐτοῦ βασιλεία πάντων δεσπόζει.

12. For the Fragments of Numenius, the English is my translation of the Greek found in Numenius, *Fragments*, ed. and trans. É. Des Places (Paris: Belles Lettres, 1973).

allegoresis of Scripture, Origen valued Numenius more than Celsus, who, like Porphyry, did not admit to biblical allegoresis.

Origen engaged in the interpretation of Plato's dialogues, including the *Republic* and the *Timaeus*, and was committed to their allegoresis. The interpretations of Plato's works that Proclus reports in his commentary on the *Timaeus* as provided by Origen are likely ascribable to the Christian philosopher, all the more so since at school Origen explained the works of Greek philosophers, among whom Plato had special prominence (Eusebius, *Hist. eccl.* 6.17). Likewise, Origen tackled the explanation of Plato's dialogues.

The first relevant passage from Proclus's commentary (1.31) comes in a debate on the purpose and meaning (σκοπός) of Plato's *Republic*. Longinus and Origen disagreed on the kind of constitution (πολιτεία) with which Socrates/Plato is dealing. According to Longinus, it was the middle πολιτεία, since its guardians were soldiers; according to Origen, it was the first, because its guardians were educated in various disciplines, including the liberal arts. These were paramount in Origen's formation and teaching. He obviously stressed their importance in Plato's *Republic* (πολιτεία), which thus symbolizes a state of knowledge and the government of souls. Longinus and Origen knew each other; Longinus mentions Origen as a Platonist of extraordinary intelligence whom he had long frequented (Porphyry, *Vit. Plot.* 20).[13] Longinus associates Origen with Ammonius, certainly because he was a disciple of Ammonius. Longinus, probably born in 212 CE, may have attended Origen's school at Caesarea in the late 230s. This leaves the door open for the identification of Origen with the Christian Platonist; it is the same Origen as mentioned in Porphyry's *Vit. Plot.* 14, since in both passages his *On Spirits* is cited. Moreover, Longinus probably knew Origen's exegesis of the Johannine Prologue.[14]

Another exegetical dissension between Longinus and Origen reported by Proclus in *Comm. Tim.* 1.76–77 concerns the interpretation of the Atlantis myth. The *Timaeus* was well known to the Christian Origen, who, like Philo and Bardaisan,[15] read Genesis through its lens. For Longinus,

---

13. Longinus praises Ammonius and Origen as being "by far superior to all their contemporaries in intelligence." See n. 11 above.

14. See Ilaria Ramelli, "Commentaries: Intersections between 'Pagan' and Christian Platonism in Late Antiquity" (paper presented at the Annual Meeting of the Society of Classical Studies, San Francisco, CA, 7–9 January 2016).

15. See Ilaria Ramelli, *Bardaisan of Edessa: A Reassessment of the Evidence and a*

this myth expressed the order of the cosmos with its planets and fixed stars, but for Origen it was an allegory of rational creatures, some good and some evil. Origen preferred a spiritual allegorization of Plato's myth: it is not about physics but about spirits. Rational creatures were the core of the Christian Origen's protology, philosophy of history, eschatology, and theodicy. He read Plato's Atlantis myth (an originally happy state of a population suddenly destroyed by a catastrophe) in light of the original life of rational creatures before the fall. These creatures are called here δαίμονες as in the title of one of the two treatises that Origen wrote on the basis of Ammonius's doctrines. It was typical of the Christian Origen to allegorize cosmological descriptions in reference, not to physics, but to spirits. For instance, he considered the "upper waters" in Genesis to symbolize good spirits and the inferior waters symbolic of evil spirits. This allegorization of the cosmological myth of Scripture is analogous to that of Origen the Neoplatonist's interpretation of Plato's cosmological myth. This also supports the identification of the two Origens.

Proclus includes Origen among those who interpreted Plato's *Timaeus* myth (the expression of "Egyptian" wisdom) allegorically, together with Numenius, Amelius, and Porphyry, all of whom were known to the Christian Origen. Crantor, instead, read the *Timaeus* myth as history, without accepting any allegorization (while Proclus later, like Iamblichus and Syrianus, upheld both the historical and allegorical meaning of this myth). The Christian Origen, indeed, read in an exclusively allegorical way both Plato's protological and eschatological myths and the Bible's protological and eschatological narratives. The most important protological myth of Plato was precisely that of his *Timaeus*.

Another disagreement between Longinus and Origen is reported by Proclus in *Comm. Tim.* 1.162. According to Longinus, the good condition of the body and soul depends on earthly factors such as a good land and climate. For Origen, however, it was dependent upon the circular movement of the sky, which he argued on the basis of his exegesis of Plato, *Resp.* 8.546A. Proclus's interpretation of the framework of the *Timaeus* myth as the expression of a double creation parallels Origen's own scheme of

---

New Interpretation (Piscataway, NJ: Gorgias, 2009); and Ramelli, "Philosophical Allegoresis of Scripture in Philo and Its Legacy in Gregory of Nyssa," *SPhiloA* 20 (2008): 55–99. On Philo, I limit myself to citing David Runia, "Philon d'Alexandrie," in *De Paccius à Plotin*, vol. 5a of *Dictionnaire des philosophes antiques*, ed. Richard Goulet (Paris: Editions du Centre National de la Recherche Scientifique, 2011), 362–90.

double creation: Proclus observes that the myth recounted by the Egyptian priest describes the "more ancient" act of creation, where all the forms were in harmony, while Solon's knowledge, which concerns constantly changing situations, is the "later" creation of the physical world in constant flux (*Tim.* 28F).[16] The same division between first and second creation (chronologically, metaphysically, and axiologically) was posited by Origen and his followers, such as Gregory of Nyssa and Evagrius. Origen precisely described physical realities as in constant flux.

Other passages from Proclus's commentary mentioning Origen can also be explained in the light of the Christian Origen's interest in allegoresis and philology. In his view, allegoresis maintained both Scripture's "soul" and its "body," that is, its spiritual and literal-historical levels. Similarly, two mentions of Origen's ideas in Proclus's commentary on the *Timaeus* perfectly suit Origen's philological, rhetorical, and literary interests related to allegoresis. Origen valued the style of Plato's dialogues (*Comm. Tim.* 1.68). He contended that such expressions as "Heracles's strength" instead of "Heracles" also befit prose, not only poetry. He assimilated Plato's prose to poetry; one aspect of this is reading symbolic meanings in Plato's dialogues. In *Comm. Tim.* 1.93, Proclus reports Origen's investigation into the different meanings of ἐλευθερώτατον in *Tim.* 21C. This parallels Origen's analyses of the meanings of terms in his scriptural commentaries. This is what Origen meant with the principle, "interpreting Scripture with Scripture," indebted to the Alexandrian philological principle, "interpreting Homer with Homer."[17] What is more, Proclus in *Comm. Tim.* 1.60 is dealing with the interpretation of Plato's metaphors. This was paramount for an allegorist like Origen. According to Origen, Proclus observes, metaphors in Plato's dialogues had a cognitive and ethical value; their goal was

---

16. See Andrew Smith, "The Image of Egypt in the Platonic Tradition," in *Plato Revived: Essays on Ancient Platonism in Honour of Dominic J. O'Meara*, ed. Filip Karfík and Euree Song (Berlin: de Gruyter, 2013), 319–25.

17. Miyako Demura underlines how Origen intended to interpret Scripture with Scripture in a coherent whole; see "Origen's Allegorical Interpretation and the Philological Tradition of Alexandria," in *Origeniana Nona: Origen and the Religious Practice of His Time; Papers of the 9th International Origen Congress, Pécs, Hungary, 29 August–2 September 2005*, ed. György Heidl and Róbert Somos (Leuven: Peeters, 2009), 149–58. The coherence of Origen's scriptural exegesis is also highlighted by John McGuckin, "Origen as a Literary Critic in the Alexandrian Tradition," in *Origeniana Octava: Origen and the Alexandria Tradition; Papers of the 8th International Origen Congress, Pisa 27–31 August 2001*, ed. Lorenzo Perrone (Leuven: Peeters, 2003), 125.

not to please—although Origen admitted that Plato appreciated stylistic elegance—but to represent passions for eliminating them. This interpretation corresponds to Origen's ethics, characterized by the ideal of impassivity (ἀπάθεια) and critical of Epicurean pleasure (ἡδονή),[18] and to his esteem of Plato's myths and allegory.

In *Comm. Tim.* 1.83, 86, a similar case regards the exegesis of Plato's myths. Longinus deemed them ornamental or psychagogical; Origen regarded them as endowed with gnoseological value and, like Plato's metaphors, not intended to produce pleasure. Proclus notes the affinity of Origen's position with Numenius, whose works Origen the Christian read assiduously. Numenius's *oeuvre* was also one of Plotinus's favorite readings, to such an extent that Plotinus was accused of plagiarizing Numenius and was defended by Amelius. This passage of Proclus even better accords with Origen's ethics and allegorical reading of Plato.

Again *Comm. Tim.* 1.63–64 features Origen as allegorizer of Plato. Proclus reports Origen's interpretation of *Tim.* 19D–E. The question of whether Plato includes Homer among the ancient poets is relevant to the issue of the symbolic meaning of Plato's dialogues. Proclus bases his account on Porphyry, who knew Origen and was interested in the allegoresis of Homer and Plato. Porphyry may have learned this anecdote from Plotinus, Longinus, or someone of that school. Origen was at pains for three days solving this problem. The description of Origen's sweating and sustained mental and physical effort corresponds to the image of Origen the Christian as an exceptional hard-worker, by which he earns the title Philoponos/Philoponotatos (lover of labor, hard worker/hard worker to the utmost degree) in Athanasius[19] and Eusebius, as well as the epithet Adamantios, "man of diamond/stainless steel," which Origen himself might have elected and was used by his Christian followers.[20] Origen's labors are often stressed by Eusebius,[21] who, like Athanasius, attaches the epithet Philoponotatos to Origen (*Ecl. proph.* 3.6). In the passage from Proclus, Porphyry attests that

---

18. See Ilaria Ramelli, "Epicureanism and Early Christianity," in *Oxford Handbook of Epicureanism*, ed. Phillip Mistis (Oxford: Oxford University Press, forthcoming).

19. Athanasius, *In illud Qui dixerit verbum in Filium* (PG 26:649,21); *Decr.* 27.1–2; *apud* Socrates Scholasticus, *Hist. eccl.* 6.13.

20. He and the Christians preferred this epithet to his "pagan" name. See Ilaria Ramelli, "The Philosophical Stance of Allegory in Stoicism and Its Reception in Platonism, Pagan and Christian," *IJCT* 18 (2011): 335–71.

21. Eusebius, *Hist. eccl.* 6.2.7; 6.2.9; 6.3.7; 6.3.11; 6.3.13; 6.8.6; 6.15.11, etc.

Origen valued Homer's poetry, because it inspired courageous deeds. Plato invited defenders of poetry to show "that it is not only sweet but beneficial to regimes and human life" (*Resp.* 607E), which is what Middle and Neoplatonists did.[22] These were concerned with the reconciliation of Plato and Homer,[23] which was facilitated by the allegorization of both.[24]

Porphyry's account of Origen the Neoplatonist's attitude toward Homer corresponds to Origen the Christian's attitude, which again suggests that they were the same person. In his extant Greek works, Origen refers to Homer, mentioning him more than thirty times, never in his biblical commentaries or homilies, but only in *Against Celsus*, where his interlocutor is a "pagan" Middle Platonist.[25] This is consistent with the division of sources with respect to Origen's Christian and philosophical works, the former cited by Christians, the latter by Neoplatonists. The author, however, was the same. In 7.6.28–37, Origen depicts Homer as "the best of the poets" and adduces his ideas on demons/spirits (the object of Origen's treatise based on Ammonius's teaching) to support his own argument. Notably, Origen also uses a Pythagorean exegesis of that Homeric passage. He tended to read Plato through Pythagorean lenses and interpreted his dialogues symbolically, as he also interpreted Scripture. Likewise, in 4.91.8, Origen describes Homer as "incredibly good at poetry" and cites a long Homeric excerpt. In 4.36.32, Plato's attitude to Homer and other poets is discussed—the same issue treated by Origen the Neoplatonist, according to Proclus. Plato, Origen maintains, was right to exclude from his state poets who corrupted the young such as Hesiod in *Theogony* (see 7.54.16). Origen's parameter is ethical (see 8.68.32), like that of Proclus's Origen. Origen the Neoplatonist's appreciation of Homer for the edifying

---

22. Rana S. Liebert, "Apian Imagery and the Critique of Poetic Sweetness in Plato's *Republic*," *TAPA* 140 (2010): 97–116.

23. Homer in antiquity was also attacked by others besides Plato, e.g., Heraclitus and the Cynic Zoilus; see Giuseppe Solaro, "Denigrare Omero," *ANost* 9 (2011): 81–86. On Plato's ambivalent attitude toward poetry, see Andrea Capra, *Plato's Four Muses: The Phaedrus and the Poetics of Philosophy*, HellSS 67 (Washington, DC: Center for Hellenic Studies, 2015).

24. See Ilaria Ramelli, *L'età classica*, vol. 1 of *Allegoria* (Milan: Vita e Pensiero, 2004), chs. 1 and 7.

25. Homeric quotes abound in this work; see Andrea Villani, "Homer in the Debate between Celsus and Origen," *REAug* 58 (2012): 113–39, who classifies the quotations into three function types: ornamental, polemical, or as support for an argument.

contents of his poems is also found in 6.7.2. The latter just adds that morally elevated messages are also found in Moses, who came before Homer.

In *Cels.* 4.91.5, Origen adduces an example from Homer: if birds had prophetic faculties, as Celsus maintains, a bird in a simile of Homer's would have foreseen that a snake was about to kill her and her chicks. The same strategy is found in 4.94.1–14: Origen adduces two other Homeric quotations to counter Celsus's claim that birds have divine souls. In 7.36.30, Origen discusses Homer from the literary-rhetorical viewpoint (the same applied to Plato by Proclus's Origen) with reference to the construction of his characters. In 4.21.16–29, Homer comes again to the fore with two examples within a dispute over Homer's or Moses's priority. In 6.43.4, he declares that Moses's words on the devil's fall cannot have been inspired by Homer due to Moses's anteriority. In 1.16.17, Homer's Galactophagi, or "Milk-Eaters," are cited by Celsus with the druids and other wise ancient peoples; only the Hebrews—Origen laments—are excluded from the categories of antiquity and wisdom. This was a crucial point in the debate between "pagan" and Christian Platonists, bearing on the legitimacy of allegoresis in biblical interpretation,[26] which paralleled the allegorization of Plato's dialogues. Celsus, Porphyry, and other "pagan" Platonists denied that Scripture hid philosophical truths under an allegorical veil, while they admitted this for mythologies of other "barbarian" peoples as well as for Homer and Plato.[27]

Origen cites Homer for his myths in connection with Celsus's assimilation of Jesus's blood to the gods' ichor (*Cels.* 1.66.11; 2.36.6).[28] In 6.42.35–65 Origen criticizes Celsus's allegoresis of a Homeric passage, in which Zeus's words to Hera are interpreted as God's words addressed to matter. Physical allegoresis, a heritage from Stoicism, was not Origen's favorite. In 7.41.12, Origen criticizes the thesis of Homer's and other poets' divine inspiration.

---

26. See Ramelli, "Philosophical Stance of Allegory."
27. See Ramelli, "Origen, Patristic Philosophy, and Christian Platonism"; Ramelli, "Origene allegorista cristiano: Il duplice attacco e la simmetria tra filosofia cristiana e allegoresi biblica," *InvLuc* 31 (2009): 141–56; Ramelli, "Philosophical Stance of Allegory"; Wolfram Kinzig, "The Pagans and the Christian Bible," in vol. 1 of *The New Cambridge History of the Bible*, ed. J. Schaper and J. Carleton Paget (Cambridge: Cambridge University Press, 2013), 752–74.
28. In *Cels.* 2.76.57, 61, three Homeric verses are quoted, in which Hermes speaks to Odysseus concerning the Sirens. In *Cels.* 7.28.8, Origen report Celsus's quotation from Homer.

Homer and Homeric philology and exegesis deeply influenced Origen. In his *Hexapla*, he imported the diacritic symbols of Aristarchus's Homeric edition. And he took up Homeric allegoresis and applied it to Biblical exegesis—already Philo's move[29]—as well as to the exegesis of Plato, which Neopythagoreans and Neoplatonists also did. Origen's principle of "interpreting Scripture by Scripture" was already used by the Alexandrian grammarians to interpret Homer and by philosophers to interpret Aristotle or Plato. Origen's attitude toward Homer is similar to that of Philo, who read Homer allegorically and saw much in common between Homer and Scripture.[30] Some predecessors of Philo assimilated—like Origen—biblical myths to Greek myths, for example, the myth of the Tower of Babel to the Homeric myth of the Aloaedes, applying literary criticism to both Homer and Scripture.[31]

This analysis, along with many other clues, suggests that the philosopher Origen cited by Proclus—like the philosopher Origen in Porphyry's *Vita Plotini* and in Hierocles—may be Origen the Christian philosopher and that this Christian Middle/Neoplatonist practiced an allegorical/symbolic reading of Plato's dialogues.

Plato and Scripture: Protology and Eschatology in Parallel Myths as Symbolic Accounts

Origen appreciated Plato's myths methodologically and drew an epistemological parallel between Plato's protological and eschatological myths and the biblical protological and eschatological accounts. These are the

---

29. See Ramelli, "Philosophical Allegoresis of Scripture in Philo."

30. See Katell Berthelot, "Philon d'Alexandrie, lecteur d'Homère: Quelques éléments de réflexion," in *Prolongements et renouvellements de la tradition classique*, ed. Anne Balansard, Gilles Dorival, and Mireille Loubet (Aix-en-Provence: Université de Provence, 2011), 145–57. On Philo's reception of Homer, also Maren R. Niehoff, *Jewish Exegesis and Homeric Scholarship in Alexandria* (Cambridge: Cambridge University Press, 2011); Pura Nieto Hernández, "Philo and Greek Poetry," *SPhiloA* 26 (2014): 135–49.

31. See Maren Niehoff, "Recherche homérique et exégèse biblique à Alexandrie," in *Philon d'Alexandrie: Un penseur à l'intersection des cultures gréco-romaine, orientale, juive et chrétienne; Actes du colloque international organisé par le Centre interdisciplinaire d'étude des religions et de la laïcité de l'Université libre de Bruxelles (Bruxelles, 26–28 juin 2007)*, ed. Sabrina Inowlocki and Baudouin Decharneux (Turnhout: Brepols, 2011), 83–103.

only sections, in Plato's dialogues and in Scripture, endowed with an *exclusively allegorical/symbolic* sense, being deprived of a literal/historical meaning. The rest of Scripture, and of Plato's dialogues, have both a literal and an allegorical/noetic/spiritual meaning.[32] Origen, exegete, theorist of exegesis, and philosopher, thought that Scripture has a literal-historical meaning, besides spiritual ones, in almost all cases. His twofold scriptural exegesis reflects the Platonic pattern of two levels of reality, which he even highlights in a biblical commentary (*Comm. Cant.* 2.8.17).[33] Only a few biblical passages have no literal meaning (*Princ.* 4.2.5, 9), due to logical absurdities, paradoxes, or impossibilities (*Princ.* 4.3.1–4). Many more passages possess a literal meaning than those which only have a spiritual sense (*apud* Pamphilus, *Apol.* 123). The story of the patriarchs and the miracle of Joshua really happened (*apud* Pamphilus, *Apol.* 125). But God's anthropomorphisms, incongruities (*Princ.* 4.3.1), and legal prescriptions that were impossible to fulfil have "bare spiritual meanings," not wrapped in a literal sense, to indicate that it is necessary to search for deeper meanings: "Sometimes even impossible things are prescribed by the Law, for the sake of those more expert and particularly fond of *investigation*, that, applying themselves to the toil of the *examination* of scriptures, they may be *persuaded by reason* that in scriptures it is necessary to look for a meaning *worthy of God*" (*Princ.* 4.2.9).

Here and elsewhere, Origen applies the terminology of philosophical investigation to exegesis because for him scriptural allegoresis, no less than the allegoresis of Plato's dialogues, is part of *philosophy* (as allegoresis of myths was for the Stoics).[34] Therefore he included his theorization

---

32. The historical account remains useless if it has no moral teaching, as Origen remarks, e.g., in *Hom. Jer.* 1.2: τί οὖν πρὸς ἐμὲ αὕτη ἡ ἱστορία; ... τί οὖν διὰ τούτων διδασκόμεθα; Yet the importance of the historical narrative of Scripture for Origen is rightly emphasized, e.g., by Karl Shuve, "Origen's 'Dramatic' Approach to Scripture in the Homilies on Jeremiah," in *Tertullian to Tyconius: Egypt before Nicaea; Athanasius and His Opponents*, vol. 3 of *Studia Patristica: Papers Presented at the Fifteenth International Conference on Patristic Studies Held in Oxford, 2007*, ed. J. Baun, A. Cameron, M. Edwards, and M. Vinzent, StPatr 46 (Leuven: Peeters, 2010): 235–40.

33. *Aurum verum in illis quae incorporea sunt et invisibilia ac spiritalia intelligatur; similitudo vero auri, inquo, non est ipsa veritas, sed umbra veritatis, ista corporea et visibilia accipiantur.*

34. See Ramelli, *Età classica*; Ramelli, "Origen and the Stoic Allegorical Tradition: Continuity and Innovation," *InvLuc* 28 (2006): 195–226; Ramelli, "Philosophical Stance of Allegory."

of scriptural allegoresis in his *philosophical* masterpiece. While he maintained the historicity of the biblical text that he also interpreted allegorically, Stoic and Middle/Neoplatonic allegorists of myths did not maintain their historicity just as "gnostic" allegorists discarded Scripture's historical plane.[35]

But in Origen, as in Plato, the accounts of the origin of the world and eschatology are subject to special hermeneutical rules. Early passages in Genesis and Revelation escape the literal and allegorical interpretive model. In the prologue to his *Commentary on the Song of Songs*, Origen ascribes a special status to the beginning of Genesis: like the Song, this must come last in one's studies after one has studied the rest of Scripture. The Genesis account of creation, just as the Song of Songs and Revelation, can be interpreted only allegorically.[36]

Besides the influence of Platonizing Philo,[37] Plato's own impact on Origen can be hypothesized with regard to the exclusively allegorical interpretation of the ἀρχή and τέλος accounts. Origen praised Plato's myths because he was aware that only mythical, not theoretical, accounts could be used of protology and eschatology. The former was tackled in Plato's *Timaeus*[38] and the latter in his eschatological myths. Origen reflected on the epistemological status of Plato's myths, praising Plato because he resorted to myths to hide the truth from "the majority," revealing it to "those who know" (*Cels.* 4.39). Origen quotes Plato's myth of Poros (*Symp.*

---

35. See Ramelli, "Philosophical Stance of Allegory."

36. *Eas quas* δευτερώσεις *appellant ad ultimum quattuor ista reservari, id est principium Genesis, in quo mundi creatura describitur, et Ezechiel prophetae principia, in quibus de Chrubin refertur, et finem, in quo Templi aedificatio continetur, et hunc Cantici Canticorum libro* (*Comm. Cant.* prol. 1.7). Origen refers to the beginning with the creation of the world in Genesis, the first principles with the vision of God's Glory in Ezekiel (Ezek 10), and the end with the heavenly temple of Ezek 40 and Revelation (the temple of "spiritual stones"), and the path that culminates into θέωσις and union with God (Song of Songs). The Song is deprived of literal-historical meaning to the point that, as is, it is a theatrical piece, not a historical account; thus it must be interpreted only spiritually (*Comm. Cant.* 4.2.4).

37. On which, see, e.g., Ramelli, "Philosophical Allegoresis of Scripture in Philo."

38. Origen was familiar with it, like the Middle Platonists. See, e.g., George Boys-Stones, "Time, Creation, and the Mind of God: The Afterlife of a Platonist Theory in Origen," *OSAP* 40 (2011): 319–37; Ilaria Ramelli, "Atticus and Origen on the Soul of God the Creator: From the Pagan to the Christian Side of Middle Platonism," *JRp* 10 (2011): 13–35.

203B–E) and remarks that its readers will either understand it literally and deride it, which Christians should not do given Plato's greatness, or allegorize it, knowing that Plato veiled his thought behind myths to reveal it only to philosophers: "If they *investigate philosophically the contents expressed mythically*, and can thereby *discover what Plato meant*, they will see how he could hide under the appearance of myth those doctrines which seemed to him especially sublime, due to the majority, and at the same time revealed them, as is fit, to *those who know how to discover* from myths what the author meant concerning *the truth*" (*Cels.* 4.39).

Origen presents again allegoresis as a *philosophical* exercise, be it applied to Scripture's or Plato's myths. Soon after, Origen assimilates Plato's Poros myth to Scripture's paradise story: "I have reported this myth, found in Plato, because Zeus's garden therein seems to have *something very similar* to God's garden, Penia can be *assimilated* to the serpent in the garden, and Poros, the victim of Penia's plot, to the human being, the victim of the serpent's plot" (*Cels.* 4.39, emphasis added). This assimilation was found not only in Origen's debate with the Middle Platonist Celsus but also in his *Commentary on Genesis*, which addressed a Christian learned public. According to Origen, there it was even more developed: "Now it was not the right occasion for *going through both Plato's myth* and the story of the serpent and God's garden and what happened there according to scripture. For *I have already treated all this in depth, as the main subject, in my commentary on Genesis*" (*Cels.* 4.39, emphasis added). Origen in that commentary extensively compared Plato's myth and the Genesis story. The short comparison in *Cels.* 4.39 is but a summary of the lengthy discussion in the lost commentary. In another commentary, Origen praises Plato's *Symposium*, where the Poros myth is encapsulated.[39] In *Cels.* 4.39, Origen remarks that if Christians should do what Celsus does with Scripture's myths—refuse to read them allegorically—they could laugh at Plato's Poros myth and ridicule Plato. But if they examine philosophically what is said mythically to discover what Plato meant, then they will admire Plato's allegory, just as "pagan" Platonists should admire Scripture's allegory.

---

39. *Apud Graecos quidem plurimi eruditorum virorum, volentes investigare veritatis indaginem, de amoris natura multa ac diversa etiam dialogorum stilo scripta protulerunt, conantes ostendere non aliud esse amoris vim nisi quae animam de terris ad fastigia caeli celsa perducat ... quaestiones de hoc quasi in conviviis propositae referuntur, inter eos, puto, inter quos non ciborum, se verborum convivium gerebatur* (*Comm. Cant.* prol. 2.1).

Likewise, Origen assimilates Hesiod's Pandora myth to the Genesis account of the creation of the woman: both must be allegorized (*Cels.* 4.38).[40] He declares that the Genesis story of humanity's receiving the "skin tunics," that is, mortal corporeality, has no literal, but symbolic meaning, which he assimilates again to the symbolic meaning of Plato's myth of the soul's descent (*Cels.* 4.40).

Origen compares the Genesis myth to Plato's myths of Poros and the soul's fall, in that they express the same content; both myths—Scripture's and Plato's—having no historical meaning, must be allegorized to find philosophical truths therein. Origen's *Commentary on Genesis* is lost, but *Cels.* 4.39 indicates that he extensively assimilated Scripture's and Plato's myths and shows how he accounted for such similarities: "It is not quite clear whether this story [the Poros myth] occurred to Plato's mind by chance or, as some believe,[41] during his sojourn in Egypt Plato also came across people who adhered to the Jews' philosophy; he learned from them, then retained some things and altered others, careful to avoid offending the Greeks by sticking to the Jews' wisdom entirely and in every respect." Origen says, "Jewish philosophy," rather than "religion," because from it stemmed what he depicted as Christian philosophy and because he considered scriptural allegoresis a *philosophical* task, already performed by Jewish exegetes. Origen observes that Celsus's attack on biblical allegoresis is directed not only against *Christian*, but also against *Jewish* allegorists, such as Philo and Aristobulus (*Cels.* 4.51). For his scriptural-philosophical allegoresis, Origen claims pre-Christian antecedents, deliberately ignored by Platonists who delegitimized scriptural allegoresis.

Both Plato and Scripture spoke mythically, that is, symbolically of protology and eschatology, which exceed historical experience.[42] The church's doctrine left protology and eschatology undefined (*Princ.* prol. 7), not even angels "can fully know the beginning and the end of all" (Pamphilus, *Apol.* 82; cf. *Princ.* 4.3.14); a fortiori these transcend human knowledge and experience: thus, Scripture speaks of them only symbolically—like Plato. This is why Origen's interpretation of the creation narrative is allegorical. Adam symbolizes all humanity (*Cels.* 4.40). The Genesis account "concerns not so much a single human as the whole of humanity"; it is

---

40. Οὐδὲ τὴν λέξιν ἐκθέμενος ... μετὰ τροπολογίας εἴρηται.

41. E.g., Clement, *Strom.* 1.1.10.2.

42. On myth dealing with what is anterior to historical record, see Jörg Rüpke, *Il crocevia del mito: Religione e narrazione nel mondo antico* (Bologna: EDB, 2014), 22.

only apparently historical, but it never happened "corporeally" or "literally" (*Princ.* 4.3.1). Origen's production offers numerous examples of exclusively allegorical exegesis of the paradise account,[43] such as his first *Homily on Genesis*. Also, in *Hom. Ps.* 1, 36 he declares that the creation account must be allegorized.

Origen interpreted allegorically not only the beginning of Genesis, but also Revelation—the biblical eschatological myth, paralleling it with Plato's eschatological myths. Origen and his followers disliked literal readings of Revelation, which smelled like millenarianism. Unlike many Origenians, Origen regarded Revelation as Scripture but interpreted it *only* allegorically. His exegesis survives partially in scholia[44] and in his *Commentaries on John* and *Matthew*, *Homilies on Jeremiah*, *First Principles*, and elsewhere. He arraigns a literal interpretation of Revelation by those who identified the eschatological beatitude with worldly pleasures and the heavenly Jerusalem with an earthly city of gems (*Princ.* 2.11.2–3). For Origen, that Jerusalem will be made, not of stones, but of saints; everyone will be instructed there to become a living precious stone; so, rational creatures will be restored to God's original plan.[45] Likewise, Origen's follower, Dionysius of Alexandria, argued that Revelation must be interpreted *only* allegorically (Eusebius, *Hist. eccl.* 7.24.3–25.26).

---

43. E.g., *Hom. Gen.* 2.4; *Sel. Num.* (PG 12:581B); *Fr. Gen.* 236; see Karin Metzler, *Die Kommentierung des Buches Genesis*, Origenes Werke mit deutscher Übersetzung 1.1 (New York: de Gruyter, 2010), frag. D15.

44. Panayiotis Tzamalikos, *An Ancient Commentary on the Book of Revelation: A Critical Edition of the* Scholia in Apocalypsin (Cambridge: Cambridge University Press, 2013), suggests that these scholia were compiled by Cassian the Sabaite based on Didymus's commentary on Revelation. The ideas would mostly go back to Origen, on whose exegesis Didymus drew. An early medieval prologue to an Irish commentary on Revelation attests to the existence of twelve homilies on Revelation by Origen preserved at that time. See J. F. T. Kelly, "Early Medieval Evidence for Twelve Homilies by Origen on the Apocalypse," *VC* 39 (1985): 273–79.

45. See Ilaria Ramelli, "Origen and Apokatastasis: A Reassessment," in *Origeniana Decima: Origen as Writer; Papers of the 10th International Origen Congress, University School of Philosophy and Education "Ignatianum," Kraków, Poland, 31 August–4 September 2009*, ed. Sylwya Kaczmarek and Henryk Pietras (Leuven: Peeters, 2011), 649–70, and Ramelli, "Origen, Greek Philosophy, and the Birth of the Trinitarian Meaning of Hypostasis," *HTR* 105 (2012): 302–50.

Origen's "Corrections" to Plato's Protological and Eschatological Myths

Origen also "corrected" Plato's protological and eschatological myths in light of scripture. In eschatology, he corrected Plato's notion of "incurable" souls, which contravened his doctrine of universal restoration (ἀποκατάστασις). For Plato, souls that have committed the gravest evils are "incurable" and cannot be healed through suffering and restored to contemplation; rather, they are eternally tormented in Tartarus (*Phaed.* 113E2; *Gorg.* 525C2; *Resp.* 615E3). Origen corrects Plato: no being is incurable for its Creator. Christ-Logos will be able to heal all of his creatures from the illness of evil (*Princ.* 3.6.5). The argument from God's omnipotence comes from Scripture (esp. Matt 19:25–26; Mark 10:26–27). Origen also "corrected" *metensomatosis*, the transmigration of souls, which Plato presented mythically but Platonists understood theoretically. Origen rejected *metensomatosis* as doctrine,[46] accepting it only as myth—that is, an allegory of how vicious people become *like* animals—and rather supported *ensomatosis*, the "incorporation" of a soul in just one body. He considers Platonic psychology in *Comm. Jo.* 6.85, stating that one must examine:

> the question of the essence of the soul, the principle of its existence, its joining this earthly body ... whether it is possible that it enters a body for a second time, whether this will happen during the same cycle and arrangement, in the same body or another, and, if in the same, whether this will remain identical to itself in its substance only acquiring different qualities, or it will remain the same in both substance and qualities, and whether the soul will always use the same body or this will change.

One must investigate this, because Scripture and the apostolic teaching have left the origin of souls unclarified (*Princ.* 1 preface 5). Likewise it must be researched whether the soul is incorporeal, whether it is simple or composed of two, three, or more parts, and whether it is created.[47] Origen finds the latter theory risible[48] and turns to an alternative: "Should one

---

46. Yet he was accused of supporting it, e.g., by Justinian and Photius, *Bibl. Cod.* 8.3b–4a.

47. *Utrum nuper creata [anima] veniat et tunc primum facta cum corpus videtur esse formatum, ut causa facturae eius animandi corporis necessitas exstitisse credatur* (*Comm. Cant.* 2.5.23).

48. In his exegesis of Titus preserved in a question to Barsanuphius (PG 86:891–

think that the soul was created much earlier and then, for some reason, comes to take up a body? And if one believes that it is reduced to this on account of a cause, what is this cause?"[49] Rational creatures existed before the "casting down" (καταβολή) of the cosmos (*Comm. Cant.* 2.8.4). Matter was created together with rational creatures: "When scripture states that God created all 'by number and measure,' we shall be correct to apply the word 'number' to rational creatures or minds ... and 'measure' to bodily matter.... These are the things we must believe were created by God in the beginning, before anything else" (*Princ.* 2.9.1). Bodies are not posterior to *noes* but were created with them—not mortal, but spiritual. After sin and the expulsion from paradise, spiritual bodies became mortal and heavy, apt to dwelling on earth. Bodies change qualities according to the place they are in (from the lost *De resurrectione*, quoted by Pamphilus, *Apol.* 134): on earth they must be thick and heavy (*Comm. Cant.* 3.5.16). In his *Mart.* 3 (248 CE), Origen expressly speaks of two kinds of bodies, earthly and not earthly. The subtle, immortal body at the beginning parallels that of the resurrection, after the deposition of the "skin tunic" added to the original immortal body (from Origen's lost commentary on Ps 6, quoted by Pamphilus, *Apol.* 157).[50]

Origen often conversed with Plato's creation myth, reading Genesis in light of the *Timaeus*, as Philo and the Christian Middle Platonist Bardaisan[51] did. Nevertheless, Origen corrected Plato on the preexistence of matter. More precisely, he corrected the Platonists who—unlike Plato, who treated it mythically—taught matter's preexistence dogmatically. Origen highlights this distance between his own position and Greek philosophy on this point (*Hom. Gen.* 14.3) and performs a *reductio ad absurdum* of matter's coeternity with God (*Princ.* 2.4.3). He surely discussed this in his *Commentary on Genesis*.

---

94), Origen said that "the doctrine that souls exist before bodies is justified neither by the apostles nor by the ecclesiastical tradition." Origen further "characterized whoever maintains this doctrine as a heretic."

49. *An prius et olim facta ob aliquam causam ad corpus sumendum venire aestimetur. Etsi ex causa aliqua in hoc deduci creditur, quae illa sit causa* (*Comm. Cant.* 2.5.21–23).

50. *Cum corpus humanum, crassitudinis huius indumento deposito, uelut nudum coeperit sustinere tormenta.*

51. See Ramelli, *Bardaisan of Edessa*.

A reaction arose from Christians against Origen's symbolic reading of Gen 1–3 in his commentary—hence its loss. These polemics are echoed in Epiphanius, *Pan.* 55.1–2, 58.6–8 and in the Antiochenes. Not only pagans but also Christians levelled accusations against Origen for his scriptural allegoresis,[52] already during his life. He defended himself even in his homilies (see *Hom. Ezech.* 6.8). By allegorizing the Old Testament, Origen refuted "gnostic" and Marcionite claims that this had to be separated from the New Testament as a product of a lesser deity and could not contain philosophical truths that allegoresis could unveil. In *Hom. Ps.* 5.36.5, Origen refers to Marcionites and some "gnostics": "when the heretics imagine a certain other God superior to God the Creator and deny that the God who created all is the good God ... if they are so mistaken in their thoughts it is because they interpret the Law *exclusively in a literal sense*, and ignore that *the Law is spiritual*" (emphasis added). Marcionites and "gnostics" were deceived, because they did not read the Old Testament allegorically.

Origen, like Philo,[53] also blamed extreme biblical allegorists who liquidated Scripture's historicity by an exclusively allegorical exegesis of all of it, turning all facts in Scripture into myths. But Origen, drawing on Plato's myths, distinguished the protological and eschatological accounts from the rest of Scripture: only these are susceptible of exclusively symbolic exegesis. Since Origen ascribed the same epistemological status to Plato's protological and eschatological myths as he did to the protological and eschatological accounts found in Scripture, for the latter he abandoned his general rule of keeping the literal plane along with the allegorical, as Plato abandoned his theoretical exposition to hint mythically at truths that could not be expressed otherwise. Moreover, Origen, who was deeply appreciative of Numenius's Neopythagorean exegesis, interpreted Plato's dialogues symbolically. While, however, he kept both the literal and the allegorical sense for the whole of them, he applied to his myths, just as to scripture's myths, an exclusively symbolic exegesis.

Origen read so much of Plato's myths into Christian doctrine as to use Plato's mythological terminology—for example, πτερορρυέω for the loss of the soul's wings—while expounding his Christian view of the fall of rational creatures after Satan's: "evil came about from the fact that some rational

---

52. Cf. Ramelli, "Origene allegorista cristiano," 141–56.
53. Origen opposed radical allegorists such as Gnostics (Heracleon), who annihilated the historical plane of Scripture. Philo had already polemicized thusly (*Migr.* 89).

beings *lost their wings* and followed the first who had lost his wings" (*Cels.* 6.43, emphasis added).

Epilogue

If the allegorizer of Plato's *Timaeus* cited by Proclus was the same as the author of the first scholarly biblical commentaries, *First Principles*, and *Against Celsus*, this is momentous also regarding the extra-Christian reception of Origen. Proclus, who had scarce sympathy for Christians, regarded the exegesis of Plato by a Christian Platonist worthy of study—probably knowing, like Porphyry, that Origen was a Christian. Proclus regarded Origen's "Ammonian" writings as part of an authoritative Neoplatonist body of texts, but he probably also knew Christian philosophical texts by Origen such as *First Principles* and the *Commentary on John*, which was likely known already to Amelius in Plotinus's circle.[54] Some of Origen's texts not accounted for in the Christian reception of Origen, circulated among Neoplatonists likely along some of his Christian philosophical and scholarly works.

Indeed, Hierocles and Proclus refer to doctrines expressed in *First Principles*, not only in Origen's "Ammonian" treatises, which could be attributed to the "pagan" Origen. Porphyry ascribes Greek doctrines to the Christian Origen in metaphysics and theology ("in his view of the existing realities and God his thoughts were those of a Greek [κατὰ δὲ τὰς περὶ τῶν πραγμάτων καὶ τοῦ θείου δόξας ἑλληνίζων], and he turned Greek ideas into a substratum of alien myths"; Prophyry, frag. 39)—the same doctrines to which Hierocles and Proclus refer. Proclus, like Hierocles, commented on Origen's philosophy, not his religious beliefs. Albeit disagreeing on some points, they held Origen as a philosopher in high esteem (for example, Porphyry took up Origen's notion of hypostasis and attached it to Plotinus; Proclus had Origen in mind about *apokatastasis* and first bodies[55]). Significantly, Justinian (d. 565) attacked both Origen's legacy and the Athenian Neoplatonists.

---

54. Ramelli, "Commentaries."
55. On Porphyry, see Ramelli, "Origen, Greek Philosophy, and the Birth of the Trinitarian Meaning of Hypostasis"; on Proclus, see Ramelli, "Proclus and Christian Neoplatonism," in *The Ways of Byzantine Philosophy*, ed. Mikonja Knežević (Alhambra, CA: Sebastian Press, 2015), 43–82.

Origen participated in competing circles in the philosophical field, being at the same time problematic and attractive for both Christians and Platonists. Even Porphyry recognized and respected Origen's knowledge of philosophical texts but criticized his mixing of Greek and barbarian in his practice of Christianity and application of allegoresis to Hebrew texts (frag. 39). If Proclus's Origen is Porphyry's Origen, then we see in fifth-century Platonist circles the reception of a de-Christianized Origen whose reading of Plato was held as authoritative. This is interesting given the fate of Origen's legacy, since precisely towards the end of the fifth century the Origenist controversy brewing in Christian circles led to Origen's condemnation by Justinian.

The Neoplatonic Transmission of Ancient Wisdom

Gregory Shaw

> If there is any community between us and the gods, it is constituted most of all through this virtue (wisdom), and it is in accordance with it that we are assimilated to them.... It is reasonable to assert, therefore, that wisdom makes those who possess it godlike. (Iamblichus, *To Asphalius, On Wisdom*)[1]

> Goods that are indivisible can be present to more than one person at the same time, and no one has a lesser share in their regard on account of possession by others.... (Proclus, *Comm. Alc.*)[2]

Wisdom and Religious Competition

It may be helpful to begin by pointing out that scholars today do not believe in ancient wisdom. To be more direct, we do not believe in wisdom at all. We know that Neoplatonists believed that wisdom allowed them to become divine and reveal the gods in their very bodies,[3] but we do

---

1. Modified translation from Iamblichus, *The Letters*, ed. and trans. John Dillon and Wolfgang Polleichtner, WGRW 19 (Atlanta: Society of Biblical Literature, 2009), 13.

2. Translation from Proclus, *Commentary on the First Alcibiades*, ed. and trans. L. G. Westerink and William O'Neill, PTT 6 (Dilton Marsh: Prometheus Trust, 2011), 193.

3. The second-century Platonist Calvenus Taurus put it this way: "the purpose of the souls' descent is to reveal the divine life, for this is the will of the gods: to reveal themselves. *For the gods come forth into bodily appearance and reveal themselves in the pure and faultless lives of human souls.*" See Iamblichus, *De Anima*, ed. and trans. John F. Finamore and John M. Dillon, PhA 92 (Leiden: Brill 2002), 54,20–26. The translation of this passage is my own, but I have consulted the translations by Finamore and Dillon as well as that by Dillon, *The Middle Platonists: 80 B.C. to A.D. 220* (London: Duckworth, 1977), 245.

not believe that anymore. Today we do not believe in wisdom, and we do not believe in gods—in or out of our bodies—but we are highly skilled at describing how ancient philosophers and theologians believed in gods, wisdom, and the divine life.

However, rather than assume our lack of understanding in these matters, we assume theirs. Our reasoning works as follows: since we *know* that there is no wisdom in the deep and deifying sense described by the Platonists, we conclude that, when they extolled the virtues of wisdom, they were involved in sophisticated forms of self-deception—"illusions" as Sigmund Freud put it, speaking for the "wisdom" of our age—yet we are nevertheless convinced that the rhetoric of ancient wisdom served a real purpose and value, one that we recognize as valid: *it gave them social and political power*. So scholars today ask how philosophers and theologians of antiquity maintained their prestige and power by using the trope of "ancient wisdom." Once we have reframed the rhetoric of wisdom for what we think it really is, a *strategy of persuasion to gain power*, we are in a position to see how these different rhetorical strategies—these theologies of wisdom—were in competition. We explore ancient religions through the values that shape our own worldview: politics and consumerism.

In the fourth century, the Neoplatonist Iamblichus observed that ancient wisdom was at risk of being corrupted by a habit of thought he recognized among his Platonic contemporaries. It was not power politics or consumerism but the destructive habit of misplaced concreteness, one that replaces reality with abstract formulations and ignores the presence of gods in the physical world. For example, Porphyry said that gods cannot be contacted in material rituals because, in his conceptualization, gods dwell beyond the cosmos and are far removed from the material world (see Iamblichus, *Myst.* 23.9–13).[4] To this Iamblichus replies, "This opinion spells the ruin of all holy ritual and theurgic communion between gods and men, since it places the presence of superior beings outside the earth. It amounts to saying that the divine is at a distance from the earth and cannot mingle with men, and that this lower region is a desert, without

---

4. References come from Iamblichus, *On the Mysteries*, ed. and trans. Emma C. Clarke, John Dillon, and Jackson P. Hershbell, WGRW 4 (Atlanta: Society of Biblical Literature, 2003). My translations are based on this translation. Following Clarke, Dillon, and Hershbell, all references here will follow the pagination in Gustav Parthey's edition of the text (*Jamblichi De Mysteriis liber* [Berlin: Nicolai, 1857]), preceded by *Myst.* (*De Mysteriis*).

gods" (*Myst.* 28.6–11).⁵ Porphyry's way of thinking eventually won the day, as should be evident from our own culture, poetically described by T. S. Eliot as a spiritual wasteland. In this habit of thinking, which is our own, what is important is not the indescribable reality and beauty of the world or the traditions and rituals that engage it; what is important to us is our thoughts, our theories, and our reflections. Lamenting such self-absorbed intellectualism, Iamblichus criticized the thinkers of his own era. He says:

> The reason everything has fallen into a state of decay—both in our words and prayers—is because they are continually being changed by the endless innovations and lawlessness of the Greeks. For the Greeks are naturally followers of the latest trends and are eagerly carried off in any direction; they possess no stability. Whatever they receive from other traditions they do not preserve; even this they immediately reject and change everything through their unstable habit of seeking the latest terms.⁶ (*Myst.* 259.4–10)

Our contemporary reframing of "ancient wisdom" as a strategy to achieve social power is a perfect example of this kind of thinking. We reduce "wisdom" to a discursive strategy or a rhetorical trope, something with which we are quite familiar. Like Iamblichus's Greeks, our academic culture places the highest value on our thinking, theories, and interpretations.

According to Iamblichus, however, ancient wisdom was not a doctrine, a theory, or a belief. It was not a credo or a dogma and thus was not part of a rhetorical strategy competing with other dogmas. For the later Platonists like Iamblichus, Proclus, and Damascius, ancient wisdom was not even ancient in a chronological sense; it was *ontologically* prior. It opened the soul to an awareness that *precedes* discursive activity. As conceived by these Platonists, ancient wisdom is therefore as much present in our world as it was in antiquity. They describe it as an awareness that is not divided

---

5. The translation is by Peter Brown, *The Making of Late Antiquity* (Cambridge: Harvard University Press, 1978), 101. I have modified his translation.

6. A similar criticism of the Greeks in contrast to the Egyptians is found in the Hermetic corpus: "For the Greeks, O King, who make logical demonstrations, use words emptied of power, and this very activity is what constitutes their philosophy, a mere noise of words. But we [Egyptians] do not [so much] use words [λόγων] but sounds [φωναῖς] which are full of effects" (Corp. herm. 16.2). Adapted from André-Jean Festugière, trans., and Arthur Darby Nock, ed., *Corpus Hermeticum*, 4 vols. (Paris: Belles Lettres, 1954–1960; repr. 1972–1983), 232.

and fixed but fluid, spontaneous, and always being discovered.[7] From the time of Plato, this wisdom was realized only through catharsis, purging the soul of mental and emotional habits (*Phaed.* 79B–D). As Proclus put it, once we attain to wisdom, we are "united with the ineffable principle of all things" (*Theo. Plat.* 1.3.22–24). It is incapable of being grasped intellectually, but we can nevertheless embody and express it. It is a kind of "innate gnosis," not a discursive knowing; it is more a breathing than a thinking awareness.[8] To paraphrase Plotinus, using insider's language that we may find frustrating, "he who has experienced it knows what I mean" (*Enn.* 1.6.7.2–3).[9] I want to explore how Neoplatonists understood this wisdom and see what it might mean to those of us who not only find it hard to fathom but cannot imagine that it was more than a "discursive strategy."

The ancient wisdom of the later Platonists is not "thinking" as we understand it; it is noetic and nondualistic, which is to say, it precedes and sustains discursive thinking. Recognizing this, they disciplined their thinking into patterns able to reveal what Iamblichus calls the "more ancient" principle within us.[10] The delicacy and challenge of this tradition is that it is precisely through discursive thinking that later Platonists were able to create receptacles for wisdom that is not discursive but con-

---

7. Iamblichus says that opposed to "discursive knowledge," which is always divided, our connection with the gods is unitary: "prior to the knowledge that knows another as being itself other, there is a unitary connection with the gods that is spontaneous (αὐτοφυής)" (*Myst.* 8.1–5). That is, *before we become self-conscious or think at all* we are enveloped in the gods and have an "innate awareness" (σύμφθτος κατανόησις) of them (*Myst.* 9.8–10). Recovering this innate awareness is to recover "ancient" (i.e., innate) wisdom. νόησις derives, as Socrates says in the *Crat.* 411E, from νέου + ἔσις, the soul longing for the new and *generating* world. Iamblichus maintains that our innate *gnōsis* of the gods comes through our longing (ἐφέσιν) for the Good (*Myst.* 8.1) and to share in its generous ἐνέργεια—demiurgy.

8. Iamblichus says "an innate gnosis (ἔμφθτος γνῶσις) of the gods co-exists with our very nature" (*Myst.* 7.11–12). See Carlos Steel's explanation of this innate gnosis in Proclus: "Breathing Thought: Proclus on the Innate Knowledge of the Soul," in *The Perennial Tradition of Neoplatonism*, ed. J. J. Cleary (Leuven: Leuven University Press, 1997), 298.

9. Plotinus is speaking of our experience of Beauty, but since, for Platonists, wisdom is the pinnacle of human beauty, deference to the experiential still applies.

10. Iamblichus explains that contact with the gods through divination comes through a "certain divine good" that is "older" than our nature and "preordained" (*Myst.* 165.13–14). That is, like ancient wisdom, this "more ancient divine good" has an "ontological" not a temporal priority.

cealed—and often betrayed—by discursive thinking.¹¹ It is no wonder that Iamblichus praises Hermes as his guide and inspiration, for Hermes captures perfectly the ambiguity of the role of thinking for Platonists (*Myst.* 1.3–2.3). Hermes is a trickster, a revealer, a psychopomp, and a liar.¹² For these Platonists, every revelation is false when taken literally, when frozen into truth. The purpose of their voluminous writing, therefore, was not to describe or explain the divine but to lead readers into its hidden activity. Their doctrines were not meant to be believed; they were incantations to free us from discursive habits. Philosophy was mystagogy.¹³

The *Nomina Barbara* and Deification

The way in which mystagogic wisdom should be transmitted comes to light through a specific issue on which Porphyry and Iamblichus disagree: the "meaning" of the ὀνόματα βάρβαρα/ἄσημα ὀνόματα, the names of gods invoked in theurgic chants that are foreign and unknowable to us. In his *Letter to Anebo*, Porphyry asks:

> What is the point of [chanting] meaningless names [ἄσημα ὀνόματα]? And why, of these meaningless names, do you prefer the barbarian [βάρβαρα] to our own? For a listener looks to their meaning, so surely what matters is that the concept remain the same whatever word is used.

---

11. Sara Rappe explores the tension among Platonists between their voluminous discursive endeavors and their acknowledgement that the wisdom they seek is incapable of being discursively grasped; see Rappe, *Reading Neoplatonism: Non-discursive Thinking in the Texts of Plotinus, Proclus, and Damascius* (Cambridge: Cambridge University Press, 2000), ix–xvii.

12. According to Plato, Hermes is the god of speech and father of all things (*Pan*); he makes them circulate and "is twofold, true *and* false" (*Crat.* 408C1–4). That Iamblichus's Hermes is the Egyptian Hermes identified with the god Thoth supports this as well for Thoth, like Hermes, was a god of trickery, revelation and paradox; see Garth Fowden, *The Egyptian Hermes: A Historical Approach to the Late Pagan Mind* (Cambridge: Cambridge University Press, 1986), 23–24.

13. This was not an aberration of Plato's thinking but its continuation. In the *Seventh Letter* (341C-D), Plato characterizes the most important aspect of his philosophy in virtually identical terms. For philosophic arguments as incantations/spells, see Plotinus: "We must call up yet another incantation [ἐπᾳστέον] to find some relief for the soul's labor pains. Might there be some relief from what we have said already if we sang it over and over again? What spell [ἐπῳδή] can we find that has something new in it?" (*Enn.* 5.3.17.15–21). For Plato as mystagogue, see Proclus, *Theo. Plat.* 1.5.16–1.6.3.

For the god invoked is surely not Egyptian by birth, and even if he were, he would not use Egyptian or any human language.[14] (*Aneb.*)

These questions sound eminently reasonable. They should. We are Porphyry's children; we think the same way. Words and names to us are conventional; they arise within the specific context of different cultures. Thus, as Porphyry says, different languages use different words for the same concept. Most scholars of religion would agree with Porphyry's suggestion that these names of gods have no *intrinsic* connection with the divine but are "imaginary forgeries ... devices created by our own passions and attributed to the divine" (*Myst.* 258.7–10). Porphyry, as we have seen, had already removed gods from the material world, so it is hardly surprising that he would also separate the gods from their culturally derived names.[15]

Iamblichus has a radically different understanding of the names of the gods. The divine names invoked by theurgists are symbols and συνθήματα (divine signatures) simultaneously revealing and veiling the gods. For theurgists, they serve as ritual foyers to deifying activity. Just as the gods of theurgy are revealed through their signatures in the material world, so they are revealed in the divine names employed by sacred races like Egyptians and Assyrians. Iamblichus thus replies to Porphyry's question:

> The situation is not as you suppose. For if the names were established by convention [κατὰ συνθήκην], it would make no difference whether some names were used instead of others. But if these names are tied to the nature of reality, those names which are more adapted to it would no doubt be more pleasing to the gods. (*Myst.* 257.3–8)

Iamblichus employs a "mystical reason" (μυστικὸς λόγος, *Myst.* 256.4) to explain the intrinsic connection of the sacred names and sounds used in

---

14. Porphyry's question begins at *Myst.* 254.11–12, but I have supplemented what Iamblichus leaves out of Porphyry's remarks with Eusebius's record of Porphyry's letter (Eusebius, *Praep. ev.* 5.10.8). See Porphyry, *Lettre à Anébon L'Égyptien*, ed. and trans. Henri Dominque Saffrey and Alain-Philippe Segonds (Paris: Belles Lettres, 2012), frag. 77, pp. 71–72. It is quite clear that Iamblichus replies to this question in the *De mysteriis*.

15. In our culture today, we have simply extended this porphyrian trajectory by erasing all notions of divinity whatsoever. We think that if something is not literally and physically real then *we made it up*; it is a "forgery," a projection of our own emotional needs.

hieratic discourse. The names of gods *are* the gods in audible form, properly received and vocalized; they are symbols that unite theurgists to their divine principles within—so long as they are prepared to receive them. Through the chanting of these names, theurgists enter the ἐνέργεια (activity) of the gods by which the cosmos comes into existence. For them, it is less an "understanding" than it is an "embodying-chanting-breathing" of the gods. Thus, Porphyry's interest in the *meaning* of names entirely misses the point. He is more interested in our concepts and explanations *about* the gods than he is in experiencing and embodying them. Addressing Porphyry's attachment to the discursive, Iamblichus says:

> It is necessary to remove all concepts and logical deductions from divine names... It is the *symbolic* character of divine resemblance, noetic and divine that must be assumed in these names. And, indeed, although it is unknowable to us [ἄγνωστος ἡμῖν] this very fact is its most sacred aspect: for it is too exalted to be divided into knowledge. (*Myst.* 255.5–11)

Iamblichus reveals how these names are theurgically potent; they awaken the divinity within. He says: "We preserve in their entirety the mystical and ineffable images of the gods in our soul; and we raise our soul up through these towards the gods and, as far as is possible, when elevated, we experience union with them" (255.14–256.2). When theurgists chant the names of the gods (their audible images), they enter into undivided union with them, which is to say, they participate in their unifying and demiurgic activity. Theurgists then no longer "think" about the gods; they embody the gods.

To ensure that these rites remain pure, Iamblichus emphasizes repeatedly that union with the god is not initiated or understood by us, for the soul—as discursively oriented—is incapable of understanding union. That the ἄσημα ὀνόματα are meaningless is therefore not a deficiency but a virtue; they possess the power to awaken us to the divine images in our souls "too exalted to be divided into knowledge." What is often overlooked in studies of later Neoplatonism or of Platonism generally is the fact that it is a mystagogic tradition, an initiation to participation in divinity, and the first requirement in Platonic mysteries is catharsis, a purging of the soul. This requires an acute awareness of our emotional and discursive habits: our fears, hungers, our instinctual contractions and expansions. In short, it requires a kind of discipline entirely forgotten in contemporary forms of education. Without undergoing catharsis, we cannot understand their texts let alone their theurgic rituals. Yet we believe the Platonists were somehow "like us," immersed in the same emotional and discursive habits, and so their "wisdom" has been reframed in terms we can understand.[16]

Divine Names, Competition, and Empire-Building

Later Platonists would have given little serious attention to competition among theologies. Neoplatonic theurgy was imagined within a polytheistic and pluralistic cosmos: the varieties of culture and geography corresponding to the diversity of theurgic societies. This was consistent with Iamblichus's metaphysics where the utterly ineffable One can be "known" only in the Many, the henophany of each culture both veiling and revealing its ineffable source. To privilege any one of these henophanies over the others, to proclaim that it alone is true, is an assertion that would have been treated with contempt by theurgic Neoplatonists.[17] Anyone convinced that he or she possessed the truth or the true doctrine would thereby demonstrate their utter ignorance of Platonic mystagogy and wisdom,[18] one that must always remain hidden and that, by definition, *cannot* be the possession of a single religion or culture. From Plato, they knew that the One is

---

16. Either that or we declare that "all we can discuss as historians of religions is [their] rhetoric; *if there be any experience*, it remains beyond our reach" (Ilinca Tanaseanu–Döbler, *Theurgy in Late Antiquity*, BERG 1 [Vandenhoeck & Ruprecht, 2013], 285, emphasis added). Yet we do presume to discuss their experiences when we interpret their texts. The problem is that we do not take the risk of entering their mystagogy, of being changed by their texts, and so we change the meaning of the texts to fit *our* assumptions. I am reminded of Socrates's comment to Callicles: "You are lucky Callicles, in having been initiated in the Great Mysteries before the Little; I did not think it was permitted" (*Gorg.* 497C). Scholars today are like Callicles, for we presume to interpret mystagogic texts but skip over the challenge of catharsis, the lesser mysteries.

17. Thus, Julian's effort to re-Hellenize the empire based on Iamblichean teachings was inevitably a distortion of Iamblichus's less hegemonic vision. Yet it is one thing to serve as a sage like Iamblichus, surrounded by one's students in Apamea; it is quite another to attempt to govern an Empire. The social context is inevitably important in shaping one's metaphysical system. See Radek Chlup's interesting comments on this issue among later Platonists in *Proclus: An Introduction* (Cambridge: Cambridge University Press, 2012), 255–78.

18. This is essentially the thesis of Polymnia Athanassiadi who refers to "l'hérésie de l'intellectualisme" against which Iamblichus directed his efforts; see *La Lutte pour l'orthodoxie dans le platonisme tardif: De Numénius à Damascius* (Paris: Les Belles Lettres, 2006), 213.

not revealed as "one" but as many, and so it is with all revelation.[19] To hold to a single revelation would create a discursive idol and this, I believe, is why Iamblichus dismisses the Christians of his time who "do not deserve to be mentioned in discussions about the gods for they are ignorant of the distinction between truth and falsity … [and] are unable to discern the principles from which these come to be" (*Myst.* 179.10–180.3). Any claim to possess the Truth betrays the very principle of theurgy understood as cosmogonic activity rooted in an *ineffable* source, one that necessarily expresses itself in *multiple* forms of demiurgic generosity. Theurgists would find claims to an exclusive possession of truth equivalent to the deranged assertion that "the sun shines only in my backyard"! Platonic mystagogy was a delicate hermetic discipline not well-suited to empire-building.

In his *Commentary on the First Alcibiades,* Proclus addresses the hunger for empire-building exemplified in Alcibiades and sees it against the larger metaphysical context in which the soul moves from a particular to a universal perspective by entering theurgic and philosophic mystagogy (149.17–150.22). Proclus explores how we can become godlike and attain universal power through wisdom. But, as is the case with Alcibiades, the soul that wants to attain universal power without catharsis falls into misguided and monstrous ignorance (and the same might be said for any culture or religion). Yet Proclus does not disparage Alcibiades's *desire* for universal power. In fact, he believes that such desire has been "seeded" into all souls. *The problem is that we do not know how to properly express that desire.* In explicating this crucial aspect of Platonic pedagogy, Proclus refers to the "divine names" imbedded in the soul. He says:

> To strive for power over all men is a sign of unlimited desire, but also of a grand conception and mental anguish that refers to the truly exalted and divine power which has filled all men with itself, is continuously present to all things and holds sway over all that lies within the world. The desire "to fill all mankind with one's name" bears a surprising resemblance to

---

19. Adrian Mihai has recently argued that Damascius's approving survey of various religious systems near the end of his *Princ.* (3.159.6–3.167.25) is not a defensive posture against Christian hegemony, nor is it missionary zeal, but an attempt to show that the multiplicity of expressions of divine revelation is "presque épistémologique," as Damascius's Neoplatonic metaphysics would require; see "Comparatism in the Neoplatonic Pantheon of Late Antiquity: Damascius, *De Princ.* III 159.6–167.25," *Numen* 61 (2014): 457–83.

this. For the ineffable names of the gods have filled the whole world, as the theurgists say.…[20] The gods, then, have filled the whole world both with themselves and their own names, and, having contemplated these before their birth, and yearning to resemble the gods, but *not knowing the way* [τρόπον] *of achieving this*, souls become lovers of command and long for the mere representations of those realities and to fill the whole race of men with their name and power. The conceptions of such souls are grand and admirable, but when put into practice they become petty, ignoble, and vaporous because they are pursued without insight [ἐπιστήμη]. Their aspirations are in accord with nature and appropriate, but their actions are unnatural; their grand ideas arise from … what has been inseminated into us but their expression of it comes from oblivion and ignorance. (*Comm. Alc.* 150.4–23, slightly modified)

Here Proclus explains the root cause of our striving for universal power and our failure to achieve it: it is because we do not know the "way" (τρόπον); we are possessed of the right idea, but do not know how to receive it, live it, express it. Alcibiades stands for all souls who fail to discover this way and who compete with other souls to acquire power. Alcibiades fails to enter the mystagogy, and Proclus's critique applies just as much to imperial theologians or politicians who pursue vaporous "representations" of reality. Our problem with understanding Proclus's critique is this: because of our fixation on things (whether physical or conceptual), we misconstrue the ineffable One of the Neoplatonists as if it were a Supreme Being. We imagine that the Platonists constructed a metaphysical nursery where they placed themselves in the warm lap of this Supreme Being. We imagine this Being as "somewhere else," that the One—imagined as a single and supreme object—is dissociated from multiplicity and materiality. We imagine that Platonists hungered for a purity and unity far above our soiled and evanescent world. *But this is not at all what the Platonists hungered for.* As Plotinus warned us, we have been bewitched by our discursive thinking (*Enn.* 4.4.43.16.). Under this spell, we create grand concepts and glorious ideas and feel exalted by them. This is precisely the failure of Alcibiades and, I would argue, the Christian appropriation of Platonism in its striving for imperial power. We no longer know the way by which we can share in godlike and universal activity.

---

20. Proclus refers to the *Chaldean Oracles*, frag. 108, which states "For the Paternal Nous has sown symbols throughout the cosmos." See Ruth Majercik, *The Chaldean Oracles, Text, Translation and Commentary*, SGRR 5 (Leiden: Brill, 1989).

So, we might well ask, what is the alternative to our habit of wanting to grasp the whole conceptually, of titanically trying to put that which escapes knowledge into knowledge, to present unity as duality? I have argued that our way of trying to engage the ineffable is misguided, that we are like Alcibiades when see ancient wisdom merely as a discursive strategy for building an empire. So, then, what might be the proper τρόπον? According to these Platonists, it is to engage the One not as a concept or as a Supreme Cause but as unifying activity. It is not, then, the concepts or metaphysical structure that matter; it is not ritual objects—dense or subtle—that should hold our attention. It is the *activity* triggered by these objects in whatever context in so far as it unites us and weaves us into the Whole. The focus is more on our breath and the sound of our voices than on the meanings we ascribe to these sounds. Yet, as embodied souls and therefore "self-alienated" by virtue of our rank in the cosmos, we live in meanings.[21] It is within the vaporous house of meaning that we are challenged to find ways of receiving and expressing activities that escape meaning. According to Iamblichus and Proclus, the "one in us" (symbolized by the "name of the god that fills the whole world") is known only as *activity*, by what it produces, and that, paradoxically, includes our self-alienated identity. So, for human souls, to be like the utterly unique and spontaneous One, we must *not* strive to be like our grand conception of it; we must become a completely new creature. It is only when we are *uniquely* rooted and live, as Ralph Waldo Emerson put it, from our own spontaneous and aboriginal Self, that we discover our τρόπον and enter the stream of divine activity that creates the world and our own self-alienated identity.[22] The metaphysics of these Platonists, which seems to capture virtually all our attention,

---

21. As Iamblichus puts it, as embodied souls, we are "made other" (ἑτεροιοῦσθαι) to ourselves. "Self-alienation" (ἀλλοτριωθὲν) constitutes our existence. For citations, see Gregory Shaw, *Theurgy and the Soul: The Neoplatonism of Iamblichus* (University Park: Pennsylvania State University Press, 1995, repr., Kettering, OH: Angelico, 2014), 102. The necessary self-alienation of the embodied soul is perhaps the most difficult and essential element of Iamblichean Platonism. I only allude to it here. The best study of this theme is the brilliant monograph by Carlos Steel, *The Changing Self: A Study on the Soul in Later Neoplatonism: Iamblichus, Damascius, and Priscianus*, trans. E. Haasl (Brussels: Paleis der Academiën, 1978).

22. Ralph Waldo Emerson, *Self-Reliance and Other Essays* (New York: Dover, 1993), 37. The French Neoplatonic scholar, Jean Trouillard, explored this paradoxical theme in one of his last publications, "Proclos et la joie de quitter le ciel," *Diotima* 11 (1983): 182–92.

is purposeful only when it leads souls into this activity. This is the insight (ἐπιστήμη) that Proclus says we lack.

Julian's Philosophy and His Religious Program*

Laura B. Dingeldein

In the study of late antique philosophy and religious competition, all roads lead to the fourth century Roman emperor Julian. Commonly dubbed "the Apostate" for his rejection of the Christian God, Julian is recognized for his devotion to a brand of philosophy known as theurgic Neoplatonism as well as his attempts to institute an empire-wide religious program rivaling Christianity.[1] The relationship between these two notable aspects of Julian's life—his philosophy and religious program—has been a key point of interest among Julianic scholars over the past several decades. Polymnia Athanassiadi, for example, argued in 1981 that Julian's theurgic Neoplatonism thoroughly informed the dogmatic articulation and physical organization of his religious program.[2] In more recent years, scholars such as Rowland Smith and Ilinca Tanaseanu-Döbler have pushed back against this view, highlighting Julian's promotion of generalized philosophical concepts and traditional Roman religious practices in his reforms. These analyses have

---

* I am grateful to Stanley Stowers, Gregory Shaw, and the editors of this volume for their helpful feedback on earlier drafts of this essay.

1. For the purposes of this essay, I use "theurgic Neoplatonism" to refer to the brand of Platonism articulated and defended by the Neoplatonist Iamblichus of Chalcis during the late third and early fourth centuries CE. Julian revered Iamblichus and occasionally mentions the philosopher in his writings; see, e.g., Julian, Or. 4.146A, 150D, 157C–158A. I consider Julian's religious program to consist of the actions, edicts, letters, and orations through which he attempted to encourage traditional Greek and Roman religious practices during his time as sole ruler of the Roman Empire (from approximately November 361 to June 363 CE).

2. Polymnia Athanassiadi, *Julian and Hellenism: An Intellectual Biography* (Oxford: Clarendon, 1981), esp. 134, 153, 160, 181, 186, and 191.

resulted in claims that Julian consigned theurgic Neoplatonism to his personal piety or private religiosity.[3]

In this essay, I chart a middle path between these two positions, maintaining that while Julian did not base his religious program solely on theurgic Neoplatonism or require participants to understand this philosophy, it is inaccurate to describe Julian as limiting theurgic Neoplatonism to his personal piety or private religiosity.[4] I argue that Julian's philosophy influenced his public religious program insofar as Julian used theurgic Neoplatonic concepts in his writings to legitimate and promote what he considered the true meanings of the practices that constituted his religious reforms. Julian conceived of these meanings as essential elements of these religious practices, regardless of whether the average Roman understood or agreed with them. In this sense, Julian's theurgic Neoplatonic meaning-making was not personal or private. It is important to highlight this aspect of the relationship between Julian's philosophy and his religious reforms because it enables us to see more clearly the ways in which Julian competed with contemporary literate Christian bishops, who authorized their religious meaning-making in part through the philosophical prowess displayed in their writings.

---

3. Rowland Smith claims "Iamblichan theurgy impinged on [Julian] deeply, to be sure; but it was part of his personal credo, not the whole of it. It belonged principally to the philosophic piety of the private man" (*Julian's Gods: Religion and Philosophy in the Thought and Action of Julian the Apostate* [New York: Routledge, 1995], 113). Ilinca Tanaseanu-Döbler argues that theurgy was a type of private elite religiosity for Julian, whereas the religiosity that Julian advocates in his public program is more generally philosophic; see *Theurgy in Late Antiquity: The Invention of a Ritual Tradition*, BERG 1 (Göttingen: Vandenhoeck & Ruprecht, 2013), 148, 281. Prior to the publication of Athanassiadi's biography of Julian, G. W. Bowersock expressed a similar sentiment: "The Neo-Platonic background is important for Julian only in the study of his emotional life and of those self-revelations which he not very artfully concealed in his reflective treatises" (*Julian the Apostate* [Cambridge: Harvard University Press, 1978], xi).

4. The blurred and muddied boundaries between "private" and "public" in ancient Mediterranean religion have been well documented and analyzed by Kim Bowes, *Private Worship, Public Values, and Religious Change in Late Antiquity* (New York: Cambridge University Press, 2008), esp. 12–14, 18–60. For the purposes of this essay, I conceive of "private" ancient Mediterranean religion as religious activities that occurred outside the space and/or supervision of institutional religions and the experts associated with them (see Bowes, *Private Worship*, 14).

My argument is organized into two parts. In the first part of this essay, I outline a quad-modal categorization of ancient Mediterranean religious activity developed by Stanley Stowers. This theoretical model provides language and analytical tools that prove useful in demonstrating that the influence of Julian's philosophy extended beyond his personal or private religiosity. In the second part of this essay, I use Stowers's theoretical model to analyze the influence of Julian's theurgic Neoplatonism on one element of his religious program: a dietary prescription associated with the worship of Magna Mater. This analysis is intended as a case study of the influence of Julian's theurgic Neoplatonism on his religious reforms; a full exploration of the relationship between Julian's philosophy and his religious program would require a more exhaustive examination of the Julianic corpus. I end this essay by briefly gesturing to the ways in which Julian's use of philosophy in his writings on religion enabled him to compete with burgeoning fourth century Christianity.

Stowers's Four Modes of Religious Activity

Inhabitants of the ancient Mediterranean basin participated in religion in varied ways. Stowers distinguishes between four key modes of religious activity: (1) the religion of everyday social exchange, (2) the religion of the literate cultural producer, (3) civic religion, and (4) the religion of the literate cultural producer and political power.[5] This four-fold categorization is a tool of analysis that highlights the ways in which meanings were ascribed to religious practices and the different types of power that legitimated and authorized these meanings.[6] According to Stowers, the first mode of ancient Mediterranean religion, that of everyday social exchange,

---

5. Stowers develops his fourfold categorization most fully in "The Religion of Plant and Animal Offerings versus the Religion of Meanings, Essences, and Textual Mysteries," in *Ancient Mediterranean Sacrifice*, ed. Jennifer Wright Knust and Zsuzsanna Várhelyi (New York: Oxford University Press, 2011), 35–56. Stowers more thoroughly elaborates on the fourth mode of religion in "Why Expert versus Nonexpert is Not Elite versus Popular Religion: The Case of the Third Century" (paper presented at the Annual Meeting of the Society of Biblical Literature, San Diego, CA, 24 November 2014), 1–17; the revised version of this paper appears in this volume.

6. This categorization is not a rigid classification system into which all ancient Mediterranean religious activity may be neatly and cleanly sorted. Rather, it is an analytical framework that helps account for the open-ended, mutable quality of religious practice by actively rejecting the notion that any given religious practice is inherently

was characterized by "default" or mundane religious practices informed by local, basic knowledge about the gods. Humans who operated in this mode of religion based their interactions with the gods on the sensibilities of everyday social exchanges among humans. Just as humans prepared food for one another, sought advice from their associates, or exchanged gifts, so too did humans interact with the gods. Often centered on the family and household, this first mode of religion was comprised of religious practices such as plant and animal offerings, divination, prayer, relic veneration, and communal meals.[7] Christians, Jews, and practitioners of other Greek and Roman religions all participated in this mode of religious activity.

Stowers's second mode of religious activity, the religion of literate cultural producers, was characterized by textual practices in which specialists defended, refined, critiqued, or modified basic, local understandings of everyday religious behaviors. In this sense, the religion of literate cultural producers depended upon and modified the first mode of religion. Literate specialists viewed meaning as the essential or primary element of religious practice, and they competed with one another in their meaning-making activities. These literate experts—who often operated as philosophers, astrologers, theologians, poets, or religious entrepreneurs—derived power, prestige, and legitimacy from their literacy and skills of textual interpretation, sometimes displaying disinterest in money or political power.[8]

Civic religion, the third mode of ancient Mediterranean religious activity, was analytically distinguishable from everyday religion in its emphasis on and promotion of civic interests. These civic interests primarily included the legitimization, control, and maintenance of social formations that were larger and more complex than the basic household, such as towns, cities, and provinces.[9] Practices constituting this mode included sacrifices on behalf of townspeople or communal feasts in honor of tutelary deities. Key participants were local landowners, town councilors, and aristocrats. Civic religion depended upon everyday religion insofar as it elaborated upon this first mode with regard to civic interests. Civic reli-

---

bound to a particular idea or possesses some intrinsic meaning (Stowers, "Religion of Plant and Animal Offerings," 35–36).

7. Ibid., 36–41.

8. Ibid., 41–49.

9. Such social formations were typically defined by place of residence, citizenship, and/or ancestry. As Stowers notes, such social formations exceeded all but the most powerful households in size ("Expert versus Non-expert," 15).

gion differed from the mode of literate cultural production in that participants legitimated and authorized their religious activities through the power derived from their political positions and their promotion of civic interests, not textual practices.[10]

When those endowed with political power used textual practices to legitimate and promote their interpretations of mundane religious practices, they operated in what Stowers identifies as the fourth mode of religious activity: the religion of literate specialists and political power. Like the experts of the second mode, participants in this fourth mode sought to defend, refine, critique, or modify mundane understandings of everyday religion through textual practices, and they competed against other literate specialists in doing so. Unlike literate specialists of the second mode, however, literate specialists of the fourth mode often operated with civic interests in mind, and they derived the power to authorize their ideas through a combination of their textual skills and their political positions.[11] Literate specialists operating in this fourth mode were found in a variety of political offices, sometimes holding the position of priest, bishop, or even emperor.

The religion of everyday social exchange, therefore, was the primary mode of ancient Mediterranean religion insofar as the second, third, and fourth modes of religion elaborated on the practices that constituted the first mode.[12] Thus the meaning-making of literate specialists in the second and fourth modes, though conducted by a small portion of the population, was not typically a personal or private affair. Literate experts' meaning-making was always aimed at, and sometimes succeeded in, defending, critiquing, or modifying the "default" religion of others (though participants did not likely conceive of their actions in these terms). In this sense, literate specialists' meaning-making was not personal. Literate experts' meaning-making was not private, either, at least in those instances in which these experts elaborated on the meanings of civic religion. Some literate specialists might have had larger, more diverse, or more dispersed audiences than

---

10. Stowers, "Religion of Plant and Animal Offerings," 40–41, 49–50.
11. Stowers, "Expert versus Non-expert," 7. This fourth mode is analytically distinguishable from both the second and third modes, and it is not considered merely a cross between these two modes, because the power that participants derive from their combination of textual skills and political positions is substantially different from the power accorded those operating in the second and third modes of religion.
12. Stowers, "Religion of Plant and Animal Offerings," 41–42, 49–50.

others, but it is difficult to imagine situations in which literate specialists, particularly those with great political power, wrote and produced meaning only to relegate their ideas to their personal piety or private religiosity.

Interpreting Julian's Religious Program

In 361 CE, Julian became sole ruler of the Roman Empire, freed from sharing the *imperium* with the Christian Constantius II. Endowed with the political power afforded him as emperor and *pontifex maximus*, Julian immediately began restoring what he believed to be the proper worship of the gods, rebuilding defunct temples and encouraging traditional Roman religious practices such as sacrifice and divination.[13] Julian also began writing extensively about religion, crafting treatises about the nature of the gods and the meanings of the everyday practices associated with the worship of these gods. During a particularly concentrated bout of writing in March of 362 CE, Julian composed an oration in celebration of the springtime festival dedicated to the goddess Magna Mater and her consort, Attis.[14] In this oration, known as *Hymn to the Mother of the Gods*, Julian elucidates the meanings of the myths and practices associated with this Metroac festival, dedicating the last portion of his work to defending adherence to a diet prescribed during the celebration.

According to Julian, a sacred law associated with Metroac purification rites states that participants may eat meat, but are forbidden the consumption of particular grains, fruits, and vegetables (*Or.* 5.173D–174A). Julian's contemporaries consider this sacred law ludicrous: after all, meat is less pure than plant matter, and animal sacrifices, unlike offerings of plant matter, inflict pain on organisms (5.174A–B). But Julian disagrees with these popular attacks on the sacred law, arguing for the propriety of the festive diet by drawing attention to a different set of principles (5.174D). According to Julian, the ultimate goal of the purifying practices associated with Magna Mater's worship is the ascent of practitioners' souls from the

---

13. Julian, *Ep.* 8.415C–D; Libanius, *Or.* 18.121, 125–29; Ammianus Marcellinus, *Res gest.* 22.5.1–2.

14. On the circumstances surrounding Julian's composition of the hymn, see Julian, *Or.* 5.161C, 178D; Libanius, *Or.* 18.157; Susanna Elm, *Sons of Hellenism, Fathers of the Church: Emperor Julian, Gregory of Nazianzus, and the Vision of Rome* (Berkeley: University of California Press, 2012), 118–19; and Robert Browning, *The Emperor Julian* (Berkeley: University of California Press, 1976), 142.

material world and their assimilation to the immaterial divine (5.169C, 175B, 178B–C). The consumption of plants that grow down into the earth counters this process of ascent because the earth is the lowest of created things and associated with evil. As Julian writes, drawing upon Plato for support:

> The end and aim of the rite of purification is the ascent of our souls. For this reason then the ordinance forbids us first to eat those fruits that grow downwards in the earth. For the earth is the last and lowest of things. And Plato also says that evil, exiled from the gods, now moves on earth; and in the oracles the gods often call the earth refuse, and exhort us to escape thence. And so, in the first place, the life-generating god who is our providence does not allow us to use to nourish our bodies fruits that grow under the earth. (*Or.* 5.175B–C [Wright, LCL])

Thus the consumption of plants that are rooted in the soil is typically forbidden during Metroac rites of purification because these plants hinder the soul's ascent from the material world.[15] Foods that are intimately associated with earthen matter are avoided for the same reason. For instance, Julian notes that the pomegranate fruit, though it hangs on shrubs and is not rooted in the soil, belongs to the underworld. It is therefore too intimately tied to matter to be consumed during purifying rites.[16] Earthen-associated meats such as fish and pork should also be avoided during Metroac purification practices. Fish should not be consumed in part because they swim in the depths of the earth. Pork is forbidden because the shape, nature, and day-to-day activities of swine are oriented toward the ground. Participants must follow such regulations, Julian argues, if they hope to unify their souls with the divine (*Or.* 5.177A–D).

In assigning these meanings to the purifying diet associated with Magna Mater's festival, Julian draws upon concepts that are distinctive to Neoplatonism and its theurgic instantiation.[17] Theurgic Neoplatonists, like their nontheurgic colleagues, considered the goal of life to be divine assimilation: these philosophers desired to unify their souls with the

---

15. Cf. Julian's exception of turnip greens in *Or.* 5.175D–176A.

16. Other fruits, such as apples and dates, are not permitted for consumption, because they are sacred symbols (Julian, *Or.* 5.176A–B).

17. Cf. Athanassiadi, *Julian and Hellenism*, 141–48; Smith, *Julian's Gods*, 162; Elm, *Sons of Hellenism*, 118–36; Tanaseanu-Döbler, *Theurgy in Late Antiquity*, 138–44.

immaterial gods and, if possible, the supreme One.[18] Julian equates this Neoplatonic goal with the aim of Metroac purifying practices. Theurgic Neoplatonists also contended that union with the gods required participation in theurgy: a set of practices described in the hermetic literature of prior centuries, through which practitioners were united with the divine through the power of the gods. Such activities included prayer, sacrifice, statue animation, and divination.[19] This was in direct opposition to non-theurgic Neoplatonists, who argued that divine assimilation was achieved through contemplation alone.[20] Julian follows theurgic Neoplatonism in considering religious practices other than contemplation necessary for effecting union with the gods. Though Julian does not describe the esoteric activities that constitute Metroac purification rites, he considers these practices and their associated diet to be closely tied to participation in the entire festival, which includes temple processions, sacrifice, and communal meals (*Or.* 5.168C–169D).[21] Participants' assimilation to the divine, therefore, is not achieved solely through contemplation, but through participation in cultic practices. Though Julian's arguments about the meaning of the Metroac purifying diet lack the theoretical precision present in the arguments of proper philosophers, Julian does use basic theurgic

---

18. Iamblichus, *Myst.* 10.5.290–10.6.292, views assimilation to the divine as a gradual process that involves successive unifications with various classes of divine powers that emanate from the Good (that is, the self-begotten, absolute principle).

19. Iamblichus, *Myst.* 1.11.38, 2.11.96–99; see also the concise definition of theurgy provided by Tanaseanu-Döbler, *Theurgy in Late Antiquity*, 9.

20. Iamblichus, in articulating the tenets of theurgic Neoplatonism, argued that humans could not assimilate to the immaterial divine solely through contemplation, because their souls were fully descended into and imprisoned by the mortal, material realm. Humans required the aid of the gods in order to escape the bonds of generation and enact deification, and this aid was delivered in the form of theurgy (*Myst.* 1.11.40; 3.20.148–49; 4.3.184–86; 8.6.269). See also Gregory Shaw, "Divination in the Neoplatonism of Iamblichus," in *Mediators of the Divine: Horizons of Prophecy, Divination, Dreams and Theurgy in Mediterranean Antiquity*, ed. Robert M. Berchman, SFSHJ 163 (Atlanta: Scholars Press, 1998), 236, 240–48.

21. For reconstructions of the schedule of rites that constituted this festival, see Duncan Fishwick, "The Cannophori and the March Festival of Magna Mater," *TPAPA* 97 (1966): 202; Jaime Alvar, *Romanising Oriental Gods: Myth, Salvation and Ethics in the Cults of Cybele, Isis and Mithras*, ed. and trans. Richard Gordon, RGRW 165 (Boston: Brill, 2008), 276–92; and Jacob Latham, "'Fabulous Clap-Trap': Roman Masculinity, the Cult of Magna Mater, and Literary Constructions of the *galli* at Rome from the Late Republic to Late Antiquity," *JR* 92 (2012): 107–8.

Neoplatonic concepts to critique common understandings of the Metroac festive diet and to legitimate the "true" meaning that he ascribes to this religious practice.

In writing an oration about this theurgic Neoplatonic meaning-making, Julian operates in the fourth mode of religion identified by Stowers: that of literate specialists and political power. While Julian's religious activity in this fourth mode is certainly esoteric, it is neither personal nor private. As Julian himself recognizes at several points throughout his fifth oration, his theurgic Neoplatonic interpretations of Metroac worship are intelligible and attractive to a limited number of people.[22] Nevertheless, Julian conceives of these theurgic Neoplatonic meanings as intrinsic elements of Metroac purification practices, regardless of who understands or performs them. Julian's interpretations are not limited to his or a private group's worship of Magna Mater: they are the meanings of Metroac worship, and Julian articulates these meanings in the hope that he will enable others to increase their knowledge of the gods (*Or.* 5.180A–B). Moreover, though not all inhabitants of the Roman Empire engaged in the purifying practices associated with the mysteries of Magna Mater, this Metroac dietary practice was a well-known aspect of a civic cult. Certainly the Metroac cult's esotericism, priesthood, and foreign import set it apart from other Roman civic cults, and Metroac initiates may have experienced personal or private moments during worship. But the cult of Magna Mater had enjoyed official status in Rome for centuries. Thus the late antique Roman cult of Magna Mater was not a private religion, nor was its associated dietary prescription a private practice.[23] Viewed from this perspective, in the case of the Metroac festive diet, Julian did not relegate his theurgic Neoplatonism to his personal life or some private religiosity. Rather, Julian wrote an oration in which he uses theurgic Neoplatonic concepts to articulate and promote among others the "true" meaning of a sacred law

---

22. In *Or.* 5.161B, 170B, 172D–173A, and 177C–D, Julian claims that there are two different ways of interpreting the myths and practices associated with the March festival dedicated to Magna Mater. There is a basic level of interpretation, which consists of everyday understandings appropriate to commoners, who derive some sort of benefit from this level of interpretation. A second, deeper level of interpretation is cultivated by the wise, among whom are theurgic Neoplatonists and Julian. See also Tanaseanu-Döbler, *Theurgy in Late Antiquity*, 138–39; Smith, *Julian's Gods*, 37.

23. Mary Beard, John North, and Simon Price, *A History*, vol. 1 of *Religions of Rome* (New York: Cambridge University Press, 1998), 337–38; Bowes, *Private Worship*, 38, 239 n. 130. Cf. Smith, *Julian's Gods*, 163, 171–72.

associated with a well-known civic cult. Julian viewed this meaning as an intrinsic part of the festive diet, even if those dieting did not understand or agree with this meaning.

A Competing Religious Program

By interpreting Julian's religious activity in this passage as the esoteric meaning-making of a literate specialist with political power rather than the private religiosity of an erudite emperor, we are able to more fully understand the ways in which Julian's religious program competed with Christianity. Fourth-century Christianity was in part produced by literate and philosophically trained bishops such as Gregory of Nazianzus and Basil of Caesarea—both of whom, incidentally, were acquaintances of Julian. Such learned bishops defined and shaped Christianity by defending, modifying, and contesting everyday understandings of mundane religion in part through their use of philosophy and textual practices. When these Christian specialists authorized their production of Christianity with the power derived from their political positions as bishops and their skills of textual interpretation and philosophy, they operated in the fourth mode of religion: that of literate specialists and political power. They drew upon these sources of power to compete with other literate specialists, both Christian and non-Christian, over the meanings of religious practices. Though the vast majority of fourth century Christians did not understand the interpretations promoted by these literate bishops, we do not consider these bishops' meaning-making to be personal or private. We should not consider the meaning-making of Julian to be so either.

By virtue of his position as sole Augustus and highest priest of the Roman Empire, Julian already possessed a great deal of political and religious power, and this undoubtedly helped him authorize and promote his religious program. Yet, by writing orations in which he used theurgic Neoplatonic concepts to elucidate the meaning of civic religion, Julian was able to legitimate and authorize his religious reforms through the power and prestige accrued from a combination of his political offices, philosophical prowess, and textual skills. Thus Julian's use of his philosophy in crafting his religious program helped him to compete with Christian bishops in a way that would not have been possible if Julian had relied solely upon the power afforded him as emperor and *pontifex maximus*.

Conclusion

Interpreting Julian's philosophy as consigned to his personal or private religiosity prevents us from noticing this aspect of Julian's religious competition with Christians. Whether or not Julian conceived of his own philosophical meaning-making this way, theurgic Neoplatonism allowed Julian to legitimate and authorize his religious program in a manner analogous to the authorization strategies of literate Christian bishops. Julian did not envision all participants in his religious program donning the mantle of theurgic Neoplatonist, nor did he relegate theurgic Neoplatonism to private religiosity. Rather, Julian used theurgic Neoplatonism in his writings to legitimate and promote particular interpretations of the everyday practices that constituted his religious program, and in doing so he was better positioned to compete with literate Christian bishops in shaping the religious practices of the public.

Part 3
Religious Experts and Popular Religion

Introduction:
Competition Between Experts and Nonexperts

Daniel Ullucci

In 2010, the Pew Research Center conducted a major survey of "religious knowledge" in the United States.[1] The survey showed that, while a significant majority of Americans self-identify as religious, the majority of Americans lack even elementary knowledge about religions, including their own. Participants were asked a series of factual questions about world religions, such as the names of the four Gospels, the birthplace of Jesus, which religion uses the Qur'an, and whether "do on to others as you would have them do on to you" was one of the Ten Commandments. Responses to questions on different religious traditions were then correlated with participants' self-identifications. Participants who self-identified as Protestant answered 46 percent of the questions on the Bible incorrectly and 62 percent of questions on other religions incorrectly. Catholics answered 55 percent of questions on the Bible incorrectly and 61 percent of questions on other religions incorrectly. The highest score was, in fact, from the group that self-identified as "atheist or agnostics," yet even they averaged only 20.9 correct answers out of 32, or 65 percent—a solid D. This survey seems to show an alarming degree of ignorance, apathy, or abject laziness on the part of the American public. It suggests that Americans are not simply ignorant of other people's religions but, more shockingly, that they cannot even be bothered to learn the basics of their own. The publication of the survey resulted in the renewal of a long tradition of bemoaning the religious "illiteracy" of Americans.[2]

---

1. "U.S. Religious Knowledge Survey: Executive Summary," Pew Research Center, Washington DC, http://www.pewforum.org/2010/09/28/u-s-religious-knowledge-survey. The total number of survey participants was 3,412.

2. Diane Winston, "What Americans Really Need to Know About Religion," *The*

I would suggest, however, that this survey illustrates something else—something more interesting to us as scholars of religion and of enormous significance for the study of ancient Mediterranean religion. All of the questions posed in the Pew survey focus on explicit knowledge of religious doctrines and texts. What the Pew survey really illustrates is that the day-to-day religious beliefs and practices of Americans are not informed by knowledge of such texts and doctrines. In other words, they are not based on the ideas of religious experts who produce written texts and theological dogma. Take, for example, the significant number of participants who self-identified as Christians yet were unable to answer basic questions about the New Testament. As critical scholars, it would be absurd for us to say that these people are *lying* about their Christian identification or that they are *faking it* or that their lack of knowledge shows that they are not *really* Christians. Only the most antiquated and irresponsible anthropologist or ethnographer would take such a position. It is the job of the scholar to analyze the data, not to shame the subjects. What the survey shows, rather, is that many American Christians are not particularly interested in the actual content of the Bible. Even if they grant the text sacred authority, it is not important in their daily lives (at least not important enough to actually read).[3] Their everyday religious interests and needs are perfectly fulfilled without knowing the names of the Gospels or that the "Golden Rule" is not one of the Ten Commandments.

The Pew survey, and reactions to it, illustrates exactly the issue under consideration in this section and why it is so important. The vast majority of our evidence for ancient religions comes from written texts, and scholars have, historically, been far too willing to allow these texts to speak as

---

Huffington Post, 6 October 2010, http://www.huffingtonpost.com/diane-winston/what-americans-really-nee_b_749581.html; Mitchell Landsberg, "Atheists, Agnostics Most Knowledgeable About Religion, Survey Says," *Los Angeles Times*, September 28, 2010. On this topic, see also the work of Stephen Prothero, who was an advisor for the Pew Study: Stephen R. Prothero, *Religious Literacy: What Every American Needs to Know—And Doesn't* (San Francisco: HarperSanFrancisco, 2007). Note that Prothero's argument focuses on the need for religious literacy for nonreligious (civic) purposes.

3. There is a large body of scholarship on the use of texts as objects of authority absent any actual reading or at least absent any thorough knowledge of the text. The work of Vincent Wimbush and the Institute for Signifying Scripture ("Signifying Scriptures," Institute for Signifying Scriptures, http://www.signifyingscriptures.org) is currently focused on this issue. As representative, see Vincent Wimbush, *White Men's Magic: Scripturalization as Slavery* (New York: Oxford University Press, 2012).

if they speak for everyone.[4] The essays in this section focus on the basic question of how the practices and products of religious experts interact (often competitively) with the lives of nonexperts. It would be hard to overstate the significance of this question since it touches the heart of that body of evidence that forms the basis of much of our work as scholars. In studying ancient religion, are we getting at the ideas and practices of a significant portion of ancient people, or are we really just studying the esoteric formulations of a very small and very atypical portion of the ancient population? Failure to take seriously this question and its consequences would, I argue, call into question the usefulness and significance of our field of study *in toto*.

The results of the Pew survey are not an anomaly, nor do they reflect some unique phenomenon in twenty-first-century America.[5] Rather, they simply repeat what anthropologists and ethnographers have known for a long time: the ideas of religious experts are often unknown, unimportant, and uninteresting to nonexperts. The fields of anthropology and ethnography faced this problem long ago, and religious studies has much to learn from the trail they blazed. These basic scholarly habits, still very common in religious studies, should be looked at with heightened suspicion and exposed when detected: (1) the tendency to overprivilege written texts as evidence, (2) the tendency to take the ideas of experts (often derived from written texts) as broadly representative rather than esoteric, (3) the tendency to systematize various bits of evidence (often from experts) into coherent and internally consistent models of belief and practices (for example, Roman religion, ancient Judaism, Gnosticism, etc.). The first two points are, I think, clear, but the last requires explanation.

The tendency to overprivilege the work of experts really amounts to privileging certain ancient voices and silencing others. This scholarly habit gives ancient experts what they certainly wanted but never had: the position and power to dictate the practices and beliefs of everyone. It also, as Bruce Lincoln argues, transforms the scholar from an analyst of ancient religious competition to a participant in that competition, for there is

---

4. On the overprivileging of texts in religious studies, see Stanley Stowers, "The Religion of Plant and Animal Offerings versus the Religion of Meanings, Essences, and Textual Mysteries," in *Ancient Mediterranean Sacrifice*, ed. Jennifer Wright Knust and Zsuzsanna Várhelyi (Oxford: Oxford University Press, 2011), 35–56.

5. For a longer history of this situation, see Prothero, *Religious Literacy*.

no more significant form of participation than claiming the authority to declare a winner.⁶

The essays of this section broach the question of how we might theorize the competitive interaction between experts and nonexperts, as well as how we might analyze the extant evidence of specific instances of this competition. The work of Stanley Stowers provides a significant portion of the theoretical framework for this discussion. His 2012 essay "The Religion of Plant and Animal Offerings versus the Religion of Meanings, Essences, and Textual Mysteries" was groundbreaking in this area and was, in part, the impetus for the 2014 Society of Biblical Literature panel from which these papers came.⁷ Stowers's contribution to this volume builds on his 2012 essay to make the critical point that the distinction between experts and nonexperts does not map onto older distinctions, common in religious studies, between elite and so-called "popular" religion. The complex formulations of religious experts do not represent a separate tradition but are rather parasitic upon the ideas and practices of nonexperts. Experts claim to have the truth about the gods and the true interpretations of rituals in contrast to the masses whose ideas they often attack as simple, provincial, superstitious, and generally wrong.

However, it is the very intuitiveness and "stickiness" of the ideas and practices of the nonelites, based as they are on evolutionarily shaped tendencies of the human brain, that make it impossible for elites to end such practices. Literate experts may "create special versions of these practices," but they cannot stop them; in fact, they often participate in them, albeit with their own esoteric interpretations. Thus, Stowers argues, distinguishing the work of experts does not and must not mean conceptualizing two distinct entities: elite religion and popular religion. Rather, the relationship between elites and nonelites is dynamic and competitive. As in any parasitic relationship, the parasite needs the host, but the host does not

---

6. Bruce Lincoln, *Gods and Demons, Priests and Scholars: Critical Explorations in the History of Religions* (Chicago: University of Chicago Press, 2012), 2–3. On the appropriate role of analysts in critical historical study, see also Bruno Latour, *Reassembling the Social: An Introduction to Actor-Network-Theory* (New York: Oxford University Press, 2005).

7. Stowers, "Religion of Plant and Animal Offerings." See also Ramsay MacMullen, *The Second Church: Popular Christianity A.D. 200–400*, WGRWSup 1 (Atlanta: Society of Biblical Literature, 2009), though note Stowers's objections below regarding the category "popular religion."

need the parasite. Religious experts need the practices of nonexperts (their own literate theologizing depends on them), but nonexperts do not need experts. It takes effort and specific social situations and/or structures of power to get nonexperts to pay attention to the formulations of experts. Stowers's paper explores this by considering the rise of the Christian ecclesiastical hierarchy, particularly bishops, who were religious experts but who also wielded, by the third century, broader powers such as political power and institutions of social control. This combination of elite cultural production with civic power in the area of interaction with superhuman agents, Stowers argues, was an innovation of early Christianity.

The competitive practices of religious experts are also well illustrated by Christopher Hoklotubbe's analysis of the concept of piety in Plutarch, Philo, and 1 Timothy. Hoklotubbe shows how elites traded on the social capital of the concept of piety while simultaneously competing to define what exactly constituted that category. This illustrates Stowers's point well. The concept of piety is not an invention of religious elites; rather, elites claim to know what true piety really is and to display this supposed superior knowledge in practices such as writing and lecturing. The concept of piety is a perfect nexus for elite competition. It is a binary term (the concept of piety itself implies the existence of *impiety*), but it is also a created category (like *beauty*) and thus infinity redefinable.

Karl Shuve's paper explores an example of elites attempting to disseminate their ideas to nonexperts. Shuve shows how Ambrose of Milan developed a complex interpretation of the Song of Songs, which served his larger competitive goals of asserting the importance of ascetic practices in his congregation. Once again, we see the competitive practices of religious experts on display: Ambrose makes a claim to superior knowledge that supersedes the knowledge of his congregation. They must replace their own simple beliefs with his superior exegesis—at least that is Ambrose's hectoring assertion. Shuve's paper also illustrates the combination of roles and power discussed by Stowers. By Ambrose's time, the office of the Christian bishop had developed into a position that combined skills in elite textual production and discourse with actual civic power within a social network. The ritualized speech act (the sermon) in which Ambrose presents his ideas to his audience as they sit quietly and listen (thus recognizing and embodying both his intellectual and social authority) is an example of this unique Christian combination.

The same situation is evident in Loren Spielman's analysis of Jewish and Christian responses to Greco-Roman spectacles. Spielman illustrates how rabbinic texts and early Christian texts develop complex rationales for why good Jews and Christians should avoid attending spectacles in the theater. Attendance at spectacles was an important social practice in the Roman world and opting out would have had significant social consequences. Elites like the rabbis and Tertullian articulate an elite identity not by simply rejecting spectacles but by using their literary and rhetorical skills to construe their own practices as superior, both intellectually and morally.

Ultimately, the historical reality that the bulk of our data for ancient Mediterranean religion comes from elites cannot be changed, and this reality must impact and limit the kinds of arguments we can make. Failure to take this situation seriously, by failing to recognize the claims of ancient experts as *competitive*, not *descriptive*, threatens to put us as scholars in the bizarre role of *player* in a game long since over—not only perpetrators of anachronism but weedy anachronisms ourselves.

Why Expert versus Nonexpert Is Not Elite versus Popular Religion: The Case of the Third Century

Stanley K. Stowers

The third century CE presents itself as a distinctive historical moment for understanding "the rise of Christianity" and the interplay of ancient Mediterranean religion more broadly. Here I am not thinking of the false Western narrative regarding the defeat of inherently inferior polytheism by inherently superior monotheism. Rather, the third century gives us the emergence of all the modes of religion that we tend to throw together under the blanket term Christianity. Most notably, freelance and independent or semi-independent literate specialists like Paul, Justin, Valentinus, Marcion, and Athenagoras come under the control of or vainly attempt to compete with a figure who combines literate specialization with political power, the bishop. Scholars over the last decades have also shown with greater clarity that bishops from the third century on were increasingly players belonging to the arena of civic power and civic ideology, a story that I cannot tell here.[1] I agree with historians who have argued that the power of bishops in the third and fourth centuries has been exaggerated, even if the claims that bishops made were sometimes enormous.[2] In my

---

1. For what I mean by civic power and civic interests and a comparison with the power of bishops, see the appendix to this article. Also see Claudia Rapp, *Holy Bishops in Late Antiquity: The Nature of Christian Leadership in an Age of Transition* (Berkeley: University of California Press, 2005); Peter Brown, *Power and Persuasion in Late Antiquity: Towards a Christian Empire* (Madison: University of Wisconsin Press, 1992); Michele Salzman, *The Making of a Christian Aristocracy: Social and Religious Change in the Western Roman Empire* (Cambridge: Harvard University Press, 2002).

2. Rita Lizzi, "I vescovi e i *potentes* della terra: Definizione e limite del ruolo episcopale nelle due *partes imperii* fra IV e V secolo d.C.," in *L'évêque dans la cité IVe au Ve siècle: Image et autorité; Actes de la table ronde organisée par l'Istituto patristico Augustinianum et l'Ecole française de Rome; Rome 1et et 2 décembre 1995*, ed. Éric

theorizing, it was precisely the constraints of the religion of everyday social exchange, on the one hand, and the power of the wealthy and the aristocracy, the basis of traditional civic religion, on the other hand, that limited and conditioned the power of bishops. My points are not about the magnitude of bishops' power but rather the social dynamics of this power. Here I argue that both the independent expert in Christian texts and knowledge and the expert in those cultural areas with political power, epitomized by the bishop, subsisted from a more basic and persistent religiosity that cut across traditions, ethnicities, and religious movements. The two kinds of experts and the nonexpert Christians were in dynamic interaction during the third century.

This last category of mundane Mediterranean religiosity has often been vaguely noted by scholarship under the rubric of popular religion.[3] "Popular religion," widely used for numerous cultures and historical periods, is normally set in opposition to elite religion or some similar category. A list of related categories would include official/popular, great tradition/little tradition, public/private, formal/informal, universal/local, authorized/unauthorized, urban/rural. Such categories reflect an important truth, namely, that in any complex society all religion is not the same and religious practices are clustered in meaningfully distributed ways across the society.[4] A major problem apparent in the categories comes from the normative assumptions that structure the oppositions: popular religion

---

Rebillard and Claire Sotinel (Rome: École française de Rome, 1998), 81–104; Claire Sotinel, "Les évêques Italiens dans la société de l'Antiquité tardive: L'émergence d'une nouvelle élite?" in *Le transformazioni delle elites in età tardoantica*, ed. R. Lizzi Testa (Rome: L'Erma di Bretschneider, 2006), 377–404.

3. There is a large bibliography on popular and official religion, e.g., Pieter A. Vrijhof and Jacques Waardenburg, eds., *Official and Popular Religion: Analysis of a Theme for Religious Studies* (The Hague: Mouton, 1979); Stephen Teiser, "Popular Religion," *JAS* 54 (1995): 378–95. For a critical discussion, see Francesca Stavrakopoulou, "'Popular' Religion and 'Official' Religion: Practice, Perception, Portrayal," in *Religious Diversity in Ancient Israel and Judah*, ed. Francesca Stavrakopoulou and John Barton (London: T&T Clark, 2010), 37–58.

4. This distribution makes sense once it is realized that religion consists of human activities (involving representations/beliefs and perceptions), mostly social practices. Such activities cluster and link in ways that are highly significant for human sociality and experience of the world. See Stanley K. Stowers, "The Ontology of Religion," in *Introducing Religion: Essays in Honor of Jonathan Z. Smith*, ed. Willi Braun and Russell T. McCutcheon (London: Equinox, 2008), 434–49.

is a kind of deviation from what some authority deems to be normative and authorized. Scholars have, in fact, derived the categories by taking the normative perspective of the dominant groups who transmitted their ideas about what is right, true, pious, and good in writings that have come down to the scholars. In third-century Christianity, emic categories that would overlap with the scholar's popular and elite are orthodox/heretical, clerical/lay, educated/uneducated, and Christian/"pagan." These suggest the second major difficulty with "elite/popular" and the other oppositions: they pose the categories as clear cut and mutually exclusive. In what follows, I will attempt to show why this is not the case.

Rather than reproducing the normative positions of groups within particular traditions and assuming their categories to be socially accurate and useful descriptions, scholars can work toward creating their own categories of analysis that better capture the social and cultural dynamics. Elsewhere, I have proposed four analytical modes of religiosity for ancient Mediterranean religion.[5] Individuals can participate in more than one mode and often cognitively compartmentalize different modes in ways described by contemporary psychology.[6] The mode that captures much of what scholars want in the concept of popular religion is what I call the religion of everyday social exchange.[7] This is the kind of religion that most easily and widely arises, persists, and is transmitted. It does not require literacy, complex hierarchical social organization, or organized political power. In this sense, it is popular. Both cognitive and social propensities come together to produce the robust and popular quality of this religiosity. Based on experimental work with babies, children, and adults, cognitive scientists have shown that automatic intuitive ontological categories are foundational to human cognition.[8] Human cognition is keyed to find

---

5. See n. 7 below.

6. Compartmentalization is a critical concept central to contemporary cognitive and more traditional psychology, although there are numerous approaches to it from those by way of cognitive modularity to those using self-structure theories.

7. Stanley K. Stowers, "The Religion of Plant and Animal Offerings versus the Religion of Meanings, Essences and Textual Mysteries," in *Ancient Mediterranean Sacrifice*, ed. Jennifer Wright Knust and Zsuzsanna Várhelyi (Oxford: Oxford University Press, 2011), 35–56; Stowers, "Kinds of Myth, Meals and Power: Paul and the Corinthians," in *Redescribing Paul and the Corinthians*, ed. Ron Cameron and Merrill O. Miller, ECL 5 (Atlanta: Society of Biblical Literature, 2011), 105–49.

8. For an introduction to these theories, see Scott Tremlin, *Minds and Gods: The Cognitive Foundations of Religion* (New York: Oxford University Press, 2006). For a

and focus upon human-like agency. We also have developed deep abilities to readily attribute mind, that is, to attribute intentions, emotions, purposes, moods, and so on, both to other people and even to the nonhuman world.[9] As a byproduct of evolutionary adaptation, the key abilities to detect agents and attribute mind are hyperactive in most human beings and range from the ultra-hyperactivity of schizophrenia, on one pole, to the autism spectrum, on the other. This is not religion, but the propensities make it easy for most people to form concepts of gods, ghosts, and similar sorts of beings with representations that are easily acquired and stored in the memory, because they are both familiar and odd; that is to say, they consist of invisible mental beings without normal bodies who can watch us.[10]

What makes such beliefs easy and robust on the social side comes from the fact that the cognitive propensities encourage belief in beings very much like persons with whom humans can interact by means of everyday social practices.[11] Virtually everyone is skilled in these practices. Gods and similar beings in this mode of religiosity are not normally distant cosmic gods or legislators who want to control humans or emperors ruling the universe or all-knowing and all-powerful. Rather, they are interested parties whom one can approach and with whom one can establish relationships of reciprocity, ranging from occasional or friend-like relations to those appropriate to powerful patrons. The god of the Platonists or of Christian orthodoxy or of the Trinity or of Christus Victor does not fit this mode, although psychologists have shown that ordinary religious people will often imagine these high beings in unorthodox ways in terms of the religion of everyday social exchange.[12] Saints, martyrs, angels, local

---

helpful discussion of critical issues regarding agency and ontological categories, see Steven Horst, "Whose Intuitions? Which Dualism?" in *The Roots of Religion: Exploring the Cognitive Science of Religion*, ed. Roger Trigg and Justin L. Barrett (Burlington, VT: Ashgate, 2014), 37–54.

9. See n. 7.

10. For this idea of moderate counterintuitiveness, including discussion of Pascal Boyer and others, see Ilkka Pyysiäinen, *How Religion Works: Towards a New Cognitive Science of Religion* (Leiden: Brill, 2007), 18–23.

11. Stowers, "Religion of Plant and Animal Offerings," 36–40.

12. Justin L. Barrett and Frank C. Keil, "Conceptualizing a Non-natural Entity: Anthropomorphism in God Concepts," *CognPsych* 31 (1996): 219–47; Justin L. Barrett, "Theological Correctness: Cognitive Constraints and the Study of Religion," *MTSR* 11 (1999): 325–39.

gods, heroes, demons, ancestors, and the beloved dead do fit, however. As Ramsey MacMullen writes about the martyr cult: "You prayed *for* something, you were a suppliant: 'begging,' 'requesting,' 'promising.' In reply, the martyrs represented the superhuman power that was accessible to the masses of people in a way that the Triune God was not."[13] Humans generally know how to observe others for signs of their moods, emotions, and desires, to talk to others and make requests, to praise others, to exchange gifts with loved ones, friends, and others, and to share meals. The same practices imagined for gods and similar beings in this mode are divinatory signs, prayer and votives, acts of honoring, offerings, and religious meals. In such practices, the beings are imagined to be inhabitants of the local environment and approachable. People went to specific places to be near these gods and nonobvious beings, as for example, with Greek hero cults or martyr tombs, tombs of the beloved dead, Christian and Greek relic sites, and dwellings of local deities.

The creative and driving force of the Christian movement was a class of literate experts, specialists in books, in writing, in inventing literary narratives, in speech-making, in argumentation, in staking interpretive positions, and so on.[14] At the beginning of the third century, it seems likely that freelance and rather entrepreneurial literate experts like Paul, Justin, Tatian, Valentinus, Marcion, Athenagoras, and Clement of Alexandria still dominated the movement. Contemporaries, both Christian and non-Christian, widely noted that these people resembled philosophers.[15] By the end of the third century, these experts had largely come under the control of bishops, literate experts with institutional-political power.

To understand this movement led by these two types of literate experts, we need the sociological concept of a field of social formation that includes characteristic practices and arenas of competition for the

---

13. Ramsay MacMullen, *The Second Church: Popular Christianity A.D. 200–400*, WGRWSup 1 (Atlanta: Society of Biblical Literature, 2009), 106 and 174 nn. 25–28.

14. Stowers, "Religion of Plant and Animal Offerings"; Stowers, "Kinds of Myth"; Heidi Wendt, *The Religion of Freelance Experts in the Roman Empire* (New York: Oxford University Press, forthcoming).

15. For some of the large bibliography, see especially for the first two centuries, Abraham J. Malherbe, *Paul and the Popular Philosophers* (Minneapolis: Fortress, 1989), 1–9 and throughout; for later, Winrich Löhr, "Christianity as Philosophy: Problems and Perspectives of an Ancient Intellectual Project," *VC* 64 (2010): 160–88. See also Stanley K. Stowers, "Paul and the Terrain of Philosophy," *EC* 6 (2015): 141–56.

particular valued resources of a field.¹⁶ There are many kinds of experts in some form of skill or knowledge by matter of degree. Take divinatory practices:¹⁷ people in all ancient Mediterranean cultures had dreams in which one looked for messages from the gods, the beloved dead, angels, and so on. Everyone could watch the clouds or birds or peculiar events for signs and messages. Everyone could throw dice, the ancient knuckle bones (astragalomacy). But one might also consult an expert in interpreting knuckle bones. Higher up on the scale of expertise resided dream interpreters and astrologers who were sometimes literate and consulted books. Only the literate dream interpreter and the astrologer with books, I would argue, might just possibly belong to a field, although just consulting a book for recipes in one's craft would not likely make one a player in a social field.

There is an interesting problem in even applying Pierre Bourdieu's theory of fields to antiquity. The theory explains how the modern organization of society arose in the West in contrast to premodern societies.¹⁸ Before modernity, religion, the economy, art, writing culture, law, and politics were thoroughly intermeshed. Modernity occurred when these

---

16. There are several sociological field theories. I find a critically modified version of Pierre Bourdieu's theory to be helpful: Pierre Bourdieu, *The Field of Cultural Production: Essays on Art and Literature*, ed. Randal Johnson (New York: Columbia University Press, 1993); Mathieu Hilgers and Éric Mangez, eds., *Bourdieu's Theory of Social Fields: Concepts and Applications* (London: Routledge, 2015). For the purposes of this essay, I say little about habitus and symbolic or social capital, although the two are integral to his theory of fields. Bourdieu, as with many topics, said many things about fields over the course of his long career. I mostly follow what I think is accepted as his core theory.

17. Jennifer Eyl, "'By the Power of Signs and Wonders': Paul, Divinatory Practices, and Symbolic Capital" (PhD diss., Brown University, 2011).

18. Scott Lash, *Sociology of Postmodernism* (London: Routledge, 1990), 237–65. I can present only a bit of the theory here, but in Bourdieu's version a field consists of stakes that the participants in the "game" or struggle pursue for types of capital, objective conditions, and spaces for activities and meanings that go with them. Capital in the premodern era was a rather undifferentiated with the capital of honor and the centrality of personal gift exchange, in contrast to modern varied forms of capital differentiated by fields and markets. In addition, his theory of the habitus, i.e., the production, reproduction, and transformation of practical senses, is important. Further, he claims that for modernity fields are homologously organized.

areas formed semiautonomous fields. By definition then, antiquity did not have fields.[19]

The theory is quite complex, but let me illustrate it by talking about semiautonomy and the economy with the instance of art.[20] In antiquity and in the medieval period, people who produced art were craftspeople. They were paid for their creations either by the piece or by a supportive client relation. Some might become quite famous, but in relation to the economy they were like contemporary bricklayers or cement workers who certainly do not form a field. Beginning mostly in the nineteenth century, there arose the idea of a radical distinction between craft and true art among some artists. No monetary value could be placed upon the truest art. The true artist had to be free from patrons, the corruption of money, and outside control. Bourdieu calls this attitude disinterestedness. This kind of artist competed to show their purity and disinterestedness. In pursuit of authentic art, they set their own rules for true art in succeeding waves of movements like art nouveau, impressionism, surrealism, cubism, minimalism, and so on; each was a new challenge reacting to a previous orthodoxy. Bourdieu realized that not all artists were like the disinterested artists who stressed autonomy from power, the economy, and so on; not all resembled the proverbial starving bohemian artist. To be in the field at all, one had to operate with the idea that art was qualitatively different from craft, but some artists did seek rich patrons or work for state-run museums and academies. This more heteronomous pole of the field was what the artists on the other pole defined themselves against. That side had sold out. All in the field competed for social capital, that is, for prestige, honor, and recognition that gave them a certain sort of power, that is, symbolic capital.[21] They did this by staking out positions with their work in the field of

---

19. The issue can be confusing, because, in his early work revising Weber, he spoke of the premodern field of religion as the chief agent of consecration.

20. Pierre Bourdieu, *The Rules of Art: Genesis and Structure of the Literary Field*, trans. Susan Emanuel (Stanford, CA: Stanford University Press, 1996), especially 285–312; Bridget Fowler, *Pierre Bourdieu and Cultural Theory: Critical Investigations* (Thousand Oaks, CA: Sage, 1997), 103–33.

21. The idea of social capital is an enormous topic with many different schools. I am loosely following Bourdieu on social and symbolic capital. I do not use cultural capital here both because Bourdieu did not clearly distinguish it from other forms of capital and because it is most properly applied to resources such as those acquired in education. For a critical analysis of the idea of social capital, see Paul Firenze, "Value and Economies of Religious Capital" (PhD diss., Brown University, 2013).

art regarding what was authentic. Bourdieu shows that the dynamic here is one of orthodoxy and heresy. Capital accrued when new ideas about art successfully challenged old ideas. But the new ideas became the old institutionalized ideas if they persisted, and the cycle went on.

In a paper read in 2003, I argued that Bourdieu's theory captured much that is helpful and true but that Mediterranean antiquity had already developed a field that was a precursor to the fields of modernity. This field included literate experts in book knowledge with Greek and Latin *paideia*, on the heteronomous pole, and many philosophers and certain freelance experts, on the autonomous pole.[22] Very briefly, let me mention some of the field characteristics. The centrality of disinterestedness is clear for the autonomous pole. Think of Socrates, Diogenes, and many other philosophers known for their rejection of power, money, and outside control. Central to this tradition was the martyr for truth and justice. Time after time philosophers stood up against tyrants or lived ascetic lives. A second field condition came in the translocal and universalizing character of knowledge and practice.[23] Experts in knuckle bone prognostication were a local phenomenon no matter how widely they traveled. But the literate specialists lived off of the "worldwide" circulation of books and ideas among the minute but powerful network of the literate experts. Third, philosophers maintained positions in the field by competition with and relation to other philosophers contending about the truest ethical, physical, and cosmological doctrines.

With this very sketchy theory of a field in mind, let us return to the literate experts in books and knowledge who were central to the Christian movement. I cannot rehearse my arguments for how Christianity formed in the autonomous pole of the field of literate experts, but I can point out that by the third century the heroes and models of the movement were autonomous pole figures such as Jesus, apostles, martyrs, and ascetic saints. The autonomous pole teachers and schools of the second century now had to deal with the ever more dominant power of bishops and the clergy. The

---

22. Stanley K. Stowers, "Pauline Scholarship, Christian Origins and the Third Way in Social Theory" (paper presented at the Annual Meeting of the Society of Biblical Literature, Atlanta, GA, 11 November 2003). Thus I do not think that there was a premodern "field of religion." Ancient religion was heterogeneous. Bourdieu wrongly imagined all of ancient religion as like the Roman Catholic Church and North African Islam that he knew.

23. What Bourdieu calls the scholastic attitude.

bishop is someone who is supposed to be an expert in the Christian books and teachings who also embodies the ideals of the apostles and martyrs, yet ironically gets his power from heteronomous sources. In other words, while the earlier teachers and figures competed for power based only on their teachings, writings, interpretive abilities, and their display of disinterest in money, power, and worldly prestige, the bishop is made by (or also made) what Bourdieu called the symbolic power of consecration.[24] An institution of bishops and clergy supported by the patronage of the wealthy and the aristocrats bestowed symbolic capital on others like themselves, at least from the third century. The bishop had both the prestige of an institution enchanted by the past of martyrs and freelance teachers and political power. The bishop of Alexandria, Demetrius, could and did excommunicate Origen (that is, banish him and declare his Caesarean ordination invalid) or could have, but did not, consecrate him as a priest. But Origen, the independent or semi-independent literate specialist could not wield that kind of power against Demetrius.

Both are literate experts whose religion is definitively shaped by the field. The religion of the field is rationalizing and universalizing, prone to abstraction, and based upon various sorts of intellectualizing practices. Creating, justifying, holding to, and expressing the true doctrines and interpretations is central to both Origen's and Demetrius's religiosity in a way that is different from the religion of everyday social exchange. In spite of the inevitable competition and discord that came from their practices of staking positions about what is true and good, both are part of the same field of competition and are networked to other literate experts across the Mediterranean and beyond by the circulation of writings and ideas. It is no accident that Christian writers consistently engaged Greco-Roman philosophy, whether using it constructively, arguing with it, or rejecting it. Contrast that to the religion of everyday social exchange.

A prominent feature of the autonomous pole going back to the Presocratics and central to all of the philosophical schools is the critique of traditional and popular religion, the religion of everyday social exchange.[25] At the center of the Greek and Roman learning of the heteronomous pole were the poets, especially Homer and Hesiod, and the use of them in

---

24. Stephen Engler, "Modern Times: Religion, Consecration and the State in Bourdieu," *CulSt* 17 (2003): 445–67.

25. Harold W. Attridge, "The Philosophical Critique of Religion under the Early Empire," *ANRW* 16.1:45–78.

education. The philosophers attacked the false views of the gods articulated in the poets but also of popular everyday religion. They debated and wrote treatises on superstition, against various divinatory practices, and so on. One only need to read the bishops' sermons from the fourth and fifth centuries, the restrictions of the church councils against household religion, and writings against so-called pagan practices to see that bishops and clergy not only attacked the "idolatry" of the Mediterranean cultures by often using arguments taken from philosophers, but also condemned practices from everyday religion, such as kinds of divination, offerings, meals, votives, lighting lamps, apotropaic practices, and celebratory ritual.[26]

Philosophers and other independent literate experts long had an uninstitutionalized freelance relation to ancient Mediterranean religion, both civic religion and the religion of everyday social exchange. But Christianity during the third century crystallized religion that institutionalized a relation between the religion of everyday social exchange and the religion of literate specialists, with the latter attempting to control the former according to its principles. Bourdieu argued that movements within fields were always struggling to establish a monopoly within the field. Something similar happens in Christianity. Texts in ancient Mediterranean religion were marginal. In the religion of everyday social exchange, one did not follow texts to practice religion. The literate experts, both the independent and the clerical, increasingly textualized ritual, however. Correct rituals had to be approved in the Scripture and often required a text, an expert interpretation, and a literate ritual expert.

As Daniel Ullucci has argued, the developed "official" religion of the churches and bishops—seen already by the mid-third century—fits what the anthropologist Harvey Whitehouse has theorized as the doctrinal

---

26. The topic is yet to be well-thematized and studied, but on Tertullian see, Caroline Johnson Hodge, "Daily Devotions: Stowers's Modes of Religion Meet Tertullian's *ad Uxorem*," in *"The One Who Sows Bountifully": Essays in Honor of Stanley K. Stowers*, ed. Caroline Johnson Hodge et al., BJS 356 (Providence, RI: Brown Judaic Studies, 2013), 43–54; David Frankfurter, "Beyond Magic and Superstition," in *Late Ancient Christianity*, vol. 2 of *A People's History of Christianity*, ed. Virginia Burrus (Minneapolis: Fortress, 2005), 255–83; Kimberly Bowes, *Private Worship, Public Values, and Religious Change in Late Antiquity* (New York: Cambridge University Press, 2008); MacMullen, *Second Church*, 105–11.

mode of transmission.[27] While the cognitive optimum easily stores in the memory, doctrinal mode religion requires an enormous educational and ritual edifice that still does not take well with most people. "Cognitive optimum" refers to extensive experimental work by cognitive psychologists showing that certain kinds of mental representations are easily stored in the memory and easily transmitted to others, while representations with different characteristics are not. "A radiant young woman appeared to me" would be of the easily memorized type, but "God is three in one and beyond every attribute" would be of the difficult kind. The catechetical training that became standard in the third century and the constant repetition of teachings in sermons and textualized ritual are examples of this effort.

While the freelance Christian teachers who were so prominent in the first and second centuries belonged to the disinterested autonomous pole and became the saints of the movement, by the last quarter of the third century, the bishops and prominent clergy were emerging as a formation with some characteristics of an aristocracy and an aristocracy's relation to "civic religion" and "civic power."[28] The heternomous sources of the bishop's social capital posed a contradiction partly solved by the rise of martyrs' and saints' cults. In this instance, one can see the different dynamics of the religion of everyday social exchange of most of the laity and the situation of the bishops. In the everyday religion, one wanted to interact with the holy dead to heal children, ask for signs, and, in general, to receive kinds of help in life that only an approachable local god or similar being could supply. Families and individuals cultivated relationships of generalized reciprocity by giving various sorts of gifts to the saints and martyrs and even the beloved dead.[29] Or they entertained these august dead by sharing meals with them and even dancing and singing for them.[30] An

---

27. Daniel Ullucci, "Toward a Typology of Religious Experts in the Ancient Mediterranean," in Johnson Hodge et al., *"One Who Sows Bountifully,"* 89–103; Harvey Whitehouse, *Modes of Religiosity: A Cognitive Theory of Religious Transmission* (New York: AltaMira, 2004). I do not believe that the science supports Whitehouse's "Imagistic Mode" or that it plays a part in ancient Christianity.

28. See the appendix to this essay.

29. Rebillard shows the lateness of church control and the continuity of pre-Christian practice, Éric Rebillard, *The Care of the Dead in Late Antiquity*, CSCP 59 (Ithaca, NY: Cornell University Press, 2009), esp. 140–71. See also MacMullen, *Second Church*, 45–58, 76.

30. For dancing, chants, and meals, see MacMullen, *Second Church*, 9 and 153 n.

inscription from North Africa, possibly from 309 CE, well captures this mood: "The table (*mensa*) of Januarius the martyr. Drink up! Live long!"[31] Bishops often did participate in this religion of everyday social exchange but also had other interests peculiar to their position.[32] Beginning in the third and increasingly in the fourth century, bishops brought the tombs and relics of the martyrs and saints into the churches and set aside marked places for their own burial next to the saints and martyrs. The altars of priests and bishops were frequently built directly over the tombs and the relics.[33] In these ways, the bishops with all of their heteronomous social capital consecrated themselves in Bourdieu's sense with the disinterestedness of impoverished and powerless apostles, saints, and martyrs. They sought to obtain autonomous pole symbolic capital by proximity and to give their own interpretations and rules of use to the cults. But while it was easier to control what went on in churches, it was more difficult to do so in cemeteries and private chapels.[34]

But the constant attempt to impose the religion of the literate expert never completely succeeded for some very basic reasons. As argued earlier, the religion of everyday social exchange is both cognitively and socially more basic than the religion of the literate experts. The elite literate experts, the bishops for instance, could not simply leave behind the religion of the masses, of everyday social exchange, and create a purely intellectualizing and textualizing religion. Given that the religion must have human-like agents—God, gods, angels, saints, demons, and so forth—one must relate to them in the socially and cognitively optimal ways basic to the religion of mundane social exchange. This points to one of the critiques in many historical fields of the idea of popular versus elite religion. The elite may have practices and beliefs that the masses never have, but the elite always seem to be found practicing popular activities, even if they have denounced them or they are deemed deviant by the elites.

The literate experts, say bishops, can restrict prayers in rituals that they control to certain texts, said only by them. They can teach that one should

---

85 (referencing Tertullian, Clement, and Origen), 44–46.

31. Paul-Albert Février, "Le culte des martyrs en Afrique et ses plus anciens monuments," *CCARB* 17 (1970): 209–13.

32. Throughout Rebillard, *Care of the Dead*, and especially MacMullen, *Second Church*.

33. MacMullen, *Second Church*, 65 and n. 45, 83.

34. A theme found in both Bowes, *Private Worship*, and MacMullen, *Second Church*.

pray only to certain divine beings and teach that one must hold certain theological beliefs during the practice, but they cannot dispense with the basic act of praying found in everyday Mediterranean religion. They can teach that prophecy has ceased and that signs and messages likely come from demons, but they cannot stop dreams from divine beings, even their own. They can declare professional or expert diviners to be doing the work of Satan, but it is difficult for them to rule that God or an angel cannot give someone a sign about something in their life. They can say that there is only one truly legitimate religious meal—a Eucharist of the clergy—but they cannot eliminate meals in numerous contexts in which interaction with god-like beings occur, including the beloved or honored dead. In other words, literate experts, even bishops with political power, can create special versions of these practices from general, everyday Mediterranean religion, and they can try to constrain lay use, but they cannot fully control them or do without them in their own religious practice. Their own religious practice indeed consists of practices from the general Mediterranean religion of every day social exchange to which they have added distinguishing elements to set their versions off as distinct and true. But it does not go the other way. The average person did not need to be literate or to understand complex doctrine or to be interested in taking positions on true and false religion or to know the scriptural and theological warrant for a practice to carry on with these activities.

I hope that this discussion makes it clear why theorizing a distinct popular religion and a distinct elite religion is misleading. They are distinct in the sense that the cognitive and social processes that make them elite or everyday are partly different. But they are also interconnected in specific ways at the same time, above all because the elite religion is based in the optimal practices of the everyday exchange. The relation between the two is dynamic. The literate experts create a field of competition and a translocal set of networks exchanging and contesting knowledge with those in the field. But they also inhabit life outside the conditions of the field, and Christianity developed an institutionalized relation between the field and the outside. On their side, the lay practitioners were constantly translating the teachings and the practices advocated by the bishops and clergy into the idiom of everyday religiosity. It is important to understand that I am not talking about experience. The lay Christian might have venerated the bishop and experienced the different dynamics of the experts and the laity as natural. My analytical approach is about the social forces producing the two. But, of course, everyday religion and the elite religion did often come into conflict, and people did sometimes experience the tension between the different social and cognitive dynamics. Above all, to treat ancient Christianity as a kind of religion (or "a religion" as in "Judaism is a religion") bounded off from other religion in the Mediterranean is to mystify and to hide the way that the masses of activities of which it consisted actually worked.

Appendix: Bishops and Civic Power

By civic interests and power—using "civic" as a loose catchall term for power, practices, and ways of legitimating social formations beyond the size of all but the most powerful household estates—I refer most typically to towns, cities, and larger entities dominated by aristocrats or aristocrats and monarchs. Central interests include the maintenance and control of the social order constituted by human subjects and human capital and human and nonhuman property. Sources of power are, on the one hand, the prestige and legitimacy of (mostly) traditional roles and institutions of aristocrats, especially related to towns, cities, and monarchies, and, on the other hand, institutionalized powers to create and enforce norms and statuses. Creation and enforcement here come by virtue of the legitimacy of roles and institutions such as law and the power of enforcement by means of violence. Very widely across the Mediterranean, aristocracies were partly defined by their domination of the city's institutions for relating to gods and similar beings. In a variation, seen widely in West Asia, religion was dominated by hereditary priestly aristocracies (for example, in Judea and Egypt). The central legitimating notion in the civic religion dominated by aristocrats came from their claim to represent the whole civic body in their practices of reciprocity with the gods. Similarly, bishops represented the whole Christian body.

Central to the social dynamics of the church under intensive development in the third century was that it came to share some important characteristics of the civic formations while differing in important ways. Although cities and monarchs certainly employed such figures as scribes, literate experts, and advisors of various sorts, textual intellectual practices were not intrinsic to their power and interests. Power came primarily from inherited or attributed legitimacy and control of institutions of violence, such as the police force and armies. In fact, such literate experts might be slaves or former slaves trained for that kind of labor. Hereditary priestly practices and institutions often entailed the transmission and authoritative interpretation of specialized or esoteric texts and knowledge, which strongly represented the heteronomos pole of the literate field. Otherwise the power of aristocrats and monarchs did not derive from their skills in literate practices. A partial exception contributing to legitimation that should not be given too much weight comes from developments of ethnicizing *paideia* associated with the trend that included the so-called Second Sophistic. This imagined return to a classical education of a past exemplary age in rhetoric and language became one mark of the aristocratic classes, at least for males. But by contrast, the bishop, and to some extent the presbyter/priest, derived their power—legitimacy, prestige, and roles—from their status as guardians and interpreters of texts and their claim to have a monopoly on the formulation of true practice and doctrine. In theory, this involved a combination of achieved skills, like that of the freelance expert, and attributed office, like that of aristocratic power. They also claimed a monopoly on the performance of most "public" ritual but a monopoly closely related to their claims to true interpretation of Scripture, tradition, and doctrine. Clearly, the freelance literate experts like Origen posed a potential competitive threat to the bishops.

Thus, unlike the freelance experts, the clergy also had civic-like interests and power. Bishops also increasingly came from local aristocracies. The legitimacy of bishops was primarily attributed by way of the office. The church came to have its own social order of clergy and the laity that the bishops tried to maintain and control in certain respects, although it was particularly difficult to control lay aristocrats and the wealthy. Such maintenance and control was associated with the creation and enforcement of norms—rules, laws, and so forth. The powers to classify and interpret to which the freelance experts aspired had some institutional enforcement with bishops and clergy. The office of the bishop involved varying degrees of power over human subjects and human capital, namely, the clergy and laity more or less under their aegis. The third century saw the rapid accumulation of property that came to be controlled mostly by the bishops, although they also competed with privately owned and controlled property and practices such as chapels and shrines to martyrs. The accumulation of property, of course, increased dramatically after 313 CE. Unlike with civic power, the clergy did not have sources of institutionalized violence for enforcement, although powerful bishops might appeal to Christian civic authorities to aid enforcement in the fourth century and later.

Great Is the Mystery of Piety: Contested Claims to Piety in Plutarch, Philo, and 1 Timothy

T. Christopher Hoklotubbe

The author of 1 Timothy boldly describes the ideal Christian assembly (ἐκκλησία) as the "pillar and foundation of the truth" (1 Tim 3:15) that challenged competing religious experts (the so-called "heterodox" teachers, 1 Tim 1:3, 6:3) who sought to persuade the Christian assembly that they possessed knowledge of the truth about the divine (1 Tim 6:20). The author continues: "Without any doubt, great is the mystery of piety [μέγα ἐστὶν τὸ τῆς εὐσεβείας μυστήριον]: He was revealed in flesh, vindicated in spirit, seen by angels, proclaimed among Gentiles, believed throughout the world, taken up in glory" (1 Tim 3:16, NRSV with emendations). In this passage, the author introduces what appears to be a hymn celebrating the manifestation and glorification of Christ as a "mystery of piety" (τὸ τῆς εὐσεβείας μυστήριον)—an ambiguous phrase with potentially significant cultural appeal not yet appreciated by most modern scholars.

When describing the cultural background and meaning of the terms "mystery" (μυστήριον) and "piety" (εὐσέβεια), contemporary scholarship on the Pastoral Epistles has generally sought to demonstrate how the author has "Christianized" these terms.[1] Philip H. Towner is representative of most modern commentators when he interprets "mystery" (μυστήριον)[2]

---

1. On εὐσέβεια, see John J. Wainwright, "*Eusebeia*: Syncretism or Conservative Contextualization," *EvQ* 65 (1993): 211–24; Philip H. Towner, *The Letters to Titus and Timothy*, NICNT (Grand Rapids: Eerdmans, 2006), 171–74. On μυστήριον, see Jonathan Z. Smith, *Drudgery Divine: On the Comparison of Early Christianities and the Religions of Late Antiquity* (Chicago: The University of Chicago Press, 1990), esp. 54–84.

2. Μυστήριον occurs twenty-eight times in the New Testament, twenty-one times in texts ascribed to Paul (Rom 11:25; 16:25; 1 Cor. 2:1, 7; 4:1; 13:2; 14:2; 15:51; Eph 1:9; 3:3 [two times], 9; 5:32; 6:19; Col 1:26, 27; 2:2; 4:3; 2 Thess 2:7; 1 Tim 3:9, 16). With

as God's secret plan to save the world, which has now been revealed in Christ, and "piety" (εὐσέβεια)³ as encapsulating in one term "the whole of Christian existence as the vibrant interplay between the knowledge of God and the observable life that emerges from this knowledge."⁴ Taken together then, "the mystery of piety" signals God's previously hidden plan of salvation, which has now become manifest in the Christ-event detailed in the hymn and empowers the ideal Christian life.

What scholars have yet to appreciate is how 1 Timothy's conceptualization of the Christ-event as a "mystery of piety" resonates with claims to piety and to disclosures of "mysteries" made among Greek philosophers. In this essay, I will demonstrate how Philo of Alexandria (early to mid-first century CE) and Plutarch of Chaeronea (late first to early second-century CE) make claims to piety with reference to Greek and Egyptian mysteries in order to legitimate their knowledge about the divine over against competing religious experts. I suggest that when we contextualize 1 Tim 3:16 within a cultural milieu, where claims to piety and disclosure of mysteries carried a particular cultural prestige or "symbolic capital,"⁵ we can better nuance the possible social and political implications of the author's celebration of Christ's manifestation as "the mystery of piety."⁶

---

respect to the Pauline corpus (disputed and undisputed), the mystery of God (1 Cor 2:1; 4:1; Col 2:2) or of Christ (Eph 3:3; Col 4:3) generally connotes the salvific effects and consequences of Jesus's incarnation, death, and resurrection. This secret plan has been kept secret since ages past (Rom 16:25; 1 Cor 2:7; Eph 3:9) but now has been revealed through revelation (Eph 1:9; 3:3). Cf. 2 Tim 1:9-11; Titus 1:2-3, where the concept of God's hidden plan of salvation that has been revealed in Jesus is described without recourse to μυστήριον. See Gregory S. Magee, "Uncovering the 'Mystery' in 1 Timothy 3," *TJ* 29 (2008): 247-65.

3. Absent from all other New Testament writings ascribed to Paul, εὐσέβεια and its cognates occur thirteen times in the Pastorals: 1 Tim 2:2; 3:16; 4:7, 8; 5:4; 6:3, 5, 6, 11; 2 Tim 3:5, 12; Tit 1:1; 2:12; there are fourteen occurrences, if you include θεοσέβεια in 1 Tim 2:10. Εὐσέβεια appears elsewhere in the New Testament four times in Acts (3:12; 10:2, 7; 17:23) and five times in 2 Peter (1:3, 6, 7; 2:9; 3:11).

4. See Towner, *Letters to Titus and Timothy*, 171-74, 263-64, 276-77, quote from 170.

5. My use of this term is influenced by Pierre Bourdieu, who has defined "symbolic capital" as "a reputation for competence and an image of respectability and honourability that are easily converted into political positions as a local or national notable" (*Distinction: A Social Critique of the Judgment of Taste*, trans. Richard Nice [Cambridge: Harvard University Press, 1984], 291).

6. For a more thorough treatment of this argument, see T. Christopher Hok-

The Symbolic Capital of Piety and the Mysteries

Both Plutarch and Philo stand within a broad philosophical legacy of wrestling with the question of what piety entails. Ancient philosophers often sought to differentiate their understanding of the divine not only from those they described as the superstitious masses but also from competing schools of thought.[7] Entire works were devoted to answering the question, "What is piety?," including Plato's *Euthyphro*, Philodemus's *On Piety*, and quite possibly a lost work of Philo.[8] For these philosophers, true piety did not merely consist in dutiful ritual observance.[9] Rather, a correct knowledge about the divine that shunned superstitious beliefs was essential. At stake for some of these philosophers was the legacy and legitimacy of their schools. For example, the Epicurean Philodemus (middle and late first century BCE) sought to defend the piety of Epicurus, who like Socrates, was slandered with accusations of impiety.[10] The attention that philosophers devoted to defining and defending their claims to piety

---

lotubbe, "The Rhetoric of *PIETAS*: The Pastoral Epistles and Claims to Piety in the Roman Empire" (ThD diss., Harvard Divinity School, 2015). In this dissertation, I also show that appeals to piety (Latin: *pietas*) were prominent within the cultural domains of Roman politics and poetry as well as Greek civic discourse. Additionally, I discuss the possibility that early audiences may have not only heard resonances of the Ephesian exclamation, "great is the mystery of Artemis" in 1 Tim 3:16's "great is the mystery of piety," but also the claims to piety made by Ephesian cult officers who oversaw the "mystic sacrifices" (μυστικὰς θυσίας) of Artemis and described themselves as "the pious ones" (εὐσεβεῖς).

7. See Harold W. Attridge, "The Philosophical Critique of Religion under the Roman Empire," *ANRW* 16.1: 45–78; Peter Van Nuffelen, *Rethinking the Gods: Philosophical Readings of Religion in the Post-Hellenic Period* (Cambridge: Cambridge University Press, 2011).

8. According to Diogenes Laertius, Bias, Zeno, Pythagoras, and Theophrastus also wrote on the topic of piety, its inverse impiety (ἀσέβεια), and its excess superstition (δεισιδαιμονία); see *Vit. Phil.* books 1, 5.2, 7, and 8.

9. Generally, philosophers rejected the meaning ascribed to rituals and sacrifices, not the practices themselves. See Daniel Ullucci, "Contesting the Meaning of Animal Sacrifice," in *Ancient Mediterranean Sacrifice*, ed. Jennifer W. Knust and Zsuzsanna Várhelyi (Oxford: Oxford University Press, 2011), 57–74.

10. See Philodemus, *Critical Text with Commentary*, vol. 1 of *On Piety*, ed. and trans. Dirk Obbink (Oxford: Oxford University, 1996).

is indicative of the cultural prestige associated with this virtue.¹¹ For many philosophers, the defense and demonstration of their piety functioned to legitimate their expertise concerning the truth about the divine.

The conceptualization of the practice of philosophy as an initiation into the mysteries also had its own rich legacy within the cultural domain of ancient philosophy. As early as Plato's dialogue *Phaedrus*, Socrates compared the turn from vice toward virtue to the purifying initiations of the Dionysian "mystery rites" (τελεταί), which prepare one to dwell with the gods (Plato, *Phaed.* 69C).¹² According to Socrates, the ancient mystics who created these mysteries had practiced philosophy correctly (οἱ πεφιλοσοφηκότες ὀρθῶς) (Plato, *Phaed.* 69D). We find further deployment of this mystery-metaphor in Aristotle (*Eudemus* frag. 10, cited in Plutarch, *Is. Os.* 382DE), Chrysippus (*SVF* 2.42; cited in Plutarch, *Stoic. rep.* 1035AB), Cicero (*De or.* 1.206), Quintilian (*Inst.* 5.13.59–60), and Dionysius of Halicarnassus (*Comp.* 25.5–6).¹³ When ancient philosophers framed their knowledge in terms of mystery terminology, they traded upon the symbolic capital ascribed to the domain of Greek and Egyptian mysteries. The cultural prestige that the mysteries enjoyed was due not only to the popular perception that initiations into the mysteries secured divine benefits but also the assumption among intellectuals that the sacred stories and initiatory rites were in fact repositories of ancient wisdom that, if interpreted correctly, disclosed the nature of the universe.¹⁴ As Peter van Nuffelen has shown, numerous intellectuals of the early empire, including the Roman antiquarian Varro, the Stoic philosophers Chaeremon and Cornutus, and Plutarch, identified both Greek and Egyptian mysteries "as the best place to look for unadulterated ancient knowledge,

---

11. For more on piety as symbolic capital, see Hoklotubbe, "Rhetoric of *PIETAS*," 31–33, 195–99.

12. See also *Phaedr.* 249C, 250BC; *Symp.* 209E–210A; *Theaet.* 156A; see also Günter Bornkamm, "μυστήριον," *TDNT* 4:808–10.

13. See Aristotle, *Select Fragments*, vol. 12 of *The Works of Aristotle*, ed. and trans. William David Ross (Oxford: Clarendon, 1952); Roderich Kirchner, "Die Mysterien der Rhetorik: Zur Mysterienmetapher in rhetoriktheoretischen Texten," *RhM* 148 (2005): 165–80.

14. On the diversity of divine benefits associated with different "mysteries," see Jan N. Bremmer, *Initiation into the Mysteries of the Ancient World*, MVAW 1 (Berlin: de Gruyter, 2014), xiii.

the precepts of secrecy guaranteeing its quality."[15] Yet *who* possessed the expertise to properly decipher the true meaning of these stories and rites was a matter of contestation among philosophers, mystagogues, and other religious experts.

THE PURE PIETY OF PHILO

In resonance with Plato's *Phaedrus*, Philo metaphorically conceptualizes the instruction of Jewish wisdom as an initiation into the mysteries.[16] He also describes piety as the "queen of virtues" within Mosaic legislation and possessed by those worthy of the knowledge of God (Philo, *Spec.* 4.135, 147).[17] Philo's adoption of the Greek virtue of piety, a term foreign to most of the Septuagint beyond 4 Maccabees,[18] served Philo's broader agenda of building solidarity among Alexandrian Jewish intellectuals.[19] As John J. Collins has observed, "Any group that holds unusual views is inevitably under pressure to establish its plausibility, not only to win the respect of outsiders, but primarily to maintain the allegiance of its own members."[20] By demonstrating that the Jewish constitution (πολιτεία) embodied Greek civic ideals including piety, Philo also sought to undercut malicious stereotypes of Jews being spread by such intellectuals as the Alexandrian

---

15. Van Nuffelen, *Rethinking the Gods*, 37. See esp. Plutarch, *Is. Os.*, 45.369B–C, Lucian, *Fug.* 8.

16. On the meaning of "the mysteries" in Philo, see Naomi G. Cohen, "The Mystery Terminology in Philo," in *Philo und das Neue Testament: Internationales Symposium zum Corpus Judaeo-Hellenisticum May 1–3, 2003*, ed. Roland Deines and Karl-Wilhelm Niebuhr (Tübingen: Mohr Siebeck, 2004), 173–88.

17. Philo also describes piety as "the greatest" (*Praem.* 53); "the leading and greatest virtue" (*Spec.* 4.97); "the finest and most profitable" (*Mos.* 1.146); and "the source of the virtues" (*Decal.* 52). See further Gregory E. Sterling, "'The Queen of the Virtues': Piety in Philo of Alexandria," *SPhiloA* 18 (2006): 103–24, esp. 120.

18. See Prov 13:11 (where there is no Hebrew equivalent), Isa 11:2, and 33:6 (where the Hebrew has יראת יהוה, "fear of the LORD"). See Werner Foerster, "εὐσεβής, εὐσέβεια, εὐσεβέω," *TDNT* 7:179.

19. For an overview of the rhetorical situation of Philo's treatises in Alexandrian politics, see David Dawson, *Allegorical Readers and Cultural Revision in Ancient Alexandria* (Berkeley: University of California Press, 1992), 113–26. Dawson identifies the immediate audience of Philo's apologetic representation of Judaism as Philo's fellow intellectual Jews rather than curious or sympathetic non-Jews.

20. John J. Collins, *Between Athens and Jerusalem: Jewish Identity in the Hellenistic Diaspora*, 2nd ed. (Grand Rapids, MI: Eerdmans, 2000), 2.

grammarian Apion.[21] Such anti-Jewish aspersion characterized Jews as lacking any legitimate status within Alexandria, being nothing more than atheists, misanthropes, and culturally inferior barbarians (see Josephus, *C. Ap.* 2.4, 12, 14). Let us now observe how Philo trades upon the symbolic capital associated with claims to piety and mystery terminology in order to bolster his apologetic appeal.

Turning to Philo's allegorical commentary on Gen 3:24–4:1, *On the Cherubim*, we can observe the discursive juxtaposition of mystery terminology, piety, and knowledge about the divine:

> When we intend to speak about the conception of and giving birth to virtues, let the superstitious [δεισιδαίμονες] block their ears and depart; for we teach each of the divine mysteries [τελετὰς θείας] to the initiates worthy of the most sacred mysteries [τοὺς τελετῶν ἀξίους τῶν ἱερωτάτων μύστας]; they are the ones who practice a true and really unadorned piety [τὴν ἀληθῆ καὶ οὖσαν ὄντως ἀκαλλώπιστον εὐσέβειαν], without vanity. We will not lead as *hierophants* [ἱεροφαντήσομεν] those who are in the power of incurable evil and measure what is pure and holy with vanity of words [τύφῳ ῥημάτων], stickiness of verbiage [ὀνομάτων γλισχρότητι], and pedantry of customs [τερθρείας ἐθῶν], and nothing else. (Philo, *Cher.* 42, my translation)

According to Philo, Jews possess their own "sacred mysteries" that produce a genuine piety among their initiates. Philo proceeds to explain the allegorical meaning of why Scripture describes none of the patriarchs as "knowing" their wives as Adam "knew his wife Eve" (Gen 4:1). According to Philo, this implies that the patriarchs' wives were not impregnated by their husbands but by God (*Cher.* 45–47). Moreover, the women collectively represent virtue and demonstrate that virtue ultimately receives its divine seed, its generative principle, from God, who impregnates virtue into human souls (44–46, 52). Philo, "having been initiated into the greater mysteries of Moses" (μυηθεὶς τὰ μεγάλα μυστήρια, 49), is privy to this secret wisdom. Equipped with "the most beautiful of all possessions, the knowledge of the Cause and of virtue" (48), Jewish initiates can confidently progress toward lives of virtue and piety.

Philo's conceptualization of Jewish instruction as both an initiation into the mysteries and productive of true piety coalesces to create a Judaism

---

21. See Philo of Alexandria, *On Virtues: Introduction, Translation, and Commentary*, trans. Walter T. Wilson, PACS 3 (Leiden: Brill, 2011), 33–34.

plausible to a cultured Hellenistic society.²² As David Dawson observes, "Philo uses this elitist language of the Greek mysteries to convince his Hellenized Jewish readership that the pinnacle of Greco-Roman religious culture was now available in the form of their very own Jewish scripture—if only they could understand its deeper meaning and significance."²³

Furthermore, Philo's rhetoric of piety and metaphorical use of mystery distinguishes his knowledge of the divine from others. Naomi Cohen has identified Philo's "superstitious" opponents as "fundamental-literalists" whose critical resistance to Philo's teaching and authority clearly agitated the philosopher.²⁴ Within this polemical contest over the right interpretation of the Septuagint, Philo's claim to piety functions to differentiate his instruction from that of other rival teachers, whom he denigrates as inferior. Philo's evocation of mystery terminology also elevates the authority of his own authorial voice. Not only does Philo's rhetoric present himself as communicating with philosophical mastery but also as instructing with the gravitas of a *hierophant*. Hence, Philo's deployment of piety and mystery metaphors effectively monopolizes the cultural prestige associated with the expertise of philosophers and hierophants, thus legitimating his particular understanding of an ideal Judaism.

PLUTARCH'S REVERENT READING OF MYSTERIES

Similar to Philo, Plutarch presents his interpretation of the divine as constituting piety or reverence (ὁσιότης).²⁵ In *On Isis and Osiris*, Plutarch does not merely metaphorically conceptualize the instruction of philosophy as an initiation.²⁶ Rather, he turns directly toward the sacred stories (ἱεροὶ

---

22. Cf. Philo, *Spec.* 1.319–323, for Philo's hostile criticism of ancient mysteries as lacking virtue and truth. On Philo's seemingly paradoxical attitude toward mysteries, see esp. Van Nuffelen, *Rethinking the Gods*, 201–5.

23. Dawson, *Allegorical Readers*, 121.

24. Cohen, "Mystery Terminology in Philo," 186.

25. For Plutarch, ὁσιότης carries a close valence to εὐσέβεια. On the interchangeably of these terms, see Sterling, "Queen of the Virtues," 112–13 n. 48; see also Plato's *Euthyphro*. Cf. Plutarch, *De superstitione*, where εὐσέβεια, rather than ὁσιότης, is the golden mean between atheism and superstition (*Superst.* 14.171F).

26. In other works, Plutarch employs this mystery metaphor; see Plutarch, *Tranq. an.* 77C–E; *Virt. prof.* 81D–E. See Geert Roskam, "'And a Great Silence Filled the Temple…': Plutarch on the Connections between Mystery Cults and Philosophy," in *Estudios Sobre Plutarco: Misticismo y religiones místéricas en la obra de Plutarco*;

λόγοι), ascetic practices, and rites associated with the mysteries of Isis and Osiris as depositories of ancient wisdom. In *On Isis and Osiris,* Plutarch argues that the stories of Osiris's death and afterlife and of Isis's struggle against Typhon should be properly interpreted as allegories detailing middle-Platonic metaphysics. According to Daniel S. Richter, Plutarch appropriates these sacred stories in order to show "the priority of Greek philosophy over Egyptian cult."[27] Of interest to this essay is how Plutarch distinguishes his expertise from that of popular opinions that produce superstition and atheism:

> Thus men make use of consecrated symbols [συμβόλοις ... καθιερωμένοις], some employing symbols that are obscure, but others those that are clearer, in guiding the intelligence toward divine things, though not without a certain hazard. For some go completely astray and become engulfed in superstition [δεισιδαιμονίαν]; and others, while they fly from superstition as from a quagmire, on the other hand unwittingly fall, as it were, over a precipice into atheism [ἀθεότητα]. Wherefore in the study of these matters it is especially necessary that we adopt, as our guide into these mysteries [μυσταγωγὸν], the reasoning [λόγον] that comes from philosophy [ἐκ φιλοσοφίας] and consider reverently [ὁσίως διανοεῖσθαι] each one of the things said and done. (*Is. Os.* 67–68.378A–B [Babbit, LCL])

Plutarch describes philosophical reasoning as having the inside track on truth as our mystagogue, revealing hidden wisdom to her initiates. It is *only* a philosophical reading of the mystery rites that enables reverent reflection and true devotion to Isis.[28] Philosophy and reverence therefore go hand in hand.[29]

Actas del VII Simposio Español sobre Plutarco (Palma de Mallorca, 2–4 de noviembre de 2000), ed. Aurelio Pérez Jiménez and Francesc Casadesús Bordoy (Madrid: Ediciones Clásicas, 2001), 221–32.

27. Daniel S. Richter, "Plutarch on Isis and Osiris: Text, Cult, and Cultural Appropriation," *TAPA* 131 (2001): 191–216, esp. 194.

28. See esp. Plutarch, *Is. Os.* 3.352C, where Plutarch describes true devotees of Isis (Ἰσιακός) as those who examine the rites and stories of Isis with philosophical reasoning.

29. See also Plutarch, *Is. Os.* 2.352A; 11.355C–D. In the latter reference, Plutarch describes his philosophical reading as *the singular* reverent manner (ὁσίως) of understanding sacred lore.

Plutarch's reclamation of sacred lore and redescription of piety according to his middle-Platonic cosmological principles distinguishes his knowledge of the divine—or what could be described as his "intellectual goods"—from competing philosophers and other religious experts of this day, including mystagogues. Plutarch is careful to point out that it is not just *any* philosophical reading that will lead you to the truth about the gods; indeed, there are many other Stoic, Pythagorean, and Platonic interpretations of the Isis lore available as documented in *On Isis and Osiris*. Rather, it is *his* interpretation that best unpacks the virtues and dualistic cosmology hidden in these stories and rites (*Is Os.* 45.369A–B; 64.377A–B). For Plutarch, sacred stories and rites are pedagogical, not propitiatory. That is to say, the mythical symbols found in these stories and rites should direct our minds to contemplate "the truth about the gods" and the cosmos (*Is. Os.* 2.351F–352A). According to Plutarch, competing views of the divine are less philosophically rigorous at best, and superstitious or atheistic at worst, but by no means do they constitute true reverence or piety.

Both Philo and Plutarch, then, attempt to persuade their audiences of the legitimacy of their own philosophical understanding of the divine by trading upon the symbolic capital associated with ancient mysteries, whether referring to them directly or metaphorically. By rhetorically locating their philosophical tenets within the cultural domain of the mysteries, these philosophers sought to monopolize the symbolic capital ascribed to mysteries, capitalizing upon the positive value associated with their alluring secrecy and ascribed ancient insight into the nature of the cosmos. The same could be suggested about 1 Tim 3:16.

The Mystery of Pastoral Piety

When we read 1 Tim 3:16 alongside Philo and Plutarch, we can begin to appreciate how "the mystery of piety" distinguishes and legitimates the author's truth about the divine. Like Philo and Plutarch, 1 Timothy's description of the divine stands in tension with the prevailing cultural opinions about the gods. Like Philo, 1 Timothy promotes the virtue of εὐσέβεια as characteristic of the Christian assembly in order to reassure his audience of the legitimacy of the "spiritual goods" associated with those beliefs and practices promoted by the author. Like both philosophers, 1 Timothy trades upon the cultural appeal of mysteries to distinguish his conception of the divine from others.

Scholars have already recognized that the Pastoral Epistles evidence a deep familiarity with terms and concepts from the cultural domain of philosophy, including use of medical imagery associated with philosophical psychagogy,[30] stereotypical invective against sophists,[31] and a conscription of the so-called philosophical cardinal virtues.[32] Given the Pastoral Epistles' broad engagement with this philosophical discourse, it becomes all the more imperative to read the constellation of piety and mystery terminology found in 1 Tim 3:16 as appropriating analogous strategies of legitimization at home within the cultural domain of ancient philosophy, as evidenced in Philo and Plutarch.

First Timothy 3:14–16 has been described as providing the heartbeat that animates the epistle's paraenetic instructions toward virtue and order in the household of God.[33] Positioned between the author's descriptions of ideal leaders (1 Tim 3:1–13) and threatening false teachers (1 Tim 4:1–5), the "mystery of piety" defines the character and behavior of the true Christian assembly. In the verses that follow, the author admonishes his audience against having anything to do with "irreverent and silly myths" but instead to "train yourself in piety [εὐσέβειαν]" (1 Tim 4:7). This admonition resonates with Plutarch's differentiation between his reverent reading of sacred stories and the misunderstanding of the superstitious masses. Furthermore, in 1 Tim 6:3–5, the author disparages the empty piety of his inscribed opponents whose false teachings obscure one's knowledge of the divine and produce vice. Similar to the self-representations of Philo and Plutarch, the author as Paul presents himself as a proprietor of true piety that corresponds to a definitive understanding of the divine (and of Paul), one that trumps the opinions of the masses and other competing religious experts. So, 1 Timothy resonates with the rhetoric of piety within the cul-

---

30. E.g., Abraham J. Malherbe, "Medical Imagery in the Pastoral Epistles," in *Texts and Testaments: Critical Essays on the Bible and Early Church Fathers; A Volume in Honor of Stuart Dickson Currie*, ed. W. Eugene March (San Antonio, TX: Trinity University Press, 1980), 19–35; repr. in Abraham J. Malherbe, *Paul and the Popular Philosophers* (Minneapolis: Fortress, 1989) 121–37.

31. E.g., Robert J. Karris, "The Background and Significance of the Polemic of the Pastoral Epistles," *JBL* 92 (1973): 549–64.

32. See, e.g., Stephen C. Mott, "Greek Ethics and Christian Conversion: The Philonic Background of Titus II 10–14 and III 3–7," *NovT* 20 (1978): 22–48.

33. See William D. Mounce, *Pastoral Epistles*, WBC 46 (Nashville: Nelson, 1999), 214.

tural domain of philosophy in its insistence that a correct understanding of the divine is essential for true piety.

I further suggest that the author's capitalization of the prestige of terms and concepts associated with the authoritative status and expertise of philosophers and mystagogues may have functioned to assure audiences of the cultural legitimacy of the Christian faith, in which both piety and mysteries find their culmination, as we saw with Philo. Furthermore, the author's choice of terms and imagery were possibly received as signaling his expertise and philosophical competency among audiences familiar with the various philosophers that occupied the civic space competing for the public's attention and patronage. Thus, the author represents himself as precisely the type of authoritative figure who can and ought to teach about matters including virtue and the nature of the divine.

Conclusion

In this essay I have suggested that 1 Tim 3:16 establishes its own contentious position within a marketplace of competing claims about piety and the nature of the divine. The author reappropriates an elite philosophical discourse that functioned to distinguish philosophers' intellectual goods over against other competing intellectuals and religious experts. Both the author's rhetoric of piety and conceptualization of the Christological hymn as a mystery serve to legitimate not only the teaching but also the authorial voice of the author for audiences habituated to discern the symbolic capital or cultural prestige associated with such terms and concepts. This short foray into reading 1 Timothy alongside a broader historical scope of tactics of persuasion employed by contemporary philosophers demonstrates the fresh interpretative horizons and questions made possible by such a mode of analysis.

Nuptial Imagery, Christian Devotion, and the Marriage Debate in Late Roman Society*

Karl Shuve

In his groundbreaking monograph *The Cult of the Saints*, Peter Brown shattered the perception that offering devotion to the relics of holy Christians was a "vulgar" or "popular" phenomenon, demonstrating the manifold ways in which the religious "elite"—by which he means well-educated and well-born bishops and ascetics—participated in a massive cultural transformation that positioned the dead bodies of saints as the link between heaven and earth.[1] Central to Brown's critique is the notion that the "elite"/"popular" binary is little more than a ruse that is "rarely, if ever, concerned to explain religious change other than among the elite."[2] By masterfully demonstrating the ways in which the veneration of dead bodies broke "most of the imaginative boundaries which ancient men had placed between heaven and earth," Brown highlights the implausibility of the cult of the saints having been borne aloft on what he calls "the lazy ocean of 'popular belief.'"[3] He instead opts to consider the rise of these cultic practices as "part of a great whole—the lurching forward of an increasing proportion of late antique society toward radically new forms of reverence."[4]

---

* A portion of this essay has been reproduced by permission of Oxford University Press from Karl Shuve, *The Song of Songs and the Fashioning of Identity in Early Latin Christianity* (Oxford: Oxford University Press, 2016), 138–72.

1. Peter Brown, *The Cult of the Saints: Its Rise and Function in Latin Christianity* (Chicago: University of Chicago Press, 1981), esp. 1–22.

2. Ibid., 18.

3. Ibid., 21.

4. Ibid., 21–22.

In this essay I would like to draw on Brown's theoretical apparatus in order to rethink another important aspect of early Christian devotion, one predicated on a similar redrawing of the social map, but to do so, as it were, from the opposite direction. By the late fourth century, nuptial imagery, drawn particularly from the Song of Songs, had become ubiquitous in Christian discourse for conceptualizing union with God. In modern scholarship, this discourse is frequently portrayed as the province of the religious "elite"—or "specialists," to borrow a carefully-articulated term from Stanley Stowers—who alone possessed both the education and the leisure to pursue contemplation of the divine.[5] For example, the noted medievalist Ann Matter traces the veritable explosion of early medieval Latin commentaries on the Song of Songs to what she calls the "rarified intellectual atmosphere" of Origen's Alexandria, which was disconnected from the concerns of ordinary Christians.[6] But this is to overlook the way in which nuptial imagery, in general, and the Song of Songs, in particular, became bound up with debates over the goodness of marriage and the appropriateness of chastity in fourth-century Christian society, particularly in the West; these debates cut across our imagined binary of popular/elite.

As David Hunter has so compellingly shown in his study of the Jovinianist controversy, which unfolded at Rome in the 390s CE, the process by which Christians came to rank virginity above marriage in the hierarchy of goods was a slow and gradual one.[7] The triad of family, wealth, and *honores* was deeply ingrained in the Roman psyche, from the middling Christian families of Ambrose's Milan to unimaginably wealthy senators like Petronius Probus.[8] Dissent was expressed from multiple fields within

---

5. See Stanley Stowers, "The Religion of Plant and Animal Offerings versus the Religion of Meanings, Essences, and Textual Mysteries," in *Ancient Mediterranean Sacrifice*, ed. Jennifer Wright Knust and Zsuzsanna Várhelyi (New York: Oxford University Press, 2011), 35–56.

6. E. Ann Matter, *The Voice of My Beloved: The Song of Songs in Western Medieval Christianity* (Philadelphia: University of Pennsylvania Press, 1990), 20. We find a similar emphasis on the scholastic/contemplative concerns of Origen in Ann Astell, *The Song of Songs in the Middle Ages* (Ithaca, NY: Cornell University Press, 1995), and Denys Turner, *Eros and Allegory: Medieval Exegesis of the Song of Songs* (Kalamazoo, MI: Cistercian, 1995).

7. David G. Hunter, *Marriage, Celibacy, and Heresy in Ancient Christianity: The Jovinianist Controversy* (Oxford: Oxford University Press, 2007).

8. For an illuminating discussion of Probus's religiosity, see John Matthews, *Western Aristocracies and Imperial Court A.D. 364–425* (Oxford: Clarendon, 1975), 195–97.

society: Ambrose's parishioners confronted him for withdrawing eligible women from the marriage economy by consecrating them as virgins; the monk Jovinian circulated a treatise in Rome that posited the equality of virgins, widows, and married women; the senator Pammachius pulled Jerome's *Against Jovinian* from circulation and demanded from him an account of the goodness of marriage; and Julian, the bishop of Eclanum in Campania, labeled Augustine a Manichee for his assertion that sexual expression is tainted by carnal concupiscence.[9] We cannot imagine this social conflict in binary terms.

We would do best, I argue, to adopt Brown's perspective and view the transformation as "the lurching forward of an increasing proportion of late antique society" toward a radically new understanding of marriage and, indeed, of Roman identity itself, which was predicated on the exemplarity of ascetic practice.[10] The physical *integritas* of virgins came to represent the spiritual purity demanded of all Christians, rendering soteriology unintelligible outside of a worldview that idealized renunciation. This transformation did not, however, represent a whole-cloth rejection of the traditional understanding of marriage. Indeed, the opposite was the case. The ascetic life came to be portrayed as a kind of marriage, except that the practitioner was espoused to Christ rather than to an ordinary human being. This held particularly true for women. In the late fourth century in Italy—and, it appears, North Africa as well—female virgins were veiled with the *flammeum* in an elaborate consecration ceremony that established them as true "brides of Christ."[11] The Song of Songs was one of the key resources used to buttress this new ideal of spiritualized marriage: verses

---

9. Ambrose, *Virginit.* 1.1–7.41; Jovinian *apud* Jerome, *Jov.* 1.3; Jerome, *Epist.* 48.2 (for Pammachius's pulling of his work from circulation); Julian *apud* Augustine, *C. Jul. op. imp.* 4.5.

10. Brown, *Cult of the Saints*, 21.

11. Raymond d'Izarny, "Mariage et consécration virginale au IVe siècle," *VSpir-Supp* 24 (1953): 92–107; Hunter, *Jovinianist Controversy*, 224–30. Recent scholarship has begun to examine the role of dress, particularly women's dress, in the construction of early Christian identities. See especially Carly Daniel-Hughes, *The Salvation of the Flesh in Tertullian of Carthage: Dressing for the Resurrection* (New York: Palgrave Macmillan, 2011); Kristi Upson-Saia, *Early Christian Dress: Gender, Virtue, and Authority*, RSAH 3 (New York: Routledge, 2011); and Kate Wilkinson, *Women and Modesty in Late Antiquity* (Cambridge: Cambridge University Press, 2015).

were chanted as part of the veiling ceremony itself and were employed by advocates in sermons, letters, and treatises.[12]

In what follows, I will undertake a close analysis of a single text—*Isaac, or The Soul*—which was originally delivered as a series of homilies by Ambrose, bishop of Milan, one of the most influential proponents of ascetic ideology in the late Roman West.[13] My aim is to show how in this text Ambrose uses the Song of Songs, and by extension the nuptial metaphor itself, to renegotiate the social landscape and redefine what it meant both to be "Roman" and "Christian."[14] *Isaac, or The Soul*, is a particularly instructive text for several reasons. First, it is usually treated as the *locus classicus* of Ambrose's "mystical theology"—that is, as a kind of purely intellectual exercise in achieving union with the divine, one divorced from the vicissitudes of Milanese ecclesiastical politics.[15] This is buttressed by demonstrations of Ambrose's heavy reliance upon Plotinus and Origen, revealing his indebtedness to Greek philosophical notions of the soul's ascent.[16] But a careful investigation of Ambrose's use of his

---

12. On the antiphonal chanting of the Song of Songs in the ceremony, see Nathalie Henry, "The Song of Songs and the Liturgy of the *Velatio* in the Fourth Century: From Literary Metaphor to Liturgical Reality," in *Continuity and Change in Christian Worship: Papers Read at the 1997 Summer Meeting and the 1998 Winter Meeting of the Ecclesiastical History Society*, ed. R. N. Swanson, SCH 35 (Woodbridge: Boydell, 1999), 18–28. Jerome, in his letter to the aristocratic virgin Demetrias, notes that Song 1:4 and Ps 45:13 were both recited at the veiling ceremony (*Epist.* 130.2).

13. For the homiletic origins of this treatise, see Pierre Courcelle, *Recherches sur les Confessions de saint Augustin* (Paris: de Bocard, 1950), 122–36.

14. Ambrose's attempt to use the nuptial metaphor to articulate a new account of Christian identity was by no means restricted to *Isaac, or The Soul*. For the broader context, see my book, *Song of Songs and the Fashioning of Identity*, 109–72.

15. A prime example of this can be found in Bernard McGinn, *The Foundations of Mysticism: Origins to the Fifth Century* (New York: Crossroad, 1991), 202–16, who separates the "ecclesiological mysticism" of *Isaac, or The Soul*, from the ascetic focus of the treatises on virginity. We find a rare example of resistance to treating *Isaac, or The Soul*, as a speculative work in Marcia Colish, *Ambrose's Patriarchs: Ethics for the Common Man* (South Bend, IN: University of Notre Dame Press, 2005), 87–89, where it is argued that the treatise offers an articulation of virtue ethics for the general Christian community. I part ways with Colish, however, in her claim that *Isaac, or The Soul*, is anti-ascetic, which I believe is strongly contradicted by the evidence.

16. The most famous example is Courcelle, *Recherche*, 106–38, but see also Pierre Hadot, "Platon et Plotin dans trois sermons de saint Ambroise," *REL* 34 (1956): 202–20; Goulven Madec, *Saint Ambroise et la philosophie* (Paris: Études augustiniennes,

sources, particularly Origen, reveals that he is interested in defining the Christian life in ascetic terms. Secondly, the text has its roots in public discourse, and indeed it appears to have been directed to catechumens. It is true that this group would likely not have included the *humiliores* in Milan. As Leslie Dossey, following Ramsey MacMullen, has noted in her study of North African sermons, urban bishops spoke frequently to an upper-class audience consisting of "property owners, merchants, lawyers, and a smattering of artisans."[17] But it does consist of a much broader range of people than we might ordinarily consider to be recipients of instruction in the Song of Songs.

I thus find useful the distinction that Stowers has made between "specialist" and "nonspecialist" religion. Admittedly, his focus is quite different from mine, since he is interested in disaggregating theories of sacrifice from an "underlying and un-theorized practical system of sacrificial exchange," and my project lies squarely in the realm of theory and does not intersect directly with any underlying practice. But his binary provides such a precise way of conceptualizing religious expertise that I have employed it here. He defines these specialist producers as those belonging to the "perhaps 2 percent or less of people who were literate enough to produce and authoritatively interpret complex, written texts."[18] Study of the history of the Song's interpretation is usually confined to this group of privileged clergy and ascetics who composed interpretive and dogmatic texts and circulated them within bounded networks.[19] The problem is not that scholars have chosen to focus on texts produced by these specialists—for there are no others to examine—but rather that they have presumed that the Song was an esoteric text to be consumed only by those within this group. My inquiry may not allow us to glimpse how nuptial devotion was understood—if at all—by slaves or farmers, but it will allow us to see how a much broader share of Christians was expected to understand this text and apply it to their lives. Ambrose did not intend for the Song of Songs to be consumed

---

1974); McGinn, *Foundations of Mysticism*, 205–12; Lorenzo Taormina, "Sant' Ambrogio e Plotino," *MSLCA* 4 (1953): 41–85.

17. Leslie Dossey, *Peasant and Empire in Christian North Africa* (Berkeley: University of California Press, 2010), 152; cf. Ramsey MacMullen, *The Second Church: Popular Christianity AD 200–400*, WGRWSup 1 (Atlanta: Society of Biblical Literature, 2009).

18. Stowers, "Religion of Plant and Animal Offerings," 41.

19. See n. 6 above.

only by his fellow specialists; rather, he intended for it to shape the identities of all those who heard his preaching. Moreover, Ambrose employed the Song in the context of debate with those in his Milanese congregation who resisted his privileging of the ascetic life. We can thus catch strains of alternative visions of Christian identity in Ambrose's prose.

Two of Ambrose's earliest works—*On Virgins* and *On Virginity*—make it quite clear that many Milanese Christians were not enthusiastic about his promotion of consecrated virginity. This opposition is but a subtext in *On Virgins*, the earlier of the two. He laments that some young women who wish to be consecrated are held back by their mothers and bemoans the fact that despite singing the praises of virginity daily, "I accomplish nothing [*proficio nihil*]" (*Virg*. 1.10.57).[20] *On Virginity* is far more defensive in tone. It appears that certain parents who had allowed their daughters to take the veil from Ambrose later wished to have them married off to human spouses, and they were taken aback when the bishop declared that this would constitute adultery, a grave sin that would bar them from participating in the sacraments. He asserts that he has been accused of the "crime [*crimen*]" of "advis[ing] chastity [*suadeo castitatem*]"—a charge to which he can only reply, "I wish the results of so great a crime could be shown [*tanti criminis probaretur effectus*]" (*Virginit*. 5.24–25). There is a dialogic quality to Ambrose's early ascetic writings, which reveal a struggle between his own vision of the Christian life and that presupposed by what Brown has called the "'middling' persons" of the Milanese *populus*.[21]

Ambrose defends himself by arguing that virgins are "like the angels" and that they bring the heavenly life down to earth (*Virg*. 1.3.11).[22] Through the integrity of their holy bodies, the spiritual purity required of

---

20. Latin text for *De virginibus* and *De virginitate* is from Ambrose, *De Virginibus; De viduis; De virginitate; De institutione virginis; Exhortatio virginitatis*, ed. Franco Gori, SAEMO 14.1, 2 (Milan: Biblioteca Ambrosiana, 1989.). All translations in this paragraph are my own

21. Peter Brown, *Through the Eye of the Needle: Wealth, the Fall of Rome, and the Making of Christianity in the West, 350-550 AD* (Princeton: Princeton University Press, 2012), 125. He notes that there was no strong "aristocratic presence" in Milan, which was rather a "city of minor bureaucrats and of provision merchants." Surely it must have been these men and women of modest wealth who were Ambrose's interlocutors, for the transfer of property of one generation to the next, secured by the presence of legitimate heirs, would have been a particular concern to them.

22. Modified English translation from Boniface Ramsey, *Ambrose*, ECF (London: Routledge, 1997), 76.

the souls of all Christians is made manifest. The text on which Ambrose relies the most in describing the purity demanded of virgins is the Song of Songs. He focuses particularly on images that stress the bride's enclosure: she is a "garden enclosed and fountain sealed" (Song 4:12) and protected by a "wall ... [with] silver towers" (Song 8:9) (*Virg.* 1.8.49 [Ramsey]); the virgin must wait in her bedchamber for Christ to come "and put his hand through the keyhole (*per prospectum*)" (Song 5:4) (*Virginit.* 11.60). The Song also warns of the dangers of embodied existence. In Platonic fashion, he reads the "chariot of Aminadab" (Song 6:12) as revealing that when "our soul is joined to the body [*anima nostra dum iungitur corpori*], it is like someone who seeks a charioteer [*aurigam*] and guide [*rectorem*] for the raging horses [*equorum frumentium*] of his chariot" (*Virginit.* 15.94).

In both works, although particularly in *On Virginity*, it is clear that Ambrose is interested in the *bodies* of virgins, because they function as a visible representation of the invisible soul. Although he uses the Song in his defense of virginity, this is a text that speaks to all Christians. We must bear this in mind as we turn to *Isaac, or The Soul*, a text in which he asserts that souls "do not know covenants of wedlock or the way of bodily union [*animae norunt coniugiorum foedera et usus copulae corporalis*], but they are like the angels in heaven [*sed sunt sicut angeli in caelo*]" (*Isaac* 6.51).[23] The classification of *Isaac, or The Soul*, as a work of mystical theology has obscured its connection to the ascetic debates in Milan. As I hope to show through an analysis of Ambrose's use of the Song in this text, however, *Isaac, or The Soul*, deliberately extends the ascetic ideal onto the lives of *all* Christians.

Isaac, or The Soul, follows sequentially from Ambrose's *On Abraham* as part of a series of allegorical readings of the lives of the patriarchs. He portrays Isaac, the long-awaited offspring of Abraham and Sarah, as a type of Christ, "since there were prefigured [*figura praecesserit*] in him the birth and passion of the Lord" (*Isaac* 1.1). Sarah's conception of Isaac in sterility and extreme old age provides the groundwork for belief in the virgin birth, and the aborted sacrifice of Isaac foreshadows the crucifixion. But perhaps most important for Ambrose in this treatise is Isaac's union with

---

23. For this and the following citations of *Isaac, or The Soul*, the text is from CSEL 32.1; English translation is from Ambrose, *Seven Exegetical Works: Isaac, or The Soul; Death as a Good; Jacob and the Happy Life; Joseph; The Patriarchs; Flight from the World; The Prayer of Job and David*, trans. Michael P. McHugh, FC 65 (Washington, DC: Catholic University of America Press, 1972).

Rebecca, his "alien wife [*alienigenam sponsam*]" (1.1). Their marriage provides the pattern for the redemption of collective humanity and each individual soul, and he uses the Song of Songs to express the dynamics of this union. Isaac prepared himself for meeting Rebecca, whom Ambrose takes to be "either the Church or the soul [*vel ecclesia vel anima*]," by going into a field "to become estranged from himself [*abalienare*]" (1.1–2).[24] The *sapiens*, as Ambrose calls Isaac, knows that he must "separate himself [*segregare se*] from fleshly pleasures [*a voluptatibus carnis*], lift up his soul [*elevare animam*], and draw away from the body [*a corpore abducere*]" (1.1). Only in so doing can one truly recapture something of true humanity. This fleshly covering—Ambrose will later call the body an item of clothing (*vestimentum*) that is extraneous to human identity (2.3)—with all its attendant desires and inclinations must be disciplined and ultimately left behind. The body is as much at issue in this treatise as is the soul.

But to see how deeply the currents of ascetic ideology run in *Isaac, or The Soul*, we must be prepared to enter into Ambrose's symbolic universe. The identification of the *mens* of the *competens* with the "garden enclosed, fountain sealed" of Song 4:12 at the beginning of the treatise is freighted with meaning for Ambrose, and its significance would have been apparent to anyone who had heard the bishop preach over the past decade. This was the language that Ambrose had used with such great effect to praise the consecrated virgin and to exhort her to enclose herself—metaphorically and physically—and thereby to protect herself from the pollution of the world. Ambrose was now clearly gesturing that the virginal life was the pattern for the Christian life. Again, the ascetic undertones of the allusion to Luke 20:35–36—souls do not know wedlock and are "like the angels in heaven"—are unmistakable; in his *On Virgins*, as noted earlier, Ambrose had spoken of consecrated virgins "who are coupled with the Lord of angels" in precisely the same way (*Virg.* 1.3.11). The result of this union is a kind of mystical pregnancy, in which the soul, as a "spiritual womb [*utero intellegibili*]," receives the "seeds [*semenibus*]" of Christ when she "rose to open to my brother" (Song 5:5) (*Isaac* 6.53). This idea of spiritual intercourse that leads to a pregnancy of soul, connected to Song 5:5, is derived

---

24. My translation. McHugh renders the infinitive *abalienare* as "to meditate" (see Ambrose, *Seven Exegetical Works*, 11). Though perhaps less awkward, this does not capture the sense of separation indicated by the verb, which clearly anticipates his discussion of the soul's struggle to separate from the body. The use of *abalienare* without a direct or indirect object is also highly unusual.

with little change from *Virg.* 11.60–66, which was directed specifically at female virgins.

To get a real sense of the degree to which the problems of corporeality infused the Milanese bishop's interpretation of the Song of Songs, it will be helpful to compare his treatment of the poem's first chapter with that of Origen.[25] For Ambrose, the very first words of the Song, "Let him kiss me with the kisses of his mouth," express a desperate and protracted longing for union with Christ. "Think either upon the Church [*considera vel ecclesia*]," he begins, "in suspense over many ages at the coming of the Lord, long promised her through the prophets [*iam diu promisso sibi per prophetas*]. Or think upon the soul [*vel animam*], who is lifting herself up from the body [*elevans se a corpore*] and rejecting indulgence and fleshly delights and pleasures [*abdicatis luxuria atque deliciis voluptatibusque carnalibus*]" (*Isaac* 3.8, modified). It is the soul, in particular, that draws Ambrose's attention, which "desired to be infused with God's presence [*infusionem sibi divinae praesentiae*] and has desired, too, the grace of the Word of salvation, and has wasted away, because he is coming late, and has been struck down, as though *wounded with love* [*quasi vulneratam caritatis*] (Song 5:8), since she cannot endure his delays" (3.8).

The debt to Origen's *Commentary* is patent. Ambrose has absorbed the profound sense of longing that Origen sees in the bride's opening petition: "Because the bridegroom delays his coming for so long, she, grieved with longing for his love [*sollicitari eam desiderio amoris eius*], is pining at home and doing all she can to bring herself at last to see her spouse [*quatenus possit aliquando videre sponsum suum*], and to enjoy his kisses [*osculis eius perfrui*]" (*Comm. Cant.* 1.1.3).[26] The parallels can, however, be drawn even more closely. In Ambrose's terse description of the church's "suspense over many ages at the coming of the Lord," we see the influence of Origen's much fuller account of the church enduring the mediation of

---

25. Even though Ambrose read Origen in Greek, in most instances, I will cite from the Latin translation of Origen's *Commentary* by Rufinus (ca. 410 CE), since it is the only complete extant text available (to Song 2:15). Where Greek fragments are available for the passage in question, I will cite those, since they will inevitably be much closer to the text Ambrose had before him.

26. Latin text from Origen, *Commentaire sur le cantique des cantiques: Texte de la version Latine de rufin*, trans. Luc Brésard and Henri Crouzel with Marcel Borret, SC 375 (Paris: Cerf, 1991); English translation from Origen, *The Song of Songs: Commentary and Homilies*, trans. R. P. Lawson, ACW 26 (Westminster, MD: Newman, 1957).

first the law and then the prophets, thrilling in the knowledge that the "age is almost ended [*saeculum iam paene finitum*]" and yet impatient for a direct encounter with the Word (1.1.7). Even more specifically than this, Ambrose follows Origen in invoking the wound of love from Song 5:8 to describe the depths of the bride's desire (1.1.4).

But there is one crucial difference between how Ambrose and Origen speak of the soul. For Origen, the soul is prepared for union with Christ by receiving the "betrothal gifts [*dotalia munera*]" of "natural law and reason and free will [*lex naturae et rationabilis sensu ac libertas arbitrii*]," which parallels the church's reception of the "volumes of the Law and the Prophets [*legis et prophetarum volumina*]" (*Comm. Cant.* 1.1.9). Ambrose, however, constructs the parallel between the church and the soul rather differently. For him, the soul has an active rather than passive role in her own preparation, which she undertakes by "lifting herself up from the body" (*Isaac* 3.8). Where Origen has a pedagogical focus, Ambrose has an ascetic one.

The contrast appears even more clearly in Ambrose's interpretation of Song 1:4, "The king has brought me into his chamber." For Origen, this verse signifies the soul's sharing in the "governing part [ἡγεμονικόν]" of Christ, drawing on the Pauline dictum, "We have the mind of Christ that we may know the things that are given to us from God (1 Cor 2:16)."[27] The soul is inducted into God's hidden knowledge, receiving a revelation akin to that of Paul when he "had been rapt to the third heaven, and thence to Paradise, and had heard unspeakable words that it is not lawful for a man to utter (2 Cor 12:2, 4)" (*Comm. Cant.* 1.5.6). Ambrose, surely under the influence of Origen, also compares entering into the chamber with Paul's rapture, but he inflects it very differently. He focuses on Paul's claim that he did not know "whether he had been caught up in the body or out of the body (cf. 2 Cor 12:3–4)" (*Isaac* 4.11), a portion of the quotation that does not appear in Rufinus's translation.[28] But it is a crucial phrase for Ambrose, who asserts that the Apostle's "soul had risen up from the body [*adsurrexerat enim anima eius de corpore*], had withdrawn from the vitals and bonds of the flesh [*a visceribus et vinculis carnis abduxerati*], and had lifted herself up [*elevaverat*]" (4.11). This is precisely what it means to enter into

---

27. Origen *apud* Procopius, *Comm. Cant.* 1.4 (PG 17:253C).

28. It is possible that Origen cited the whole of vv. 2–4 and that Rufinus abridged it, allowing v. 3 to drop out, but there is no compelling reason to think this. Even if it is the case, v. 3, which is central for Ambrose, would have been peripheral to Origen.

the *cubiculum*: "Rising up from the body [*insurgens de corpore*], [the soul] becomes more distant from all [*ab omnibus fit remotior*], and she searches and seeks within herself [*intra semet*], if in any way she can pursue the divine [*divinum ... insequi*]" (4.11).

Ambrose then omits any consideration of Song 1:5 and passes directly to 1:6, keeping with the same theme of flight from the body. He asserts that the bride is to be thought of as "black and beautiful" (Song 1:5), because she has been "darkened by her fellowship with the body [*corporis societate fuscatam*]" (*Isaac* 4.13, modified). It is the "passions of the body [*corporis passions*]" and the "allurements of the flesh [*carnis inlecebrae*]" that have besieged her (4.13). This is strikingly different from Origen, for whom the Bride has been darkened, because she has "no illustrious nor enlightened fathers [ἐκ λαμπρῶν μηδὲ πεφωτισμένων πατέρων]."[29] When Origen turns to speak of the soul, he makes a general reference to the stain of sinfulness. Ambrose is entirely more specific than this. It is the body that casts a dark shadow over the gleaming brilliance of the soul (*Comm. Cant.* 2.1.56–7).

The Song of Songs was no esoteric text for Ambrose. Far from the rarefied intellectual environment of Alexandria, this poem was a tool in the service of self-definition that helped him extend the virginal ideal onto the whole of his congregation. We cannot know how thoroughly Ambrose's message was absorbed by his hearers, nor do we know if his interpretation of the Song itself was contested—these are the limitations of using "elite" or "specialist" writings to gain some purchase on "popular" or "nonspecialist" religion—but it was certainly his intention that the Song shape the ways in which his congregation thought about the right use of their bodies and the right expression of their desires.

---

29. Origen *apud* Procopius, *Comm. Cant.* 1.5 (PG 17:256B). For the English translation, see Origen, *Song of Songs*, 92.

Competing for the Competitors: Jewish and Christian Responses to Spectacle

Loren R. Spielman

Introduction

Both ancient and modern critics have derided the many festivals of the Roman Empire, with their flamboyant displays of excess and largesse as "bread and circuses," claiming that handouts and shows distracted the populace both from the cruel yoke of imperial rule and from more elevated civic and political life. Recent scholarship, on the other hand, has stressed that games and spectacles in the Roman Empire played a social function that transcended mere entertainment. The theater and the amphitheater operated as a sort of safety valve for the anxieties of both rich and poor, where the tensions of living under the threat of constant violence could be relaxed, and the crowd, watching the execution of prisoners and slaves, could take comfort in and affirm their status as free citizens. The events held at theaters, amphitheaters, circuses, and hippodromes were used by provincial elites to represent *Romanitas*, the very essence of being Roman.[1] The buildings themselves, often the first public structures constructed in a new or resettled Roman city, were powerful indicators of Roman identity.[2]

---

1. Keith Hopkins, *Death and Renewal*, SSRH 2 (Cambridge: Cambridge University Press, 1983); Thomas Wiedemann, *Emperors and Gladiators* (London: Routledge, 1992); Magnus Wistrand, *Entertainment and Violence in Ancient Rome: The Attitudes of Roman Writers of the First Century A.D.*, SGLG 56 (Göteborg: Acta Universitatis Gothoburgensis, 1992); Richard C. Beacham, *Spectacle Entertainments of Early Imperial Rome* (New Haven: Yale University Press, 1999); Alison Futrell, *Blood in the Arena: The Spectacle of Roman Power* (Austin: University of Texas Press, 2001).

2. Greg Woolf, *Becoming Roman: The Origins of Provincial Civilization in Gaul* (Cambridge: Cambridge University Press, 1998), 121.

Festivals and games served as arenas to express rivalries between cities and to promote civic solidarity. Attending the games and spectacles hosted by prominent citizens demonstrated a willingness to be counted among the Roman crowd. Since the seating in these entertainment structures was divided according to status and tickets were provided by patrons and voluntary organizations rather than by means of purchase, attending games and other spectacles also provided an unparalleled opportunity to express subgroup identities, whether as a client of a particular patron, a member of a guild, or a constituent of an ethnic or religious minority.[3]

Early Christianity and rabbinic Judaism came of age amid this culture of spectacular entertainment. The emerging leadership of both groups, the early church fathers and rabbis, faced similar challenges. As Christianity gained more adherents among the urban pagan populations of the Roman Empire during the second and third centuries CE, the overwhelming popularity of the spectacles and their rootedness in urban life became a significant thorn in the side of Christian theologians.[4] The more than thirty-five theaters, stadia, and amphitheaters built in Roman Palestine and the many references to them in Palestinian rabbinic literature demonstrate that, by the mid-third century, spectacle entertainments were as popular in Roman Palestine as they were in the rest of the Roman Empire, save perhaps for Rome and a few other Italian cities.[5] The important role which the theater and amphitheater played in the development of group and subgroup identities, let alone their extraordinary popularity, presented serious challenges to Jewish and Christian leaders who eschewed more traditional avenues for establishing personal authority. It must have been extremely difficult for them to compete with urban patrons who were

---

3. Garrett G. Fagan, *The Lure of the Arena: Social Psychology and the Crowd at the Roman Games* (Cambridge: Cambridge University Press, 2011); Louis Robert, *Les gladiateurs dans l'Orient grec* (Amsterdam: Hakkert, 1971), Inscription no. 48 mentions, for example, a Dionysiac association. Inscription no. 97 mentions a corporation of launderers. On ticketing in the arena, see Futrell, *Blood in the Arena*, 160–67.

4. Timothy D. Barnes, "Christians and the Theater," in *Roman Theater and Society: E. Togo Salmon Papers I*, ed. William J. Slater (Ann Arbor: University of Michigan Press, 2004), 161–81.

5. Zeev Weiss, *Public Spectacles in Roman and Late Antique Palestine* (Cambridge: Harvard University Press, 2014), esp. 57–66; Arthur Segal, *Theatres in Roman Palestine and Provincia Arabia* (Leiden: Brill, 1995); Martin Jacobs, "Theatres and Performances as Reflected in the Talmud Yerushalmi," in *Talmud Yerushalmi and Graeco-Roman Culture*, ed. Peter Schäfer, TSAJ 71 (Tübingen: Mohr Siebeck, 1998), 327–47.

responsible for the presentation of gladiator shows and beast hunts or with the city councilors who sponsored agonistic festivals.[6] As a result, the early church fathers and Palestinian rabbis were profoundly disturbed by the ways that theater entertainments and gladiatorial combat threatened to blur the very categories of religious and secular authority that both groups sought to differentiate and monopolize.

Since no biblical injunction expressly forbade attending theaters or other entertainment, Christian and Jewish scholars were forced to exert considerable creative energy developing exegetical and homiletical responses to the popularity of spectacles and shows among their coreligionists. Rooted in a shared language of Scripture, the strategies of the church fathers and the early rabbis intersected in interesting ways; at times, their critiques of the theater seized upon the same verses from the Bible. Reading the discourses of second- and third-century Christian apologists and orators alongside the dicta contained in second- and third-century rabbinic texts like the Mishnah, Tosefta, and the early midrash compilations reveals a remarkable confluence of scriptural language and moral ideology. Both groups essentially constituted orthodoxies, demanding a rigor that few others would have been able to uphold. In their eyes, Roman spectacles reeked of idolatry and perversion. The games were immoral distractions and bloody displays of unchecked power. Worst of all, their popularity consumed what little free time most urbanites could muster and drained the elite of resources that could have been directed towards other communal needs, such as the care of the poor.[7]

"Their Customs":
Theater as Foreign in Early Christian and Jewish Texts

The earliest Christian polemics against Roman spectacle appeared as brief asides in apologetic tracts, mostly as defense against pagan accusations of

---

6. Loren Spielman, "Sitting with Scorners: Jewish Attitudes toward Roman Spectacle Entertainment from the Herodian Period through the Muslim Conquest" (PhD diss., The Jewish Theological Seminary of America, 2010), 126–55; Weiss, *Public Spectacles*, 171–94.

7. Blake Leyerle, *Theatrical Shows and Ascetic Lives: John Chrysostom's Attack on Spiritual Marriage* (Berkeley: University of California Press, 2001), 33–36. On rabbinic attitudes toward charity, see Gregg E. Gardner, *The Origins of Organized Charity in Rabbinic Judaism* (Cambridge: Cambridge University Press, 2015).

cannibalism and murder. After refuting these ridiculous charges, Christian apologists like Tatian sought to point out their inherent hypocrisy.[8] In his *Oration to the Greeks*, Tatian turns the charge of cannibalism against his would-be detractors: "You slaughter animals for the purpose of eating their flesh," he exclaims, "and you purchase men to supply a cannibal banquet for the soul" (*Or. Graec.* 23).[9] In two brief paragraphs, he lashes out against every form of Roman entertainment: the duplicitous illusion of drama, the lewd and suggestive movements of dancers and mimes, the dangerous enchantment of music, and the bloodlust of spectators at gladiator shows. Men pretended to be women, even gods; they played murderers, adulterers, and madmen before a crowd that was held captive, mouths agape, transfixed in their gaze (23). Here Tatian collapses these disparate genres of spectacle entertainment—the theatrical and amphitheatrical events, athletics, pugilism, theater, and mime—into a single despicable category, a strategy that would eventually come to dominate the Christian approach to spectacle.

Tatian's conglomerative reproach of spectacle entertainment was a novelty. There had always been pagan critics of sport and spectacle, but their negative evaluation generally applied to only one form of entertainment. Rarely did they perceive spectacle entertainment as a generic category, as merely different forms of the same base instinct. So, for example, the Roman politician Pliny in his panegyric of the emperor Trajan could praise arena events for demonstrating the pinnacle of Roman virtue, yet rant about the immorality of pantomime dancers or the frenzy of the crowd at chariot races (*Pan.* 31.1, 34.4, 46.2).[10] Each event was worthy of its own attention, and Roman moralists saw very little similarity between the false representation of the theater stage and the very real drama of the arena floor.

Christian apologetics, on the other hand, held out spectacle entertainment *en masse* as the very antithesis of Christian piety and wore their separation from such events as a proud badge of difference. Tatian took up the argument that the Christian "philosophy" was older than "Greek practices." The Greeks had gotten all of their culture from barbarians: astron-

---

8. Ruth Webb, *Demons and Dancers: Performance in Late Antiquity* (Cambridge: Harvard University Press, 2008), 32. See Athenagoras, *Leg.* 35; Theophilus, *Autol.* 3:15.

9. Translations of Tatian adapted from Tatian, *Address to the Greeks*, trans. J. E. Ryland, *ANF* 2:65–82. English translation of Tertullian is adapted from Tertullian, *De Spectaclulis*, trans. T. R. Glover, LCL 250 (Cambridge: Harvard University Press, 1998). Translation of rabbinic texts are my own.

10. See also Wistrand, *Entertainment and Violence*, 11–13, 30.

omy from the Babylonians, magic from the Persians, geometry from the Egyptians, and the alphabet from the Phoenicians (*Or. Graec.* 1).[11] In a final word about the theater, Tatian remarks to the Greeks, "We leave you to these worthless things; and you, either believe your doctrines, or, like us, give up yours for ours" (24). Dwelling on the foreign or "barbarian" nature of the spectacles provided these early apologists with an opportunity to distinguish Christian culture from its Greek roots. They ignored the basic fact that Christians, who largely came from pagan roots themselves, might also engage in the very behaviors that Tatian and others chastised. Spectacles, like the rest of Greek and Roman culture, were wholly "other." One might describe their criticism of Roman theater and games as "externally directed," towards a culture in which they may have lived, but which they categorized as completely foreign.

A similar strategy can be found in the early rabbinic midrash known as the Mekilta de Arayot, which is found only as an interpolation in most manuscripts of the Sipra on Leviticus.[12] The Mekilta de Arayot comments on an apparent redundancy between two passages, Lev 18:3 and Deut 18:10–11. The verses from Deuteronomy prohibit various practices of divination on the grounds that, because the Canaanites devoted themselves to these abhorrent practices, God dispossessed them of the land and ceded it to the Israelites. The midrash considers Lev 18:3, on the other hand, to be a general prohibition of foreign practices.[13] It resolves the redundancy between the general and specific prohibitions by interpreting Lev 18:3 as directed specifically against customary practices that might not fall under strict definitions of divination, necromancy, and, by extension, any of the

---

11. See also Francis Young, "Greek Apologists of the Second Century," in *Apologetics in the Roman Empire: Pagans, Jews, and Christians*, ed. Mark J. Edwards, Martin Goodman, Simon R. F. Price, and Christopher Rowland (Oxford: Oxford University Press, 1999), 94.

12. On some of the important differences between the Mekilta de Arayot and the rest of the Sipra, see Beth A. Berkowitz, *Defining Jewish Difference: From Antiquity to the Present* (Cambridge: Cambridge University Press, 2012), 77–112; and Berkowitz, "The Limits of 'Their Laws': Ancient Rabbinic Controversies about Jewishness (and Non-Jewishness)," *JQR* 99 (2009): 121–57.

13. In its original context, the verse introduces a list of prohibited sexual practices, which includes offering up one's child to Molech. Deuteronomy 12:31 and 18:10 mention burning children as an offering but do not mention Molech. A connection between the two practices is made in 2 Kgs 23:10, which complicates the Sipra's resolution of the redundancy between the two verses.

other idolatrous practices specifically forbidden in Deut 18:10–11 or, for that matter, elsewhere in Scripture:

> [*You shall not copy the practices of the land of Egypt where you dwelt, or the land of Canaan to which I am taking you*] *nor shall you follow their laws* ... (Lev 18:3). And what does this verse say that has not already been said? Has it not already been stated: *Let no one be found among you who consigns his son or daughter to the fire ... or who is a charmer* (Deut 18:10–11)? Thus Scripture teaches, *Nor shall you follow their laws* [*ḥuqôt*]—that you should not follow their laws [*nimûsôt*] in matters inscribed [*haqûqin*] for them, for example, theaters, circuses, and stadiums.[14] R. Meir says: These things are "the ways of the Amorites" as classified by the sages. R. Judah b. Batera says: That one should not perforate,[15] grow the locks, or get a Roman haircut. Perhaps you might say, "They have customs and we do not have customs?" Thus Scripture says: *My rules alone shall you observe and my laws shall you follow* (Lev 18:4). Still, there is room for the evil impulse to worry and say: "Their laws are nicer than ours." Thus Scripture says: *Observe them faithfully, for that will be proof of your wisdom and discernment* [*to other peoples*] (Deut 4:6). (Sipra Achare Mot 13.9 [Finkelstein])

The Mekilta de Arayot hinges this interpretation on the translation of the biblical Hebrew word for laws, *ḥuqôt*, into rabbinic parlance, *nimûsôt*, a Greek loanword (from νόμος) that can mean either "law" or "custom" in the rabbinic corpus. A further word play glosses the word *ḥuqôt* by relating it to the root of the verb *ḥqq* meaning "to inscribe" or "to engrave." By playing with the Hebrew root for both "law" and "inscribe" as well as the ambiguous meaning of the word for law in Greek, the Mekilta de Arayot creates a category of customs that do not quite fit into the realm of established or authorized practices but do nonetheless fall under the general ban implied by the midrashic understanding of Lev 18:3. As examples, the Sipra offers the various buildings that housed Roman spectacles: theaters, circuses, and stadia.

Through the mechanism of "the ways of the Amorites," the Mekilta de Arayot applies the biblical strictures against following Canaanite customs

---

14. Following the marginal correction in Codex Assemani 66. See Berkowitz, "Limits of 'Their Laws,'" 135 n. 35.

15. The precise meaning of this verb is difficult to construe. Various alternatives have been offered, but none is entirely convincing. Following the Ra'avad, Berkowitz suggests that this refers to "foppish dress" or excessive self-beautification. See Berkowitz, "Limits of 'Their Laws,'" 146 esp. n. 67–69.

to the theater, the circus, and the stadium as well as to a variety of other cultural practices including haircuts or modes of dress, which appear to be characteristically Roman but fall short of being demonstrably related to idolatrous worship or immoral content. In this brief list of entertainment buildings, the Mekilta, not unlike Tatian, collapses the broad array of spectacles into a single category, which functions as metonymy for the whole of Roman culture. The repetition of possessive pronouns and adjectives in binary pairs (such as they/we or theirs/ours) places emphasis on the opposition between Jewish culture and this loose set of foreign practices. Like Tatian who dismisses spectacles as foreign and leaves the worthless spectacles to "you Greeks," the Mekilta de Arayot adopts spectacle entertainment as a symbol to highlight the distinction between Israel, whose cultural heritage depends on the observance of the torah law, and the nations, whose cultural practices are to be avoided simply because they are foreign.

Tatian's *Oration to the Greeks* and the Mekilta de Arayot's midrash share what I call an externally directed critique against spectacles. Both are obsessed with separating *us*, a community of believers, and *them*, a population which can be best described by their devotion to the urban culture of the Roman Empire, represented in both texts by images of theatrical indulgence and idle spectatorship. Both Tatian and this midrash are concerned with putting Roman passion for mass entertainment to the service of essentially apologetic aims. For Tatian, the spectacles present key evidence for the moral inferiority of his pagan detractors. For all their desire to distinguish themselves from barbarians, Tatian argues, the bloody gladiator bouts and the intentional falseness of the theater demonstrate that the Christians, and not the Greeks, are culturally superior. The rabbis in the Sipra put forward a similar argument. But their version of the apologetic differs from Tatian in one important respect: the Mekilta de Arayot seems to have nothing in particular against the theater or Roman haircuts for that matter, except for the fact that they are foreign. Unlike Tatian, there is little moral judgment involved in the Mekilta de Arayot's cultural distinction between the spectators and the Jews. Rather than fixate on the theater's possible idolatrous associations or on the impropriety of spectatorship, the Mekilta de Arayot's anxieties stem instead from a sense of cultural inadequacy (perhaps "their laws" are better than "our laws").[16]

---

16. This same strategy of acknowledging the benefits of Roman culture, while simultaneously engaging in a polemic against it, can be seen in b. Šabb. 33b, where R. Judah and R. Simeon argue about whether or not Roman roads, baths, and bridges

Sitting with Scorners: Moral Condemnation of Spectators in Early Christian and Rabbinic Literature

Later Christian discourse about the theater built upon some of the themes established by the apologists. Like Athenagoras (*Leg.* 35), Tertullian argued that gladiatorial combat constituted murder (*Idol.* 11:3–5), and John Chrysostom echoed Tatian's criticism that the theater was a site of moral depravity (e.g. *Theatr.* 2).[17] But by the early third century, Christian antitheatrical rhetoric ceased to see the theater as "barbaric" or "foreign." Christian orators like Tertullian, John Chrysostom, and Augustine focused on the fact that the content of Roman spectacle was fundamentally immoral and therefore completely inappropriate for Christians to attend. Their antitheatrical rhetoric tended to be directed internally, towards Christians who might attend the theater, rather than externally, towards a pagan culture that delighted in depravities. Chrysostom went so far as to claim that Christians who attended the theater did spiritual damage to themselves. As a result, he refused to let anyone who stepped into a theater enter into his church or share in communion (*Theatr.* 46).[18]

This turn from an outwardly to an inwardly directed critique against spectacle rejected Christian spectators because of their involvement in something that was abhorrent and morally bereft rather than foreign. This process occurred, at least in part, as Christian clergy began more and more to view themselves as an exclusive elite who ought to serve as exemplars of ascetic behavior. Opting out of the civic culture surrounding the theater would have had serious consequences, since it constituted one of the only places in the city where a crowd might be able to successfully give voice to its concerns and demands. Though turning away from a culture of spectacles was often celebrated as the beginning of asceticism and an important step towards a more orthopraxic lifestyle, rejection of spectacles as centers of popular influence must have coincided with the development of alternative modes of constructing authority.[19] Christian oratory increasingly

---

should be considered praiseworthy. See also Mireille Hadas-Lebel, *Jerusalem against Rome*, trans. Robyn Fréchet, ISACR 7 (Leuven: Peeters, 2005), 365–414; Sacha Stern, *Jewish Identity in Early Rabbinic Writings* (Leiden: Brill, 1994), 42–45.

17. For John Chrysostom's view of the theater, see Leyerle, *Theatrical Shows and Ascetic Lives*, 13–74.

18. See also Barnes, "Christians and the Theater," 176.

19. E.g., in Jerome's *Vit. Hil.* 2 (*NPNF* 2/6:303), the young Christian Hilarion

came to think of the theater not so much as an abhorrent gentile institution but as an internal threat to the church.[20]

Tertullian, a Christian convert from a pagan background, living and preaching in Carthage, North Africa, during the early third century CE, devoted an entire discourse to the problem of Roman spectacles. Known for his almost maniacal rigor and his biting invective, Tertullian launched a vituperative attack against the whole array of Roman entertainments. His *De spectaculis* was most likely a sermon before the baptismal rite addressed to baptismal candidates and those who had recently been baptized. In it, he argues that spectacles are forbidden to Christians by faith, by truth, and by discipline. Thus, he claims, it is fitting that he should direct this discourse to those who were just about to enter the fold and those who have just done so. For Tertullian, the baptismal vow requires, above all else, the renunciation of idolatry, including the spectacles that are in their very origins and operation completely linked to pagan religion. Christian devotion to truth requires a repudiation of all falsehood; since the theater depends on illusion, it must be avoided. Christian discipline also requires the renunciation of pleasures (*voluptates*), which corrode the soul. Chief among these are the spectacles, which Tertullian sees as "the heart of all wickedness, the center of all evil" (*Spect.* 1).

The rabbis did not show nearly as much interest in combating the influence of spectacles amongst their coreligionists as did the irascible Tertullian. There are only a few scattered references in early rabbinic literature; one of these, which we have already mentioned above, deals directly with the games. Nothing remotely compares to the full-length diatribe composed by the Carthaginian church father. Nevertheless, some compelling intersections do exist between Tertullian's *De spectaculis* and rabbinic texts prohibiting spectacles.

---

singles himself out as a believer in Christ, because "his only pleasure was, not in the excitement of the circus, the blood of the arena, or the decadence of the theater but in the congregation of the church." Hilarion's next step included taking up the habit as a disciple of the celebrated Egyptian monk Anthony before venturing out on his own with a few disciples. One can easily imagine that in the relatively urban context that most rabbis would come to inhabit, abstinence from Roman spectacles would have been a relatively simple, yet dramatic way for a would-be disciple to publicize his inclination towards greater piety.

20. Leyerle, *Theatrical Shows and Ascetic Lives*, 42–74; Webb, *Demons and Dancers*, 197–216.

The most explicit reference to a rabbinic ban against theater attendance comes from the Tosefta.[21] The Tosefta raises the issue of spectacle entertainment within the larger context of the sorts of financial and social interactions that a Jew must avoid due to the general ban against idolatry. Interestingly, though, it grounds its prohibition of the theater not as a part of this general ban but as a specific prohibition that requires separate justification:

> It is forbidden for one to go up to the theaters of the gentiles on account of idolatry—these are the words of R. Meir. But the sages say, when they sacrifice it is forbidden on account of idolatry. When they do not sacrifice, it is forbidden because of "sitting with scorners." If one goes to stadiums and *castra* (circuses?)[22] and sees the diviners and magicians, *buccion, mukion, mullion, sagilarion, sagilaria*,[23] behold, this is "sitting

---

21. Though we could quibble somewhat about the proper dating of this rabbinic collection, the excerpt we are discussing appears to date from before the completion of the Palestinian Talmud, sometime in the fourth century, roughly contemporaneous with the floruit of Tertullian. It thus stands as a relatively good and oft-quoted comparandum. For a good English summary of the scholarship on the Tosefta and its relationship to the Mishnah and other rabbinic collections, see Paul Mandel, "The Tosefta," in *The Late Roman-Rabbinic Period*, vol. 4 of *The Cambridge History of Judaism*, ed. Steven T. Katz (Cambridge: Cambridge University Press, 2006), 316–35; Abraham Goldberg, "The Tosefta: Companion to the Mishnah," in *Oral Tora, Halakha, Mishna, Tosefta, Talmud, External Tractates*, vol. 1 of *The Literature of the Sages*, CRINT 2.3.1, ed. Shmuel Safrai (Philadelphia: Fortress; Assen: Van Gorcum, 1987), esp. 283, 285–89; Shamma Friedman, "The Primacy of Tosefta to Mishnah in Synoptic Parallels," in *Introducing Tosefta: Textual, Intratextual, and Intertextual Studies*, ed. Harry Fox, Tirzah Meacham, and Diane Kriger (Hoboken, NJ: Ktav, 1999), 99–121.

22. The precise meaning of *karqom* is unclear. Following Marcus Jastrow, *A Dictionary of the Targumim, the Talmud Babli and Yerushalmi, and the Midrashic Literature* (New York: Pardes, 1950), 669, most assume that this is loanword from the Greek χαράκωμα, meaning "palisaded enclosure or entrenched camp." The word may also result from a corruption of the Latin *circus*, though no manuscript supports this reading.

23. The first three terms are often taken to be references to popular performers from the *fabula atellana*, a type of popular farce involving a series of stock characters. See, e.g., Samuel Krauss, *Griechische und lateinische Lehnwörter im Talmud, Midrasch, und Targum*, 2 vols. (Berlin: Calvary, 1898–1899), 1.319; Jacobs, "Theatres and Performances," 333; Weiss, "Games and Spectacles," 124. The last two may be references to the *ludi saeculares*, a set of games established every hundred years or so to be celebrated with gladiatorial combat and circus races. For a more skeptical view of these identifications, see G. Veltri, "Magic, Sex and Politics: The Media Power of

with scorners." As it is written: [*Happy is the man who has not followed the counsel of the wicked, or taken the path of sinners] nor sat in the seat of scorners; rather, the teaching of the Lord is his delight* (Ps. 1:1–2). This teaches that they bring man to neglect <the study of> Torah.[24]

If one went up to the theaters of the gentiles and shouted because of the needs of the state, behold this is permitted. If he is counted among them,[25] behold this is forbidden. One who sits in the stadium, behold this is spilling blood. R. Natan permits [going to the stadium] on account of the fact that one might call out and save, and to the *castra* on account of welfare of the state, but if he is counted among them, behold it is forbidden. (t. 'Abod. Zar. 2:2–5)

The passage begins with a disagreement between R. Meir and the anonymous majority of sages as to the reason why attendance at spectacles is forbidden. According to R. Meir (who functions as a literary character playing the role of the foil), attending performances at the theater is forbidden, because these performances are in fact equivalent to idolatry. R. Meir might have agreed with Tertullian that "in origin, name, equipment, place and art [*de originibus, de titulis, de apparatibus, de locis, de*

Theatre Amusements in the Mirror of Rabbinic Literature," in *The Words of a Wise Man's Mouth Are Gracious (Qoh 10, 12): Festschrift for Günter Stemberger on the Occasion of His 65th Birthday*, ed. Mauro Perani (Berlin: de Gruyter, 2005), 243–56.

24. Cf. y. 'Abod. Zar. 1:7, which omits "the study of."

25. The meaning of the verb *mithashev* is unclear and the subject of some debate. Jacob Neusner translates, "If he took account [of what is happening therein]." See Jacob Neusner, *The Tosefta* (Hoboken, NJ: Ktav, 1977–1986), ad loc., and Neusner, *The Talmud of the Land of Israel: A Preliminary Translation and Explanation*, 33 vols, CSHJ (Chicago: University of Chicago, 1982–1993), ad loc. Alternatively, Saul Lieberman, *Meḥkarim be-Torat Erets-Yiśra'el*, ed. D. Rosenthal (Jerusalem: Magnes, 1991), 380, explains *mithashev* (as a participle functioning adjectivally?) as referring to "an important person in the eyes of the nation," whose model others will follow. Following Samuel Krauss, *Talmudische Archäologie*, 3 vols. (Leipzig: Fock, 1910–1912), 3:119, Jacobs, "Theatres and Performances," 333 n. 39, conjectures that this is a reference to gambling. Berkowitz, "Limits of 'Their Laws,'" 140–41 n. 51 resolves the contradictions between these two points of view with cautious indeterminacy and states, "This could mean either mental account (the audience member is mesmerized by the performance) or financial account (the audience member makes a bet on the performance)." Elsewhere in the Tosefta (t. Bek. 7:3), the verb is used only in a discussion about the tithe of cattle as specified by Lev 27:32 and clearly means "to be counted, reckoned, or considered." I have tried to use this sense of the verb in my translation here.

artificiis], in every conceivable way" spectacles involve idolatry (*Spect.* 13.1). But since he uses the frustratingly vague term *avodah zarah* (literally "alien service"), which can refer to either a specific act of non-Jewish sacrifice, including the burning of incense, the pouring of a libation, or a physical object like an idol, or be used more generally as a catch-all phrase for idolatry, we cannot know with certainty what R. Meir's specific problem is with the theater. He might be alluding to the fact that it was quite common for performances in the theater to begin with a sacrifice, either at a temporary altar dedicated to the imperial cult that was brought out at the beginning of the proceedings or at a permanent altar or shrine associated with the theater. Alternatively, R. Meir may be referring to the content of the shows that were presented in the theater, since they were often based on mythological content. Or he may have been influenced by the origins of the Greek theater as Dionysiac ritual, an association which lasted to some degree well into late antiquity. Perhaps it is best to simply view his comment as general derision, rather than as a reference to any specific practice.

R. Meir's explanation of the prohibition is ultimately rejected by the anonymous majority of sages who acknowledge that sacrifice, though common, was not an essential feature of Roman spectacles. Since, according to the rules of rabbinic legislation, in almost all cases an anonymous opinion is considered preferable to a named one, anyone trained in rabbinic hermeneutics would be well aware that R. Meir's concern about the inherent idolatry of Roman spectacles is meant to be cast by the way side. In the place of R. Meir's general prohibition on attending these entertainments on the grounds that they constituted idolatry, the Tosefta applies a verse from Ps 1:1 as a proof text for a general ban on the theater. The Tosefta then lists what it imagines as the content of the performances in theaters, a list that includes snake charmers, magicians, and a few other confused references to Roman performance and ritual.[26] The proof text from Ps 1:1 then receives a further gloss, revealing that the meaning of the phrase "sitting in the seat of scorners" refers to the fact that these entertainments distract man from loftier pursuits; that is, from the study of torah.

---

26. For a brief explanation of some of the issues surrounding these terms, see Spielman, "Sitting with Scorners," 279–90.

Psalm 1:1 in Jewish and Christian Attacks on the Theater

As opposed to the externally directed apologetic arguments of Tatian and the Mekhilta de Arayot, the Tosefta shares with Tertullian what I call an internally directed critique. The Tosefta directs its rebuke at the individual Jew involved in specific acts of transgression (one who goes up to the theater, one who sits in the stadium, and so forth) rather than outward as a critique of foreign or non-Jewish practice. The exegesis of Ps 1:1–2 also highlights the juxtaposition between the righteous and the wicked, a predominant theme in the rest of Ps 1. According to the psalm, the righteous "find delight in the Teaching of the Lord and study that teaching night and day." In the Tosefta, then, the theater functions as a specific threat to the rabbinic lifestyle. By attending the performances in the theater or the contests in the stadium, Jews neglect the torah, because they ought to have been studying torah night and day; this leaves no time for leisure or frivolity.[27] Similarly, Tertullian addresses certain "game-lovers" (*suaviludii*), those Christians who argue that the spectacles are nowhere forbidden by Scripture. When pushed to offer scriptural proof for the prohibition of the theater, Tertullian concedes that Scripture offers no specific prohibition. Instead, he offers up a verse which he finds particularly relevant, the very same verse from Psalms that served as a proof text in the Tosefta: "Happy is the man who has not gone to the gathering of the ungodly, nor stood in the ways of sinners, nor sat in the chair of pestilence" (Ps 1:1).[28] The plain meaning of the verse clearly has nothing to do with theater entertainments. In its literal sense, the psalm advocates distancing oneself from impious and wicked influences and cleaving to the community of the righteous. But for Tertullian, the verse is perfectly suited to the spectacles. For, he claims, at the public shows, people sit in the seats of honor in the first few rows of the audience and stand in the *viae*, the ways, the alleys, and corridors that circle around the arena and separate the common seating from those reserved for equestrians and senators. All the more so, then, is every spectacle a "gathering of the ungodly" (*Spect.* 3).

---

27. The application of the phrase מושב לצים, or "sitting with scorners," depends first on the allusion to sitting in a theater but also perhaps on the wordplay between the biblical Hebrew root ליץ, meaning "to mock or scorn," and the rabbinic Hebrew construction לצית, which might mean "sport or pleasure." See, e.g., t. Šabb. 6(7):4.

28. Whatever Latin translation Tertullian had on hand renders Ps 1:1 as *nec in cathedra pestium sedit*, as does the Vulgate.

It is not easy to explain how these two different traditions came to adopt this same, seemingly irrelevant scrap of Scripture as a piece of rhetorical invective against Roman spectacle. Perhaps Tertullian heard the rabbinic exegesis of Ps 1 through contact with Jews in Carthage, in much the same way that Jerome managed to pick up scraps of rabbinic interpretation from his Jewish contacts in Palestine.[29] Or the rabbis could have come across Tertullian's writings in Palestine. Either suggestion is possible, but neither is terribly likely. Tertullian and the rabbis seem to have seized upon the verse independently. The verse would have been attractive not only because it refers to "sitting among scorners" or mockers, which could be taken as an allusion to the performers of the theater (though the Greek and Latin translations of the verse available to Tertullian seem not to capture this sense from the original Hebrew). The verse from Ps 1 was useful more for its stark juxtaposition between the community of the righteous and the council of the wicked, which provided the perfect opportunity for both Tertullian and the early rabbis to construct imaginary borders between their own circles and the throngs who filled the theaters.

Ultimately, though, rabbinic and Christian exegesis of this verse moved in different trajectories. Dismissing his exegesis as "mere quibbling," Tertullian gives primacy to another argument. Christian discipline, he argues, demands complete separation from games, because they are completely rooted in idolatry. In fact, the greater part of his discourse is devoted to proving that every single aspect of every form of spectacle consists of nothing but the worship of demons and spirits. Delving into every obscurity of pagan literature, he discusses the origins of every event, demonstrating first that each began as either a festival devoted to a divinity, a celebration of royal birthdays, a remembrance of victories of the state, or an occasion for municipal feasts.

While Tertullian privileges the renunciation of idolatry over any exegetical argument, the Tosefta, in contrast, de-emphasizes the religious aspects of the spectacles and instead favors an argument rooted in scriptural exegesis. The rabbinic interpretation of Ps 1 stresses a decidedly rabbinic agenda

---

29. Hillel I. Newman, "Jerome and the Jews" [Hebrew] (PhD diss, Hebrew University of Jerusalem, 1997); Megan H. Williams, "Lessons from Jerome's Jewish Teachers: Exegesis and Cultural Interaction in Late Antique Palestine," in *Jewish Biblical Interpretation and Cultural Exchange: Comparative Exegesis in Context*, ed. Natalie B. Dohrmann and David Stern (Philadelphia: University of Pennsylvania Press, 2008), 66–86.

over and above any other concern. While Tertullian places his emphasis on the first clause of the verse from Psalms, the Tosefta draws attention to its final clause, "sitting with scorners."[30] The purpose of quoting the last clause is that it connects "sitting with scorners," that is, sitting with the throngs in the stadium, to the concept of torah study. The Tosefta demands constant study of the torah through the rabbinic curriculum and precludes the use of leisure time for fruitless activities as a result.

This oppositional movement of rabbinic and Christian exegesis demonstrates a key difference in the symbolic usage of spectacles in early rabbinic texts. For Christians, the spectacles functioned mostly as a subset of Graeco-Roman paganism. In the West, Christian polemics continued to rail against the inherent idolatry of the theater and the arena long after imperial legislation purged the idolatrous elements from them. For Christians like Tertullian, coming from pagan roots and addressing primarily pagan converts, the idolatrous overtones of theater became a key concern, because renunciation of idolatry was a central feature of Christian identity. In the absence of a unified pagan "church," the artificial agglomeration of different forms of spectacles provided, in the words of Ruth Webb, "a perfect foil against which the institution of the Church could define itself."[31] Tertullian found in the shows the perfect symbol through which he could illustrate two opposing ways of life: a life lived in communion with God or in communion with demons.[32]

The theater and the circus served a similar rhetorical function in early rabbinic literature. To the exclusion of other typically Roman institutions like baths, the theater often appears in rabbinic literature as a synecdoche for all of Rome and represents a way of life that is antithetical to torah. In rabbinic thought, the torah—both as symbol and as an institution—functioned as the defining feature of rabbinic identity. Not only did the torah serve as the sole factor that distinguished Israel from the nations, torah study as a "practice embedded in a social and material setting" functioned as the core activity that defined one's status as a sage.[33] Within the various rabbinic disciple circles or "textual communities" that studied

---

30. The Tosefta quotes only the last clause of the verse "sitting in the seat of scorners." The first clause would actually have been a better fit given that the verb the Tosefta uses to describe theater attendance refers to "going" rather than "sitting."

31. Webb, *Demons and Dancers*, 198.

32. Robert Sider, "Tertullian, On the Shows: An Analysis," *JTS* 29 (1978): 363.

33. See, e.g., Sipra Behukotai 8:10; m. Avot 3:14. See also Stern, *Jewish Identity*,

and discussed the torah together, membership and status depended on one's level of torah learning, including not only the mastery of the written text but also the set of traditions handed down from master to disciple. In claiming a functional opposition between the study of torah and "sitting with scorners" at the theater, the rabbis of the Tosefta stressed their absence from the theater, much like Tertullian and his fellow Christians, as a defining characteristic of their communal identity.

Conclusion

Christian and rabbinic criticism of the theater in the late second and early third centuries CE essentially shared two arguments. Some, like Tatian and the Mekhilta de Arayot, engaged in apologetic arguments that viewed sport and spectacle as foreign contaminants. Others, like Tertullian and the Tosefta, turned their critique inwards and demanded of their Christian and Jewish adherents total abstention from the world of Roman spectacle.

In both of these cases, criticism of the theater usually served other aims. Tertullian's oration was not intended to convince Christians to abandon their favorite pastimes. Rather, his immediate goal at the very least was to steel up the will of a small group of Christians who were taking their baptismal vows. In this context, the theater and the circus represented the world that the baptismal candidates were leaving behind. A new world with its own spectacles awaited them. In the close of his discourse, Tertullian declares, "But what a spectacle is already at hand—the return of the Lord.... Yes, and there are still to come other spectacles—that last, that eternal day of Judgment.... How vast the spectacle that day, and how wide" (*Spect.* 30). Rabbinic exegetical and homiletical responses to the theater also employed the theater as a potent symbol in the construction of rabbinic identity. As is in Tatian and Tertullian, the theater served as a convenient foil against which the rabbis could inscribe their own values—torah mastery and discipleship.

By the mid-third through the early fourth century, Jewish and Christian criticism of the theater seems to have taken an inward turn. The externally directed critique adopted by the Mekhilta de Arayot and Christian apologists like Tatian was abandoned in favor of a moral corrective

---

74–76; Catherine Hezser, *The Social Structure of the Rabbinic Movement in Roman Palestine*, TSAJ 66 (Tübingen: Mohr Siebeck, 1997), 124.

that was directed internally towards initiates and disciples who might be tempted to stray from the path of discipline.[34] Rather than use the games to criticize a foreign or Roman lifestyle, antitheatrical discourse tends to be bound up with issues of religious identity. Influenced largely by Tertullian, later Christian attacks on the theater concentrate more on issues related to Christian piety, such as the abandonment of worldly pleasures or the renunciation of falsity, than on the content of the spectacle. Later rabbinic literature preserves only the Tosefta's version—based on Ps 1:1—of a ban against theater attendance and not the Mekhilta's explanation of Lev 18:3. In later rabbinic compilations, the theater increasingly functions as a symbol that distinguishes between "scorners" and scholars rather than between Israel and the nations.

---

34. E.g., y. Ber. 4:2. See also Spielman, "Sitting with Scorners," 318–73.

Part 4
Competition and Relics

Introduction:
The Competition for Relics in Late Antiquity

Susan Ashbrook Harvey

The four papers here collected speak to common ritual habits that linked religious behavior regarding relics across the ancient Mediterranean world.[1] In these papers, we move from Greek healing shrines dedicated to Asklepios, through late antique Christian holy spaces, and into literary depictions of early Muslim devotional practices. One could easily expand these offerings to include Jewish places and practices and those of other religions in the broader Mediterranean world.[2] Yet the commonality of these behaviors does not reduce these "case studies" to a homogeneous sameness. Rather, the specificities of each case tell us something distinct—even incisively so—about the different religions, their adherents, their contexts, their opportunities, and their needs. Each case offers a particular and vivid articulation of religious process within a particular movement, and each time, we learn. Starting from the commonalities, it is the differences here that merit our attention.

Holy relics offered powerful instruments for participation in the fierce religious competitions of the late antique Mediterranean. Those competitions could be contestations between competing sites: between

---

1. I am grateful to Nathaniel P. DesRosiers and Arthur Urbano for inviting my participation in the original conference session at which these papers were delivered. Thanks also to my colleague Nancy Khalek, with whom I discussed the materials and ideas here put forward.
2. See, e.g., Michael Satlow, "Giving for Return: Jewish Offerings in Late Antiquity," in *Religion and the Self in Antiquity*, ed. David Brakke, Michael Satlow, and Steven Weitzman (Bloomington: Indiana University Press, 2005), 91–108. On the broadly shared religious culture of the Roman Mediterranean, see James Rives, *Religion in the Roman Empire* (Malden, MA: Blackwell, 2007).

the cathedral in Antioch where the body of Simeon the Stylite was enshrined over and against Qal'at Sim'an, the pilgrimage site some four days' travel distant, that grew up around the pillar on which he had stood for decades (Dina Boero); or between the martyr chapels outside the walls of Rome that housed the bodily relics of those revered figures and the titular churches inside the city walls that lacked bodily remains but offered other holy substances instead (Mary Joan Winn Leith and Allyson Everingham Sheckler). The competition could be between early Sunni and Shi'ia claims regarding access to Muhammad's sacred authority, played out in stories about the Prophet's hair or other bodily remains collected during his lifetime; or between articulations of such devotional piety for Muslims, over and against the devotional habits of their rival religionists (Adam Bursi). It could be played out in the claims to efficacy marked by votive offerings left at Christian healing churches and shrines over and against continuing pagan holy sites—a practice that signaled continuity as much as it affirmed competition (Gary Vikan). At stake were rivalries and negotiations between competing modes of religious authority, structures, and identity.

In the distinctive case studies offered by these papers, two shared motifs merit particular notice. First is the degree to which each of these papers demonstrates relic cult and devotion as a materially expansive form of religious practice. Of seeming infinite variety, relics by their presence, absence, or substitutions provided singular efficacy to heal, soothe, empower, protect, perform, attack, and resolve the needs, fears, and concerns of their faithful devotees. These chapters treat a diversity of relic types. Relics could be bodily: the hair or fingernail clippings of a holy person collected while alive or after death, which continued to be efficacious beyond the boundary of death; or they could be bones or body parts from the dead holy person. They could be substances rendered powerful by contact with the holy one: dirt, dust, stones, water, oil, or cloth carried away from the holy site, which were seen as conduits of divine power authenticated and activated by virtue of direct contact with the holy body. They could be substances blessed at the holy place by religious authorities: bread, water, or contact relics (*brandea*), items receiving their miraculous qualities by means of ritual processes performed by ritual agents, whether lay or ordained. They demonstrated that power perceived as holy could radiate out from specific sources or places, connecting people, locations, and events across ever-expanding territories. Relics that worked were relics that would require increasing and extended access for growing numbers of people, not only because of competition but also because of success. These chapters attest to an impressive capacity for reduplication, extension, expansion, and transferability in the substances that performed the functionality of relics. No matter the type of object or community involved, what we see in each of these chapters is significant expansion in what constituted relics or functioned as relics and how they worked, emerging through contexts of competition, contestation, and affirmation.

Second, in every case the piety of relics in whatever form they took engaged a multisensory experience for the participants. That sensory richness was twofold: at once generated by the relic as object and also received by the faithful believer who encountered it. On the one hand, relics themselves—whether body parts or contact substances—represented a striking valuation of materiality. Matter carried enormous capacity to operate across human and divine domains and to convey powers to heal and protect. This notable aspect of late antique piety has been much discussed in recent scholarship and commands the attention of religionists. Religion is not simply an embodied activity; it is furthermore an engagement with materiality itself.[3]

At the same time, pilgrims and devotees encountered and venerated relics through a rich, synaesthetic sensory engagement.[4] Vikan describes the atmosphere of healing shrines as "narcotic," filled as they were with sacred images, incense, votive lamps, recitation of holy stories, words and pictures adorning the walls, and the collective psychology of ill, desperate, or needy people. But even the pilgrim token or blessed substance carried elsewhere elicited a multisensory encounter, however simple. Relic piety involved much more than the concrete encounter of touch. Tactility in broader terms was fundamental. Ancient understandings of optics, for

---

3. For late antiquity, see especially Patricia Cox Miller, *The Corporeal Imagination: Signifying the Holy in Late Ancient Christianity* (Philadelphia: University of Pennsylvania Press, 2009); Susan Ashbrook Harvey, *Scenting Salvation: Ancient Christianity and the Olfactory Imagination* (Berkeley: University of California Press, 2006). I have been much helped by Caroline Walker Bynum, *Christian Materiality: An Essay on Religion in Late Medieval Europe* (New York: Zone, 2011); and Sally M. Promey, *Sensational Religion: Sensory Cultures in Material Practice* (New Haven: Yale University Press, 2014).

4. By synaesthetic, I do not mean an abnormal sensory confusion but rather the complex and multiple sensations that characterize any sensory encounter. See now Shane Butler and Alex Purves, *Synaesthesia and the Ancient Senses* (Durham: Acumen, 2013).

example, provided the notion that eyes reached out to touch what they saw; sounds literally *struck* the ears. Smells were received, sometimes viscerally, by olfactory receptors that carried the atoms to the brain. Ingestion of blessed substances involved taste when substances were eaten or drunk; but penetration to the believer's interior was also gained by rubbing, anointment, or even simple proximity. Domains divine and human were constantly porous to one another, and the believer's body experienced that porousness through sensory encounter with the relic. The encounter was tactile in a variety of ways and invariably much more than that.[5]

Relic veneration was a ritual habit that continually opened the bodily senses to larger realities beyond the immediate physical realm. Moreover, sensory encounters with the relic engaged the participant in a tangible, palpable experience of physical transformation: the merely bodily or human, through experienced sensory means, became the conduit of divine presence and force. Sensory change marked that effect. Hair and sweat from the Prophet Muhammad's body became a sweet perfume (Bursi), as did ḥnānā, a grimy, oily substance made from the dirt at the base of Simeon the Stylite's pillar (Boero). Palm prints marked the clay tokens and votives of healing shrines (Vikan). Bread became more than bread (Leith and Sheckler). These substances—mundane, even repellant markers of transient mortality—were rendered fragrant, sweet, and efficacious by virtue of the sacred power they gained as relics.

Ritually marked by their source and location and ritually activated by the ritual agents who produced them and those who received them, relics differentiated spaces, persons, substances, identities. By direct encounter with the physicality of the ordinary, the extraordinary could be grasped with one's own body. Such ritual practices were not borrowings, appropriations, or concessions to popular piety. They were deeply ingrained cultural habits, shared across the religions of the Mediterranean. They represented

---

5. On modes of perception as understood by ancient Mediterranean cultures, see, e.g., Ashley Clements, "The Senses in Philosophy and Science: Five Conceptions from Heraclitus to Plato," in *A Cultural History of the Senses in Antiquity*, ed. Jerry P. Toner (London: Bloomsbury, 2014), 115–37. At the end of her essay, Clements traces the trajectory for science of the senses through Aristotle, the Hellenistic philosophers, and Galen, into the late antique period. On the matter of tactility as a fundamental quality of sensation, views remained fairly constant across these schools of thought. The scholarship is extensive, and available in the above-cited works by Miller, Harvey, and Butler and Purves.

profound and fundamental cultural patterns regarding bodiliness, materiality, and the negotiation of divine-human relations. Each of the contributions in this section provides vivid demonstration of how devotion to relics contributed to the culture of religious competition and contestation that characterized the late antique Mediterranean world. In the variegated realm of relic piety they open for us, we have much to learn.

Relics? What Relics?

Mary Joan Winn Leith and Allyson Everingham Sheckler

Our perspective on religious competition arises from what can seem like a current scholarly obsession with relics in early Christianity. The focus of our work has been the early fifth-century basilica of Santa Sabina, built 423–433 CE by Bishop Celestine I and the wealthy priest Peter the Illyrian on the Aventine Hill in Rome.[1] The seeming importance of early Christian relics to current scholars led us to ask of Santa Sabina: Why were there no relics in this church? This in turn begged the same question regarding the other churches built in Rome in the first half of the fifth century, Santa Pudenziana, Santa Maria Maggiore, San Pietro in Vincoli.[2] Recent scholarship suggests that martyr veneration was slow to develop at Rome, and Roman Christians had no historical tradition of local martyr veneration before the fourth century. Only by the mid-fourth century does martyr veneration begin to make a mark.[3] When later in the century Damasus (366–384) publicized outside Rome, he seems to have invented many of his martyrs.[4] Rome's Aurelian Walls are a central factor in this question

---

1. Good images of Santa Sabina may be viewed at Ron Reznick, "Rome: Ancient Churches," digital-images.net, http://tinyurl.com/SBL4210a.
2. For the churches, see Hugo Brandenburg, *Ancient Churches of Rome from the Fourth to the Seventh Century: The Dawn of Christian Architecture in the West* (Turnhout: Brepols, 2005).
3. For Roman martyrs, see Michele Salzman, *On Roman Time: The Codex-Calendar of 354 and the Rhythms of Urban Life in Late Antiquity*, TCH 14 (Berkeley: University of California Press, 1990).
4. Alan Thacker, "Rome of the Martyrs: Saints, Cults and Relics, Fourth to Seventh Centuries," in *Roma Felix: Formation and Reflections of Medieval Rome*, ed. Éamonn Ó Carragáin and Carol Neuman de Vegvar (Aldershot, UK: Ashgate, 2007), 20–26, and Dennis Trout, "Damasus and the Invention of Early Christian Rome," *JMEMS* 33 (2003): 522–23.

since for centuries burial within Rome's walls was prohibited.[5] The Codex Calendar of 354 indicates that all Roman martyr veneration took place in the extramural funerary basilicas that surrounded the walls.[6] In the early fifth century, martyr cults with bodily relics were still flourishing and well attended. According to Alan Thacker, "In its earliest phases, at the very least, up to the mid-fifth century, martyr cult in Rome was undoubtedly associated primarily if not exclusively with extramural sites."[7] Fifth-century Roman Christians looked for their safety to the "concentric layering of the 'thresholds of the saints' over the 'pomerial' boundary at the Wall."[8] The saints, like Roman generals and their legions, were restricted from entering the city itself. Inside the walls, then, some mode of parallel worship—perhaps even a degree of competition—was arguably just as active and attractive to fifth-century Roman Christians. For Romans "the buildings in the two zones separated by the Wall pertained to diverse architectural patrimonies," and behavior and even dress in the two zones differed.[9] If we look inside the Aurelian walls, we find little evidence for bodily relics of any kind in Roman churches.

What Was Inside the Walls?

The large fourth-century funerary basilicas built outside Rome's walls accommodated great numbers of people at the tomb sites who visited deceased family members as part of the uninterrupted tradition of ancestor veneration; they also participated there in the evolving tradition of martyr worship.[10] Inside the walls, the Lateran was the only church that

---

5. Technically, burial was prohibited within Rome's *pomerium*, or religious boundary, which the walls came to signify in late antiquity.

6. Salzman, *Roman Time*, 42.

7. Alan Thacker, "Martyr Cult within Walls: Saints and Relics in the Roman 'Tituli of Fourth to Seventh Centuries," in *Text, Image and Interpretation: Studies in Anglo-Saxon Literature and its Insular Context in Honour of Éamonn Ó. Carrigáin*, ed. Alastair J. Minnis and Jane Roberts, SEMA 18 (Turnhout: Brepols, 2007), 31; Hendrik W. Dey, *The Aurelian Wall and the Refashioning of Imperial Rome, AD 271–855* (Cambridge: Cambridge University Press, 2011), 218, indicates that martyr shrines flourished until the middle of the sixth century in open air cemeteries even though the catacombs gradually went out of use after approximately 400 CE.

8. Dey, *Aurelian Wall*, 221–22, citing a letter of Sidonius Apollinaris dated to 467.

9. Dey, *Aurelian Wall*, 215.

10. For Christian worship at Rome's funereal basilicas, see Ramsay MacMullen,

matched the size of the extramural funerary basilicas; and there were no martyr remains or relics there. Rather, intramural titular churches shared consecrated hosts from the Lateran, the *fermentum*,[11] a practice meant to establish unity across the city while binding each church to the Lateran and the bishop of Rome.[12] While the cult of the dead in the fourth century is, archaeologically speaking, the most visible form of Roman Christianity, we know that worship took place within the walls of the city in meeting places that once existed but are no longer archaeologically visible.[13] These meeting places were by necessity hidden before the Peace of the Church and have remained so to this day.

Evidence of private Christian worship spaces in elite homes inside the city of Rome is similarly lacking. Various sources indicate that some elite private homes contained worship spaces,[14] but our actual knowledge of these spaces rests on a single small, private Christian worship space

---

The Second Church: Popular Christianity A.D. 200–400, WGRWSup 1 (Atlanta: Society of Biblical Literature, 2009). See also R. Ross Holloway, *Constantine and Rome* (New Haven: Yale University Press, 2004), esp. 57–119.

11. See Innocent I's letter (416 CE) to Decentius, Bishop of Gubbio, in Lawrence J. Johnson, *Worship in the Early Church: An Anthology of Historical Sources*, vol. 3 (Collegeville, MN: Liturgical Press, 2009), 101. We take the consensus position that the *fermentum* was distributed to titular churches and that their presbyters distributed it to the people. As we know from the councils and canons of the period (canon 2 of the Council of Antioch of 341 CE; *Apostolic Constitutions*, 8.47.9; *Canons of the Holy Apostles*, First Council of Toledo [400 CE]), the church felt the need to require more frequent communion in the fourth and fifth centuries. It is probable that those complaining about and reporting the drop in eucharistic participation would have been presbyters in Roman titular churches who were distributing communion to their congregations.

12. Thacker, "Martyr Cult," 60; John F. Baldovin, "The *Fermentum* at Rome in the Fifth Century: A Reconsideration," *Worship* 79 (2005): 38–53.

13. See F. Guidobaldi, "Roma, il tessuto abitativo, le *domus* e i *tituli*," in *L'età tardoantica*, part 2 of *I luoghi e le culture*, vol. 3 of *Storia di Roma*, ed. Andrea Carandini, Lellia Cracco Ruggini, and Andrea Giardina (Turin: Einaudi, 1993), 76.

14. See Kim Bowes, *Private Worship, Public Values, and Religious Change in Late Antiquity* (New York: Cambridge University Press, 2008), 61–103. See also Julia Hillner, "Families, Patronage, and the Titular Churches of Rome, c. 300–c. 600," in *Religion, Dynasty, and Patronage in Early Christian Rome, 300–900*, ed. Kate Cooper and Julia Hillner (Cambridge: Cambridge University Press, 2007), 260, and Gillian Mackie, *Early Christian Chapels in the West: Decoration, Function and Patronage* (Toronto: University of Toronto Press, 2003), 62.

preserved under the church of San Giovanni e Paolo.[15] This shrine is precious, because it is private and preserves Christian art dated to the second half of the fourth century, one register of which may constitute the earliest extant scene of Christian martyrdom.[16] The shrine space is too small to be anything but private, and there is no evidence for a tomb of any sort underneath the chapel space.[17] The imposition of the later sixth-century *passio* of the martyrs onto the existing space distorts the perspective on earlier use of the space.[18] This chapel was subsequently filled in when the early fifth-century basilica was built. The claims about San Giovanni e Paolo as an early Christian house church located at the site of two intramural martyrs' tombs have muddied the waters in the scholarly investigation into relics and the fourth- and fifth-century Roman Church.[19]

Further examples of confusion may be found in the claims for corporeal martyr remains in intramural churches and beneath their altars

---

15. Kim Bowes, *Private Worship*, 88–92. See also Beat Brenk, "Microstoria sotto la chiesa del ss. Giovanni e Paolo: La cristianizzione di una casa privata," *RIASA* 18 (1995): 169–205, and Brandenburg, *Ancient Churches*, 155–62.

16. We have questions about this particular fresco, which has yet to be scientifically examined.

17. Brenk, "Microstoria sotto la chiesa," 192 and 194. The supposed window is really a closed niche along the lines of a traditional *lararium*. See also Brandenburg, *Ancient Churches*, 159. This fact has escaped the notice of many reputable scholars, e.g., Thacker, "Martyr Cult," 59; Mackie, *Early Christian Chapels*, 63; Caroline J. Goodson, "Roman Archaeology and Medieval Rome," in *Rome: Continuing Encounters between Past and Present*, ed. Dorigen Caldwell and Lesley Caldwell (Burlington, VT: Ashgate, 2011), 28; however, Goodson corrected herself in "Archaeology and the Cult of Saints in the Early Middle Ages: Accessing the Sacred," *MEFRM* 126 (2014): 124–48.

18. Because the land where the chapel had been and on which the basilica of San Giovanni e Paolo arose was privately owned, the property must have been donated to the church in order to build the basilica. When the basilica was constructed, ca. 410 CE, the private chapel was no longer a cult place as its burial in the foundation of the 410 CE basilica suggests. In addition, there is no evidence that the chapel, when operative, was frequented by anyone other than the family and friends of the original homeowner. Brenk ("Microstoria sotto la chiesa," 197) suggests that the space was rediscovered in the sixth century when the *passio* of the two martyrs became current. See also Kim Bowes, *Private Worship*, 88–92.

19. On the martyr *passio*, see Conrad Leyser, "'A Church in the House of the Saints': Property and Power in the Passion of John and Paul," in *Religion, Dynasty, and Patronage in Early Christian Rome, 300–900*, ed. Kate Cooper and Julia Hillner (Cambridge: Cambridge University Press, 2007), 140–62.

in the fourth and the fifth century.[20] Some of the confusion comes from Ambrose's translation of the remains of Saints Protasius and Gervasius to a church in Milan, and the assumption that the same would be true for Rome. Ambrose, however, is a special case, and he deposited his martyrs in his own funerary church (later Sant'Ambrogio), outside the walls of Milan. Such translations did not occur in Rome. In addition, credulous claims made in later centuries that churches had contained relics from an early date have often been taken at face value. As we know, however, Gregory the Great (late sixth century) refused permission to move martyr remains from their graves outside Rome's walls, insisting that *brandea* (contact relics) were sufficient for a church dedication.[21] Therefore, Roman saints buried outside Rome remained immobile and untouched through the early seventh century; the requirement for bodily relics in altars only dates from the eighth century.[22] In the first half of the fifth century, no martyrs were buried in Roman churches, nor were there corporeal relics inside the city.

Confusion also reigns with regard to noncorporeal relics in Rome at this time.[23] For example, claims that the imperial chapel, later named Santa Croce in Gerusalemme, that all but straddled the city walls possessed a piece of the true cross are problematic; as Thacker points out, the church was first called Gerusalemme and not Santa Croce, suggesting the relic may have come later.[24] When Rome's San Pietro in Vincoli was founded

---

20. Paul F. Bradshaw, *Early Christian Worship: A Basic Introduction to Ideas and Practice*, 2nd ed. (Collegeville, MN: Liturgical Press, 2010), 100. This is the most recent edition and Bradshaw, in his introduction, says that no chapter of the earlier edition went unrevised. See also John Crook, *The Architectural Setting of the Cult of Saints in the Early Christian West c.300–c.1200* (Oxford: Oxford University Press, 2000), 13. R. A. Markus, "How on Earth Could Places Become Holy? Origins of the Christian Idea of Holy Places," *JECS* 2 (1994): 270.

21. John M. McCulloh, "The Cult of Relics in the Letters and 'Dialogues' of Pope Gregory the Great: A Lexicographical Study," *Traditio* 32 (1976): 149, 152, 155.

22. Caroline Goodson, "The Relic Translations of Paschal I: Transforming City and Cult," in *Roman Bodies*, ed. Andrew Hopkins and Maria Wyke (London: British School at Rome, 2005), 125.

23. The Lateran baptistery chapels whose dates fall outside the scope of our investigation contained only noncorporeal relics of saints and a piece of the True Cross. See Thacker, "Martyr Cult," 44–45; and Mackie, *Early Christian Chapels*, 195–211.

24. Thacker, "Martyr Cult," 44; see also Dey, *Aurelian Wall*, 219, where he discusses the council of Braga in 562 CE prohibiting intramural burial.

(mid-fifth century), the Empress Eudoxia donated from Constantinople the chains of Saint Peter, a noncorporeal relic.[25]

A further red herring in the historical understanding of the period is the "sack" of Rome in 410 CE. Contrary to a longstanding assumption, new archaeological excavations and reassessments of contemporary sources indicate that 410 was not a game-changing cataclysm for the city.[26] The events in 410 did not prevent church building in Rome over the next few decades. As Richard Krautheimer observed, after 410 there was an upsurge of church building within the walls, especially after 433 under Sixtus III.[27] Their monumentality and opulence were an innovation in the landscape of Roman Christian worship, even as the martyr cult continued outside the walls in the funerary basilicas. These urban *tutuli* (Santa Maria Maggiore, Santa Sabina, San Pietro in Vincoli, etc.) made no claims to have bodily relics. Notably, the Lateran, the pope's church, was dedicated to Christ and had no relics in the first half of the fifth century. In sum, there was no need for martyr relics, regardless of whether the church was a *titulus*, an imperially sponsored church, or a papal foundation.[28]

---

25. Alan Thacker, "The Origin and Early Development of Rome's Intramural Cults: A Context for the Cult of Sant'Agnese in Agone," *MEFRM* 126 (2014): 1–27. Thacker reports that this relic tradition is only documented as of the sixth century CE.

26. For the reevaluation of the impact of Alaric's 410 CE attack on Rome, see Johannes Lipps, Carlos Machado, and Philipp von Rummel, eds., *The Sack of Rome in 410 AD: The Event, Its Context and Its Impact; Proceedings of the Conference Held at the German Archaeological Institute at Rome, 04–06 November 2010* (Wiesbaden: Reichert, 2013), and especially Philipp von Rummel's chapter in that volume, "Eriegnis und Narrativ: Erzählungen der Plünderung Roms im August 410 zwischen Textüberlieferung und Archäologie," 26. Augustine's *City of God*, a major source for this assumption, is not social history but theology; see Peter Brown's nuanced analysis of this period in *Through the Eye of a Needle: Wealth, the Fall of Rome, and the Making of Christianity in the West, 350–550 AD* (Princeton: Princeton University Press, 2012).

27. Richard Krautheimer, *Three Christian Capitals: Topography and Politics* (Berkeley: University of California Press, 1983), 103–21.

28. Marios Costambeys, "Burial Topography and the Power of the Church in Fifth- and Sixth-Century Rome," *PBSR* 69 (2001): 169–89. He points out that throughout the fifth century burials inside the walls increased (171–73); connections between burials and churches, however, are tenuous at best.

Why Build Fifth-Century Intramural Churches?

Regarding religious competition, we suggest that these fifth-century churches were built *in part* to compete with the extramural funerary basilicas, although it is also possible Roman Christians would have considered these two sets of contemporary Christian places of worship to be the Christian equivalent of apples and oranges; in other words, Romans chose to participate in one or the other or both depending on the festal calendar and their own circumstances. Turning to Innocent I's letter of 416 to Decentius, it is worth noting that Innocent draws a clear distinction in essence between churches inside Rome and the funerary basilicas outside. When Innocent says "churches," he means the titular churches of Rome. When he later mentions the "various cemetery churches," he clearly puts them in a different category from the intramural Roman churches,[29] precisely as expected given the Roman perception of the ontological difference between the intra- and extramural zones. Clearly these new churches were built for the use of Roman Christians and offered something of meaning for them. Whereas martyr cult took place on specified days such as the *natale* (technically, the death day) of the martyr,[30] the intramural churches offered daily worship and, on Sundays and Easter, the Eucharist.[31] Patterns of ritual and behavior also differed inside and outside the walls. Inside the walls, decorum prevailed; outside the walls, according to both eastern and western sources (Augustine, Jerome, John Chrysostom, Vigilantius, Ambrose, etc.), martyr and family worship involved all-night vigils with singing, dancing, drinking, feasting, and cohabitational hijinks.[32] In contrast to the intramural churches, Jean-Michel Spieser even proposes that religious practice in the cemeteries belonged to what might be called the private and family sphere.[33]

---

29. Johnson, *Worship in the Early Church*, 101–2.
30. Bradshaw, *Early Christian Worship*, 99.
31. Johnson, *Worship in the Early Church*, 101–2.
32. Jean-Michel Spieser, "Ambrose's Foundations at Milan and the Question of Martyria," in *Urban and Religious Spaces in Late Antiquity and Early Byzantium*, VCS 706, ed. Jean-Michel Spieser (Burlington, VT: Ashgate, 2001), 8. This is the English translation of Spieser's earlier article, "Les fondations d'Ambroise à Milan et la question des martyria," *DChAE* 20 (1998): 29–34.
33. Spieser, "Ambrose's Foundations."

Churches functioned as places of worship. Within this context, what also made these intramural churches attractive to ordinary Roman Christians was their easy access to splendid interiors evoking elite villa decoration and, in the regular and dignified liturgy, the spectacle of worship. Although the latest studies of early liturgy emphasize our lack of data for liturgical practice before the late fifth century,[34] at the least we know of psalm singing, public naming of benefactors, naming of the dead, processions and vestments, and Sunday Eucharist with the *fermentum* distributed throughout the city by the bishop of Rome from the Lateran.[35] It is also likely that some of these *tituli*, such as Santa Sabina, had baptisteries that accommodated the growing number of converts who taxed the Lateran baptistery's capacity.[36]

Already in the mid-fourth century, the trend in Roman liturgy was toward greater spectacle to impress worshipers. Centering his research exclusively on fourth-century *eastern* Christian documents, Robert Taft promoted the concept that at this time the Eucharistic liturgy increasingly used the forbidding language of "fear and awe" in part to capture the attention of new converts whose piety was assumed to be less devoted.[37] Georg Kretschmar, however, cautions that in the *West* this was less the case.[38] For example, Johannes Quasten noted that Ambrose "likens the relationship of the soul to the Eucharist to the relationship between the bride and groom. The Eucharistic meal was a banquet uniting body and soul."[39] However, it was probably true in Rome that, as Paul Bradshaw writes, "eucharistic

---

34. Costambeys, "Burial Topography," 183.

35. Baldovin, "*Fermentum* at Rome," 38–52; and Dey, *Aurelian Wall*, 217–18.

36. Brandenburg, *Ancient Churches*, 175, citing the *Liber Pontificalis* on Sixtus III. On the Santa Sabina baptistery, see Ivan Foletti, "Le porte lignee di Santa Sabina all'Aventino: Tra liturgia stazionaria e funzione iniziatica (il nartece di Santa Sabina, II)," *Hortus atrium medievalium: Journal of the International Research Center for Late Antiquity and Middle Ages* 20.2 (2014): 710.

37. Robert Taft, "The Lord's Prayer in the Eucharistic Liturgy: When and Why?," *EccOr* 14 (1997): 153. See also Baldovin, "*Fermentum* at Rome," 51, and Bradshaw, *Early Christian Worship*, 70.

38. Georg Kretschmar, "Abendmahl III/1: Alte Kirche," *TRE* 1:78.

39. Johannes Quasten, "The Liturgical Mysticism of Theodore of Mopsuestia," *TS* 15 (1954): 431; see also Auxentios Chrysostomos and James Thornton, *Four Essays on Orthodox Liturgical Issues: A Collection of Liturgical Commentaries Written from a Traditionalist Orthodox Perspective* (Etna, CA: Center for Traditionalist Orthodox Studies, 1996), ch. 3.

celebrations ... became much more formal and elaborate; they used such things as ceremonial actions, gesture, processions, and music in order to make an impression upon the congregation."[40] Bradshaw also suggests "a strong dramatizing of the baptismal ceremonies in order to produce a profound emotional effect upon the candidates."[41]

The interior opulence of the new churches, such as Santa Sabina, were on par with the most luxurious elite Roman interiors, whether private homes, mausolea, or imperial palaces. More importantly, however, worshipers would experience sensory overload conducive to an encounter with a numinous presence. Inside, Santa Sabina glowed with diffused light from over two-dozen large arched windows[42] and from hanging lamps and candles. The basilica boasted a rare matched set of twenty four gleaming imported columns of white Proconnesian marble with Corinthian capitals of the late second century that came from an imperial marble depot; such costly materials could not be released without imperial authorization, a strong indication of the level of grandeur which the new basilica commanded.[43] The elegant *opus sectile* (cut marble inlays) designs that survive in the spandrels of the nave arcade constituted the most expensive form of contemporary decoration. Between the columns there were probably rich hangings.[44] The floors would have been marble *opus sectile*. The apse contained a glittering mosaic of Christ and saints, which was lost in the sixteenth century to Zuccaro's replacement fresco[45] but whose glittering monumentality may be inferred from the apse mosaic of Santa Pudenziana. The mosaics of the apse arch portrayed Christ and the apostles in *clipei* (round shields) rising up over images of Bethlehem and Jerusalem

---

40. Bradshaw, *Early Christian Worship*, 70.
41. Ibid.
42. Richard Krautheimer, *Rome: Profile of a City, 312–1308* (Princeton: Princeton University Press, 1980), 45.
43. Hugo Brandenburg, "The Use of Older Elements in the Architecture of Fourth- and Fifth-Century Rome: A Contribution to the Evaluation of Spolia," in *Reuse Value: Spolia and Appropriation in Art and Architecture from Constantine to Sherrie Levine*, ed. Richard Brilliant and Dale Kinney (Burlington, VA: Ashgate, 2011), 54. See also Paolo Liverani, "Reading *Spolia* in Late Antiquity and Contemporary Perception," in Brilliant and Kinney, *Reuse Value*, 33–51. The columns are no longer considered *spolia* from an earlier temple on the Aventine, *pace* Krautheimer, *Rome*, 4.
44. Brandenburg, "Use of Older Elements," 98.
45. Jean-Michel Spieser, "The Representation of Christ in the Apses of Early Christian Churches," *Gesta* 37 (1998): 65.

at either end of the arch.[46] The sanctuary would have been separated from the rest of the nave by a gleaming marble *transenna* (low screen denoting the altar space). Turning to exit through the western doors, worshipers faced arched windows, at either end of which were mosaics of Peter and Paul and whose spandrels contained the symbols of the four evangelists.[47] Spanning the space below the windows is the extant monumental mosaic inscription whose large gold letters on a blue field connoted "imperial splendor and victory and, at the same time, [created] a new framework of visual reception geared specifically at the Christian viewer."[48]

Animated by the changing daylight, the candles and the oil lamps, the mosaics, columns, marble *transenna*, and liturgical vessels would all have flickered and shimmered, suffusing the worship space with a mystical radiance. In a world where seeing was itself conceived of as tactile, with the eye "reaching out" to touch what it saw,[49] the worshiper would have experienced an otherworldly space dissolving the barriers between earth and heaven.[50]

Remarkable work has been done on the visual rhetoric and experience of saints' shrines.[51] We propose that a similar rhetorical dynamic was at

---

46. As recorded by Giovanni Ciampini in the seventeenth century. See Erik Thunø, "Looking at Letters: 'Living Writing' in S. Sabina in Rome," *MJK* 34 (2007): 30 and fig. 13.

47. Ibid., 22 and fig. 5.

48. Ibid., 28.

49. See Robert S. Nelson on ancient concepts of seeing in "Descartes's Cow and Other Domestications of the Visual," in *Visuality before and beyond the Renaissance: Seeing as Others Saw*, ed. Robert S. Nelson (Cambridge: Cambridge University Press, 2000), 1–21.

50. Bissera Pentcheva contrasts the deadening effect of steady uniform "museum" lighting with the animation produced on gleaming surfaces by flickering light from hanging lamps and candles ("The Performative Icon," *ABull* 88 [2006]: 631–55). Her remarks are focused on middle-Byzantine relief icons but are salient for earlier periods as well. She writes, "In its original setting, the icon performed through its materiality. The radiance of light reflected from the gilded surfaces, the flicker of candles and oil lamps placed before the image, the sweetly fragrant incense, the sounds of prayer and music—these inundated all senses. In saturating the material and sensorial to excess, the experience of the icon led to a transcendence of this very materiality and gave access to the intangible, invisible, and noetic" (631). She goes on to note the "late antique tradition of saturating the senses" (632).

51. See Cynthia Hahn, "Seeing and Believing: The Construction of Sanctity in Early-Medieval Saints' Shrines," *Spec* 72 (1997): 1079–1106; Patricia Cox Miller *The*

work in the urban churches. In other words, the ways of seeing and the spiritual satisfaction operative at saints' shrines, such as that of Felix at Nola, apply no less to the experience of the worshiper in Roman fifth-century churches, not because Roman churches had martyr shrines, but because they offered a comparable spiritual and sensorial "bang for the buck." As Cynthia Hahn writes, "the first characteristic of visual rhetoric, the purposeful creation of the miraculous or the unique, means that all elements of a shrine, including location and spatial organization, were carefully orchestrated for their effect upon the viewer.... Saints' shrines were conceived, built and ornamented as glorious sites where it could be seen that heaven touched earth and that the saints supported and glorified the universal church made up of its living members."[52] In his description of Paulinus's Felix shrine, Dennis Trout refers to "an alluring multi-media program of architecture, art and performance."[53]

Hahn cites a poem of Paulinus (ca. 400 CE) celebrating the building of the new basilica around Felix's shrine as evidence of pilgrims' experience at the saint's reliquary shrine.[54] However, this poem actually refers to space around the shrine and not just the shrine itself.

> Fresh light and extended space now open the shrine of Felix to men's eyes.... This place was earlier confined and small for celebrating the sacred ritual. It did not allow those at prayer to raise wide their arms. But now it affords the congregation a shrine with plenty of room for their sacred duties, embraced by the martyr at the centre. All things renewed are pleasing to God; Christ is ever renewing all things, and ennobling them to enhance His light. So He has honoured the tomb of His beloved Felix by improving both its brightness and its access.[55]

Corporeal Imagination: Signifying the Holy in Late Ancient Christianity (Philadelphia: University of Pennsylvania Press, 2009); Georgia Frank, "'Taste and See': The Eucharist and the Eyes of Faith in the Fourth Century," *CH* 70 (2001): 619–43.

52. Hahn, "Seeing and Believing," 1080.

53. Dennis Trout, "Town, Countryside, and Christianization at Paulinus' Nola," in *Shifting Frontiers in Late Antiquity*, ed. Ralph W. Mathisen and Hagith Sivan (Burlington, VT: Ashgate, 1996), 181.

54. Cynthia Hahn, "What Do Reliquaries Do for Relics?" *Numen* 57 (2010): 291.

55. Poem 30 in Paulinus of Nola, *The Poems of St. Paulinus of Nola*, trans. P. G. Walsh, ACW 40 (New York: Newman, 1975), 308.

Paulinus's references to brightness, light, and space could apply to any splendid church in which the "sacred duties" would have focused not on the martyr's "shrine at the centre" but on the liturgical spectacle.

In light of this trend toward liturgical drama and spectacle, Santa Sabina's magnificent interior space serves as a parade example. Whereas the relic's saint linked the pilgrim to heaven, the liturgy and its splendid spatial setting served the same purpose in easily accessible intramural Roman churches. One might suppose the Eucharist, Christ's presence, to have been the focus of awe; however this was probably not the case.[56] Rather, given the documented drop in communion participation beginning in the late fourth century,[57] other elements of the liturgy within the ritual space of the church—processions, hymns, prayers and most importantly, as Taft emphasizes, the blessings[58]—rivaled the rituals and interior splendor of buildings that enclosed the martyr relics on which Hahn focuses.

Despite the "apples and oranges" difference we noted earlier, did the church along with its elite and imperial supporters[59] intend this new splendor specifically to offer worship space and rituals that rivaled those of the extramural martyr shrines? It is perhaps no wonder that the famous and, as we argue elsewhere, unprecedented wooden doors of Santa Sabina appear at this moment.[60] Did they, as Trout writes of Paulinus's celebrated doorways at Nola, create for the Roman *titulus* a kind of "'supercharged' atmosphere?"[61] The first indicator of Santa Sabina's magnificence that a worshiper would have encountered were the monumental wooden doors, at that time brightly painted and decorated.[62] In addition to astounding

---

56. Andrew McGowan, "Rethinking Eucharistic Origins," *Pacifica* 23 (2010): 173–91.

57. Canon 2 of the Council of Antioch of 341 CE; *Apostolic Constitutions* 8.47.9; *Canons of the Holy Apostles* [ca. 400 CE]; and Canon 13, First Council of Toledo [400 CE]; see Baldovin, "Fermentum at Rome," 52.

58. Robert Taft, "The Inclination Prayer before Communion in the Byzantine Liturgy of St. John Chrysostom: A Study in Comparative Liturgy," *Ecclesia Orans* 3 (1986): 57–58.

59. Brown's (*Through the Eye of a Needle*) stresses throughout the complexities of elite support of church building in Rome.

60. Allyson Everingham Sheckler and Mary Joan Winn Leith, "The Crucifixion Conundrum and the Santa Sabina Doors," *HTR* 103 (2010), 67–88.

61. Trout, "Town, Countryside," 179 n. 24, also citing Paulinus, *Ep.* 32.12-15.

62. The study of color on ancient wood, ivory, and stone reliefs is still in its infancy. For an overview of the challenges, see Carolyn L. Connor, "Color on Late Antique and

the viewer with their gem-like colors, the doors presented worshipers with familiar Christian scenes that they had observed in funerary contexts: catacomb chapels, gold glass roundels, and sarcophagus reliefs. If we consider Christ the archetypal martyr,[63] the first public depiction of his crucifixion on the Santa Sabina doors should come as no surprise. The church is the martyr shrine for Christ and his martyrdom is depicted to prepare the worshiper to encounter Christ the triumphant martyr within the church—in the apse, on the apse arch, and on the ceremonial vessels, curtains, and vestments.

Despite all the attractions of these fifth-century intramural *tituli*, it would appear that, in the long run, saints and relics were a better draw. By the end of the century, Rome's churches began to transfer relics—admittedly *brandea* and not corporeal ones—into their magnificent sanctuaries.

Byzantine Ivories: Problems and Challenges of Conservation," in *Spätantike und byzantinische Elfenbeinbildwerke im Diskurs*, ed. Gudrun Bühl, Anthony Cutler, and Arne Effenberger (Wiesbaden: Reichert, 2008), 31–36.

63. Notably, in 429 CE John Cassian accused Nestorians in Rome of equating martyrs and saints with Christ (John Cassian, *De Incarnatione* 5.3). Note also that Candida Moss argues that there were "groups whose practices—if not their confessional statements—treated the martyrs as though they were Christs" (*The Other Christs: Imitating Jesus in Ancient Christian Ideologies of Martyrdom* [Oxford: Oxford University Press, 2010], 169).

A Hair's Breadth:
The Prophet Muhammad's Hair
as Relic in Early Islamic Texts*

Adam Bursi

Arabic biographical and historiographical texts recount many stories of pious Muslims collecting and utilizing objects associated with the Prophet Muhammad, including such bodily relics as Muhammad's hair. An example of this phenomenon appears in a non-Muslim's bewildered testimony about the interactions observed between the Prophet and his followers: "He [the Prophet] did not perform ablution without their running to get the water he had used; he did not spit out saliva without their running to it; and none of his hairs fell without their taking it.... I have been to Chosroes, Caesar, and the Negus, and by God I have never seen a king among a people like Muḥammad among his Companions!"[1] Out of great reverence for him, Muhammad's followers (called within Islamic texts his "Companions," ṣaḥāba) scoop up his used ablution water, his spit, and his fallen hairs. Indeed, their zeal for these relics is further emphasized in reports that the Companions "nearly come to blows" over the Prophet's discarded ablution water and "pour it upon their heads, taking it as a blessing."[2]

---

* This essay is based in part upon material from my doctoral dissertation, "Holy Spit and Magic Spells: Religion, Magic and the Body in Late Ancient Judaism, Christianity, and Islam" (PhD diss., Cornell University, 2015). I thank Kim Haines-Eitzen, David S. Powers, Ross Brann, Susan Ashbrook Harvey, Hamza M. Zafer, Nathaniel P. DesRosiers, Lily C. Vuong, and the anonymous reviewer for their comments on past versions of this paper. All errors are my own.

1. Abū Muḥammad 'Abd al-Malik Ibn Hishām, *Sīrat Rasūl Allāh: Das Leben Muhammed's nach Muhammed Ibn Isḥāk bearbeitet von Abd el-Malik Ibn Hischām*, ed. Ferdinand Wüstenfeld, 2 vols. (Göttingen: Dieterichsche Universitäts-Buchhandlung, 1858–1860), 744–45.

2. 'Abd al-Razzāq b. Hammām al-Ṣan'ānī, *al-Muṣannaf*, ed. Ḥabīb al-Raḥmān

These stories of the Companions scrambling after Prophetic fragments parallel those of late ancient Christians desperately seeking to acquire objects (and body parts) associated with holy men and women to keep as blessings or phylacteries.[3] In such Christian hagiographical narratives, we find dramatic expression of the importance of the saint and his/her relics in late antiquity. In this period, saints and their relics served as ideological embodiments of the values and traditions of Christian communities, functioning as unifying symbols as well as objects of pilgrimage and devotion for religious communities.[4] The shrines, hymns, *vitae*, and icons associated with saint and relic veneration provided powerful sites of identity formation and maintenance for late ancient Christian communities, even as those identities evolved with historical developments and ruptures.[5]

Early Muslims assigned great significance and, as we will see, power to the bodily remains of holy persons, much as their Christian contempo-

---

al-Aʿẓamī, 11 vols. (Beirut: Al-Maktab al-Islāmī, 1983), 5:336 (no. 9720); Abū Bakr ʿAbd Allāh b. Muḥammad Ibn Abī Shayba, *al-Muṣannaf*, ed. Ḥamad ibn ʿAbd Allāh al-Jumʿa and Muḥammad ibn Ibrāhīm al-Laḥīdān, 16 vols. (Riyadh: Maktabat al-Rushd Nāshirūn, 2006), 13:330 (no. 37836). The Arabic word here translated as "blessing" is *ḥanān*, a cognate with Syriac *ḥnānā*, i.e., water or oil that has come into contact with holy relics. See Christelle Jullien and Florence Jullien, "Du *ḥnana* ou la bénédiction contestée," in *Sur les pas des Araméens chrétiens: Mélanges offerts à Alain Desreumaux*, ed. Françoise Briquel Chatonnet and Muriel Debié (Paris: Geuthner, 2010), 333–49. I thank Dina Boero for this reference.

3. David Frankfurter, "On Sacrifices and Residues: Processing the Potent Body," in *Religion in Cultural Discourse: Essays in Honor of Hans G. Kippenberg on the Occasion of His 65th Birthday*, ed. Brigitte Luchesi and Kocku von Stuckrad (Berlin: de Gruyter, 2004), 514–15.

4. Significant studies include Peter Brown, *The Cult of the Saints: Its Rise and Function in Latin Christianity* (Chicago: University of Chicago Press, 1981); Brown, *Society and the Holy in Late Antiquity* (Berkeley: University of California Press, 1982); Caroline Walker Bynum, *The Resurrection of the Body in Western Christianity, 200–1336* (New York: Columbia University Press, 1995); Pierre Maraval, *Lieux saints et pèlerinages d'Orient: Histoire et géographie des origines à la conquête arabe* (Paris: Cerf, 1985); Patricia Cox Miller, *The Corporeal Imagination: Signifying the Holy in Late Antiquity* (Philadelphia: University of Pennsylvania Press, 2009); Thomas Sizgorich, *Violence and Belief in Late Antiquity: Militant Devotion in Christianity and Islam* (Philadelphia: University of Pennsylvania Press, 2009); Raymond Van Dam, *Leadership and Community in Late Antique Gaul* (Berkeley: University of California Press, 1985).

5. Arietta Papaconstantinou, "The Cult of Saints: A Haven of Continuity in a Changing World?" in *Egypt in the Byzantine World, 300–700*, ed. Roger S. Bagnall (Cambridge: Cambridge University Press, 2007), 350–67.

raries did. Despite these similarities, discussions of relics have often used iconoclastic "orthodox Islam" as an austere foil for the extensive significance of saints' relics, shrines, and stories within late ancient and medieval Christianity.[6] Within Islamic studies, too, the veneration of the relics of Muhammad and other Islamic figures was long dismissed as "an expression of individual piety and superstition" or a "low fetishistic form among the common populace."[7] Recent work has, however, demonstrated the significance of relic veneration from very early in the history of Islam. For example, Nancy Khalek argues that the cult of John the Baptist's relics in Damascus was "part of the early Islamic process of identity formation as publicly articulated" by the Umayyad administration of the late seventh and early eighth centuries CE.[8] Josef W. Meri demonstrates that relics "were a fundamental aspect of Muslim and Christian daily life throughout the Islamic lands of the Near East and North Africa during the Middle Ages."[9] In fact, a great area of overlap appears to have existed in the important role that corporeal relics played in the elaboration of identities in these different religious communities.

That the Prophet Muhammad's relics were venerated by Muslims in the medieval period has been discussed in several recent studies, but considerably less attention has been given to the role of relics within the early, formative period of Islam.[10] Moreover, when examining this earlier

---

6. For examples, see Brown, *Cult of the Saints*, 10; Caroline Walker Bynum, *Christian Materiality: An Essay on Religion in Late Medieval Europe* (New York: Zone, 2011), 273–79.

7. Ignaz Goldziher, "Veneration of Saints in Islam," in *Muslim Studies*, ed. S. M. Stern, trans. C. R. Barber and S. M. Stern, 2 vols. (London: Allen & Unwin, 1967), 1:322–29. Samuel M. Zwemer, "Hairs of the Prophet," in *Ignace Goldziher Memorial Volume*, ed. Samuel Löwinger and Joseph Somogyi, 2 vols. (Budapest: Globus, 1948), 1:48–54. Regarding Islamic Studies' historical inattention to relics, see Josef W. Meri, "Relics of Piety and Power in Medieval Islam," in *Relics and Remains*, ed. Alexandra Walsham, P&Psup 5 (Oxford: Oxford University Press, 2010), 97–99.

8. Nancy Khalek, *Damascus after the Muslim Conquest: Text and Image in Early Islam* (Oxford: Oxford University Press, 2011), 94.

9. Meri, "Relics of Piety," 100.

10. For example, Daniella Talmon-Heller states, "In early Islam, the cult of relics was considered to be a despicable *bid'a*" (citing Goldziher) before she then describes the much later, Ayyūbid-era cult of relics; see *Islamic Piety in Medieval Syria: Mosques, Cemeteries and Sermons under the Zangids and Ayyūbids (1146–1260)* (Leiden: Brill, 2007), 55. Other studies of relics in the medieval period include: Josef W. Meri, *The Cult of Saints among Muslims and Jews in Medieval Syria* (Oxford: Oxford University

period, scholars have often focused on the Umayyad and early 'Abbāsid caliphs' deployment of the Prophet's relics for the purposes of political legitimacy, as indications of these dynasties' rightful inheritance of the Prophet's authority.[11] Fewer scholars have examined how early Islamic texts describe Muslims using the Prophet's relics in ritual, especially as signifiers of Islamic identity.[12] The formation and maintenance of Christian communal identities in the late ancient Mediterranean world was closely tied to Christians' material and ideological engagements with saints' shrines, relics, and stories.[13] Did the Prophet Muhammad's relics, and stories about them, perform a similar role for Muslims within early Islam?

In this essay, I suggest that the stories of individuals collecting and using the Prophet's hair offer evidence of the importance of relic veneration within the literary construction of Islamic practice and identity in the early Islamic period. Muslims used stories about Muhammad's hairs—and likely the hairs themselves—to construct Islamic identity in the late seventh and eighth centuries CE, a critical and formative period for nascent Islam. Because belief in Muhammad's status as Prophet was a crucial means of differentiating Muslims from other monotheists in this period, veneration of the Prophet's hair functioned as a visible sign of Islamic identity. Stories of famous Muslims' interactions with the Prophet's hair provided models of

---

Press, 2002); Christopher S. Taylor, *In the Vicinity of the Righteous: Ziyāra and the Veneration of Muslim Saints in Late Medieval Egypt*, IHC 22 (Leiden: Brill, 1999).

11. Finbarr Barry Flood, *The Great Mosque of Damascus: Studies on the Makings of an Umayyad Visual Culture* (Leiden: Brill, 2001), 107–8. Goldizher, "Veneration of Saints in Islam," 330. David S. Margoliouth, "The Relics of the Prophet Mohammed," *MW* 27 (1937): 20–27. Meri, "Relics of Piety," 103, 112–16. Brannon M. Wheeler, *Mecca and Eden: Ritual, Relics, and Territory in Islam* (Chicago: University of Chicago Press, 2006), 74, 81, 87. On competition between the 'Abbāsid and Fāṭimid dynasties over relics, see Paul E. Walker, "Purloined Symbols of the Past: The Theft of Souvenirs and Sacred Relics in the Rivalry between the Abbasids and Fatimids," in *Culture and Memory in Medieval Islam: Essays in Honour of Wilferd Madelung*, ed. Farhad Daftary and Josef W. Meri (New York: Tauris, 2003), 364–87; Yūsuf Rāġib, "Un épisode obscur d'histoire fatimide," *SIs* 48 (1978): 125–32.

12. Interesting studies of the role of the Prophet Muhammad's relics in early Islam include Brannon M. Wheeler, "Gift of the Body in Islam: The Prophet Muhammad's Camel Sacrifice and Distribution of Hair and Nails at his Farewell Pilgrimage," *Numen* 57 (2010): 341–88; Wheeler, *Mecca and Eden*, 71–98.

13. Miller, *Corporeal Imagination*, 82–101. Giselle de Nie, "Seeing and Believing in the Early Middle Ages: A Preliminary Investigation," in *The Pictured Word*, ed. Martin Heusser et al., WII 2 (Amsterdam: Rodopi, 1998), 67–76.

behavior for how to "perform Muslim-ness" in a period when the elaboration of a distinctly Islamic identity was still evolving.

Not a Strand Fell: Stories of the Prophet's Hair

A historicizing impulse pervades the traditions about the Companions and the Prophet's hair. Rather than supernatural *inventiones* that uncover long-lost relics of ancient figures, these stories narrate the specific occasions for the collection of the Prophet's hairs, placing them within the hands of the Companions from the moment they leave the Prophet's head. Several traditions situate the Companions' collection of the Prophet's hairs at important dates in the sacred history of the primordial Islamic community, such as when the Companions "circled [the Prophet], not allowing any of his hair to fall but into a man's hands" as he was shaved during the Farewell Pilgrimage to Mecca in 10/632.[14] According to some of these reports, the Prophet himself encourages his followers to take this shaved hair, as when he commands the Companion Abū Ṭalḥa al-Anṣārī, "Divide it amongst the people."[15] Elsewhere, such relic collection occurs within more intimate circumstances, as when Umm Sulaym (a prominent female Companion) collects the Prophet's hair and sweat as he sleeps in her house.[16]

Beside these narrations of hairs being collected from the living Prophet, other traditions depict Companions wielding the hairs for apotropaic and amuletic purposes after the Prophet's death. For example, Umm Salama, one of the most revered of the Prophet's wives, keeps a reliquary used for medicinal purposes: "Umm Salama had a small silver bell containing hairs

---

14. Abū ʿAbd Allāh Muḥammad Ibn Saʿd, *Kitāb al-Ṭabaqāt al-Kabīr*, ed. Eduard Sachau et al., 9 vols. (Leiden: Brill, 1904–1940), 1.2:135. Muslim b. al-Ḥajjāj, *Ṣaḥīḥ Muslim*, ed. Muḥammad Fuʾād ʿAbd al-Bāqī, 5 vols. (Cairo: Dār Iḥyā al-Kutub al-ʿArabiyya, 1955–1956), 4:1812 (no. 2325). See Wheeler, "Gift of the Body in Islam," 341–44. Dates given correspond to the Islamic Hijrī calendar (before the slash) and the Common Era (after the slash).

15. Muslim, *Ṣaḥīḥ*, 2:947–48 (no. 1305). The Prophet's favorite wife ʿĀʾisha cites this distribution as the occasion when she acquired her strands of the Prophet's hair; see Muḥammad b. ʿUmar al-Wāqidī, *Kitāb al-Maghāzī*, ed. J. Marsden Jones, 3 vols. (Oxford: Oxford University Press, 1966), 3:1109.

16. Abū ʿAbd Allāh Muḥammad b. Ismāʿīl al-Bukhārī, *Kitāb Jāmiʿ al-Ṣaḥīḥ*, ed. L. Krehl and T. W. Juynboll, 4 vols. (Leiden: Brill, 1862–1908), 4:180–81 (*kitāb* 79, *bāb* 41). Muslim, *Ṣaḥīḥ*, 4:1815–16 (no. 2331). Ibn Saʿd, *Ṭabaqāt*, 8:313–14. See Meri, "Relics of Piety," 104–5; Wheeler, "Gift of the Body in Islam," 360–64.

of the Prophet. Whenever someone was sick or had been struck by an evil eye, he would bring a vessel of water [to Umm Salama] and put the hair in it, then drink from it and perform ablutions with it."[17] Umm Salama here retains the Prophet's hairs in a silver container, used by those looking for respite from illness. Dipping the hair in water transmits blessing to the liquid, which can then be drunk and used for ablutions in order to heal an afflicted individual. Hairs of the Prophet owned by the Companion Umm ʿUmāra Nusayba bt. Kaʿb are likewise "washed for the sick," seemingly referencing the same kind of healing ritual.[18]

Umm Salama uses as a receptacle for the Prophet's hairs a "small bell" (*juljul*), a word used elsewhere for objects hung around the necks of sheep or camels. While not explicitly stated, this is perhaps meant to convey that she wore the Prophet's hair upon her body. Such an amuletic usage of the Prophet's hair appears in traditions alleging that the Muslim conquests of Syria and Iraq were successful due to the Companion Khālid b. al-Walīd's wearing a cap (*qalansuwa*) containing hairs of the Prophet as he led the Muslim armies. For example, on the day of the important Muslim defeat of the Byzantine army at al-Yarmūk in Syria in 15/636, Khālid loses his cap in battle and runs after it. Asked by his soldiers why he would bother to look for his cap in the midst of battle, Khālid recalls his story of receiving the Prophet's hair during the Farewell Pilgrimage and notes, "I have not witnessed any battle when it was with me without my being given victory."[19] Blessed by his wearing the Prophet's hair, Khālid is able to lead the Muslims to crucial military successes.

This powerful touch of the Prophet's hair also appears in traditions that describe prominent Companions being buried with Prophetic relics. The Prophet's servant Anas b. Mālik (d. ca. 91/710) absorbs fragments of the Prophet into his own body in death: in a variety of sources, he is said to have been embalmed with a perfume (*sukk*) containing the sweat and

---

17. Isḥāq b. Ibrāhīm b. Makhlad al-Ḥanẓalī al-Marwazī, *Musnad Isḥāq bin Rāhwayh*, ed. ʿAbd al-Ghafūr ʿAbd al-Ḥaqq Ḥusayn Burr al-Balūshī, 5 vols. (Medina: Tawzīʿ Maktabat al-Īmān: 1990–1995), 4:141–42 (no. 1913), 172–73 (no. 1958). Similar versions appear in: ʿUmar Ibn Shabba, *Taʾrīkh al-madīna al-munawwara*, ed. Fuhaym Muḥammad Shaltūt, 4 vols. (Mecca: Dār al-Turāth, 1979), 2:618; Bukhārī, *Ṣaḥīḥ*, 4:96 (*kitāb* 77, *bāb* 66). On this tradition, see Meri, "Relics of Piety," 105.

18. Wāqidī, *Maghāzī*, 2:615.

19. Wāqidī, *Maghāzī*, 3:883–84.

hair of the Prophet.[20] Similarly, the Companion and caliph Muʿāwiya b. Abī Sufyān (d. 60/680) reportedly asked to be buried in a cloak that the Prophet had given him and that the Prophet's nail clippings be sprinkled over his eyes and into his mouth after his death, intimately mixing these relics with Muʿāwiya's own body. The intercessory power understood to reside within the relics of the Prophet's body is explicitly indicated by Muʿāwiya's request that the nail clippings be placed in his mouth and eyes, "for perhaps God will have mercy on me through their blessing."[21]

In these traditions, Muhammad's hairs function as objects of power: curing illnesses, bringing victory in battle, and providing blessing after death. Keeping the hairs in a silver reliquary or tucked into a cap, Muhammad's contemporaries use these relics much as late ancient Christians use the relics of saints: "as locus[es] and mediator[s] of spiritual presence and power."[22] Muhammad's hairs could rival such relics as the hairs of Saint Symeon the Younger that heal illnesses or the thumb of Saint Sergius that repels enemies "as if they had been vanquished by the martyr's miraculous power."[23] These commonalities point to a set of ideas shared with Christians regarding the holiness of the (in Peter Brown's words) "very special dead": Christians and Muslims both seem to have participated in a set of beliefs regarding the potential of holy individuals' powerful remains.

Hair-Dos: Performing Islamic Identity with Prophetic Relics

While the representations of the Prophet's hair point to shared ideas between Muslims and Christians regarding corporeal relics, in several cases these traditions also mark the veneration of Muhammad's hair as a component in the performance of a specifically Islamic identity. The stories of Khālid b. al-Walīd's cap, for example, place Muhammad's relics centrally within the narratives of the Islamic conquests, events crucial to

---

20. Ibn Abī Shayba, *Muṣannaf*, 4:418 (no. 11132). Ibn Saʿd, *Ṭabaqāt*, 7.1:16. Bukhārī, *Ṣaḥīḥ*, 4:180–81 (*kitāb* 79, *bāb* 41).

21. Abū Jaʿfar Muḥammad b. Jarīr al-Ṭabarī, *Taʾrīkh al-rusul waʾl mulūk*, ed. M. J. de Goeje et al., 15 vols. (Leiden: Brill, 1879–1901), 2.1:201.

22. Miller, *Corporeal Imagination*, 2.

23. Paul van den Ven, ed., *La vie ancienne de S. Syméon Stylite le Jeune (521–592)*, 2 vols., SubHag 32 (Brussels: Société des Bollandistes, 1962–1970), 1:122–23, 209. Gregory of Tours, *The History of the Franks*, trans. Lewis Thorpe (Harmondsworth: Penguin, 1974), 413.

early Islamic narratives about the creation of the Muslim community.[24] These world-shaking military victories are explained as emerging from the intervention of the Prophet's hair, making the hair a synecdoche not only of the Prophet but of the divine favor that enabled the Muslims to conquer (and subsequently govern) a sprawling empire. Khālid's pious veneration of Muḥammad's hair becomes a symbol of the kind of Islamic practice that led the Muslims to divinely-inspired dominion over other monotheistic communities.

Indeed, in some traditions about the Companions, rather than "an expression of individual piety and superstition," veneration of the Prophet's hair functions as a public sign of Islamic identity. In a pair of reports, the first Islamic caliph Abū Bakr al-Ṣiddīq describes two former pagan opponents of the Prophet—Khālid b. al-Walīd and Suhayl b. 'Amr—each collecting the Prophet's hair during the Farewell Pilgrimage. As he watches Khālid "take the forelock of the Messenger of God and place it on his mouth and eyes," Abū Bakr compares the scene before him with Khālid's previously antagonist relations with the Muslim community, when "we [the Muslims] had battled him at ... every place where we encountered him."[25] Similarly, Abū Bakr observes Suhayl b. 'Amr, a former denier of Muḥammad's prophecy, "pick up [the Prophet's] hair ... and place it on his eyes." Seeing Suhayl do this, Abū Bakr praises God for having "brought him [Suhayl] to Islam."[26]

These stories cast Khālid and Suhayl as Muslims precisely by their usage of the Prophet's hairs. Like the Companions who rub the Prophet's phlegm into their skin, Khālid and Suhayl touch the hair to their faces. In doing so, they not only acquire the hair's blessing but also signal (to a viewer such as Abū Bakr) their devotion to the Prophet and thus their abandonments of their previous, non-Muslim statuses. Veneration of Muḥammad's hair is a public performance of Khālid's and Suhayl's Muslim identities, distinguishing their present commitments from their previous hostilities.

---

24. Fred Donner, *Narratives of Islamic Origins: The Beginnings of Islamic Historical Writing* (Princeton: Darwin, 1998), 174–81. Thomas Sizgorich, "Narrative and Community in Islamic Late Antiquity," *P&P* 185 (2004): 9–42.

25. Wāqidī, *Maghāzī*, 3:1108–9.

26. Ibid., 2:610.

Dating the Prophet's Hair

These stories represent the Companions—the Muslims closest to the Prophet in history—keeping the Prophet's hairs and using them for different ritual purposes. Even the Prophet himself authorizes the Companions to take his hairs as he is shaved. These stories thus depict the veneration of the Prophet's relics as part of the Islamic practice, or *sunna*, as performed by the members of the primordial Islamic community, who function as models of correct Islamic practice for later generations.

Yet what can we actually gather from these reports about the ritual practice of early Muslims? The traditions studied above come from texts compiled in the ninth century CE that claim to transmit oral traditions stretching back to the period of the Prophet. However, like late ancient Christian sources ("texts of a highly literary, rhetorical, and ideological nature"),[27] early Islamic sources "often tell us more about their date of composition than they do about the events they purport to relate" and are difficult to use for historical reconstruction.[28] Because of the important rhetorical function of the Companions in the legitimation of Islamic practice, the ascription of relic practices to these figures is likely more prescriptive than descriptive.[29]

If veneration of the Prophet's hair did not emerge among the Prophet's Companions, when might it have begun? While it is difficult to date with any precision these and other literary traditions about the Prophet and the early Muslim community, I would suggest that these reports about veneration of the Prophet's hair likely emerged in conjunction with other seventh- and eighth-century processes that witness "evidence of an emergent cult of Muḥammad's person ... cultivated by the Umayyads."[30] As Fred Donner and others have noted, declarations of Muhammad's prophethood

---

27. Elizabeth Clark, *History, Theory, Text: Historians and the Linguistic Turn* (Cambridge: Harvard University Press, 2004), 159.

28. Chase Robinson, *Islamic Historiography*, TIH (New York: Cambridge University Press, 2003), 51.

29. Nancy Khalek, "'He Was Tall and Slender, and His Virtues Were Numerous': Byzantine Hagiographical Topoi and the Companions of Muḥammad in al-Azdī's *Futūḥ al-Shām*," in *Writing "True Stories": Historians and Hagiographers in the Late Antique and Early Medieval Near East*, ed. Arietta Papaconstantinou, Muriel Debié, and Hugh Kennedy (Turnhout: Brepols, 2010), 106–10.

30. Aziz Al-Azmeh, *The Emergence of Islam in Late Antiquity: Allāh and His People* (New York: Cambridge University Press, 2014), 426.

suddenly begin to appear on Arabic inscriptions, coins, and administrative documents only in the late seventh century CE, during the rule of the Umayyad regime.³¹ The systematic collection (and Umayyad patronage) of reports about the Prophet's biography likewise emerged in this period,³² as did imperial elaboration of the Prophet's tomb and related sites in Medina.³³ While the specific motivations for these actions are debated, these developments all appear to be related to Umayyad efforts to promulgate publically a distinctly "Islamic" identity, with veneration of Muhammad and the Qur'ān as some of the clearest signs of difference from contemporaneous Jewish and Christian practice and belief.³⁴

The Prophet's relics were significant symbols of this emergent Islamic identity, witnessed in Umayyad attempts to utilize the Prophet's *minbar* (pulpit), staff, and tomb in asserting the caliph's status as ruler.³⁵ The symbolic value of the Prophet's relics for Islamic identity was not restricted to caliphal authority, however. Notably, in one of the few extant stories of early eighth-century conversions to Islam, a man travels to Muhammad's tomb in Medina after the Umayyad caliph Sulaymān b. ʿAbd al-Malik (r. 96/714–99/717) tells him that the tomb is the most "illustrious" place to convert.³⁶ Proximity to the Prophet's remains appears here as a uniquely

---

31. Fred M. Donner, *Muhammad and the Believers: At the Origins of Islam* (Cambridge: Harvard University Press, 2010), 111–12, 203–8. Donner, *Narratives*, 87–90. Leor Halevi, *Muhammad's Grave: Death Rites and the Making of Islamic Society* (New York: Columbia University Press, 2007), 14–21. Robert Hoyland, "New Documentary Texts and the Early Islamic State," *BSOAS* 69 (2006): 396–97. Jeremy Johns, "Archaeology and the History of Early Islam: The First Seventy Years," *JESHO* 46 (2003): 416.

32. G. H. A. Juynboll, *Muslim Tradition: Studies in Chronology, Provenance and Authorship of Early Ḥadīth* (Cambridge: Cambridge University Press, 1983), 30–39. Wael Hallaq, *The Origins and Evolution of Islamic Law* (Cambridge: Cambridge University Press, 2004), 42–56, 69–78.

33. Harry Munt, *The Holy City of Medina: Sacred Space in Early Islamic Arabia* (New York: Cambridge University Press, 2014), 103–15, 129–47. Miklos Muranyi, "The Emergence of Holy Places in Early Islam: On the Prophet's Track," *JSAI* 39 (2012): 165–71. Stephen J. Shoemaker, *The Death of a Prophet: The End of Muhammad's Life and the Beginnings of Islam* (Philadelphia: University of Pennsylvania Press, 2011), 260.

34. For differing explanations, see Donner, *Muhammad and the Believers*, 202–11; Hoyland, "New Documentary Texts," 397.

35. Munt, *Holy City*, 104. See n.11 above.

36. Ḥamza b. Yūsuf al-Sahmī, *Taʾrīkh Jurjān*, ed. M. A. Muʿīd Khān, 2nd ed. (Hyderabad: Maṭbaʿat Majlis Dāʾirat al-Maʿārif al-ʿUthmāniyya, 1967), 247 (no. 381).

powerful signifier of conversion to Islam. Another story records Byzantine artisans working in Medina as part of the Umayyad construction efforts there who convert to Islam after one of their fellows is miraculously killed as he plans to desecrate the Prophet's tomb.[37] The Prophet's tomb here distinguishes between Christian impiety and Muslim piety, clearly demarcating religious boundaries.[38] While both stories are likely apocryphal, they nonetheless indicate the symbolic value attached to Muhammad's relics in the performance of Islamic identity in this period.

It is within this historical environment of marked attention to Muhammad's symbolic value for Islamic identity that veneration of his hair likely flourished. The plausibility of this dating is further indicated by a cluster of traditions that witness late seventh- and early eighth-century Muslims collecting hairs of the Prophet. The Medinan jurist Rabīʿa b. Abī ʿAbd al-Raḥmān (d. 130/747 or 136/753) claims to have seen hairs of the Prophet, while the Meccan ʿIkrima b. Khālid (d. after 115/733) says that he actually possesses some.[39] When told of the Baṣran scholar Muḥammad b. Sīrīn (d. 110/728) receiving a hair of the Prophet as a gift, the Kūfan ʿAbīda b. ʿAmr al-Salmānī (d. 72/691–2) reportedly responded, "If I had one of his hairs, it would be dearer to me than all the gold and silver in the world" or, more dramatically, "it would be dearer to me than the world and everything in it."[40] The appearance of these traditions indicates that the Muslims of this period saw great value in the hairs of the Prophet.

Not only did they venerate the Prophet's hair, but early eighth-century Muslims even reportedly practiced some of the specific relic rituals that are elsewhere ascribed to the time of the Companions. For example, like Umm Salama's silver-encased hairs of the Prophet used for healing, Ibrāhīm b. Muḥammad b. Saʿd (grandson of the Companion Saʿd b. Abī Waqqāṣ) reports, "We had a small golden bell containing the Messenger

---

Translated in Richard Bulliet, *Islam: The View from the Edge* (New York: Columbia University Press, 1994), 43–44.

37. Abū ʿAlī Aḥmad b. ʿUmar Ibn Rusta, *Kitāb al-Aʿlāk al-Nafīsa*, ed. M. J. de Goeje, BGA 7 (Leiden: Brill, 1892), 69.

38. For similar Christian stories, see Arietta Papaconstantinou, "Saints and Saracens: On Some Miracle Accounts of the Early Arab Period," in *Byzantine Religious Culture: Studies in Honor of Alice-Mary Talbot*, ed. Denis Sullivan, Elizabeth Fisher, and Stratis Papaioannou, MMed 92 (Leiden: Brill, 2012), 328–30.

39. Ibn Saʿd, *Ṭabaqāt*, 1.2:139.

40. Ibid., 3.2:65. Bukhārī, *Ṣaḥīḥ*, 1:56 (*kitāb* 4, *bāb* 33). Meri, "Relics of Piety," 104.

of God's hair that people would wash."⁴¹ The Egyptian scholar Zuhra b. Maʿbad (d. 127/743 or 135/751) similarly claims that he "saw a hair of the Messenger of God ... and [one] would dip it in water and drink that water."⁴² Like the Companions Anas b. Mālik and Muʿāwiya b. Abī Sufyān, the Umayyad caliph ʿUmar b. ʿAbd al-ʿAzīz (d. 101/720) is also said to have been buried with the hair and nails of the Prophet.⁴³ Though these representations of early eighth-century Muslims may have been based upon the transmitted stories of the Companions, it appears more likely that late seventh- and early-eighth century Muslims themselves provided models for the remembered practices of the Companions.

Conclusion

While many of the narratives of Muhammad's hair are set during the lifetime of the Prophet and/or his Companions, these traditions likely emerged in the late seventh and early eighth centuries CE. With Muhammad's rising significance for Islamic identity, rituals and stories associated with the Prophet's relics allowed Muslims to perform their being "brought to Islam" through their acknowledgement and veneration of Muhammad. The traditions of the Prophet's Companions likely circulated alongside, and legitimated, rituals that placed such power in the Prophet's hairs. Rather than historical records, the stories of the Companions and the Prophet's hair might be compared to the written and oral texts that circulated alongside late ancient Christian relics "that trace [the relics'] movement from time to time and place to place, and ... in turn serve to authorize the relics' authenticity and power."⁴⁴ Saying that prominent Companions both kept and used the Prophet's hairs authenticated both the practices and the relics themselves, as coming from the period of the primordial Islamic community. We might imagine late seventh- or eighth-century Muslims listening to these stories of the Companions and performing similar rituals themselves, enacting their Muslim statuses with the Prophet's hair.

Even if only the stories of the Prophet's relics circulated without actual relics accompanying the stories' recitation, the narratives themselves

---

41. Ibn Saʿd, *Ṭabaqāt*, 1.2:139.
42. Ibn Shabba, *Taʾrīkh*, 2:621.
43. Ibn Saʿd, *Ṭabaqāt*, 5:300. Cited in Halevi, *Muhammad's Grave*, 289.
44. Kevin Trainor, "*Pars pro toto*: On Comparing Religious Relic Practices," *Numen* 57 (2010): 269.

focused attention upon the Prophet as a uniquely important embodiment of divine power and thus contributed to the articulation of a distinctly Islamic identity.[45] Early Islamic texts' descriptions of practices associated with the Prophet's hair thus suggest both dialogue and competition between Muslims and Christians. The shared literary and cultural milieu of the late ancient Near East allowed for similar Christian and Islamic literary representations of the holy person's relics and ritual usages of those relics' power and significance. Yet exactly *which* saint's, martyr's, or prophet's relic was literarily described or ritually manipulated was likely a juncture at which communal identities were clearly distinguished and where the competition between Christian and Muslim identities was felt most acutely.

---

45. I thank Christine Shepardson for articulating this point in conversation with me.

Promoting a Cult Site without Bodily Relics: Sacred Substances and Imagined Topography in *The Syriac Life of Symeon the Stylite*

Dina Boero

The text of Theodoret's life of Symeon the Stylite in his *History of the Monks of Syria* concludes,

> Thus, even after death does victory remain united to the contestants according to Christ. Certainly cures of disease of every kind, miracles, and acts of divine power are accomplished even now, just as when he was alive, not only at the tomb of the holy relics but also by the memorial of his heroism and long contending—I mean the great and celebrated pillar of this righteous and much-lauded Symeon—, by whose holy intercession we pray both that we ourselves may be preserved and made firm in the true faith. (*Phil. hist.* 26.28 [Price])

This passage is an interpolation, found only in one set of manuscripts.[1] Although not original to the text, it is important nevertheless, since it

---

1. Theodoret composed his *History of the Monks of Syria* between 440 and 444 CE, approximately fifteen to twenty years before Symeon's death. At a later date, he added an epilogue, although the date of the epilogue is unclear. Given that Theodoret ends his narrative before Symeon's death, this passage most certainly is an interpolation. For a critical edition of the text, see Theodoret of Cyrrhus, *Histoire des moines de Syrie: Histoire Philothée*, ed. and trans. Pierre Canivet and Alice Leroy-Molinghen, 2 vols. SC 234, 257 (Paris: Cerf, 1977–1979). For an English introduction and translation of the text, see *A History of the Monks of Syria*, trans. R. M. Price, CSS 88 (Kalamazoo, MI: Cistercian, 1985). On the text's manuscript tradition, see Canivet and Leroy-Molinghen, *Histoire des moines de Syrie*, 1:58–113; and Alice Leroy-Molinghen, "Les manuscrits de l''Histoire Philothée' de Théodoret de Cyr," *Byzantion* 34 (1964): 27–47. Canivet, Leroy-Molinghen, and Price agree that this passage is an interpolation.

documents a period in the history of Symeon's cult when multiple cult sites claimed to be the locus of Symeon's intercessory power. This passage emphasizes two sites: Symeon's tomb in Antioch, where Symeon's body was transferred and buried following his death in 459 CE, and Symeon's shrine at Telneshe (Telanissos in Greek, modern Deir Sim'an), a four day journey from Antioch, where Symeon had stood upon his column for approximately forty years.[2] In the minds of his followers, this column allowed Symeon to dwell among angels. It made him a penitent philosopher, a new Moses, a bearer of the sins of the world, and an effective intercessor for the many pilgrims who sought his help.[3]

The interpolation in *A History of the Monks of Syria* allots each cult site equal spiritual authority, but it is unlikely that all devotees of Symeon shared this assessment. The militarized procession by which Symeon's body was conveyed to Antioch points to very real contestation over where

---

2. Symeon's body was transported to the Great Church in Antioch following his death, potentially relocated to the Church of Cassian in Antioch, and finally interred in a martyrium built specifically to house Symeon's relics. No archaeological evidence of any of these structures survives. For discussion of the primary sources documenting these shifts, see Wendy Mayer and Pauline Allen, *The Churches of Syrian Antioch (300–638 CE)* (Leuven: Peeters, 2012), 104–7. For an introduction to the archaeological remains of Symeon's cult site in Telneshe, see Georges Tchalenko, *Villages antiques de la Syrie du nord: Le massif du Bélus à l'époque romaine*, 3 vols. (Paris: Geuthner, 1953–1958), 1:223–76, and Jean-Pierre Sodini and Jean-Luc Biscop, "Qal'at Sem'an et Deir Sem'an: Naissance et développement d'un lieu de pèlerinage durant l'Antiquité tardive," in *Architecture paléochrétienne*, ed. J. M. Spieser (Gollion: Infolio, 2011), 11–59. Excavations of the monumental pilgrimage complex in Telneshe unearthed fragments of a reliquary in the cruciform basilica; the reliquary was installed in the first phase of construction (approximately 475–495 CE) or later. Marie-Christine Comte, *Les Reliquaires du Proche-Orient et de Chypre à la période protobyzantine (ive–viiie siècles): Formes, emplacements, fonctions et cultes* (Turnhout: Brepols, 2012), 342–43. To the cult sites in Antioch and Telneshe can be added the cult site in Constantinople mentioned in *The Life of Daniel the Stylite*. For an edition of this text, see Hippolyte Delehaye, *Les Saints Stylites*, SubHag 14 (Paris: Picard, 1923), 1–94. For a translation, see Elizabeth A. S. Dawes and Norman Hepburn Baynes, trans., *Three Byzantine Saints: Contemporary Biographies of St. Daniel the Stylite, St. Theodore of Sykeon, and St. John the Almsgiver* (Oxford: Blackwell, 1948).

3. Susan Ashbrook Harvey, "The Sense of a Stylite: Perspectives on Simeon the Elder," *VC* 42 (1988): 376–94; Peter Brown, "The Rise and Function of the Holy Man in Late Antiquity," *JRS* 61 (1971): 80–101. The image of Symeon dwelling among angels appears repeatedly in the Syriac literature on Symeon and in sixth-century visual representations of Symeon.

his remains would ultimately reside.[4] For those who administered Symeon's cult site in Telneshe, this transfer must have posed a challenge. While the site in Telneshe was certainly not the only cult site to lack a saint's bodily relics—Thecla's pilgrimage complex in Seleucia also lacked bodily relics—the possession of a saint's remains enhanced a cult site's authority and prestige.[5] Now that Symeon had died and his body had been interred in Antioch, his cult-keepers in Telneshe faced a set of critical questions. How were devotees to have contact with the saint? Where would they contact him? Was Telneshe still the center of cult life?

Written only fourteen years after Symeon's death by two otherwise unknown devotees of Symeon, Bar-Ḥaṭar and Simeon bar-Eupolemos, *The Syriac Life of Symeon the Elder* offers insight into how a set of cult-keepers promoted a cult site that lacked bodily relics.[6] To promote the site, the authors took a bifold approach. First, Bar-Ḥaṭar and Simeon bar-Eupolemos describe the distribution of material substances such as dust, water, and oil as a method for accessing the saint's intercessory power in place of contact with Symeon's body. Second, the authors specify that these substances played a broader role within the imagined topography of the cult site and the Near Eastern landscape. In addition to offering healing and protection, these substances, and in particular a paste mixture

---

4. Details of this procession are discussed below.

5. For an introduction to relics in late antique and medieval religious practice, see Martina Bagnoli et al., eds., *Treasures of Heaven: Saints, Relics, and Devotion in Medieval Europe* (New Haven: Yale University Press, 2010), and Cynthia J. Hahn and Holger A. Klein, eds., *Saints and Sacred Matter: The Cult of Relics in Byzantium and Beyond* (Washington DC: Dumbarton Oaks, 2015). For Thecla's cult site in Seleucia, see Stephen J. Davis, *The Cult of Saint Thecla: A Tradition of Women's Piety in Late Antiquity* (Oxford: Oxford University Press, 2001), 36–80.

6. This version of *The Syriac Life of Symeon* dates to 473 CE and is preserved in Vatican Syriac Manuscript 160, fols. 1–79. Stefano Evodio Assemani transcribed the manuscript and translated it into Latin; see *Acta Sanctorum Martyrum Orientalium et Occidentalium*, 2 vols. (Rome: Collini, 1748), 2:268–398. Robert Doran translated this version of the *The Syriac Life of Symeon* into English: *The Lives of Simeon Stylites*, CSS 112 (Kalamazoo, MI: Cistercian Publications, 1992), 103–98. I follow Doran's chapter divisions. Doran gives a synoptic chart of his chapter divisions, the Vatican Manuscript's folio numbers, and Assemani's page and line numbers on pp. 201–5 of his publication. On Telneshe as the location of production for the manuscript and its close association with pilgrimage infrastructure, see Dina Boero, "The Context of Production of the Vatican Manuscript of the *Syriac Life of Symeon the Stylite*," *Hug* 18 (2015): 319–59.

called *ḥnānā* in Syriac, delineated new spaces in the landscape marked by Symeon's sanctity. The distribution of these substances created a center and periphery for cultic devotion, placing Telneshe and the cult site at the center and creating ritually-constituted territorial links between the cult site at Telneshe, satellite sites, and the Great Church in Antioch, where Symeon's body was interred. This approach integrated devotion to Symeon across an expansive landscape, while also differentiating Telneshe's cult community and placing it in a superior hierarchical relationship with his tomb in Antioch.[7]

Sacred Substances

The Syriac Life of Symeon places a premium on the distribution of dust, water, oil, and *ḥnānā* as well as other substances originating from or blessed at the cult site. *Ḥnānā* consisted of a mixture of dust and other accumulation at the shrine combined with oil and water. Out of approximately thirty-two miracles in *The Syriac Life of Symeon*, Bar-Ḥaṭar and Simeon bar-Eupolemos include references to such substances in approximately twenty-five miracle accounts, a remarkable number in comparison to other late antique hagiographies.[8] The two authors refer to water most often, a total of twelve times (chs. 35, 38, 56, 79, 81, 82, 83, 84, 87, 89, 91, and 97), followed by *ḥnānā* eight times (chs. 38, 39, 61, 63, 64, 71, 72, and 88), dust seven times (chs. 33, 34, 35, 36, 89, 91, and 93), oil twice

---

7. Catherine Bell's work on ritualization serves at the theoretical foundation for my approach to substances from Symeon's cult site. See *Ritual Theory, Ritual Practice* (Oxford: Oxford University Press, 1992). For her discussion of spatial systems, see pp. 124–30. Recent research by Christine C. Shepardson (*Controlling Contested Places: Late Antique Antioch and the Spatial Politics of Religious Controversy* [Berkeley: University of California Press, 2014]) has illuminated the importance of physical and rhetorical contestation over space in late antiquity.

8. Using thirty-three Greek hagiographies, Daniel Caner has compiled a quantitative assessment of references to "blessings," the category in which the dust, water, oil, and *ḥnānā* fall. In his count, the two hagiographies with the largest number of "blessings" are *The Life of Saint Nicholas of Sion* with thirteen references to "blessings" and John Moschus's *Spiritual Meadow* with twenty references. A far earlier hagiography than these two texts, *The Syriac Life of Symeon* exceeds both in count. See Daniel Caner, "Alms, Blessings, Offerings: The Repertoire of Christian Gifts in Early Byzantium," in *The Gift in Antiquity*, ed. Michael L. Satlow (Hoboken, NJ: Wiley-Blackwell, 2013), 32.

(chs. 29 and 88), pebbles once (ch. 64), stones once (ch. 86), and finally a shawl (ch. 80).[9]

As scholars have noted previously and as Gary Vikan discusses in this volume, the distribution of these substances reflects wider traditions of relic veneration and pilgrimage practice in late antiquity, both within the Limestone Massif specifically and the Mediterranean world more broadly.[10] In northern Syria, reliquaries were designed so that devotees could pour water, oil, and other liquids through the central receptacle that housed the saint's bones, providing direct contact with the saint.[11] At the shrine of Abu Menas in Egypt and the shrine of Saint John in Asia Minor, pilgrims purchased stamped, terracotta flasks in which they carried away the shrine's dust, water, and oil.[12] In late antiquity, nonbodily relics could be equally as potent as bodily relics; there was not necessarily a clear distinction between the two.[13] These materials gave expression to pilgrims' belief that sacred power was physically concentrated in objects.[14] Ampullae and their contents also afforded a tactile experience of the divine, in which the localized sacred could be transferred through the experience of touch.[15]

At the same time, the procurement of materials from individual pilgrimage sites was constructed around particular social, political, and economic contexts. While Bar-Ḥaṭar and Simeon bar-Eupolemos's references to the distribution of sacred substances at the cult site participate in broader traditions of relic veneration and pilgrimage practice, the authors

---

9. In certain miracle accounts, multiple substances are used in the same miracle.

10. Gary Vikan, *Early Byzantine Pilgrimage Art* (Washington, DC: Dumbarton Oaks, 2010), and Laura Veneskey, "Alternative Topographies: Loca Sancta Surrogates and Site Circulation in Late Antiquity and Byzantium" (PhD diss., Northwestern University, 2012), 43–65. Venesky focuses on dust above other substances from the cult site at Telneshe.

11. Comte, *Reliquaires du Proche-Orient*, 41–52.

12. Vikan, *Early Byzantine Pilgrimage Art*, 33–35; Davis, *Cult of Saint Thecla*, 114–26 and 195–200; Andreas Pülz, "Archaeological Evidence of Christian Pilgrimage in Ephesus," *Herom* 1 (2012): 225–60.

13. Julia Smith, "Relics: An Evolving Tradition in Latin Christianity," in *Saints and Sacred Matter: The Cult of Relics in Byzantium and Beyond*, eds. Cynthia J. Hahn and Holger A. Klein (Washington, DC: Dumbarton Oaks, 2015).

14. Vikan, *Early Byzantine Pilgrimage Art*, 23–25.

15. Heather Hunter-Crawley, "Pilgrimage Made Portable: A Sensory Archaeology of the Monza-Bobbio Ampullae," *Herom* 1 (2012): 135–56.

also engage in a process of innovating upon this tradition.[16] *The Syriac Life of Symeon* offers an opportunity to move away from general discussions of pilgrimage practice and examine the approach to and use of sacred substances within a specific historical situation.

The Syriac Life of Symeon was composed at a transitional moment in the history of Symeon's cult, that is, after Symeon's body had been removed from Telneshe and interred in the Great Church in Antioch in 459 CE but before the Telneshe cult site was established as the central place for veneration of Symeon, with the construction of the monumental pilgrimage complex between approximately 475 and 490 CE. Bar-Ḥaṭar and Simeon bar-Eupolemos emphasize the use of dust, water, oil, and *ḥnānā* in healing, exorcism, and ritual cleansing to promote their much-loved place of veneration. The distribution of these substances offered a method for accessing the saint's intercessory power in place of Symeon's body. By encouraging the use of substances specifically procured at the cult site, the authors endorse the centrality of the cult site in seeking Symeon's intercessory powers. They advocate its uniqueness and, thus, differentiate it from the cult site in Antioch.

Imagined Topography

In addition to making the material substances of the cult site central to accessing the saint's intercessory powers, Bar-Ḥaṭar and Simeon bar-Eupolemos put forward that these substances, and *ḥnānā* in particular, could be used to bless new places protected by Symeon. The authors present the topography of Symeon's sanctity as stemming from Symeon's enclosure, radiating outward though Telneshe, and extending across the Near Eastern countryside. Whereas previous scholarship has focused on the medical, apotropaic, and defensive qualities of *ḥnānā*, the use of *ḥnānā* to dedicate spaces as protected by the saint has, on the whole, gone unnoticed.[17] Yet, in the imagination of Bar-Ḥaṭar and Simeon bar-Eupolemos, *ḥnānā* more than any other substance contained the power to imbue new

---

16. Bell, *Ritual Theory, Ritual Practice*, 118–20, addresses continuity and change in the construction of tradition.

17. For the medical, apotropaic, and defensive qualities of *ḥnānā* and other *eulogiae*, see Gary Vikan, "Art, Medicine, and Magic in Early Byzantium," *DOP* 38 (1984): 65–86. For an overview of *ḥnānā* as it appears in Syriac literature, see Christelle Jullien and Florence Jullien, "Du 'ḥnana' ou la bénédiction contestée," in *Sur les pas des*

places with Symeon's saintly presence and to construct a link between the cult site and additional loci in the landscape protected by Symeon.[18]

For the authors of the *The Syriac Life of Symeon*, Symeon's sanctity originated from Symeon's enclosure. Bar-Ḥaṭar and Simeon bar-Eupolemos pay special attention to specifying the boundaries and arrangement of this enclosure. The plot of land which came to comprise Symeon's enclosure was originally owned by the priest Daniel (ch. 28). The enclosure was a concretely defined space, with walls, a eucharistic niche, and a door (chs. 98 and 99). The organization of the space changed several times during Symeon's life, with the pulling down of walls and the construction of various columns (chs. 76 and 113). During Lent, Symeon isolated himself in his enclosure, ordering the door to be closed to his devotees and his disciples (chs. 51–52, 54, 61, and 112). When the door to the enclosure was open, men could enter but not women (ch. 33).[19]

Bar-Ḥaṭar and Simeon bar-Eupolemos depict Symeon's power as emanating from the enclosure and extending to Telneshe's village boundaries. In one miracle account, the authors relate how three men ruined a cucumber patch belonging to a poor farmer who lived outside of Aleppo (ch. 39). In punishment, the first assailant was consumed with elephantiasis, and the third was smitten with an evil spirit. The body of the second swelled,

---

araméens chrétiens: Mélanges offerts à Alain Desreumaux, ed. Françoise Briquel-Chatonnet and Muriel Debié (Paris: Geuthner, 2010), 333–49.

18. Comprised not simply of dust but more specifically the material that had fallen off of and accumulated around Symeon's column over his extended residence there, ḥnānā possessed a ritualized association with Symeon beyond the dust, water, oil, pebbles, and stones obtained at the cult site. In recounting an early miracle in Symeon's career, the authors specify, "For there was no oil there to give, nor was it yet the custom to give ḥnānā for he had been there only fourteen months" (ch. 33 [Doran]).

19. Although late fifth- and early sixth-century buildings at Qal'at Sem'an obscure many of the site's earliest structures, at least one of the features mentioned in *The Syriac Life of Symeon* is documented archaeologically. The bases of two different columns are still extant, one inside the cruciform basilica and another in a courtyard between the south and east arms of the basilica (Sodini and Biscop, "Qal'at Sem'an," 15–17 and figs. 4 and 5). Ch. 33 specifies that when a man brought his paralyzed daughter to be healed by the saint, he laid her down north of the saint's enclosure while her father supplicated the saint on her behalf. After she was healed, she never entered the boundaries of the shrine to thank Symeon, even though the miraculous event inspired her to join a monastery. This suggests that women were not admitted into the cult site. Theodoret corroborates the ban on women at the cult site (*Phil. hist.* 26.21).

and walking caused him much pain. He went to see the saint, but when he crossed Telneshe's boundary stone, he stumbled and fell. His belly burst open, and he immediately died. The authors present the sanctity that imbued Telneshe as too potent for the villain to bear, exacting justice on the evildoer who attempted to enter the village and defending the devotee in question.

The authors also emphasize the portability of Symeon's sanctity and its capacity to initiate new places under Symeon's protection. To continue with the case of the cucumber farmer from Aleppo, in addition to punishing the three villains who had destroyed the farmer's field, Symeon instructed the farmer to carry away some *ḥnānā* from the cult site and use it to mark his field with three crosses. This act would bless his field and ensure its productivity. By physically layering Symeon's *ḥnānā* onto his own soil, the farmer marked a new point in the landscape protected by Symeon, thus extending the radius of Symeon's sanctity from the cult site and Telneshe to his own farm outside Aleppo.

The incident with the cucumber farmer is not the only case in which Bar-Ḥaṭar and Simeon bar-Eupolemos depict supplicants using *ḥnānā* to delineate a new space under Symeon's protection. In chapters 62 and 63, the authors recount how a crowd came to Symeon from a village in Lebanon. Members of the crowd explained to the saint that wild animals roamed the mountains. They attacked villagers, entered their homes, and ate their children. To remedy the situation, Symeon directed the villagers to bless the boundaries of the village using substances from the cult site. He prescribed in detail that the villagers take *ḥnānā*, set up four stones at each boundary of the village, make three crosses on each stone using the *ḥnānā*, and keep vigil there for three days. Just as the authors emphasize the boundary stones of Telneshe as the limit to Symeon's radiating power, so also in the village in Lebanon the newly hallowed boundary stones circumscribed the space protected by Symeon. Threatening beasts could not cross them; some beasts even fell down and burst open in front of them—the same punishment born by the assailant of the cucumber farm upon his entry to Telneshe. In thanksgiving, the Lebanese villagers gave Symeon the skins of three animals which had died at the village's boundary, hanging them on the door of Symeon's enclosure like hunting trophies. This public display affirmed the centrality of Telneshe as the place from which Symeon's sanctity originated. It reinforced the boundaries of the cult site. Finally, it expressed a social bond and a territorial link between the village in Lebanon and the Telneshe cult site, envisioning a new topography of cultic devotion.

Such accounts of individuals carrying away *ḥnānā* and other substances from the cult site and dedicating new places as protected by Symeon abound in *The Syriac Life of Symeon*. Bar-Ḥaṭar and Simeon bar-Eupolemos imagine a landscape dotted with loci dedicated to Symeon. When a ship traveling to Syria was about to sink, one of the travelers carrying the saint's *ḥnānā* made a cross with the *ḥnānā* on the mast of the ship and rubbed handfuls of it on the ship's sides. After the traveler marked the ship, Symeon materialized out of thin air and fought off the evil spirit who was causing the ship to sink (ch. 71). When a man was tormented by an evil spirit, Symeon instructed the man to make three crosses on his house in order to purify the space (ch. 36). When a spring had dried up in Gindaros, Symeon ordered the villagers: take three pebbles, make crosses on them, and throw them down when the spring gushes forth; take *ḥnānā*, make crosses on the *ḥnānā*, and throw the clump of *ḥnānā* into the spring as well; finally place crosses on the sides of the spring and keep vigil in the church. Water was subsequently restored to the spring (ch. 64).

The reader must be careful not to assume that the mention of these newly protected places—the farmer's cucumber patch outside Aleppo, the village in Lebanon, and the spring in Gindaros—documents the actual distribution of devotion to Symeon in or before 473 CE (the date of composition of *The Syriac Life of Symeon*). There is no corroborating evidence which suggests that Symeon was venerated in these places above and beyond other saints.[20] Rather, the mention of these places constructs an imagined topography of Symeon's sanctity which originated in Telneshe and radiated outward across the Syrian landscape. In the imagination of the authors, the distribution of *ḥnānā* and other substances from the cult site and the initiation of new places protected by Symeon's power created ritually-constituted territorial links between the cult site in Telneshe and new places endowed with Symeon's protection. While these new places benefited from Symeon's protection, they themselves were not generative of Symeon's powers. These newly protected places always point back to the cult site in Telneshe. In this way, the authors integrate devotion to

---

20. In his archaeological report on Gindaros, Nobert Kramer argues that the stylite had direct influence over Gindaros. However, his assessment is based solely on the passage in *The Syriac Life of Symeon*; he admits that there is no other archaeological or literary evidence for devotion to Symeon after his death; see *Gindaros: Geschichte und Archäologie einer Siedlung im nordwestlichen Syrien vom hellenistischer bis in frühbyzantinische Zeit* (Rahden: Leidorf, 2004), 333–35.

Symeon across an expansive landscape, while also constructing a center and periphery for cultic devotion.

Integration and Hierarchy: The Procession to Antioch

The culminating extension of Symeon's sanctity was his burial procession and interment in Antioch. Upon Symeon's death, the city of Antioch petitioned Ardabur, the son of Aspar, the commander of the East, that Symeon's body be transported to Antioch so that Symeon might become its fortified wall and that he might defend the city with his prayer. Ardabur oversaw the transport of Symeon's body in a procession accompanied by twenty-one prefects, tribunes, and soldiers.[21] The militarized nature of the procession, in combination with the fact that the village of Telneshe was under the jurisdiction of Antioch both politically and ecclesiastically, suggests that the community in Telneshe had little say regarding the fate of Symeon's remains. They were also in a weak position to express public discontent with the turn of events.

Treading carefully in this difficult situation, Bar-Ḥatar and Simeon bar-Eupolemos smooth over any hint of tension between Antioch and the community at Telneshe. In their telling of the event, the veneration of Symeon in a regional capital further demonstrated the saint's authority. The authors explain that Symeon's burial in Antioch was "devised by the Lord to show how much glory he meted out to one who glorified him with good works and righteous deeds" (ch. 125 [Doran]). The military component of the procession demonstrated Symeon's territorial power and authority, calling to mind triumphs and celebratory processions of emperors and military victors.[22] At the same time, the authors describe the procession to and the burial of Symeon's body in Antioch as forging a link between the cult site in Telneshe and the cult site in Antioch. This subtle move presented a positive relationship between the two cult sites, while it simultaneously positioned the cult site in Telneshe as the originating source of Symeon's power.

---

21. J. R. Martindale, *A.D. 395-527*, vol. 2 of *The Prosopography of the Later Roman Empire* (Cambridge: Cambridge University Press, 1980), 135–37.

22. Sabine MacCormack, *Art and Ceremony in Late Antiquity* (Berkeley: University of California Press, 1981), 15–91; Franz Alto Bauer, "Urban Space and Ritual: Constantinople in Late Antiquity," *AAAHP* 15 (2001): 27–61.

The authors integrate the procession to and interment in Antioch into the imagined topography of the text. After departing from Telneshe, the procession's first stop was the village of Shih (ch. 125).[23] The villagers at Shih had previously witnessed one of Symeon's miracles; thus, they already shared a special relationship with the saint (ch. 38). The same villagers venerated the saint in ritual fashion, burning incense and lighting candles as they sought his blessing (ch. 125). This incense, which appears at important moments throughout the text—Symeon's prayer in his youth, his ascent to the column, and his death—demonstrated this community's correct and rightful devotion to the saint.[24] The community placed Symeon's coffin on a chariot and displayed it for commanders, prefects, soldiers, and villagers. The visual display interwove Symeon's spiritual, political, and even military power.[25] The procession then departed from the village, making commemorative stops at villages between Telneshe and Antioch over the course of five days (ch. 26). Each stop created a spatial link between the cult site in Telneshe and subsequent villages which Symeon's body graced. The authors set forth a lateral relationship between various locals while also assuming the hierarchical authority of Telneshe.

Finally, the procession arrived at Antioch, the end point of the punctuated route. The language of Antioch's petition, seeking that Symeon be its "fortified wall," calls to mind the use of substances to bless the boundary stones of the cucumber farmer's plot of land, the village in Lebanon, and other points in the Syrian landscape protected by Symeon. In this case,

---

23. Jean-Luc Biscop and Jean-Pierre Sodini, "L'accès nord au domaine de Syméon le Stylite: Le village de Shih (Sheikh ed Deir-Shader, Bardakhan)," in Desreumaux, Briquel-Chatonnet, and Debié, *Sur les pas des Araméens chrétiens*, 259–68.

24. Susan Ashbrook Harvey, *Scenting Salvation: Ancient Christianity and the Olfactory Imagination* (Berkeley: University of California Press, 2006), 192–94.

25. The importance of saints in military affairs is well-documented in late antiquity. Sergius makes an excellent example. Elizabeth Key Fowden, *The Barbarian Plain: Saint Sergius between Rome and Iran* (Berkeley: University of California Press, 1999). Evagrius Scholasticus also emphasizes Symeon's capabilities in assuring military success, recounting how Symeon's head was removed from its tomb and sent to Philippicus for the protection of the eastern armies (*Hist. eccl.* 1.13). For the critical edition of Evagrius' text, see Evagrius Scholasticus, *Historia ecclesiastica/Kirchengeschichte*, ed. and trans. Adelheid Hübner, Joseph Bidez, and Léon Parmentier, FChr 57 (Turnhout: Brepols, 2007). For an English translation, see Evagrius Scholasticus, *The Ecclesiastical History of Evagrius Scholasticus*, trans. Michael Whitby, TTH 33 (Liverpool: Liverpool University Press, 2000).

The Syriac Life of Symeon quite possibly preserves the actual language of the petition (ch. 125).[26] The Antiochene audience acclaimed Symeon's entrance into the city by chanting psalms and casting precious spices upon Symeon and all who accompanied him. They burnt incense and lit candles, reproducing the ritual at Shih. The procession then entered the Great Church in Antioch built by Constantine, the domain of the imperially recognized bishop and his congregation in the fourth and fifth centuries. The choice to bury Symeon in the Great Church made evident the city's regard for the saint; no prophets, saints, or martyrs had previously been buried there.[27] Every day, the archbishop and his clergy sang and chanted before Symeon's tomb. Silver censers imbued the space before the tomb with rich fragrances, honoring Symeon while also calling to mind previous celebrations of Symeon at Telneshe, Shih, and Antioch's gates (ch. 126).

The narrative makes the Great Church in Antioch the concluding point in an expansive landscape that benefited from Symeon's presence, in this case a presence made manifest through Symeon's body rather than his *ḥnānā*, dust, oil, or water. The authors link the cult centers in Telneshe and Antioch: the two complement one another in the honor which they express for Symeon. This approach integrated the divided landscape of Symeon's cult and, as a result, minimized potential conflict between Telneshe and its patriarchate. At the same time, the authors deem the Great Church a subsidiary cult center, whose source of authority radiated from the cult site in Telneshe. This maximized the importance of the cult site in Telneshe and constructed a hierarchy between the two cult sites.[28]

Conclusion

As stated at the outset, Bar-Ḥaṭar and Simeon bar-Eupolemos wrote *The Syriac Life of Symeon* in a transitional moment in the history of Symeon's

---

26. In his description of Symeon's death and the procession into Antioch, Evagrius Scholasticus uses almost identical language as *The Syriac Life of Symeon the Stylite*, albeit in Greek not Syriac (*Hist. eccl.* 1.13). This indicates that either Evagrius and the authors of *The Syriac Life of Symeon* relied on the same source or that Evagrius may have used *The Syriac Life of Symeon* as a source for his *Ecclesiastical History*. See Evagrius Scholasticus, *Ecclesiastical History of Evagrius Scholasticus*, 37 n. 132.

27. Mayer and Allen, *Churches of Syrian Antioch*, 68–80; Shepardson, *Controlling Contested Places*, 54.

28. Bell, *Ritual Theory, Ritual Practice*, 123–25.

cult. After Symeon had died and his body had been removed, there was no guarantee that the cult site in Telneshe would be the authoritative center of cultic activity. The authors engage in the process of restructuring the sacred geography of Symeon's cult by placing Symeon's sanctuary and Telneshe in a hierarchical relationship with Antioch. They make Symeon's sanctuary and the town of Telneshe the center for efficacious cultic activity from which all other devotion originates and radiates outwards. The substances distributed at Symeon's site make it possible to transport Symeon's sanctity beyond the cult site and mark new spaces dedicated to Symeon. These new loci of Symeon's power act as satellite sites emanating from the enclosure in Telneshe. The authors make Antioch and the Great Church that housed Symeon a subsidiary cult center, whose source of authority was closely associated with the cult site and Telneshe. In this way, they promote the cult site in Telneshe as the primary place to access Symeon's intercessory powers while also integrating devotion to Symeon across a broad topography. The authors recognize the importance of Antioch while insisting upon the primacy of the Telneshe cult site. In this way, they asserted their authority in their nascent saint's cult even without the saint's body.

From Asclepius to Simeon:
Votives and Sacred Healing in Late Antiquity

Gary Vikan

Early Byzantine Votives

The category of early Byzantine pilgrims' material culture that follows the εὐλογία or material (sacred oil, earth, water, etc.) "blessing" in significance is the votive; while the former was taken away, the latter was usually left behind. Some votives were simply items of value that were left at the shrine, either in thanks for a miracle or in the hope that a miracle would follow. There were herds of pigs and camels left at the Menas shrine, and the alabaster pot under the altar that supplied pilgrims with Menas oil was eventually nearly filled with more than 8,600 small bronze votive coins.[1] Pilgrim votive inscriptions were common at early Byzantine pilgrim shrines. Many simply recorded the names of the pilgrims themselves or of friends or relatives who were unable to make the journey; others acknowledged help received. The patriarch of Jerusalem, Sophronius (560–638 CE), describes a votive scribbled in fiery red paint at the entrance to the incubation healing shrine of Cyrus and John: "I, John from the city of Rome, a blind man, waited eight years here faithfully and recovered my sight through the power of Saints Cyrus and John" (*Mir. Cyr. John* 69).[2]

---

1. The first part of this paper provides a summary of the section of my book devoted to votives: Gary Vikan, *Early Byzantine Pilgrimage Art* (Washington, DC: Dumbarton Oaks Research Library and Collection 2010), 71–78; rev. and enl. ed. of Vikan, *Byzantine Pilgrimage Art* (Washington, DC: Dumbarton Oaks, 1982). My earlier work provides a foil for what follows, as I show that early Christian votives and votive practices perpetuated those of the pre-Christian world of sacred healing, including the distinctive iconographic motifs of the healing snake and the healing hand.

2. Translations of Sophronius's *Miracles of Cyrus and John* are from Dominic

Even anonymous votive inscriptions may have been left to acknowledge specific miracles. For example, the Life of Daniel Stylites (ca. 409–493 CE) records the healing of the elder daughter of the former consul Kyros, in thanks for which he inscribed on the saint's column generic honorific verses, including "Great Simeon's rival [is] he" (L. Daniel Styl. 36).[3] Many inscriptional votives took the form of an invocation, making permanent the suppliant's prayer for help. An incised bronze cross at Dumbarton Oaks shows, at the upper center, a bust-length portrait of Thecla in the orant pose of intercession, while across its surface is an invocation on behalf of four individuals, one of whom was named after the saint: "Saint Thecla, Help Simonios and Sinesois and Mary and Thecla."[4] A bronze cross in the Cabinet des Médailles—bearing the analogous, generic invocation "Saint George help …"—takes the iconography one step farther by showing the donor supplicating the saint. These two bronze crosses are iconographic votives; a more elaborate example of silver votives is described in the Life of Daniel Stylites:

> As thank offering he dedicated a silver icon, ten pounds in weight, on which was represented the holy man and themselves [the suppliant's family] writing these words below, "Oh father, beseech God to pardon us our sins against thee." This memorial is preserved to the present day near the altar. (L. Daniel Styl. 59)

The Life of Simeon the Younger includes reference to an iconographic votive set up in Antioch by an artisan who had been exorcised by the saint at his shrine: "Having returned home, he set up to the saint, by way of thanksgiving, an image in a public place and in full view of the city, above the entry to his workshop" (L. Simeon Young. 158).[5] Sophronius describes

---

Montserrat, "Pilgrimage to the Shrine of SS Cyrus and John at Menouthis in Late Antiquity," in *Pilgrimage and Holy Space in Late Antique Egypt*, ed. David Frankfurter, RGRW 134 (Leiden: Brill 1998), 272–73.

3. This and subsequent translations are from Elizabeth A. S. Dawes and Norman Hepburn Baynes, trans., *Three Byzantine Saints: Contemporary Biographies of St. Daniel the Stylite, St. Theodore of Sykeon, and St. John the Almsgiver* (Oxford: Blackwell, 1948).

4. Vikan, *Early Byzantine Pilgrimage Art*, 72, fig. 51.

5. English translation based on Paul van den Ven, *La vie ancienne de S. Syméon Stylite le Jeune (521–592)*, 2 vols., SubHag 32 (Brussels: Société des Bollandistes 1962–1970).

the votive of a former prefect named Nemesion at the healing shrine of Cyrus and John; he commissioned a mosaic near the tomb showing Christ, John the Baptist, Cyrus and John, and Nemesion himself, announcing his thanks (*Mir. Cyr. John* 28).

These three texts describe iconographic votives; those dedicated to Daniel and Simeon were likely relatively small and portable, while the mosaic dedicated to Cyrus and John was large and fixed in place. The Daniel votive may have resembled the silver-gilt votive of Simeon the Elder in the Louvre, which is inscribed: "In thanksgiving to God and to Saint Simeon, I have offered [this]."[6] But probably closer still is a later Georgian votive that includes, in addition to the saint on his column (here, Simeon the Younger) and a dedicatory inscription, a portrait of the donor-supplicant.[7] Mosaic votives covered the walls of the Church of Saint Demetrios in Thessalonike before the disastrous fire of 1917, though it is not clear whether these were intended to acknowledge or to invoke the saint's help. Their textual counterpart among the saint's *miracula* is more explicit, as it tells the story of the prefect Marianos who commissioned a mosaic for the exterior of the sanctuary showing the saint healing him of paralysis (Mir. Dem. 1.24).[8] One among the miracles of Cosmas and Damian is similarly explicit, as it describes a suppliant who, after having been healed of a fistula, arranges to have the miracle portrayed "in the church of the saints, in the colonnade at the left, above the entrance to the side chapel" (Mir. Cos. Dam. 30).[9] Again, the votive was likely a mural, permanently fixed in place, and its iconography explicitly documented both the healing and the individual healed. A suggestive parallel to this exists in a fresco in the Church of the Monastery of the Syrians in the Wādī Naṭrūn, which shows Cyrus healing a blind man (fig. 1). By contrast, the votive eyes at the Walters Art Museum from the Maʿarat al-Nuʿman silver treasure ("In Fulfillment of a Vow") are portable and anonymous (fig. 2). The same was

---

6. Paris, Museé du Louvre, no. Bj 2180. See image in Vikan, *Early Byzantine Pilgrimage Art*, 73, fig. 52.

7. See Vikan, *Early Byzantine Pilgrimage Art*, 45, fig. 32.

8. Text and translation based on Paul Lemerle, ed. and trans., *Le text*, vol. 1 of *Les plus anciens recueils des miracles de Saint Démétrius et la pénétration des Slaves dans les Balkans*, MdByz 2 (Paris: Éditions du Centre de la Recherche scientifique 1979–81), 56 and 67.

9. Text and translation based on André-Jean Festugière, trans., *Sainte Thècle, saints Côme et Damien, saints Cyr et Jean (extraits), saint Georges: Collections grecques de miracles* (Paris: Picard, 1971), 169–72.

likely true of the body-part votives described by Theodoret of Cyrrhus: "That they obtained [from Saint Simeon] what they so earnestly prayed for is clearly proven by their votive gifts, which proclaim the healing. Some bring images of eyes, others feet, others hands, which are sometimes of gold, other times of [silver?] (*Hell. Ther.* 8)."[10] The Daniel and Simeon votives are both identified as χαριστήρια or "thank offerings"—as distinct, for example, from ψυχικά, which would be proactive votives dedicated for the "salvation of the soul [ψυχικές]."[11] Among the miracles of Thecla is one that tells how the general Satornilos presented "many ... thank offerings [πολλά ... χαριστήρια]," apparently valuable implements or furnishings, to the saint's sanctuary in acknowledgment of her miraculous intervention on his behalf in battle (*Mir. Thec.* 13).[12] As in the case of the Daniel votive, which is said to be "silver ... ten pounds in weight," material worth was an important ingredient in the donor's piety, as it clearly was with the Louvre

Figure 1 (left). Monastery of the Syrians, Egyptpt, Wādī Naṭrūn. Reproduced with permission from Vikan, *Early Byzantine Pilgrimage Art*, 74, fig. 53. Figure 2 (right). Baltimore, the Walters Art Museum, no. 57.1865. 563. Reproduced with permission from Vikan, *Early Byzantine Pilgrimage Art*, 74, fig. 54.

---

10. Translation from John Wortley, "Iconoclasm and *Leipsanoclasm*: Leo III, Constantine V and the Relics," *ByzF* 8 (1982): 273.

11. Marlia M. Mango, *Silver Treasure from Early Byzantium: The Kaper Koraon and Related Treasures* (Baltimore: Trustees of the Walters Art Gallery 1986), 5–6.

12. Text and translation based on Gilbert Dagron, ed. and trans., *Vie et miracles de saint Thècle*, SubHag 62 (Brussels: Société des Bollandistes, 1978), 324–25.

and the Georgian silver votive plaques, the Walters silver votive eyes, and even the Menas copper coins; each, presumably, according to his or her means. The prefect Marianos, whose healing by Saint Demetrios was proclaimed in mosaic on the exterior of the church, expressed his thanks as well through the donation of gold and silver objects from among his personal possessions as well as gold coins for the poor and sick.

Although Qal'at Sem'ān was not an incubation center in the sense that the shrines of Artemios, Cyrus and John, and Cosmas and Damian were, the process of invoking the saintly presence on site, of "seeing" Simeon, especially after the holy man's death, was likely little different. Demetrios was mainly revered as patron protector of Thessalonike, but he was a healing saint as well. Although his church was not an incubation hall, it was a place where miracles sometimes took place during sleep. The prefect Marianos, for example, was instructed by the saint to "come to his house" and to sleep there, where through a vision of the saint he was eventually cured of his paralysis (Mir. Dem. 1.16). The miracles of the famous incubation centers date for the most part to the early seventh century; presumably then, when vision-facilitated miracles were taking place at those shrines, they were taking place as well at Qal'at Sem'ān. Under those circumstances, iconographic votives dedicated to Simeon, like those in Thessalonike dedicated to Demetrios, would have fulfilled a second, audience-defined function—a function toward which their image and not their material was instrumental. These votives, like the on-site images of Cosmas and Damian, Cyrus and John, and, earlier, of Asclepius, would have facilitated "sacred seeing" for the pilgrim on site after the saint's death, especially as they might be accompanied by the power of scores of devotional lamps and incense.

Pre-Christian Votives

Thank offering votives, sometimes inscribed as χαριστήρια, were common at pagan healing shrines, especially Asklepieia, until these shrines were finally superseded or supplanted by their Christian counterparts in the fifth century.[13] Given in acknowledgement—in effect, as payment—after incubation and successful treatment, some include an image of Asclepius who, mirror-

---

13. Ralph Jackson, *Doctors and Diseases in the Roman Empire* (Norman: University of Oklahoma, 1988), 145, 157; René Josef Rüttiman, "Asclepius and Jesus: The Form, Character, and Status of the Asclepius Cult in the Second Century CE and Its

ing the local cult statues, typically appears with his serpent-entwined staff. Others show the specific cure.[14] Like their later Christian counterparts, they vary widely in medium and format, depending in part on the customs at the particular shrine, from crude inscriptions and simple cakes and tokens, to animals, to body parts in various media, to coins, precious metal artifacts, and relief plaques in stone.

The silver votive eyes found with the Ma'art al-Nu'man Treasure and the various body-part dedications described by Theodoret at the shrine of Simeon the Elder perpetuate, in only slightly transmuted forms, types of votives associated with pagan healing shrines, specifically those of Asclepius.[15] A similar derivative relationship is clear on the Louvre Simeon votive from the presence of the snake entwined around the saint's column. This should be understood as a generic evocation of miraculous healing in the tradition of Asclepius and not as a reference to some episode in the saint's *vita*. A snake also appears, wrapped around a tree this time, on a contemporary stone-casting mold for medallion amulets of Phokas in the British Museum, undoubtedly because Phokas, too, could be a source of miraculous cures. In both, the snake's specific appearance and its healing message recall Greek Asklepieion votives, which in the era of the Phokas medallion and the Simeon plaque—namely, the fifth to seventh centuries—was current outside the confines of the Asklepieion on the covers of medicine boxes.[16] Finally, and more generally, the Louvre plaque parallels pre-Christian votives in both its medium, repoussé silver, and its presentation of the divine benefactor within an *aedicule*.[17] Churches were built over or near the ruins of many healing shrines. For example, the Athens Askepieion was supplanted after nine centuries, just before the end of the

---

Influence on Early Christianity" (ThD diss., Harvard University, 1987), 19, 50, 77–84, 106–8, 205–11.

14. See the Piraeus Asklepieion reproduced in Jackson, *Doctors and Diseases*, 144, fig. 38.

15. See "Thank offering of Tyche to Asklepios and Hygieia" reproduced in Antje Krug, *Heilkunst und Heilkult: Medizin in der Antike* (Munich: Beck 1985), 149 fig. 65.

16. Beat Brenk and Hugo Brandenburg, *Spätantike und frühes Christentum* (Frankfurt am Main: Propylaea, 1977), no. 168.

17. See "To Juno Regina, Marina Dedicated This, in Fulfillment of a Vow" (Vienna, Kunsthistorisches Museum, no. M8) reproduced in Rudolf Noll, *Das Inventar des Dolichenusheiligtums von Mauer und der Url (Noricum)*, vol. 30 of *Der römische Limes in Österreich* (Vienna: Österreichischen Akademie der Wissenschaften, 1980), 53–54, no. 8.

fifth century (which was when the great shrine of Qal'at Sem'ān was being built by Emperor Zeno) by a church dedicated to Cosmas and Damian that incorporated its pre-Asclepius sacred spring.[18]

The ancient votive tradition, with image as subset, had been substantially but not completely Christianized by the sixth century—thus, the persistence of the healing snake. Though as early as the second century, the apocryphal Acts of John records a votive dedication that, but for date and benefactor, might as well have come from the story of Simeon the Younger—that is, from around 600 CE. In the Life of Simeon the Younger, we are told of a woman from Cilicia who, after having been exorcised by Simeon, "put up an image of the saint in the interior of her home." (118). Now, set the clock back more than four centuries and we learn in the Acts of John about Lykomides, a praetor of Ephesos. In thanks for having been raised from the dead and converted by the Apostle, Lykomides arranged to have a portrait painted secretly of his benefactor and then "suspended it in his bedroom, and crowned it...." (Acts John 27).[19] This second-century "icon" of Saint John seems out of place by several centuries in the traditional developmental model of the Byzantine sacred image. But then again, so does the statue in Paneas believed to show Christ healing the woman with the issue of blood, as described in the early fourth century by Eusebius:

> For there stands upon an elevated stone, by the gate of her house, a brazen image of a woman kneeling, with her hands stretched out, as if she were praying. Opposite this is another upright image of a man, made of the same material ... extending his hand toward the woman. At his feet, beside the statue itself, is a certain strange plant ... and [it] is a remedy for all kinds of diseases. (*Hist. eccl.* 7.18.2 [*NPNF2* 1:304])

Eusebius takes this sculptural ensemble to be "ancient" and goes on to speak disapprovingly of the custom among "gentiles of old" of paying homage to their deliverers through such votive images. One need not accept the notion of André Grabar that these texts together attest to the

---

18. Timothy E. Gregory, "The Survival of Paganism in Christian Greece," *AJP* 107 (1986): 229–42.

19. Text and translation based on E. Junod and Jean-Daniel Kaestli, eds., *Acta Ioannis*, CCSA 2 (Turnhout: Brepols, 1983), 176–77.

continuity of authentic sacred portraiture back to the apostolic age[20] to recognize in them evidence of recent converts translating directly their traditional votive practices into a Christian idiom. The "life setting" of the Paneas statue of circa 320 CE and that of Lykomides's portrait of John of circa 140 CE is not that of the theological debates of eighth-century iconoclasm but rather that of the practical reality of divine healing in late paganism. It is the same "life setting" as that of the Tiber Island Asclepius statue of the early second century that was, in a way very similar to the Paneas statue, a source of sacred cures through the magic of contagion:

> In those days Asclepius revealed to Gaius, a blind man, that he should go to the holy base [of the statue] and there should prostrate himself; then go from the right to the left and place his five fingers on the base and raise his hand and lay it on his own eyes. And he could see again clearly, while the people stood by and rejoiced that glorious deeds lived again.[21]

Incubation and Healing Rituals

Links between the early Byzantine healing shrine and the Asklepieion went beyond votive practices and iconography. They also include the ritual of diagnosis and healing through incubation dreams, the belief in "sacred space," the magic of contagion, and the use of mundane intermediary substances like dirt to effect the miraculous. In the second century, priests at the Tiber Island Asklepieion in Rome recorded a miraculous healing achieved through a paste of wine and altar ash. It is a match both for implicit magical belief in contagion, and in its specific ritual, with what was going on at the shrine of Simeon the Elder three centuries later:

> Asclepius: To Lucius, who suffered from pleurisy and had been despaired of by all men, the god revealed that he should go and from the threefold altar lift ashes and mix them thoroughly with the wine and lay them on his side. And he was saved, and publicly offered thanks to the god....[22]

---

20. André Grabar, *Christian Iconography: A Study of Its Origins* (Princeton: Princeton University Press, 1968), 60–86.
21. Quotation from Rüttiman, "Asclepius and Jesus," 58.
22. Quotation from ibid.

Simeon: The saint ordered water to be brought. He prayed and blessed it. He ordered him [a man with a severe headache] in the name of Christ, and the man drank and even poured some over his head. The moment the water touched him his affliction fled and he never noticed it again.... He confessed and praised God.[23] (L. Simeon Styl. Eld. 79)

Hypnagogic fantasies were critical to the hearings of Askepios, as they were more generally in antiquity to making real one's encounter with the gods. In Asklepieia, as later in Christian healing shrines, suppliants imagined their benefactor in the form that his "icons"—which were usually statues—had sanctioned or even in animated versions of the statues themselves. According to the second-century dream theories of Artemidorus of Daldis, to dream of a god's statue was to dream of the god himself (*Onir.* 2.35). Aelius Aristeides, a second-century rhetorician whose votive to Asclepius—called the *Sacred Tales*—was a diary documenting his years of cure-seeking through incubation, freely interweaves Asclepius, the shrine's statuary, and himself: "I noticed in a dream a statue of me. At one momentum I saw it as if it were me, and then again it seemed to be a large and beautiful statue of Asclepius" (*S.T.* 48.18).[24]

Robert Lane Fox speaks of the narcotic atmosphere of the Asklepieion's ἄβατον or sacred space that was "intoxicated, above all, by the presence of religious works of art."[25] Sacred images, powerful and ever-present incense, scores of votive lamps, recitation of the miracle stories of the site, and their documentation in words and pictures on the wall, coupled with the force of the collective psychology of desperately ill people, would have prepared any pilgrim for his or her appropriate epiphany experience. To this extent, the pagan and Christian experiences were likely much the same. But at the Christian shrine there was as well the powerfully evocative force of incarnate sanctity: the bones of the martyr or the focal contact relic he or she left behind, such as the ciborium in Thessalonike and the column at Qalʽat Semʽan. These and the notion of intercession add critical nuance to the distinction between the late pagan and the early Christian healing shrines. Among the miracles of Artemios, there is one

---

23. Translation from Robert Doran, ed. and trans., *The Lives of Simeon Stylites*, CSS 112 (Kalamazoo, MI: Cistercian Studies 1992), 161.

24. Translation from Robin Lane Fox, *Pagans and Christians* (San Francisco: Knopf, 1986), 162.

25. Ibid., 153.

wherein a sixty-year-old suppliant wakes up after incubation with a wax seal in his hand bearing the image of the saint; he softens it and applies it to his hernia and is instantly healed (Mir. Art. 16).²⁶ Similarly, those awaking in the pagan ἄβατον might have received overnight from their god a curative token or perhaps a letter bearing a prescription. Dreams were aggressively courted and stimulated, not only by art but by fasting and heavy incense like the "incense of Epidaurus," which would be concocted from exotic recipes.

The Healing Hand

Several hundred clay healing tokens of Simeon the Elder survive, and all of them share one thing in common: the print of a human palm on their bulbous back side (fig. 3). I puzzled over this for a long time, because it seemed to me to be so "purposeful." Finally, I coupled these palm prints with an episode in the Life of Simeon the Younger, and it all made sense. In the account, a priest and his ill son are sent home from the Simeon shrine with a clay healing token and with the saint's promise that the cure will eventually be accomplished there. Once home, the priest has a visionary encounter with the saint who, disguised, elicits this revealing exchange: "What do you prefer, this eulogia that Simeon has sent you or this right hand? Don't be angry, Lord [the priest replies], for great is the power of his eulogia, but I was seeking his right hand" (L. Simeon Young. 231). I drew some support for my thinking from the fact that Oral Roberts was then combating demons over television through his right hand, with which, as an afflicted viewer, you were invited to make "contact" by pressing your right hand against your TV screen (fig. 4). Then I began to see healing hands all over the place in early Byzantium. Not only on that Phokas medallion mold with the snake but also on an incised bronze cross supported by a hand in the Metropolitan Museum dating from the fifth to seventh century.²⁷ On its four arms, it shows the Virgin and Child (top), Cosmas and Damian

---

26. See Virgil S. Crisafulli and John W. Nesbitt, eds. and trans., *The Miracles of St. Artemios: A Collection of Miracle Stories by an Anonymous Author of Seventeenth-Century Byzantium*, MMed 13 (Leiden: Brill, 1997), 107–8.

27. New York, Metropolitan Museum of Art, Cloisters Collection, no. 1974.150. Reproduced in Kurt Weitzmann, ed., *Age of Spirituality: Late Antique and Early Christian Art, Third to Seventh Century; Catalogue of the Exhibition (Nov. 19, 1977—Feb. 12, 1978)*, (New York: Metropolitan Museum of Art, 1979), 621 no. 557.

(bottom), while at its center appears Saint Stephen with a censer in one hand and an incense box in the other. There are two invocations: in large letters on the horizontal cross is the common and generic, "Christ, help [me]," and on the lower arm the uncommon and specific, "Saints Kosmas and Damianos, grant [me] your blessing." What else can that "blessing" be from these holy doctors but the blessing of health?

Figure 3. Houston, *The Menil Collection*, 79–24.199 DJ. Reproduced with permission from Vikan, *Early Byzantine Pilgrimage Art*, 56–58, figs. 17, 35.

Like only a few other surviving early Byzantine crosses, this one is supported by a hand, a striking conception that derives from pagan apotropaic hands of only slightly earlier date, like that of the Phyrigian nature god Sabazios in the St. Louis Art Museum of the third to fourth century CE (fig. 5). Although the precise meaning and use of these pre-Christian votives remains uncertain, it may be assumed that they were dedicated in shrines identified with the god and that the hand suggests both

Figure 4. Advertisement in *The Washington Post*, November 1983.

the god's power to help the donor and his promise to do so. Significantly, the benediction gesture of the hand itself is a characteristic attribute of Sabazios, who appears within the hand, raising (originally) both of his hands in that same gesture. Similarly, on the New York cross, the healing powers whose blessing are invoked raise their hands—as do Peter and Paul—in a manner matching that of the hand that holds the cross. Additionally, the cross rests on a globe, which draws on imperial iconography to reinforce the notion of imminent power and prerogative. Moreover, the votive hand and the saints' hand gestures mirror the omnipotent hand of Solomon as it then appears on contemporary amuletic rings ("Seal of Solomon"). This gives me some comfort, knowing that King Solomon, Cosmas and Damian, Simeon Stylites, and Oral Roberts are all playing on the same healing team.

Figure 5. St. Louis, The St. Louis Art Museum, no. 52.1956. Reproduced with permission from Kurt Weitzmann, *Age of Spirituality*, no. 163.

Bibliography

'Abd al-Razzāq b. Hammām al-Ṣanʿānī. *al-Muṣannaf*. Edited by Ḥabīb al-Raḥmān al-Aʿẓamī. 11 vols. Beirut: Al-Maktab al-Islāmī, 1983.

Adkins, Arthur W. H. *Merit and Responsibility: A Study in Greek Values*. Oxford: Clarendon, 1960.

Adluri, Vishwa. "Plato's Saving *Mūthos*: The Language of Salvation in the Republic." *IJPT* 8 (2014): 3–32.

Alvar, Jaime. *Romanising Oriental Gods: Myth, Salvation and Ethics in the Cults of Cybele, Isis and Mithras*. Edited and translated by Richard Gordon. RGRW 165. Boston: Brill, 2008.

Ambrose. *De Virginibus; De viduis; De virginitate; De institutione virginis; Exhortatio virginitatis*. Edited by Franco Gori. SAEMO 14.1, 2. Milan: Biblioteca Ambrosiana, 1989.

———. *Epistularum liber decimu: Epistulae extra collectionem; Gesta Concilii Aquileiensis*. Part 3 of *Epistulae et acta*. Vol. 10 of *Sancti Ambrosii Opera*. Edited by Michaela Zelzer. CSEL 82.3. Vienna: Hoelder-Pichler-Tempsky, 1982.

———. *Political Letters and Speeches*. Translated by J. H. W. G. Liebeschuetz. TTH 43. Liverpool: Liverpool University Press, 2005.

———. *Seven Exegetical Works: Isaac, or The Soul; Death as a Good; Jacob and the Happy Life; Joseph; The Patriarchs; Flight from the World; The Prayer of Job and David*. Translated by Michael P. McHugh. FC 65. Washington, DC: Catholic University of America Press, 1972.

Aristotle. *Select Fragments*. Vol. 12 of *The Works of Aristotle*. Edited and translated by William David Ross. Oxford: Clarendon, 1952.

Ashley, Kathleen M., and Véronique Plesch. "The Cultural Processes of 'Appropriation.'" *JMEMS* 32 (2002): 1–15.

Assemani, Stefano Evodio, ed. and trans. *Acta Sanctorum Martyrum Orientalium et Occidentalium*. 2 vols. Rome: Collini, 1748.

Astell, Ann. *The Song of Songs in the Middle Ages*. Ithaca, NY: Cornell University Press, 1995.

Athanassiadi, Polymnia. *Julian and Hellenism: An Intellectual Biography.* Oxford: Clarendon, 1981.

———. *La lutte pour l'orthodoxie dans le platonisme tardif: De Numénius à Damascius.* Paris: Belles Lettres, 2006.

Attridge, Harold W. "The Philosophical Critique of Religion under the Roman Empire." *ANRW* 16.1:45–78.

Austin, J. L. *How to Do Things with Words.* Cambridge: Harvard University Press, 1962.

Azmah, Aziz Al-. *The Emergence of Islam in Late Antiquity: Allāh and His People.* New York: Cambridge University Press, 2014.

Bagnoli, Martina, Holger A. Klein, C. Griffith Mann, and James Robinson, eds. *Treasures of Heaven: Saints, Relics, and Devotion in Medieval Europe.* New Haven: Yale University Press, 2010.

Baldovin, John F. "The *Fermentum* at Rome in the Fifth Century: A Reconsideration." *Worship* 79 (2005): 38–53.

Barfield, Raymond. *The Ancient Quarrel between Philosophy and Poetry.* Repr., Cambridge: Cambridge University Press, 2011.

Barnes, Timothy D. "Christians and the Theater." Pages 161–81 in *Roman Theater and Society: E. Togo Salmon Papers I.* Edited by William J. Slater. Ann Arbor: University of Michigan Press, 2004.

———. *Constantine and Eusebius.* Cambridge: Harvard University Press, 2006.

———. *The New Empire of Diocletian and Constantine.* Cambridge: Harvard University Press, 1982.

Barrett, Justin L. "Theological Correctness: Cognitive Constraints and the Study of Religion." *MTSR* 11 (1999): 325–39.

Barrett, Justin L., and Frank C. Keil. "Conceptualizing a Non-natural Entity: Anthropomorphism in God Concepts." *CognPsych* 31 (1996): 219–47.

Barthes, Roland. *The Fashion System.* Translated by Matthew Ward and Richard Howard. New York: Hill & Wang, 1983.

———. *Mythologies.* Translated by Annette Lavers. New York: Hill & Wang, 1972.

Barton, Carlin. "Being in the Eyes: Shame and Sight in Ancient Rome." Pages 216–35 in *The Roman Gaze: Vision, Power, and the Body.* Edited by David Frederick. Baltimore: Johns Hopkins University Press, 2002.

Bartsch, Shadi. *The Mirror of the Self: Sexuality, Self-Knowledge, and the Gaze in the Early Roman Empire.* Chicago: University of Chicago Press, 2006.

Batten, Alicia. "Carthaginian Critiques of Adornment." *JECH* 1 (2011): 3–21.
Bauer, Franz Alto. "Urban Space and Ritual: Constantinople in Late Antiquity." *AAAHP* 15 (2001): 27–61.
Beacham, Richard C. *Spectacle Entertainments of Early Imperial Rome*. New Haven: Yale University Press, 1999.
Beard, Mary, John North, and Simon Price. *A History*. Vol. 1 of *Religions of Rome*. New York: Cambridge University Press, 1998.
Bell, Catherine M. *Ritual Theory, Ritual Practice*. Oxford: Oxford University Press, 1992.
Berkowitz, Beth A. *Defining Jewish Difference: From Antiquity to the Present*. Cambridge: Cambridge University Press, 2012.
———. "The Limits of 'Their Laws': Ancient Rabbinic Controversies about Jewishness (and Non-Jewishness)." *JQR* 99 (2009): 121–57.
Berthelot, Katell. "Philon d'Alexandrie, lecteur d'Homère: Quelques éléments de réflexion." Pages 145–57 in *Prolongements et renouvellements de la tradition classique*. Edited by Anne Balansard, Gilles Dorival, and Mireille Loubet. Aix-en-Provence: Université de Provence, 2011.
Birk, Stine. "Man or Woman? Cross-Gendering and Individuality on Third Century Roman Sarcophagi." Pages 229–60 in *Life, Death and Representation: Some New Work on Roman Sarcophagi*. Edited by Jaś Elsner and Janet Huskinson. New York: de Gruyter, 2010.
Bisconti, Fabrizio, "Il sogno e la quiete: L'altro mondo degli Aureli." Pages 11–20 in *L'ipogeo degli Aureli in viale Manzoni: Restauri, tutela, valorizzazione e aggiornamenti interpretativi*. Edited by Fabrizio Bisconti. Vatican City: Pontificia Commissione di Archeologia Sacra, 2011.
———, ed. *L'ipogeo degli Aureli in viale Manzoni: Restauri, tutela, valorizzazione e aggiornamenti interpretativi*. Vatican City: Pontificia Commissione di Archeologia Sacra, 2011.
———. "L'ipogeo degli Aureli in viale Manzoni: Un esempio di sincresi privata." *Aug* 25 (1985): 889–903.
Biscop, Jean-Luc, and Jean-Pierre Sodini. "L'accès nord au domaine de Syméon le Stylite: Le village de Shih (Sheikh ed Deir-Shader, Bardakhan)." Pages 259–68 in *Sur les pas des Araméens chrétiens: Mélanges offerts a Alain Desreumaux*. Edited by Françoise Briquel-Chatonnet and Muriel Debié. Paris: Geuthner, 2010.
Boero, Dina. "The Context of Production of the Vatican Manuscript of the *Syriac Life of Symeon the Stylite*." *Hug* 18 (2015): 319–59.

Bourdieu, Pierre. *Distinction: A Social Critique of the Judgment of Taste.* Translated by Richard Nice. Cambridge: Harvard University Press, 1984.

——. *The Field of Cultural Production: Essays on Art and Literature.* Edited by Randal Johnson. New York: Columbia University Press, 1993.

——. *The Rules of Art: Genesis and Structure of the Literary Field.* Translated by Susan Emanuel. Stanford, CA: Stanford University Press, 1996.

Bowersock, G. W. *Julian the Apostate.* Cambridge: Harvard University Press, 1978.

Bowes, Kim. *Private Worship, Public Values, and Religious Change in Late Antiquity.* New York: Cambridge University Press, 2008.

Boys-Stones, George. "Time, Creation, and the Mind of God: The Afterlife of a Platonist Theory in Origen." *OSAP* 40 (2011): 319–37.

Bradshaw, Paul F. *Early Christian Worship: A Basic Introduction to Ideas and Practice.* 2nd ed. Collegeville, MN: Liturgical Press, 2010.

Brandenburg, Hugo. *Ancient Churches of Rome from the Fourth to the Seventh Century: The Dawn of Christian Architecture in the West.* Turnhout: Brepols, 2005.

——. "The Use of Older Elements in the Architecture of Fourth- and Fifth-Century Rome: A Contribution to the Evaluation of *Spolia*." Pages 53–73 in *Reuse Value: Spolia and Appropriation in Art and Architecture from Constantine to Sherrie Levine.* Edited by Richard Brilliant and Dale Kinney. Burlington, VT: Ashgate, 2011.

Brauer, George C., Jr. *The Age of the Soldier Emperors: Imperial Rome, A.D. 244–284.* Park Ridge, NJ: Noyes, 1975.

Bremmer, Jan N. *Initiation into the Mysteries of the Ancient World.* MVAW 1. Berlin: de Gruyter, 2014.

Brenk, Beat. "Microstoria sotto la chiesa del ss. Giovanni e Paolo: La cristianizzione di una casa privata." *RIASA* 18 (1995): 169–205.

——. "Spolia from Constantine to Charlemagne: Aesthetics versus Ideology." *DOP* 41 (1987): 103–9.

Brenk, Beat, and Hugo Brandenburg. *Spätantike und frühes Christentum.* Frankfurt am Main: Propylaea, 1977.

Brent, Allen. *Cyprian and Roman Carthage.* Cambridge: Cambridge University Press, 2010.

Brown, Peter. *The Cult of the Saints: Its Rise and Function in Latin Christianity.* Chicago: University of Chicago Press, 1981.

———. *The Making of Late Antiquity*. Cambridge: Harvard University Press, 1978.

———. *Power and Persuasion in Late Antiquity: Towards a Christian Empire*. Madison: University of Wisconsin Press, 1992.

———. "The Rise and Function of the Holy Man in Late Antiquity." *JRS* 61 (1971): 80–101.

———. *Society and the Holy in Late Antiquity*. Berkeley: University of California Press, 1982.

———. *Through the Eye of a Needle: Wealth, the Fall of Rome, and the Making of Christianity in the West, 350–550 AD*. Princeton: Princeton University Press, 2012.

Browning, Robert. *The Emperor Julian*. Berkeley: University of California Press, 1976.

Brubaker, Rogers, and Frederick Cooper. "Beyond Identity." *ThSo* 29 (2000): 1–47.

Bruun, Patrick M. *Constantine and Licinus A.D. 307–337*. Vol. 7 of *The Roman Imperial Coinage*. London: Spink & Son, 1966.

———. *Studies in Constantinian Numismatics: Papers from 1954 to 1988*. AIRF 12 Rome: Institutum Romanun Finlandiae, 1991.

Bukhārī, Abū ʿAbdallāh Muḥammad b. Ismāʿīl al-. *Kitāb al-Jāmiʿ al-Ṣaḥīḥ*. Edited by L. Krehl and T. W. Juynboll. 4 vols. Leiden: Brill, 1862–1908.

Bulliet, Richard. *Islam: The View from the Edge*. New York: Columbia University Press, 1994.

Burns, J. Patout, Jr., and Robin M. Jensen. *Christianity in Roman Africa: The Development of Its Practices and Beliefs*. Grand Rapids: Eerdmans, 2014.

Bursi, Adam. "Holy Spit and Magic Spells: Religion, Magic and the Body in Late Ancient Judaism, Christianity, and Islam." PhD diss., Cornell University, 2015.

Butler, Judith. *Excitable Speech: A Politics of the Performative*. London: Routledge, 1997.

Butler, Shane, and Alex Purves. *Synaesthesia and the Ancient Senses*. Durham: Acumen, 2013.

Bynum, Caroline Walker. *Christian Materiality: An Essay on Religion in Late Medieval Europe*. New York: Zone, 2011.

———. *The Resurrection of the Body in Western Christianity, 200–1336*. New York: Columbia University Press, 1995.

Cairns, Douglas L. *Aidos: The Psychology and Ethics of Honour and Shame in Ancient Greek Literature*. New York: Oxford University Press, 1993.

Cameron, Averil. *Christianity and the Rhetoric of Empire: The Development of Christian Discourse*. Berkeley: University of California Press, 1991.

Caner, Daniel. "Alms, Blessings, Offerings: The Repertoire of Christian Gifts in Early Byzantium." Pages 25–44 in *The Gift in Antiquity*. Edited by Michael L. Satlow. Hoboken, NJ: Wiley-Blackwell, 2013.

Capra, Andrea. *Plato's Four Muses: The Phaedrus and the Poetics of Philosophy*. HellSS 67. Washington, DC: Center for Hellenic Studies, 2014.

Carp, Richard M. "Teaching Religion and Material Culture." *TTR* 10 (2007): 2–12.

Chin, Catherine M. "The Bishop's Two Bodies: Ambrose and the Basilicas of Milan." *CH* 79 (2010): 531–55.

Chlup, Radek. *Proclus: An Introduction*. Cambridge: Cambridge University Press, 2012.

Chrysostomos, Auxentios, and James Thornton. *Four Essays on Orthodox Liturgical Issues: A Collection of Liturgical Commentaries Written from a Traditionalist Orthodox Perspective*. Etna, CA: Center for Traditionalist Orthodox Studies, 1996.

Clark, Elizabeth. *History, Theory, Text: Historians and the Linguistic Turn*. Cambridge: Harvard University Press, 2004.

Clements, Ashley. "The Senses in Philosophy and Science: Five Conceptions from Heraclitus to Plato." Pages 115–37 in *A Cultural History of the Senses in Antiquity*. Edited by Jerry P. Toner. London: Bloomsbury, 2014.

Cohen, Naomi G. "The Mystery Terminology in Philo." Pages 173–88 in *Philo und das Neue Testament: Internationales Symposium zum Corpus Judaeo-Hellenisticum May 1–3, 2003*. Edited by Roland Deines and Karl-Wilhelm Niebuhr. Tübingen: Mohr Siebeck, 2004.

Colish, Marcia. *Ambrose's Patriarchs: Ethics for the Common Man*. South Bend, IN: University of Notre Dame Press, 2005.

Collins, John J. *Between Athens and Jerusalem: Jewish Identity in the Hellenistic Diaspora*. 2nd ed. Grand Rapids, MI: Eerdmans, 2000.

Collobert, Catherine, Pierre Destrée, and Francisco J. González, eds. *Plato and Myth: Studies on the Use and Status of Platonic Myths*. Leiden: Brill, 2012.

Comte, Marie-Christine. *Les Reliquaires du Proche-Orient et de Chypre à la période protobyzantine (ive–viiie siècles): Formes, emplacements, fonctions et cultes*. Turnhout: Brepols, 2012.

Connor, Carolyn L. "Color on Late Antique and Byzantine Ivories: Problems and Challenges of Conservation." Pages 31–36 in *Spätantike und byzantinische Elfenbeinbildwerke im Diskurs*. Edited by Gudrun Bühl, Anthony Cutler, and Arne Effenberger. Wiesbaden: Reichert, 2008.

Costambeys, Marios. "Burial Topography and the Power of the Church in Fifth- and Sixth-Century Rome." *PBSR* 69 (2001): 169–89.

Courcelle, Pierre. *Recherches sur les Confessions de saint Augustin*. Paris: de Boccard, 1950.

Crawford, M. H. "Roman Imperial Coin Types and the Formation of Public Opinion." Pages 47–64 in *Studies in Numismatic Method: Presented to Philip Grierson*. Edited by C. N. L. Brooke, B. H. I. H. Stewart, J. G. Pollard, and T. R. Volk. Cambridge: Cambridge University Press, 1983.

Crisafulli, Virgil S., and John W. Nesbitt, eds. and trans. *The Miracles of St. Artemios: A Collection of Miracle Stories by an Anonymous Author of Seventeenth-Century Byzantium*. MMed 13. Leiden: Brill, 1997.

Crook, John. *The Architectural Setting of the Cult of Saints in the Early Christian West c. 300–c. 1200*. Oxford: Oxford University Press, 2000.

Croom, Alexandra T. *Roman Clothing and Fashion*. London: Tempus 2002.

Dagron, Gilbert, ed. and trans. *Vie et miracles de saint Thècle*. SubHag 62. Brussels: Société des Bollandistes, 1978.

Daniel-Hughes, Carly. "Belief." In *The Oxford Berg History of Dress*. Edited by Mary Harlow. Oxford: Oxford University Press, forthcoming.

———. *The Salvation of the Flesh in Tertullian of Carthage: Dressing for the Resurrection*. New York: Palgrave Macmillan, 2011.

Davies, Glenys. "What Made the Roman Toga *Virilis*?" Pages 121–30 in *The Clothed Body in the Ancient World*. Edited by Liza Cleland, Mary Harlow, and Lloyd Llewellyn-Jones. Oxford: Oxbow, 2005.

Davis, Stephen J. *The Cult of Saint Thecla: A Tradition of Women's Piety in Late Antiquity*. Oxford: Oxford University Press, 2001.

Dawes, Elizabeth A. S., and Norman Hepburn Baynes, trans. *Three Byzantine Saints: Contemporary Biographies of St. Daniel the Stylite, St. Theodore of Sykeon, and St. John the Almsgiver*. Oxford: Blackwell, 1948.

Dawson, David. *Allegorical Readers and Cultural Revision in Ancient Alexandria*. Berkeley: University of California Press, 1992.

Deichmann, Friedrich Wilhelm, Giuseppe Bovini, and Hugo Brandenburg. *Rom und Ostia*. Vol. 1 of *Repertorium der christlich-antiken Sarkophage*. Wiesbaden: Steiner, 1967.

Delehaye, Hippolyte. *Les Saints Stylites*. SubHag 14. Paris: Picard, 1923.

Demura, Miyako. "Origen's Allegorical Interpretation and the Philological Tradition of Alexandria." Pages 149–58 in *Origeniana Nona: Origen and the Religious Practice of His Time; Papers of the 9th International Origen Congress, Pécs, Hungary, 29 August–2 September 2005*. Edited by György Heidl and Róbert Somos. Leuven: Peeters, 2009.

Destrée, Pierre, and Fritz-Gregor Herrmann, eds. *Plato and the Poets*. Leiden: Brill, 2011.

Dey, Hendrik W. *The Aurelian Wall and the Refashioning of Imperial Rome, AD 271–855*. Cambridge: Cambridge University Press, 2011.

Dillon, John M. *The Middle Platonists: 80 B.C. to A.D. 220*. London: Duckworth, 1977.

d'Izarny, Raymond. "Mariage et consécration virginale au IVe siècle." *VSpirSup* 24 (1953): 92–118.

Donner, Fred M. *Muhammad and the Believers: At the Origins of Islam*. Cambridge: Harvard University Press, 2010.

———. *Narratives of Islamic Origins: The Beginnings of Islamic Historical Writing*. Princeton: Darwin, 1998.

Doran, Robert, ed. and trans. *The Lives of Simeon Stylites*. CSS 112. Kalamazoo, MI: Cistercian, 1992.

Dossey, Leslie. *Peasant and Empire in Christian North Africa*. Berkeley: University of California Press, 2010.

Drake, H. A. "Constantine and Consensus." *CH* 64 (1995): 1–15.

———. "Intolerance, Religious Violence, and Political Legitimacy in Late Antiquity." *JAAR* 79 (2011): 193–235.

Elm, Susanna. *Sons of Hellenism, Fathers of the Church: Emperor Julian, Gregory of Nazianzus, and the Vision of Rome*. Berkeley: University of California Press, 2012.

Elsner, Jaś. "Perspectives in Art." Pages 255–77 in *The Cambridge Companion to the Age of Constantine*. Edited by Noel Lenski. New York: Cambridge University Press, 2006.

Emerson, Ralph Waldo. *Self-Reliance and Other Essays*. New York: Dover, 1993.

Engler, Stephen. "Modern Times: Religion, Consecration and the State in Bourdieu." *CulSt* 17 (2003): 445–67.

Evagrius Scholasticus. *Ecclesiastical History*. Translated by Michael Whitby. TTH 33. Liverpool: Liverpool University Press, 2000.

———. *Historia ecclesiastica/ Kirchengeschichte*. Edited and translated by Adelheid Hübner, Joseph Bidez, and Léon Parmentier. FChr 57. Turnhout: Brepols, 2007.

Ewald, Björn Christian. *Der Philosoph als Leitbild: Ikonographische Untersuchungen an römischen Sarkophagreliefs*. Mainz: von Zabern, 1999.

Eyl, Jennifer. "'By the Power of Signs and Wonders': Paul, Divinatory Practices, and Symbolic Capital." PhD diss., Brown University, 2011.

Fagan, Garrett G. *The Lure of the Arena: Social Psychology and the Crowd at the Roman Games*. Cambridge: Cambridge University Press, 2011.

Festugière, André-Jean, trans. *Sainte Thècle, saints Côme et Damien, saints Cyr et Jean (extraits), saint Georges: Collections grecques de miracles*. Paris: Picard, 1971.

Festugière, André-Jean, trans., and Arthur Darby Nock, ed. *Corpus Hermeticum*. 4 vols. Paris: Belles Lettres, 1954–1960. Repr., 1972–1983.

Février, Paul-Albert. "Le culte des martyrs en Afrique et ses plus anciens monuments." *CCARB* 17 (1970): 191–215.

Finney, Paul Corby. *The Invisible God: The Earliest Christians on Art*. New York: Oxford University Press, 1994.

Firenze, Paul. "Value and Economies of Religious Capital." PhD diss., Brown University, 2013.

Fishwick, Duncan. "The Cannophori and the March Festival of Magna Mater." *TAPA* 97 (1966): 193–202.

Flood, Finbarr Barry. *The Great Mosque of Damascus: Studies on the Makings of an Umayyad Visual Culture*. Leiden: Brill, 2001.

Fowden, Elizabeth Key. *The Barbarian Plain: Saint Sergius between Rome and Iran*. Berkeley: University of California Press, 1999.

Fowden, Garth. *The Egyptian Hermes: A Historical Approach to the Late Pagan Mind*. Cambridge: Cambridge University Press, 1986.

Fowler, Bridget. *Pierre Bourdieu and Cultural Theory: Critical Investigations*. Thousand Oaks, CA: Sage, 1997.

Fox, Robin Lane. *Pagans and Christians*. San Francisco: Knopf, 1986.

Fraenkel, Carlos. *Philosophical Religions from Plato to Spinoza: Reason, Religion, and Autonomy*. Cambridge: Cambridge University Press, 2012.

Frakes, Robert. "The Dynasty of Constantine Down to 363." Pages 91–108 in *The Cambridge Companion to the Age of Constantine*. Edited by Noel Lenski. New York: Cambridge University Press, 2006.

Frank, Georgia. "'Taste and See': The Eucharist and the Eyes of Faith in the Fourth Century." *CH* 70 (2001): 619–43.

Frankfurter, David. "Beyond Magic and Superstition." Pages 255–83 in *Late Ancient Christianity*. Vol. 2 of *A People's History of Christianity*. Edited by Virginia Burrus. Minneapolis: Fortress, 2005.

———. "On Sacrifices and Residues: Processing the Potent Body." Pages 511–33 in *Religion in Cultural Discourse: Essays in Honor of Hans G.*

Kippenberg on the Occasion of His 65th Birthday. Edited by Brigitte Luchesi and Kocku von Stuckrad. Berlin: de Gruyter, 2004.

———. "Where the Spirits Dwell: Possession, Christianization, and Saints' Shrines in Late Antiquity." *HTR* 103 (2010): 27–46.

Friedman, Shamma. "The Primacy of Tosefta to Mishnah in Synoptic Parallels." Pages 99–121 in *Introducing Tosefta: Textual, Intratextual, and Intertextual Studies.* Edited by Harry Fox, Tirzah Meacham, and Diane Kriger. Hoboken, NJ: Ktav, 1999.

Futrell, Alison. *Blood in the Arena: The Spectacle of Roman Power.* Austin: University of Texas Press, 2001.

Gaddis, Michael. *There Is No Crime for Those Who Have Christ: Religious Violence in the Christian Roman Empire.* Berkeley: University of California Press, 2005.

Gardner, Gregg E. *The Origins of Organized Charity in Rabbinic Judaism.* Cambridge: Cambridge University Press, 2015.

Gawlinski, Laura. "'Fashioning' Initiates: Dress at the Mysteries." Pages 146–69 in *Reading a Dynamic Canvas: Adornment in the Ancient Mediterranean World.* Edited by Cynthia S. Colburn and Maura K. Heyn. Newcastle, UK: Cambridge Scholars, 2008.

———. *The Sacred Law of Andania: A New Text and Commentary.* Sozomena 2. Berlin: de Gruyter, 2012.

Giuliano, Fabio Massimo. *Platone e la Poesia: Teoria della composizione e prassi della ricezione.* IPS 22. Sankt Augustin: Academia, 2005.

Gleason, Maud. *Making Men: Sophists and Self-Presentation in Ancient Rome.* Oxford: Oxford University Press, 1995.

Goldberg, Abraham. "The Tosefta: Companion to the Mishnah." Pages 283–350 in *Oral Tora, Halakha, Mishna, Tosefta, Talmud, External Tractates.* Vol. 1 of *The Literature of the Sages.* CRINT 2.3.1. Edited by Shmuel Safrai. Philadelphia: Fortress; Assen: Van Gorcum, 1987.

Goldziher, Ignaz. "Veneration of Saints in Islam." Pages 255–341 in vol. 1 of *Muslim Studies.* Edited by S. M. Stern. Translated by C. R. Barber and S. M. Stern. London: Allen & Unwin, 1967.

Goodson, Caroline J. "Archaeology and the Cult of Saints in the Early Middle Ages: Accessing the Sacred." *MEFRM* 126 (2014): 124–48.

———. "The Relic Translations of Paschal I: Transforming City and Cult." Pages 123–41 in *Roman Bodies.* Edited by Andrew Hopkins and Maria Wyke. London: British School at Rome, 2005.

———. "Roman Archaeology and Medieval Rome." Pages 17–34 in *Rome: Continuing Encounters between Past and Present*. Edited by Dorigen Caldwell and Lesley Caldwell. Burlington, VT: Ashgate, 2011.

Gotter, Ulrich. "Zwischen Christentum und Staatsraison: Römisches Imperium und religiöse Gewalt." Pages 133–58 in *Spätantiker Staat und religiöser Konflikt: Imperiale und lokale Verwaltung und die Gewalt gegen Heiligtümer*. Edited by Johannes Hahn. Berlin: de Gruyter, 2011.

Gouldner, Alvin W. *Enter Plato: Classical Greece and the Origin of Social Theory*. New York: Basic, 1965.

Grabar, André. *Christian Iconography: A Study of Its Origins*. Princeton: Princeton University Press, 1968.

Gregory, Timothy E. "The Survival of Paganism in Christian Greece." *AJP* 107 (1986): 229–42.

Gregory of Tours. *The History of the Franks*. Translated by Lewis Thorpe. Harmondsworth: Penguin, 1974.

Guidobaldi, F. "Roma, il tessuto abitativo, le *domus* e i *tituli*." Pages 69–83 in *L'età tardoantica*. Part 2 of *I luoghi e le culture*. Vol. 3 of *Storia di Roma*. Edited by Andrea Carandini, Lellia Cracco Ruggini, and Andrea Giardina. Turin: Einaudi, 1993.

Gunderson, Erik. *Staging Masculinity: The Rhetoric of Performance in the Roman World*. Ann Arbor: University of Michigan Press, 2000.

Hadas-Lebel, Mireille. *Jerusalem against Rome*. Translated by Robyn Fréchet. ISACR 7. Leuven: Peeters, 2005.

Hadot, Pierre. "Platon et Plotin dans trois sermons de saint Ambroise." *REL* 34 (1956): 202–20.

Hahn, Cynthia J. "Seeing and Believing: The Construction of Sanctity in Early-Medieval Saints' Shrines." *Spec* 72 (1997): 1079–1106.

———. "What Do Reliquaries Do for Relics?" *Numen* 57 (2010): 284–316.

Hahn, Cynthia J., and Holger A Klein, eds. *Saints and Sacred Matter: The Cult of Relics in Byzantium and Beyond*. Washington, DC: Dumbarton Oaks, 2015.

Halevi, Leor. *Muhammad's Grave: Death Rites and the Making of Islamic Society*. New York: Columbia University Press, 2007.

Hall, Stuart G. "Some Constantinian Documents in the *Vita Constantini*." Pages 86–104 in *Constantine: History, Historiography and Legend*. Edited by Samuel N. C. Lieu and Dominic Montserrat. New York: Routledge, 1998.

Hallaq, Wael. *The Origins and Evolution of Islamic Law*. Cambridge: Cambridge University Press, 2004.

Hansen, Maria Fabricius. *The Eloquence of Appropriation: Prolegomena to an Understanding of Spolia in Early Christian Rome*. ARIDSup 33. Rome: L'Erma di Bretschneider, 2003.

Harlow, Mary. "Clothes Maketh the Man: Power Dressing and Elite Masculinity in the Later Roman Empire." Pages 44–69 in *Gender in the Early Medieval World*. Edited by Leslie Brubaker and Julia M. H. Smith. Cambridge: Cambridge University Press, 2005.

Harrill, J. Albert. "The Domestic Enemy: A Moral Polarity of Household Slaves in Early Christian Apologies and Martyrdoms." Pages 231–54 in *Early Christian Families in Context: An Interdisciplinary Dialogue*. Edited by David L. Balch and Carolyn Osiek. Grand Rapids: Eerdmans, 2003.

Harvey, Susan Ashbrook. *Scenting Salvation: Ancient Christianity and the Olfactory Imagination*. Berkeley: University of California Press, 2006.

———. "The Sense of a Stylite: Perspectives on Simeon the Elder." *VC* 42 (1988): 376–94.

Henig, Martin. *Religion in Roman Britain*. New York: Routledge, 2003.

Henry, Nathalie. "The Song of Songs and the Liturgy of the *Velatio* in the Fourth Century: From Literary Metaphor to Liturgical Reality." Pages 18–28 in *Continuity and Change in Christian Worship: Papers Read at the 1997 Summer Meeting and the 1998 Winter Meeting of the Ecclesiastical History Society*. Edited by R. N. Swanson. SCH 35. Woodbridge: Boydell, 1999.

Hernández, Purta Nieto. "Philo and Greek Poetry." *SPhiloA* 26 (2014): 135–49.

Hezser, Catherine. *The Social Structure of the Rabbinic Movement in Roman Palestine*. TSAJ 66. Tübingen: Mohr Siebeck, 1997.

Hijmans, Steven E. "Sol: The Sun in the Art and Religions of Rome." PhD diss., University of Groningen, 2009.

———. "The Sun Which Did Not Rise in the East: The Cult of Sol Invictus in the Light of Non-literary Evidence." *BABesch* 71 (1996): 115–50.

Hilgers, Mathieu, and Éric Mangez, eds. *Bourdieu's Theory of Social Fields: Concepts and Applications*. London: Routledge, 2015.

Hillner, Julia. "Families, Patronage, and the Titular Churches of Rome, c. 300–c. 600." Pages 225–61 in *Religion, Dynasty, and Patronage in Early Christian Rome, 300–900*. Edited by Kate Cooper and Julia Hillner. Cambridge: Cambridge University Press, 2007.

Himmelmann, Nikolaus. *Das Hypogäum der Aurelier am Viale Manzoni: Ikonographische Beobachtungen*. AWL 7. Wiesbaden: Steiner, 1975.

Hodder, Ian. *Entangled: An Archaeology of the Relationships between Humans and Things*. Malden, MA: Wiley-Blackwell, 2012.

Hodge, Caroline Johnson. "Daily Devotions: Stowers's Modes of Religion Meet Tertullian's *ad Uxorem*." Pages in 43–54 in *"The One Who Sows Bountifully": Essays in Honor of Stanley K. Stowers*. Edited by Caroline Johnson Hodge, Saul M. Olyan, Daniel Ullucci, and Emma Wasserman. BJS 356. Providence, RI: Brown Judaic Studies, 2013.

Hoklotubbe, T. Christopher. "The Rhetoric of *PIETAS*: The Pastoral Epistles and Claims to Piety in the Roman Empire." ThD diss., Harvard Divinity School, 2015.

Holloway, R. Ross. *Constantine and Rome*. New Haven: Yale University Press, 2004.

Hölscher, Tonio. *The Language of Images in Roman Art*. Cambridge: Cambridge University Press, 2004.

Hopkins, Keith. *Death and Renewal*. SSRH 2. Cambridge: Cambridge University Press, 1983.

Horst, Steven. "Whose Intuitions? Which Dualism?" Pages 37–54 in *The Roots of Religion: Exploring the Cognitive Science of Religion*. Edited by Roger Trigg and Justin L. Barrett. Burlington, VT: Ashgate, 2014.

Hoyland, Robert. "New Documentary Texts and the Early Islamic State." *BSOAS* 69 (2006): 395–416.

Humphries, Mark. "From Usurper to Emperor: The Politics of Legitimation in the Age of Constantine." *JLA* 1 (2008): 82–100.

Hunter, David G. *Marriage, Celibacy, and Heresy in Ancient Christianity: The Jovinianist Controversy*. Oxford: Oxford University Press, 2007.

Hunter-Crawley, Heather. "Pilgrimage Made Portable: A Sensory Archaeology of the Monza-Bobbio Ampullae." *Herom* 1 (2012): 135–56.

Huskinson, Janet. "Elite Culture and the Identity of Empire." Pages 95–123 in *Experiencing Rome: Culture, Identity and Power in the Roman Empire*. Edited by Janet Huskinson. London: Routledge, 2000.

Iamblichus. *De Anima*. Edited and translated by John F. Finamore and John M. Dillon. PhA 92. Leiden: Brill, 2002.

———. *On the Mysteries*. Edited and translated by Emma C. Clarke, John M. Dillon, and Jackson P. Hershbell. WGRW 4. Atlanta: Society of Biblical Literature, 2003.

———. *The Letters*. Edited and translated by John Dillon and Wolfgang Polleichtner. WGRW 19. Atlanta: Society of Biblical Literature, 2009.

Ibn Abī Shayba, ʿAbd Allāh b. Muḥammad. *Kitāb al-Muṣannaf*. Edited by Ḥamad ibn ʿAbd Allāh al-Jumʿa and Muḥammad ibn Ibrāhīm al-Laḥīdān. 16 vols. Riyadh: Maktabat al-Rushd Nāshirūn, 2006.

Ibn Hishām, Abū Muḥammad ʿAbd al-Malik. *Sīrat Rasūl Allāh (Das Leben Muhammed)*. Edited by Ferdinand Wüstenfeld. 2 vols. Göttingen: Dieterichsche Universitäts-Buchhandlung, 1858–1860.

Ibn Rusta, Aḥmad Ibn-ʿUmar. *Kitāb al-Aʿlāk al-Nafīsa*. Edited by M.J. de Goeje. BGA 7. Leiden: Brill, 1892.

Ibn Saʿd, Abū ʿAbd Allāh Muḥammad. *Kitāb al-tabaqāt al-kabīr*. Edited by Eduard Sachau et al. 9 vols. Leiden: Brill, 1904–1940.

Ibn Shabba, ʿUmar. *Taʾrīkh al-madīna al-munawwara*. Edited by Fuhaym Muḥammad Shaltūt. 4 vols. Mecca: Dār al-Turāth, 1979.

Ingold, Tim. *Being Alive: Essays on Movement, Knowledge, and Description*. London: Routledge, 2011.

Jackson, Ralph. *Doctors and Diseases in the Roman Empire*. Norman: University of Oklahoma Press, 1988.

Jacobs, Martin. "Theatres and Performances as Reflected in the Talmud Yerushalmi." Pages 327–47 in vol. 1 of *Talmud Yerushalmi and Graeco-Roman Culture*. Edited by Peter Schäfer. TSAJ 71. Tübingen: Mohr Siebeck, 1998.

Jastrow, Marcus. *A Dictionary of the Targumim, the Talmud Babli and Yerushalmi, and the Midrashic Literature*. New York: Pardes, 1950.

Jefferson, Lee M., and Robin Margaret Jensen, eds. *The Art of Empire: Christian Art in Its Imperial Context*. Minneapolis: Fortress, 2015.

Jensen, Robin M. "Compiling Narratives: The Visual Strategies of Early Christian Visual Art." *JECS* 23 (2015): 1–26.

Johns, Jeremy. "Archaeology and the History of Early Islam: The First Seventy Years." *JESHO* 46 (2003): 411–36.

Johnson, Lawrence J. *Worship in the Early Church: An Anthology of Historical Sources*. Vol. 3. Collegeville, MN: Liturgical Press, 2009.

Jones, A. H. M. "Numismatics and History." Pages 13–33 in *Essays in Roman Coinage Presented to Harold Mattingly*. Edited by Carol Humphrey Vivian Sutherland and Robert A. G. Carson. Oxford: Oxford University Press, 1956.

Julian. *The Works*. Translated by Wilmer C. Wright. 3 vols. LCL 13, 29, 157. Cambridge: Harvard University Press, 1913–1923.

Jullien, Christelle, and Florence Jullien. "Du ʾḥnanaʾ ou la bénédiction contestée." Pages 333–49 in *Sur les pas des araméens chrétiens: Mélanges offerts à Alain Desreumaux*. Edited by Françoise Briquel-Chatonnet and Muriel Debié. Paris: Geuthner, 2010.

Junod, E., and Jean-Daniel Kaestli, eds. *Acta Ioannis*. CCSA 2. Turnhout: Brepols, 1983.

Juynboll, G. H. A. *Muslim Tradition: Studies in Chronology, Provenance and Authorship of Early Ḥadīth*. Cambridge: Cambridge University Press, 1983.

Kalleres, Dayna S. *City of Demons: Violence, Ritual, and Christian Power in Late Antiquity*. Berkeley: University of California Press, 2015.

Karris, Robert J. "The Background and Significance of the Polemic of the Pastoral Epistles." *JBL* 92 (1973): 549–64.

Keane, Webb. "Semiotics and the Social Analysis of Material Things." *Language and Communication* 23 (2003): 409–25.

Kelly, J. F. T. "Early Medieval Evidence for Twelve Homilies by Origen on the Apocalypse." *VC* 39 (1985): 273–79.

Kennedy, J. B. *The Musical Structure of Plato's Dialogues*. Repr., New York: Routledge, 2014.

———. "Plato's Forms, Pythagorean Mathematics, and Stichometry." *Apeiron* 43 (2010): 1–32.

Khalek, Nancy. *Damascus after the Muslim Conquest: Text and Image in Early Islam*. Oxford: Oxford University Press, 2011.

———. "'He Was Tall and Slender, and His Virtues Were Numerous': Byzantine Hagiographical Topoi and the Companions of Muḥammad in al-Azdī's *Futūḥ al-Shām*." Pages 105–23 in *Writing "True Stories": Historians and Hagiographers in the Late Antique and Early Medieval Near East*. Edited by Arietta Papaconstantinou, Muriel Debié, and Hugh Kennedy. Turnhout: Brepols, 2010.

Kinney, Dale. "The Evidence for the Dating of S. Lorenzo in Milan." *JSAH* 31 (1972): 92–107.

———. "Spolia: *Damnatio* and *Renovatio Memoriae*." *MAAR* 42 (1997): 117–48.

Kinzig, Wolfram. "The Pagans and the Christian Bible." Pages 752–74 in vol. 1 of *The New Cambridge History of the Bible*. Edited by J. Schaper and J. Carleton Paget. Cambridge: Cambridge University Press, 2013.

Kirchner, Roderich. "Die Mysterien der Rhetorik: Zur Mysteriernmetapher in rhetoriktheoretischen Texten." *RhM* 148 (2005): 165–80.

Kramer, Norbert. *Gindaros: Geschichte und Archäologie einer Siedlung im nordwestlichen Syrien vom hellenistischer bis in frühbyzantinische Zeit*. Rahden: Leidorf, 2004.

Krauss, Samuel. *Griechische und lateinische Lehnwörter im Talmud, Midrasch, und Targum*. 2 vols. Berlin: Calvary, 1898–1899.

———. *Talmudische Archäologie*. 3 vols. Leipzig: Fock, 1910–1912.

Krautheimer, Richard. *Rome: Profile of a City, 312–1308*. Princeton: Princeton University Press, 1980.

———. *Three Christian Capitals: Topography and Politics*. Berkeley: University of California, 1983.

Kretschmar, Georg. "Abendmahl III/1: Alte Kirche." *TRE* 1:59–89.

Krug, Antje. *Heilkunst und Heilkult: Medizin in der Antike*. Munich: Beck 1985.

Krulak, Todd. "Θυσία and Theurgy: Sacrificial Theory in Fourth- and Fifth-Century Platonism." *ClQ* 64 (2014): 353–82.

Kuefler, Mathew. *The Manly Eunuch: Masculinity, Gender Ambiguity, and Christian Ideology in Late Antiquity*. Chicago: University of Chicago Press, 2001.

Landsberg, Mitchell. "Atheists, Agnostics Most Knowledgeable About Religion, Survey Says." *Los Angeles Times*. September 28, 2010.

Larson, Steven J. "The Trouble with Religious Tolerance in Roman Antiquity." Pages 50–59 in *Religious Competition in the Third Century CE: Jews, Christians, and the Greco-Roman World*. Edited by Jordan D. Rosenblum, Lily C. Vuong, and Nathaniel P. DesRosiers. Göttingen: Vandenhoeck & Ruprecht, 2014.

———. "What Temples Stood For: Constantine, Eusebius, and Roman Imperial Practice." PhD diss., Brown University, 2008.

Lash, Scott. *Sociology of Postmodernism*. London: Routledge, 1990.

Latham, Jacob. "'Fabulous Clap-Trap': Roman Masculinity, the Cult of Magna Mater, and Literary Constructions of the *galli* at Rome from the Late Republic to Late Antiquity." *JR* 92 (2012): 84–122.

Latour, Bruno. *Reassembling the Social: An Introduction to Actor-Network-Theory*. New York: Oxford University Press, 2005.

Lee, A. D. "Traditional Religions." Pages 159–79 in *The Cambridge Companion to the Age of Constantine*. Edited by Noel Lenski. New York: Cambridge University Press, 2006.

Lemerle, Paul, ed. and trans. *Le texte*. Vol. 1 of *Les plus anciens recueils des miracles de Saint Démétrius et la pénétration des Slaves dans les Balkans*. MdByz 2. Paris: Éditions du Centre national de la Recherche scientifique, 1979–1981.

Lenski, Noel. "The Reign of Constantine." Pages 59–90 in *The Cambridge Companion to the Age of Constantine*. Edited by Noel Lenski. New York: Cambridge University Press, 2006.

Leroy-Molinghen, Alice. "Les manuscrits de l'Histoire Philothée' de Théodoret de Cyr." *Byzantion* 34 (1964): 27–47.

Leszl, Walter G. "Plato's Attitude to Poetry and the Fine Arts, and the Origins of Aesthetics." *EPla* 1 (2004): 113–97; 2 (2006): 285–351; 3 (2006): 245–336.

Levick, Barbara. "Propaganda and the Imperial Coinage." *Antichthon* 16 (1982): 104–16.

Lewis, Suzanne. "Function and Symbolic Form in the Basilica Apostolorum in Milan." *JSAH* 28 (1969): 83–98.

Leyerle, Blake. *Theatrical Shows and Ascetic Lives: John Chrysostom's Attack on Spiritual Marriage*. Berkeley: University of California Press, 2001.

Leyser, Conrad. "'A Church in the House of the Saints': Property and Power in the Passion of John and Paul." Pages 140–62 in *Religion, Dynasty, and Patronage in Early Christian Rome, 300–900*. Edited by Kate Cooper and Julia Hillner. Cambridge: Cambridge University Press, 2007.

Lieberman, Saul. *Meḥkarim be-Torat Erets-Yiśraʾel*. Edited by D. Rosenthal. Jerusalem: Magnes, 1991.

Liebert, Rana S. "Apian Imagery and the Critique of Poetic Sweetness in Plato's *Republic*." *TAPA* 140 (2010): 97–116.

Lincoln, Bruce. *Gods and Demons, Priests and Scholars: Critical Explorations in the History of Religions*. Chicago: University of Chicago Press, 2012.

Lipps, Johannes, Carlos Machado, and Philipp von Rummel, eds. *The Sack of Rome in 410 AD: The Event, Its Context and Its Impact; Proceedings of the Conference Held at the German Archaeological Institute at Rome, 04–06 November 2010*. Wiesbaden: Reichert, 2013.

Liverani, Paolo. "Reading *Spolia* in Late Antiquity and Contemporary Perception." Pages 33–51 in *Reuse Value: Spolia and Appropriation in Art and Architecture from Constantine to Sherrie Levine*. Edited by Richard Brilliant and Dale Kinney. Burlington, VT: Ashgate, 2011.

Lizzi, Rita. "I vescovi e i potentes della terra: Definizione e limite del ruolo episcopale nelle due partes imperii fra IV e V secolo d.C." Pages 81–104 in *L'évêque dans la cité IVe au Ve siècle: Image et autorité; Actes de la table ronde organisée par l'Istituto patristico Augustinianum et l'Ecole française de Rome; Rome 1er et 2 décembre 1995*. Edited by Éric Rebillard and Claire Sotinel. Rome: École française de Rome, 1998.

Löhr, Winrich. "Christianity as Philosophy: Problems and Perspectives of an Ancient Intellectual Project." *VC* 64 (2010): 160–88.

MacCormack, Sabine. *Art and Ceremony in Late Antiquity*. Berkeley: University of California Press, 1981.

Mackie, Gillian. *Early Christian Chapels in the West: Decoration, Function and Patronage*. Toronto: University of Toronto Press, 2003.

MacMullen, Ramsay. *The Second Church: Popular Christianity A.D. 200–400*. WGRWSup 1. Atlanta: Society of Biblical Literature, 2009.

Madec, Goulven. *Saint Ambroise et la philosophie*. Paris: Études augustiniennes, 1974.

Magee, Gregory S. "Uncovering the 'Mystery' in 1 Timothy 3." *TJ* 29 (2008): 247–65.

Majercik, Ruth. *The Chaldean Oracles: Text, Translation, and Commentary*. SGRR 5. Leiden: Brill, 1989.

Malherbe, Abraham J. "Medical Imagery in the Pastoral Epistles." Pages 19–35 in *Texts and Testaments: Critical Essays on the Bible and Early Church Fathers; A Volume in Honor of Stuart Dickson Currie*. Edited by W. Eugene March. San Antonio, TX: Trinity University Press, 1980.

———. *Paul and the Popular Philosophers*. Minneapolis, MN: Fortress, 1989.

Malina, Bruce J. *The New Testament World: Insights from Cultural Anthropology*. Atlanta: John Knox, 1981.

Mandel, Paul. "The Tosefta." Pages 316–35 in *The Late Roman-Rabbinic Period*. Vol. 4 of *The Cambridge History of Judaism*. Edited by Steven T. Katz. Cambridge: Cambridge University Press, 2006.

Mango, Marlia M. *Silver Treasure from Early Byzantium: The Kaper Koraon and Related Treasures*. Baltimore: Trustees of the Walters Art Gallery, 1986.

Maraval, Pierre. *Lieux saints et pèlerinages d'Orient: Histoire et géographie des origines à la conquête arabe*. Paris: Cerf, 1985.

Margoliouth, David S. "The Relics of the Prophet Mohammed." *MW* 27 (1937): 20–27.

Markus, R. A. "How on Earth Could Places Become Holy? Origins of the Christian Idea of Holy Places." *JECS* 2 (1994): 257–71.

Marrou, Henri Irénée. *Mousikos anēr: Étude sur les scènes de la vie intellectuelle figurant sur les monuments funéraires romains*. Grenoble: Didier & Richard, 1938.

Martindale, J. R. *A.D. 395–527*. Vol. 2 of *The Prosopography of the Later Roman Empire*. Cambridge: Cambridge University Press, 1980.
Marwazī, Isḥāq ibn Ibrāhīm ibn Makhlad al-Ḥanẓalī al-. *Musnad Isḥāq bin Rāhwayh*. Edited by Abd al-Ghafūr ʿAbd al-Ḥaqq Ḥusayn Burr al-Balūshī. 5 vols. Medina: Tawzīʿ Maktabat al-Īmān, 1990–1995.
Matter, E. Ann. *The Voice of My Beloved: The Song of Songs in Western Medieval Christianity*. Philadelphia: University of Pennsylvania Press, 1990.
Matthews, John. *Western Aristocracies and Imperial Court A.D. 364–425*. Oxford: Clarendon, 1975.
Mayer, Wendy, and Pauline Allen. *The Churches of Syrian Antioch (300–638 CE)*. Leuven: Peeters, 2012.
McCulloh, John M. "The Cult of Relics in the Letters and 'Dialogues' of Pope Gregory the Great: A Lexicographical Study." *Traditio* 32 (1976): 145–84.
McGinn, Bernard. *The Foundations of Mysticism: Origins to the Fifth Century*. New York: Crossroad, 1991.
McGowan, Andrew. "Rethinking Eucharistic Origins." *Pacifica* 23 (2010): 173–91.
McGuckin, John A. "Origen as a Literary Critic in the Alexandrian Tradition." Pages 121–36 in *Origeniana Octava: Origen and the Alexandria Tradition; Papers of the 8th International Origen Congress, Pisa 27–31 August 2001*. Edited by L. Perrone. Leuven: Peeters, 2003.
McLynn, Neil B. *Ambrose of Milan: Church and Court in a Christian Capital*. Berkeley: University of California Press, 1994.
Meadows, Andrew, and Jonathan Williams. "Moneta and the Monuments: Coinage and Politics in Republican Rome." *JRS* 91 (2001): 27–49.
Meri, Josef W. *The Cult of Saints among Muslims and Jews in Medieval Syria*. Oxford: Oxford University Press, 2002.
———. "Relics of Piety and Power in Medieval Islam." Pages 97–120 in *Relics and Remains*. Edited by Alexandra Walsham. P&PSup 5. Oxford: Oxford University Press, 2010.
Metcalf, William E. "Whose *Liberalitas*? Propaganda and the Audience in the Early Roman Empire." *RIN* 95 (1993): 337–46.
Metzler, Karin. *Die Kommentierung des Buches Genesis*. Origenes Werke mit deutscher Übersetzung 1.1. New York: de Gruyter, 2010.
Mihai, Adrian. "Comparatism in the Neoplatonic Pantheon of Late Antiquity: Damascius, *De Princ. III 159.6–167.25*." *Numen* 61 (2014): 457–83.

Millar, Fergus. "Local Cultures in the Roman Empire: Libyan, Punic, and Latin in Roman Africa." *JRS* 58 (1968): 126–34.

Miller, Patricia Cox. *The Corporeal Imagination: Signifying the Holy in Late Ancient Christianity*. Philadelphia: University of Pennsylvania Press, 2009.

Mills, Harrianne. "Greek Clothing Regulations: Sacred and Profane?" *ZPE* 55 (1984): 255–65.

Montserrat, Dominic. "Pilgrimage to the Shrine of SS Cyrus and John at Menouthis in Late Antiquity." Pages 257–73 in *Pilgrimage and Holy Space in Late Antique Egypt*. Edited by David Frankfurter. RGRW 134. Leiden: Brill, 1998.

Morgan, David. "Introduction: 'The Matter of Belief.'" Pages 1–20 in *Religion and Material Culture: The Matter of Belief*. Edited by David Morgan. London: Routledge, 2010.

Moss, Candida R. *The Other Christs: Imitating Jesus in Ancient Christian Ideologies of Martyrdom*. Oxford: Oxford University Press, 2010.

Mott, Stephen C. "Greek Ethics and Christian Conversion: The Philonic Background of Titus II 10–14 and III 3–7." *NovT* 20 (1978): 22–48.

Mounce, William D. *Pastoral Epistles*. WBC 46. Nashville: Nelson, 1999.

Munt, Harry. *The Holy City of Medina: Sacred Space in Early Islamic Arabia*. New York: Cambridge University Press, 2014.

Muranyi, Miklos. "The Emergence of Holy Places in Early Islam: On the Prophet's Track." *JSAI* 39 (2012): 165–71.

Muslim, Ibn al-Ḥajjāj. *Ṣaḥīḥ Muslim*. Edited by Muḥammad Fu'ād 'Abd al-Bāqī. 5 vols. Cairo: Dār Iḥyā al-Kutub al-'Arabiyya, 1955–1956.

Musurillo, Herbert. *The Acts of the Christian Martyrs*. OECT. Oxford: Clarendon, 1972.

Nelson, Robert S. "Appropriation." Pages 162–73 in *Critical Terms for Art History*. Edited by Robert S. Nelson and Richard Schiff. 2nd ed. Chicago: University of Chicago Press, 2010.

———. "Descartes's Cow and Other Domestications of the Visual." Pages 1–21 in *Visuality before and beyond the Renaissance: Seeing as Others Saw*. Edited by Robert S. Nelson Cambridge: Cambridge University Press, 2000.

Neusner, Jacob. *The Talmud of the Land of Israel: A Preliminary Translation and Explanation*. 33 vols. CSHJ. Chicago: University of Chicago, 1982–1993.

———. *The Tosefta*. Hoboken, NJ: Ktav, 1977–1986.

Newman, Hillel I. "Jerome and the Jews" [Hebrew]. PhD diss., Hebrew University of Jerusalem, 1997.

Neyrey, Jerome H. *Honor and Shame in the Gospel of Matthew*. Louisville: Westminster John Knox, 1998

Nie, Giselle de. "Seeing and Believing in the Early Middle Ages: A Preliminary Investigation." Pages 67–76 in *The Pictured Word*. Edited by Martin Heusser, Claus Clüver, Leo Hoek, and Lauren Weingarden. WII 2. Amsterdam: Rodopi, 1998.

Niehoff, Maren R. *Jewish Exegesis and Homeric Scholarship in Alexandria*. Cambridge: Cambridge University Press, 2011.

———. "Recherche homérique et exégèse biblique à Alexandrie: Le cas de la Tour de Babel." Pages 83–103 in *Philon d'Alexandrie: Un penseur à l'intersection des cultures gréco-romaine, orientale, juive, et chrétienne; Actes du colloque international organisé par le Centre interdisciplinaire d'étude des religions et de la laïcité de l'Université libre de Bruxelles (Bruxelles, 26-28 juin 2007)*. Edited by Sabrina Inowlocki and Baudouin Decharneux. Turnhout: Brepols, 2011.

Noll, Rudolf. *Das Inventar des Dolichenusheiligtums von Mauer an der Url (Noricum)*. Vol. 30 of *Der römische Limes in Österreich*. Vienna: Österreichischen Akademie der Wissenschaften, 1980.

Numenius. *Fragments*. Edited and translated by É. Des Places. Paris: Belles Lettres, 1973.

Olson, Kelly. "Matrona and Whore: Clothing and Definition in Roman Antiquity." Pages 186–204 in *Prostitutes and Courtesans in the Ancient World*. Edited by Christopher A. Faraone and Laura K. McClure. Madison: University of Wisconsin Press, 2006.

Origen. *Commentaire sur le cantique des cantiques: Texte de la version Latine de rufin*. Translated by Luc Brésard and Henri Crouzel with Marcel Borret. SC 375. Paris: Cerf, 1991.

———. *Contra Celsum*. Translated by Henry Chadwick. Cambridge: Cambridge University Press, 1953.

———. *The Song of Songs: Commentary and Homilies*. Translated by R. P. Lawson. ACW 26. Westminster, MD: Newman, 1957.

Papaconstantinou, Arietta. "The Cult of Saints: A Haven of Continuity in a Changing World?" Pages 350–67 in *Egypt in the Byzantine World, 300-700*. Edited by Roger S. Bagnall. Cambridge: Cambridge University Press, 2007.

———. "Saints and Saracens: On Some Miracle Accounts of the Early Arab Period." Pages 323–38 in *Byzantine Religious Culture: Studies in Honor of Alice-Mary Talbot*. Edited by Dennis Sullivan, Elizabeth Fisher, and Stratis Papaioannou. MMed 92. Leiden: Brill, 2012.

Parthey, Gustav. *Jamblichi De Mysteriis liber*. Berlin: Nicolai, 1857.

Paulinus of Nola. *The Poems of St. Paulinus of Nola*. Translated by P. G. Walsh. ACW 40. New York: Newman, 1975.

Pentcheva, Bissera. "The Performative Icon." *ABull* 88 (2006): 631–55.

Pergola, Agnese. "Il quadrante delle intrepretazioni." Pages 81–124 in *L'ipogeo degli Aureli in viale Manzoni: Restauri, tutela, valorizzazione e aggiornamenti interpretative*. Edited by Fabrizio Bisconti. Vatican City: Pontificia Commissione di Archeologia Sacra, 2011.

Petraki, Zacharoula A. *The Poetics of Philosophical Language: Plato, Poets and Presocratics in the Republic*. Berlin: de Gruyter, 2011.

Pharr, Clyde, trans. *The Theodosian Code and Novels, and the Sirmondian Constitutions*. Princeton: Princeton University Press, 1952.

Philodemus. *Critical Edition with Commentary*. Vol. 1 of *On Piety*. Edited and translated by Dirk Obbink. Oxford: Oxford University, 1996.

Philo of Alexandria. *On Virtues: Introduction, Translation, and Commentary*. Translated by Walter T. Wilson. PACS 3. Leiden: Brill, 2011.

Poe, Alison Crystal. "The Third-Century Mausoleum ('Hypogaeum') of the Aurelii in Rome: Pagan or Mixed-Religion Collegium Tomb." PhD diss., Rutgers University, 2007.

Porphyry. *Lettre à Anébon L'Égyptien*. Edited and translated by Henri Dominique Saffrey and Alain-Philippe Segonds. Paris: Belles Lettres, 2012.

Pratt, Mary Louise. *Imperial Eyes: Travel Writing and Transculturation*. London: Routledge, 1992.

Price, Simon R. F. *Rituals and Power: The Roman Imperial Cult in Asia Minor*. Cambridge: Cambridge University Press, 1984.

Proclus. *Commentary on the First Alcibiades*. Edited and translated by L. G. Westerink and William O'Neill. PTT 6. Dilton Marsh: Prometheus Trust, 2011.

Promey, Sally M. *Sensational Religion: Sensory Cultures in Material Practice*. New Haven: Yale University Press, 2014.

Prothero, Stephen R. *Religious Literacy: What Every American Needs to Know—And Doesn't*. San Francisco: HarperSanFrancisco, 2007.

Pülz, Andreas. "Archaeological Evidence of Christian Pilgrimage in Ephesus." *Herom* 1 (2012): 225–60.

Pyysiäinen, Ilkka. *How Religion Works: Towards a New Cognitive Science of Religion*. Leiden: Brill, 2001.

Quasten, Johannes. "The Liturgical Mysticism of Theodore of Mopsuestia." *TS* 15 (1954): 431–39.
Rāġib, Yūsuf. "Un épisode obscur d'histoire fatimide." *SIs* 48 (1978): 125–32.
Ramelli, Ilaria. "Atticus and Origen on the Soul of God the Creator: From the Pagan to the Christian Side of Middle Platonism." *JRp* 10 (2011): 13–35.
———. *Bardaisan of Edessa: A Reassessment of the Evidence and a New Interpretation*. Piscataway, NJ: Gorgias, 2009.
———. *The Christian Doctrine of Apokatastasis: A Critical Assessment from the New Testament to Eriugena*. Leiden: Brill, 2013.
———. "Commentaries: Intersections between 'Pagan' and Christian Platonism in Late Antiquity." Paper presented at the Annual Meeting of the Society of Classical Studies. San Francisco, CA, 7–9 January 2016.
———. "Epicureanism and Early Christianity." In *Oxford Handbook of Epicureanism*. Edited by Phillip Mistis. Oxford: Oxford University Press, forthcoming.
———. *L'età classica*, vol. 1 of *Allegoria*. Milan: Vita e Pensiero, 2004.
———. "Origen and Apokatastasis: A Reassessment." Pages 649–70 in *Origeniana Decima: Origen as Writer; Papers of the 10th International Origen Congress, University School of Philosophy and Education "Ignatianum," Kraków, Poland, 31 August–4 September 2009*. Edited by Sylwya Kaczmarek and Henryk Pietras. Leuven: Peeters, 2011.
———. "Origen and the Stoic Allegorical Tradition: Continuity and Innovation." *InvLuc* 28 (2006): 195–226.
———. "Origene allegorista cristiano: Il duplice attacco e la simmetria tra filosofia cristiana e allegoresi biblica." *InvLuc* 31 (2009): 141–56.
———. "Origen, Greek Philosophy, and the Birth of the Trinitarian Meaning of Hypostasis." *HTR* 105 (2012): 302–50.
———. *Origen of Alexandria Philosopher and Theologian*. Cambridge: Cambridge University Press, forthcoming.
———. "Origen, Patristic Philosophy, and Christian Platonism: Rethinking the Christianization of Hellenism." *VC* 63 (2009): 217–63.
———. "Origen the Christian Middle/Neoplatonist." *JECH* 1 (2011): 98–130.
———. "Philosophical Allegoresis of Scripture in Philo and Its Legacy in Gregory of Nyssa." *SPhiloA* 20 (2008): 55–99.
———. "The Philosophical Stance of Allegory in Stoicism and Its Reception in Platonism, Pagan and Christian." *IJCT* 18 (2011): 335–71.

———. "Proclus and Christian Neoplatonism." Pages 43–82 in *The Ways of Byzantine Philosophy*. Edited by Mikonja Knežević. Alhambra, CA: Sebastian, 2015.

Ramsey, Boniface. *Ambrose*. ECF. London: Routledge, 1997.

Rapp, Claudia. *Holy Bishops in Late Antiquity: The Nature of Christian Leadership in an Age of Transition*. Berkeley: University of California Press, 2005.

Rappe, Sara. *Reading Neoplatonism: Non-discursive Thinking in the Texts of Plotinus, Proclus, and Damascius*. Cambridge: Cambridge University Press, 2000.

Rebillard, Éric. *Christians and Their Many Identities in Late Antiquity: North Africa, 200–450 CE*. Ithaca, NY: Cornell University Press, 2012.

———. *The Care of the Dead in Late Antiquity*. CSCP 59. Ithaca, NY: Cornell University Press, 2009.

Reznick, Ron. "Rome: Ancient Churches." digital-images.net. http://tinyurl.com/SBL4210a.

Richter, Daniel S. "Plutarch on Isis and Osiris: Text, Cult, and Cultural Appropriation." *TAPA* 131 (2001): 191–216.

Ridings, Daniel. *The Attic Moses: The Dependency Theme in Some Early Christian Writers*. Göteborg: Acta Universitatis Gothoburgensis, 1995.

Rives, James B. *Religion and Authority in Roman Carthage from Augustus to Constantine*. Oxford: Clarendon, 1995.

———. *Religion in the Roman Empire*. Malden, MA: Blackwell, 2007.

Robert, Louis. *Les gladiateurs dans l'Orient grec*. Amsterdam: Hakkert, 1971.

Robinson, Chase. *Islamic Historiography*. TIH. New York: Cambridge University Press, 2003.

Rosenblum, Jordan D., Lily C. Vuong, and Nathaniel P. DesRosiers, eds. *Religious Competition in the Third Century CE: Jews, Christians, and the Greco-Roman World*. JAJSup 15. Göttingen: Vandenhoeck & Ruprecht Press, 2014.

Roskam, Geert. "'And a Great Silence Filled the Temple...': Plutarch on the Connections between Mystery Cults and Philosophy." Pages 221–32 in *Estudios sobre Plutarco: Misticismo y religiones mistéricas en la obra de Plutarco; Actas del VII Simposio Español sobre Plutarco (Palma de Mallorca, 2–4 de noviembre de 2000)*. Edited by Aurelio Pérez Jiménez and Francesc Casadesús Bordoy. Madrid: Ediciones Clásicas, 2001.

Rummel, Philipp von. "Ereignis und Narrativ: Erzählungen der Plünderung Roms im August 410 zwischen Textüberlieferung und Archäologie." Pages 17–27 in *The Sack of Rome in 410 AD: The Event, Its Context and Its Impact; Proceedings of the Conference Held at the German Archaeological Institute at Rome, 04–06 November 2010*. Edited by Johannes Lipps, Carlos Machado, and Philipp von Rummel. Wiesbaden: Reichert Verlag, 2013.

Runia, David. "Philon d'Alexandrie." Pages 362–90 in *De Paccius à Plotin*, vol. 5a of *Dictionnaire des philosophes antiques*. Edited by Richard Goulet. Paris: Editions du Centre National de la Recherche Scientifique, 2011.

Rüpke, Jörg. *Il crocevia del mito: Religione e narrazione nel mondo antico*. Bologna: EDB, 2014.

Russell, Ben. "The Roman Sarcophagus Industry: A Reconsideration." Pages 119–48 in *Life, Death and Representation: Some New Work on Roman Sarcophagi*. Edited by Jaś Elsner and Janet Huskinson. New York: de Gruyter, 2010.

Rüttiman, René Josef. "Asclepius and Jesus: The Form, Character, and Status of the Asclepius Cult in the Second Century CE and Its Influence on Early Christianity." ThD diss., Harvard University, 1987.

Sahmī, Ḥamza b. Yūsuf al-. *Tāʾrīkh Jurjān*. Edited by M. A. Muʿīd Khān. 2nd ed. Hyderabad: Maṭbaʿat Majlis Dāʾirat al-Maʿārif al-ʿUthmāniyya, 1967.

Salzman, Michele. *The Making of a Christian Aristocracy: Social and Religious Change in the Western Roman Empire*. Cambridge: Harvard University Press, 2002.

———. *On Roman Time: The Codex-Calendar of 354 and the Rhythms of Urban Life in Late Antiquity*. TCH 14. Berkeley: University of California Press, 1990.

Satlow, Michael. "Giving for Return: Jewish Offerings in Late Antiquity." Pages 91–108 in *Religion and the Self in Antiquity*. Edited by David Brakke, Michael Satlow, and Steven Weitzman. Bloomington: Indiana University Press, 2005.

Schlezinger-Katsman, Dafna. "Clothing." Pages 362–81 in *The Oxford Handbook of Jewish Daily Life in Roman Palestine*. Edited by Catherine Hezser. Oxford: Oxford University Press, 2010.

Schott, Jeremy M. *Christianity, Empire, and the Making of Religion in Late Antiquity*. Philadelphia: University of Pennsylvania Press, 2008.

———. "Founding Platonopolis: The Platonic *Politeia* in Eusebius, Porphyry, and Iamblichus." *JECS* 11 (2003): 501–32.

———. "Language." Pages 58–79 in *Late Ancient Knowing: Explorations in Intellectual History*. Edited by Catherine M. Chin and Moulie Vidas. Oakland: University of California Press, 2015.

Schwartz, Seth. *Imperialism and Jewish Society, 200 B.C.E. to 640 C.E.* Princeton: Princeton University Press, 2001.

Segal, Arthur. *Theatres in Roman Palestine and Provincia Arabia*. Leiden: Brill, 1995.

Shaw, Gregory. "Divination in the Neoplatonism of Iamblichus." Pages 225–67 in *Mediators of the Divine: Horizons of Prophecy, Divination, Dreams and Theurgy in Mediterranean Antiquity*. Edited by Robert M. Berchman. SFSHJ 163. Atlanta: Scholars Press, 1998.

———. *Theurgy and the Soul: The Neoplatonism of Iamblichus*. University Park: Pennsylvania State University Press, 1995. Repr., Kettering, OH: Angelico, 2014.

Sheckler, Allyson Everingham, and Mary Joan Winn Leith. "The Crucifixion Conundrum and the Santa Sabina Doors." HTR 103 (2010), 67–88.

Shepardson, Christine C. *Controlling Contested Places: Late Antique Antioch and the Spatial Politics of Religious Controversy*. Berkeley: University of California Press, 2014.

Shoemaker, Stephen J. *The Death of a Prophet: The End of Muhammad's Life and the Beginnings of Islam*. Philadelphia: University of Pennsylvania Press, 2011.

Shuve, Karl. "Origen's 'Dramatic' Approach to Scripture in the Homilies on Jeremiah." Pages 235–40 in *Tertullian to Tyconius: Egypt before Nicaea; Athanasius and His Opponents*. Vol. 3 of *Studia Patristica: Papers Presented at the Fifteenth International Conference on Patristic Studies Held in Oxford, 2007*. Edited by J. Baun, A. Cameron, M. Edwards, and M. Vinzent. StPatr 46. Leuven: Peeters, 2010.

———. *The Song of Songs and the Fashioning of Identity in Early Latin Christianity*. Oxford: Oxford University Press, 2016.

Sider, Robert. "Tertullian, On the Shows: An Analysis." JTS 29 (1978): 339–65.

"Signifying Scriptures." Institute for Signifying Scriptures. http://www.signifyingscriptures.org

Sizgorich, Thomas. "Narrative and Community in Islamic Late Antiquity." P&P 185 (2004): 9–42.

———. *Violence and Belief in Late Antiquity: Militant Devotion in Christianity and Islam*. Philadelphia: University of Pennsylvania Press, 2009.

Smith, Andrew. "The Image of Egypt in the Platonic Tradition." Pages 319–25 in *Plato Revived: Essays on Ancient Platonism in Honour of Dominic J. O'Meara*. Edited by Filip Karfík and Euree Song. Berlin: de Gruyter, 2013.

Smith, Jonathan Z. *Drudgery Divine: On the Comparison of Early Christianities and the Religions of Late Antiquity*. Chicago: University of Chicago Press, 1990.

Smith, Julia. "Relics: An Evolving Tradition in Latin Christianity." Pages 41–60 in *Saints and Sacred Matter: The Cult of Relics in Byzantium and Beyond*. Edited by Cynthia J. Hahn and Holger A. Klein. Washington, DC: Dumbarton Oaks, 2015.

Smith, Rowland. *Julian's Gods: Religion and Philosophy in the Thought and Action of Julian the Apostate*. New York: Routledge, 1995.

Sodini, Jean-Pierre, and Jean-Luc Biscop. "Qal'at Sem'an et Deir Sem'an: Naissance et développement d'un lieu de pèlerinage durant l'Antiquité tardive. " Pages 11–59 in *Architecture paléochrétienne*. Edited by J. M. Spieser. Gollion: Infolio, 2011.

Solaro, Giuseppe. "Denigrare Omero." *ANost* 9 (2011): 81–86.

Sotinel, Claire. "Les évêques Italiens dans la société de l'Antiquité tardive: L'émergence d'une nouvelle élite?" Pages 377–404 in *Le transformazioni delle elites in età tardoantica*. Edited by R. Lizzi Testa. Rome: L'Erma di Bretschneider, 2006.

Spielman, Loren. "Sitting with Scorners: Jewish Attitudes toward Roman Spectacle Entertainment from the Herodian Period through the Muslim conquest." PhD diss., Jewish Theological Seminary of America, 2010.

Spieser, Jean-Michel. "Ambrose's Foundations at Milan and the Question of Martyria." Pages 1–12 in *Urban and Religious Spaces in Late Antiquity and Early Byzantium*. VCS 706. Edited by Jean-Michel Spieser. Burlington, VT: Ashgate, 2001.

———. "Les fondations d'Ambroise à Milan et la question des martyria." *DChAE* 20 (1998): 29–34.

———. "The Representation of Christ in the Apses of Early Christian Churches." *Gesta* 37 (1998): 63–73.

Stavrakopoulou, Francesca. "'Popular' Religion and 'Official' Religion: Practice, Perception, Portrayal." Pages 37–58 in *Religious Diversity in Ancient Israel and Judah*. Edited by Francesca Stavrakopoulou and John Barton. London: T&T Clark, 2010.

Steel, Carlos G. "Breathing Thought: Proclus on the Innate Knowledge of the Soul." Pages 293–309 in *The Perennial Tradition of Neoplatonism*. Edited by J. J. Cleary. Leuven: Leuven University Press, 1997.

———. *The Changing Self: A Study on the Soul in Later Neoplatonism: Iamblichus, Damascius, and Priscianus*. Translated by E. Haasl. Brussels: Paleis der Academiën, 1978.

Stephenson, Paul. *Constantine: Roman Emperor Christian Victor*. New York: Overlook, 2010.

Sterling, Gregory E. "'The Queen of the Virtues': Piety in Philo of Alexandria." *SPhiloA* 18 (2006): 103–24.

Stern, Sacha. *Jewish Identity in Early Rabbinic Writings*. Leiden: Brill, 1994.

Stowers, Stanley K. "Kinds of Myth, Meals and Power: Paul and the Corinthians." Pages 105–49 in *Redescribing Paul and the Corinthians*. Edited by Ron Cameron and Merrill O. Miller. ECL 5. Atlanta: Society of Biblical Literature, 2011.

———. "The Ontology of Religion." Pages 434–49 in *Introducing Religion: Essays in Honor of Jonathan Z. Smith*. Edited by Willi Braun and Russell T. McCutcheon. London: Equinox, 2008.

———. "Paul and the Terrain of Philosophy." *EC* 6 (2015): 141–56.

———. "Pauline Scholarship, Christian Origins and the Third Way in Social Theory." Paper presented at the Annual Meeting of the Society of Biblical Literature. Atlanta, GA, 11 November 2010.

———. "The Religion of Plant and Animal Offerings versus the Religion of Meanings, Essences, and Textual Mysteries." Pages 35–56 in *Ancient Mediterranean Sacrifice*. Edited by Jennifer Wright Knust and Zsuzsanna Várhelyi. Oxford: Oxford University Press, 2011.

———. "Why Expert versus Non-expert Is Not Elite versus Popular Religion: The Case of the Third Century." Paper presented at the Annual Meeting of the Society of Biblical Literature. San Diego, 24 November 2014.

Stroumsa, Guy G. "Tertullian and the Limits of Tolerance." Pages 173–84 in *Tolerance and Intolerance in Early Judaism and Christianity*. Edited by Graham Stanton and Guy Strousma. Cambridge: Cambridge University Press, 1998.

Struck, Peter T. *Birth of the Symbol: Ancient Readers at the Limits of Their Texts*. Princeton: Princeton University Press, 2004.

Sutherland, Carol Humphrey Vivian. *Coinage in Roman Imperial Policy, 31 B.C.–A.D. 68*. London: Methuen, 1951.

Swartz, David. *Culture and Power: The Sociology of Pierre Bourdieu*. Chicago: University of Chicago Press, 1997.
Ṭabarī, Abū Jaʻfar Muḥammad b. Jarīr al-. *Taʾrīkh al-rusul waʾl mulūk*. Edited by M. J. de Goeje et al. 15 vols. Leiden: Brill, 1879–1901.
Taft, Robert F. "The Lord's Prayer in the Eucharistic Liturgy: When and Why?" *EccOr* 14 (1997): 137–55.
———. *The Precommunion Rites*. OrChrAn 261. Rome: Pontificio istituto orientale, 2000.
Talmon-Heller, Daniella. *Islamic Piety in Medieval Syria: Mosques, Cemeteries and Sermons under the Zangids and Ayyūbids (1146–1260)*. Leiden: Brill, 2007.
Tanaseanu-Döbler, Ilinca. *Theurgy in Late Antiquity: The Invention of a Ritual Tradition*. BERG 1. Göttingen: Vandenhoeck & Ruprecht, 2013.
Taormina, Lorenzo. "Sant' Ambrogio e Plotino." *MSLCA* 4 (1953): 41–85.
Tarrant, Harold. Review of *The Musical Structure of Plato's Dialogues*, by J. B. Kennedy. *IJPT* 7 (2013): 244–45.
Taylor, Christopher S. *In the Vicinity of the Righteous: Ziyāra and the Veneration of Muslim Saints in Late Medieval Egypt*. IHC 22. Leiden: Brill, 1999.
Tchalenko, Georges. *Villages antiques de la Syrie du nord: Le massif du Bélus à l'époque romaine*. 3 vols. Paris: Geuthner, 1953–1958.
Teiser, Stephen. "Popular Religion." *JAS* 54 (1995): 378–95.
Tertullian(us). *De idolatria*. Edited by A. Reifferscheid and G. Wissowa. CCSL 2. Turnhout: Brepols, 1954.
———. *De Pallio: Translation with Commentary*. Edited and translated by Vincent Hunink. Amsterdam: Gieben, 2005.
Thacker, Alan. "Martyr Cult within Walls: Saints and Relics in the Roman 'Tituli of the Fourth to Seventh Centuries." Pages 31–70 in *Text, Image and Interpretation: Studies in Anglo-Saxon Literature and Its Insular Context in Honour of Éamonn Ó. Carrigáin*. Edited by Alastair J. Minnis and Jane Roberts. SEMA 18. Turnhout: Brepols, 2007.
———. "The Origin and Early Development of Rome's Intramural Cults: A Context for the Cult of Sant'Agnese in Agone." *MEFRM* 126 (2014): 1–27.
———. "Rome of the Martyrs: Saints, Cults and Relics, Fourth to Seventh Centuries." Pages 13–50 in *Roma Felix: Formation and Reflections of Medieval Rome*. Edited by Éamonn Ó Carragáin and Carol Neuman de Vegvar. Aldershot, UK: Ashgate, 2007.

Theodoret of Cyrus. *A History of the Monks of Syria*. Translated by R. M. Price. CSS 88. Kalamazoo, MI: Cistercian Publications, 1985.

———. *Histoire des moines de Syrie: Histoire Philothée*. Edited and translated by Pierre Canivet and Alice Leroy-Molinghen. 2 vols. SC 234, 257. Paris: Cerf, 1977–1979.

Thunø, Erik. "Looking at Letters: 'Living Writing' in S. Sabina in Rome." *MJK* 34 (2007): 19–41.

Towner, Philip H. *The Letters to Titus and Timothy*. NICNT. Grand Rapids: Eerdmans, 2006.

Trainor, Kevin. "*Pars pro toto*: On Comparing Religious Relic Practices." *Numen* 57 (2010): 267–83.

Tremlin, Scott. *Minds and Gods: The Cognitive Foundations of Religion*. New York: Oxford University Press, 2006.

Trouillard, Jean. "Proclos et la joie de quitter le ciel." *Diotima* 11 (1983): 182–92.

Trout, Dennis. "Damasus and the Invention of Early Christian Rome." *JMEMS* 33 (2003): 517–36.

———. "Town, Countryside, and Christianization at Paulinus' Nola." Pages 175–86 in *Shifting Frontiers in Late Antiquity*. Edited by Ralph W. Mathisen and Hagith Sivan. Burlington, VT: Ashgate, 1996.

Turner, Denys. *Eros and Allegory: Medieval Exegesis of the Song of Songs*. Kalamazoo, MI: Cistercian, 1995.

Tzamalikos, Panayiotis. *An Ancient Commentary on the Book of Revelation: A Critical Edition of the* Scholia in Apocalypsin. Cambridge: Cambridge University Press, 2013.

Ullucci, Daniel. "Contesting the Meaning of Animal Sacrifice." Pages 57–74 in *Ancient Mediterranean Sacrifice*. Edited by Jennifer W. Knust and Zsuzsanna Várhelyi. Oxford: Oxford University Press, 2011.

———. "Toward a Typology of Religious Experts in the Ancient Mediterranean." Pages 89–103 in *"The One Who Sows Bountifully": Essays in Honor of Stanley K. Stowers*. Edited by Caroline Johnson Hodge, Saul M. Olyan, Daniel Ullucci, and Emma Wasserman. BJS 356. Providence, RI: Brown Judaic Studies, 2013.

Upson-Saia, Kristi. *Early Christian Dress: Gender, Virtue, and Authority*. RSAH 3. New York: Routledge, 2011.

Urbano, Arthur P. "Sizing Up the Philosopher's Cloak: Christian Verbal and Visual Representations of the *Tribōn*." Pages 175–94 in *Dressing Judeans and Christians in Antiquity*. Edited by Kristi Upson-Saia, Carly Daniel-Hughes, and Alicia Batten. Surrey, UK: Ashgate, 2014.

"U.S. Religious Knowledge Survey: Executive Summary." Pew Research Center, Washington DC. http://www.pewforum.org/2010/09/28/u-s-religious-knowledge-survey.

Van Dam, Raymond. *Leadership and Community in Late Antique Gaul.* Berkeley: University of California Press, 1985.

———. *The Roman Revolution of Constantine.* New York: Cambridge University Press, 2007.

Van Nuffelen, Peter. *Rethinking the Gods: Philosophical Readings of Religion in the Post-Hellenic Period.* Cambridge: Cambridge University Press, 2011.

Van Winden, J. C. M. "Idolum and Idolatria in Tertullian." *VC* 36 (1982): 108–14.

Veltri, G. "Magic, Sex and Politics: The Media Power of Theatre Amusements in the Mirror of Rabbinic Literature." Pages 243–56 in *The Words of a Wise Man's Mouth Are Gracious (Qoh 10, 12): Festschrift for Günter Stemberger on the Occasion of His 65th Birthday.* Edited by Mauro Perani. Berlin: de Gruyter, 2005.

Ven, Paul van den, ed. *La vie ancienne de S. Syméon Stylite le Jeune (521–592).* 2 vols. SubHag 32. Brussels: Société des Bollandistes, 1962–1970.

Veneskey, Laura. "Alternative Topographies: Loca Sancta Surrogates and Site Circulation in Late Antiquity and Byzantium." PhD diss., Northwestern University, 2012.

Vikan, Gary. "Art, Medicine, and Magic in Early Byzantium." *DOP* 38 (1984): 65–86.

———. *Byzantine Pilgrimage Art.* Washington, DC: Dumbarton Oaks, 1982.

———. *Early Byzantine Pilgrimage Art.* Washington, DC: Dumbarton Oaks Research Library and Collection, 2010.

Villani, Andrea. "Homer in the Debate between Celsus and Origen." *REAug* 58 (2012): 113–39.

Vout, Caroline. "The Myth of the Toga: Understanding the History of Roman Dress." *G&R* 43 (1996): 204–20.

Vrijhof, Pieter A., and Jacques Waardenburg, eds. *Official and Popular Religion: Analysis of a Theme for Religious Studies.* The Hague: Mouton, 1979.

Wainwright, John J. "*Eusebeia*: Syncretism or Conservative Contextualization." *EvQ* 65 (1993): 211–24.

Wāķidī, Muḥammad b. ʿUmar al-. *Kitāb al-Maghāzī.* 3 vols. Edited by J. Marsden Jones. Oxford: Oxford University Press, 1966.

Walker, Paul E. "Purloined Symbols of the Past: The Theft of Souvenirs and Sacred Relics in the Rivalry between the Abbasids and Fatimids." Pages 364–87 in *Culture and Memory in Medieval Islam: Essays in Honour of Wilferd Madelung*. Edited by Farhad Daftary and Josef W. Meri. New York: Tauris, 2003.

Wallace-Hadrill, Andrew. "The Emperor and His Virtues." *Historia* 30 (1981): 298–323.

Webb, Ruth. *Demons and Dancers: Performance in Late Antiquity*. Cambridge: Harvard University Press, 2008.

Weiss, Zeev. *Public Spectacles in Roman and Late Antique Palestine*. Cambridge: Harvard University Press, 2014.

Weitzmann, Kurt, ed. *Age of Spirituality: Late Antique and Early Christian Art, Third to Seventh Century; Catalogue of the Exhibition (Nov. 19, 1977—Feb. 12, 1978)*. New York: Metropolitan Museum of Art, 1979.

Wendt, Heidi. *At the Temple Gates: The Religion of Freelance Experts in the Roman Empire*. New York: Oxford University Press, forthcoming.

Werner, Daniel S. *Myth and Philosophy in Plato's Phaedrus*. Cambridge: Cambridge University Press, 2012.

Wharton, Annabel. "The Tribune Tower: *Spolia* as Despoliation." Pages 179–98 in *Reuse Value: Spolia and Appropriation in Art and Architecture from Constantine Sherrie Levine*. Edited by Richard Brilliant and Dale Kinney. Burlington, VT: Ashgate, 2011.

Wheeler, Brannon M. "Gift of the Body in Islam: The Prophet Muhammad's Camel Sacrifice and Distribution of Hair and Nails at His Farewell Pilgrimage." *Numen* 57 (2010): 341–88.

———. *Mecca and Eden: Ritual, Relics, and Territory in Islam*. Chicago: University of Chicago Press, 2006.

White, John F. *Restorer of the World: The Roman Emperor Aurelian*. Stonehouse, UK: Spellmount, 2007.

White, L. Michael. *The Social Origins of Christian Architecture*. 2 vols. HTS 42–43. Valley Forge, PA: Trinity Press International, 1996.

Whitehouse, Harvey. *Modes of Religiosity: A Cognitive Theory of Religious Transmission*. New York: AltaMira, 2004.

Wiedemann, Thomas. *Emperors and Gladiators*. London: Routledge, 1992.

Wilhite, David E. *Tertullian the African: An Anthropological Reading of Tertullian's Context and Identities*. Berlin: de Gruyter, 2007.

Wilkinson, Kate. *Women and Modesty in Late Antiquity*. Cambridge: Cambridge University Press, 2015.

Williams, Megan H. "Lessons from Jerome's Jewish Teachers: Exegesis and Cultural Interaction in Late Antique Palestine." Pages 66–86 in *Jewish Biblical Interpretation and Cultural Exchange: Comparative Exegesis in Context*. Edited by Natalie B. Dohrmann and David Stern. Philadelphia: University of Pennsylvania Press, 2008.

Wimbush, Vincent. *White Men's Magic: Scripturalization as Slavery*. New York: Oxford University Press, 2012.

Winston, Diane. "What Americans Really Need to Know About Religion." *The Huffington Post*. 6 October 2010. http://www.huffingtonpost.com/diane-winston/what-americans-really-nee_b_749581.html.

Wistrand, Magnus. *Entertainment and Violence in Ancient Rome: The Attitudes of Roman Writers of the First Century A.D.* SGLG 56. Göteborg: Acta Universitatis Gothoburgensis, 1992.

Woolf, Greg. *Becoming Roman: The Origins of Provincial Civilization in Gaul*. Cambridge: Cambridge University Press, 1998.

Wortley, John. "Iconoclasm and *Leipsanoclasm*: Leo III, Constantine V and the Relics." *ByzF* 8 (1982): 253–79.

Wyke, Maria. "Woman in the Mirror: The Rhetoric of Adornment in the Roman World." Pages 134–51 in *Women in Ancient Societies: An Illusion of Night*. Edited by Léonie J. Archer, Susan Fischler, and Maria Wyke. London: Routledge, 1994.

Young, Francis. "Greek Apologists of the Second Century." Pages 81–104 in *Apologetics in the Roman Empire: Pagans, Jews, and Christians*. Edited by Mark J. Edwards, Martin Goodman, Simon R. F. Price, and Christopher Rowland. Oxford: Oxford University Press, 1999.

Zanker, Paul. *The Mask of Socrates: The Image of the Intellectual in Antiquity*. SCL 59. Berkeley: University of California Press, 1995.

———. *The Power of Images in the Age of Augustus*. Ann Arbor: University of Michigan Press, 1988.

Zwemer, Samuel M. "Hairs of the Prophet." Pages 48–54 in vol. 1 of *Ignace Goldziher Memorial Volume*. Edited by Samuel Löwinger and Joseph Somogyi. 2 vols. Budapest: Globus, 1948.

Contributors

Dina Boero is a Postdoctoral Research Associate at the Seeger Center for Hellenic Studies at Princeton University. In fall of 2017, she will hold the position of Assistant Professor in the Department of History at The College of New Jersey. She received her Ph.D. in Classics at the University of Southern California in 2015. She specializes in history, religion, and material culture in the late antique Near East. Her dissertation, "Symeon and the Making of the Stylite: The Construction of Sanctity in Late Antique Syria," traces the development of the cult of Symeon the Stylite the Elder in the fifth and sixth centuries. Her recent article in *Hugoye: Journal of Syriac Studies* identifies the location and context of production of a fifth-century manuscript of *The Syriac Life of Symeon the Stylite the Elder*. She is currently revising her dissertation for publication as a book as well as conducting research on the institutionalization of Syrian.

Adam Bursi is a postdoctoral fellow at the Marco Institute for Medieval and Renaissance Studies at the University of Tennessee, Knoxville. He earned his PhD in Near Eastern Studies from Cornell University in 2015. His areas of interest include early Islam, late antique and Byzantine history, and material theories of religion.

Catherine M. Chin is Associate Professor of Classics at the University of California-Davis, where she teaches courses on late antiquity, ancient religion, and Latin literature. Her research interests include early Christian intellectual history and the literary history of late antiquity. Her book *Grammar and Christianity in the Late Roman World* (University of Pennsylvania Press, 2008) discusses the ways that the teaching of literature in late antiquity shaped concepts of religion and tradition among Christian readers and writers.

Carly Daniel-Hughes is Associate Professor of Religion at Concordia University in Montréal. Editor with Kristi Upson-Saia and Alicia Batten of *Dressing Judeans and Christians in Antiquity* (Ashgate 2014) and author of *The Salvation of the Flesh in Tertullian of Carthage: Dressing for the Resurrection* (Palgrave 2011), her research focuses on the connections between social practice and early Christian theological perspectives as well as gender and sexuality in the history of Christianity.

Nathaniel P. DesRosiers is Associate Professor in Religious Studies at Stonehill College, where he teaches courses in classics, New Testament, and early Christianity. His area of research includes the history of ancient Mediterranean religions, identity formation and the modes of interaction between Greco-Roman traditions, Judaism, and Christianity, and the influences of Hellenistic philosophy and contemporary socio-religious praxes on the formation of Pauline literature and the Synoptic Gospels. He is coeditor (with Jordan Rosenblum and Lily C. Vuong) of *Religious Competition in the Third Century CE: Jews, Christians, and the Greco-Roman World* (Vandenhoeck & Ruprecht, 2014) and is presently working on a book project *Cities of the Gods*, which explores socioreligious competition in the Greek cities of Asia Minor during the Roman Empire.

Laura B. Dingeldein teaches at the University of Illinois at Chicago and Lake Forest College. Her research focuses on the historical contextualization of early Christian thought and practice, particularly through critical comparison with ancient philosophy. She received her PhD from Brown University and wrote her dissertation on the apostle Paul's use of popular philosophical concepts in his program of moral development for Christ-followers. Her other research interests include ancient Mediterranean deification practices and the reception of Paul's letters from antiquity through modernity.

Gregg E. Gardner is Assistant Professor and the Diamond Chair in Jewish Law and Ethics in the Department of Classical, Near Eastern, and Religious Studies at the University of British Columbia. He holds a PhD in Religion from Princeton University and was a Newcombe Foundation Fellow, a Starr Fellow in Judaica at Harvard University, and a Mellon/American Council of Learned Societies Fellow at Brown University. He is the author of *The Origins of Organized Charity in Rabbinic Judaism* (Cambridge University Press, 2015), coeditor of *Antiquity in Antiquity: Jewish* *and Christian Pasts in the Greco-Roman World* (Mohr Siebeck, 2008), and has published articles in such journals as *The Jewish Quarterly Review, Journal for the Study of Judaism,* and *Journal of Biblical Literature.*

Susan Ashbrook Harvey is the Royce Family Professor of Teaching Excellence and the Willard Prescott and Annie McClelland Smith Professor of Religious Studies at Brown University. She specializes in late antique and Byzantine Christianity with a special focus on Syriac studies. She is the author of *Song and Memory: Biblical Women in Syriac Tradition* (Marquette University Press, 2010); *Scenting Salvation: Ancient Christianity and the Olfactory Imagination* (University of California Press, 2006, 2015), and *Asceticism and Society in Crisis: John of Ephesus and the Lives of the Eastern Saints* (University of California Press, 1990). She is coeditor with David G. Hunter of the *Oxford Handbook of Early Christian Studies* (Oxford University Press, 2008, 2010) and coauthor with Sebastian P. Brock of *Holy Women of the Syrian Orient* (University of California Press, 1987, 1998).

T. Christopher Hoklotubbe is a Louisville Institute Postdoctoral Fellow and Instructor and Postdoctoral Faculty Fellow in Theological Studies at Loyola Marymount University. Before arriving at LMU, he served as a Visiting Assistant Professor of New Testament and Early Christian History at Andover Newton Theological School. His dissertation, "The Rhetoric of Pietas: The Pastoral Epistles and Claims to Piety in the Roman Empire" (Harvard, 2015; forthcoming with Baylor University Press, 2017), examines the multifaceted sociopolitical functions that "piety" served within various cultural fields of the ancient Mediterranean world. This study argues that contemporary discourses on piety illuminate the Pastoral Epistles' own strategies of negotiating imperial culture and brokering power among patrons and rival religious experts.

Todd Krulak teaches in the Core Texts Program at Samford University. His research focuses on late Platonist religiophilosophy and ritual and the intersection of Christian and Greek theological and philosophical discourses in late antiquity. He has published articles in the *Journal of Late Antiquity* and *Classical Quarterly* and is currently completing a monograph on divine images in late antique philosophical discourse and praxis.

Mary Joan Winn Leith is Associate Professor and Chair of the Religious Studies Department at Stonehill College. She has worked as an archaeologist in various Middle Eastern countries and is the author of *Wadi Daliyeh I: The Wadi Daliyeh Seal Impressions* (Oxford University Press, 1997) as well as articles in the areas of biblical studies and early Christian art.

Ilaria L. E. Ramelli is Professor of Theology and K. Britt Chair at the Graduate School of Theology of Sacred Heart Major Seminary (Angelicum University), Senior Visiting Professor of Church History, and Senior Research Fellow in Ancient and Patristic Philosophy at the Catholic University of Milan and at Oxford University. Her publications include: *The Christian Doctrine of Apokatastasis: A Critical Assessment from the New Testament to Eriugena* (Brill, 2013), *Hierocles the Stoic: Elements of Ethics, Fragments, and Excerpts* (Society of Biblical Literature, 2009), *Evagrius's Kephalaia Gnostika* (Society of Biblical Literature, 2015), *Early Christian and Jewish Narrative: The Role of Religion in Shaping Narrative Forms* (Mohr Siebeck, 2015), and *Social Justice and the Legitimacy of Slavery: The Role of Philosophical Asceticism from Ancient Judaism to Late Antiquity* (Oxford University Press, 2016).

Gregory Shaw is Professor of Religious Studies at Stonehill College where he teaches courses in Neoplatonism, Roman religions, and mysticism. His research interests include the religions of late antiquity and the history of divination with an emphasis on dreams. His publications include the monograph *Theurgy and the Soul: The Neoplatonism of Iamblichus* (Penn State Press, 1995) and the edited volume *Practicing Gnosis: Ritual, Magic, Theurgy, and Liturgy in Nag Hammadi, Manichaean, and Other Ancient Literature: Essays in Honor of Birger Pearson* (Brill, 2013).

Allyson Everingham Sheckler is Assistant Professor of Visual and Performing Arts at Stonehill College in Easton, MA. Her new-found interest in the late antique and early Christian period has centered on the Roman church of Santa Sabina. In 2010, she coauthored, "The Crucifixion Conundrum and the Santa Sabina Doors" published in the *Harvard Theological Review* with her colleague, Mary Joan Winn Leith.

Karl Shuve is Assistant Professor in the Department of Religious Studies where he teaches courses in the history of Christianity. His first book, *The Song of Songs and the Fashioning of Identity in Early Latin Christianity* (Oxford University Press, 2016), explores the role that the Song played in shaping attitudes towards the body and community in late antique Christianity. His present book project is a cultural history of the nuptial metaphor—the identification of the church or the individual as the "bride of Christ"—in late antiquity.

Loren R. Spielman is Assistant Professor of Religious Studies at Portland State University, where he teaches courses on the Bible, Jewish history, and rabbinic literature. His interests include the social, economic, and political history of ancient Palestine and ancient sports and spectacle. These foci are featured in his forthcoming monograph *Sitting with Scorners: Ancient Jewish Attitudes towards Sport and Spectacle*.

Stanley K. Stowers is Emeritus Professor of Religious Studies at Brown University. His research is focused in early Christian history and literature, Hellenistic philosophy and early Christianity, Greek religion, and theory of religion. His numerous publications include *A Rereading of Romans: Justice, Jews and Gentiles* (Yale University Press, 1994), *Letter Writing in Greco-Roman Antiquity* (Westminster, 1986), and *The Diatribe and Paul's Letter to the Romans* (Scholars Press, 1981).

Daniel Ullucci is an Assistant Professor of Religious Studies at Rhodes College in Memphis, TN. His research focuses on the interactions between ancient Mediterranean religions and early Christianity, particularly textual production and ritual practice. His monograph *The Christian Rejection of Animal Sacrifice* (Oxford University Press, 2012) examines the ancient debate over sacrifice and the long process by which some Christians came to reject the practice. His current work combines network theory and cognitive theory to analyze Roman euergetism and the Christian discourse on "spiritual" sacrifice.

Arthur P. Urbano Jr. is Associate Professor in the Theology Department at Providence College. He teaches courses in New Testament and early Christianity. His research focuses on the dynamic role of biographical literature and art as arenas of philosophical debate and cultural competition between Christian and Neoplatonist intellectuals in late antiquity. He is also interested in contemporary issues related to ecumenical and interreligious dialogue. His monograph, *The Philosophical Life: Biography and the Crafting of Intellectual Identity in Late Antiquity*, was published in 2013 by Catholic University of America Press. He is currently working on a study that examines philosophical imagery in early Christian art and its relation to intellectual, educational, and religious contexts.

Gary Vikan is the principal of Vikan Consulting LCC. In 2013, he stepped down as the director of Walters Art Museum of Baltimore Maryland after twenty-seven years of service. He is also a former Senior Associate at Harvard's Center for Byzantine Studies at Dumbarton Oaks. His publications include *From the Holy Land to Graceland: Sacred People, Places, and Things in Our Lives* (American Alliance of Museums Press, 2013) and *Early Byzantine Pilgrimage Art* (Dumbarton Oaks Research Library and Collection, 2011).

Lily C. Vuong is Assistant Professor of Religious Studies at Central Washington University, where she teaches courses in early Judaism and early Christianity. Her area of study is in New Testament Apocryphal and Pseudepigraphal writings. Other research interests include the relationships between Judaism, Christianity, and Greco-Roman culture, the formation of Jewish and Christian identities in late antiquity, and the representation of women in the ancient world. She is the author of *Gender and Purity in the Protevangelium of James* (Mohr Siebeck, 2013), which explores ritual and sexual purity in the portrayal of Mary, the mother of Jesus, and editor with Jordan Rosenblum and Nathaniel DesRosiers of *Religious Competition in the Third Century CE: Jews, Christians, and the Greco-Roman World* (Vandenhoeck & Ruprecht, 2014).

Ancient Sources Index

Hebrew Bible

Genesis
- 4:1   160

Exodus
- 12:35–36   32

Leviticus
- 18:3   183, 184, 195
- 18:4   184
- 27:32   189 n. 25

Deuteronomy
- 4:6   184
- 12:31   183 n. 13
- 18:10   183 n. 13, 184
- 18:10–11   183, 184

2 Kings
- 23:10   183 n. 13

Psalms
- 1   191, 192
- 1:1   190, 191, 191 n. 28, 195
- 1:1–2   189, 191

Proverbs
- 13:11   159 n. 18

Song of Songs
- 1:5   177
- 4:12   173, 174
- 5:4   173
- 5:5   174–75
- 5:8   175, 176
- 6:12   173
- 8:9   173

Isaiah
- 11:2   159 n. 18
- 33:6   159 n. 18

Ancient Jewish Writers

Josephus, *Contra Apionem*
- 2.4   160
- 2.12   160
- 2.14   160

Philo, *De cherubim*
- 42   160
- 44–46   160
- 45–47   160
- 48   160
- 49   160
- 52   160

Philo, *De decalogo*
- 52   159 n. 17

Philo, *De migration Abrahami*
- 89   103 n. 53

Philo, *De praemiis et poenis*
- 53   159 n. 17

Philo, *De specialibus legibus*
- 1.319–323   161 n. 22
- 4.97   159 n. 17

Philo, De specialibus legibus (cont.)
4.135	159
4.137	159

Philo, De vita Mosis
1.146	159 n. 17

New Testament

Matthew
19:25–26	101
22:21	43 n. 5

Mark
10:26–27	101
12:17	43 n. 5

Luke
20:24	43 n. 5
20:35–36	174

Acts
3:12	156 n. 3
10:2	156 n. 3
10:7	156 n. 3
17:23	156 n. 3

Romans
11:25	155 n. 2
16:25	155–56 n. 2

1 Corinthians
2:1	155–56 n. 2
2:7	155–56 n. 2
2:16	176
4:1	155–56 n. 2
10:21	58 n. 41
13:2	155 n. 2
14:2	155 n. 2
15:51	155 n. 2

2 Corinthians
12:2	176
12:3–4	176

Ephesians
1:9	155–56 n. 2
3:3	155–56 n. 2
3:9	155–56 n. 2
5:32	155 n. 2
6:19	155 n. 2

Colossians
1:26	155 n. 2
1:27	155 n. 2
2:2	155 n. 2
4:3	155–56 n. 2

2 Thessalonians
2:7	155 n. 2

1 Timothy
1:3	155
2:2	156 n. 3
2:10	156 n. 3
3:1–13	164
3:9	155 n. 2
3:14–16	164
3:15	155
3:16	155, 155 n. 2, 156, 157 n. 6, 163–64, 165
4:1–5	164
4:7	156 n. 3, 164
4:8	156 n. 3
5:4	156 n. 3
6:3	155, 156 n. 3
6:3–5	164
6:5	156 n. 3
6:6	156 n. 3
6:11	156 n. 3
6:20	155

2 Timothy
1:9–11	156 n. 2
3:5	156 n. 3
3:12	156 n. 3

Titus
1:1	156 n. 3
1:2–3	156 n. 2

2:12	156 n. 3	Acts of the Scillitan Martyrs	
		14	25
2 Peter		16	25
1:3	156 n. 3		
1:6	156 n. 3	Ambrose, *De Isaac*	
1:7	156 n. 3	1.1	173, 174
2:9	156 n. 3	1.1–2	174
3:11	156 n. 3	2.3	174
		3.8	175, 176
Rabbinic Works		4.11	176–77
		4.13	177
b. Shabbat		6.51	173
33b	185 n. 16	6.53	174
m. Avot		Ambrose, *De Obitu Theodosii*	
3:14	193 n. 33	75	54–55
Sipra Achare Mot		Ambrose, *De virginibus*	
13.9	184	1.3.11	172, 174
		1.8.49	173
Sipra Behukotai		1.10.57	172
10.8	193	11.60–66	175
t. ʿAvodah Zarah		Ambrose, *De virginitate*	
2:2–5	189	1.1–7.41	169 n. 9
		5.24–25	172
t. Bekhorot		11.60	173
7:3	189 n. 25	15.94	173
t. Šabbbat		Ambrose, *Epistulae*	
6(7):4	191 n. 27	74	65–75
		74.1	70
y. ʿAvodah Zarah		74.6	67, 71
1:7	189 n. 24	74.8	67, 71–72
		74.10	67–68
y. Berakhot		74.13	66
4:2	195 n. 34	74.14	67
		74.19	69, 72
Early Christian Writings		74.20	69
		74.21	70
Acts of John		74.27	67
27	253	74.31	67, 73
42	58 n. 41	74.33	73

Ambrose, *Epistulae extra collectionem*
1   71
1.28   73 n. 26

Athanasius, *De decretis*
27.1–2   92 n. 19

Athenagoras, *Legatio pro Christianos*
35   182 n. 8, 186

Augustine, *De doctrina christiana*
2.24   32

Augustine, *Epistula*
185.27   58

Clement, *Stromateis*
1.1.10.2   99

Cyprian, *Epistulae*
55.14.1   58 n. 41, 60, n. 44
59.12.2   58 n. 41
65.1   58 n. 41

Epiphanius, *Panarion*
55.1–2   103
58.6–8   103

Eusebius, *Eclogae propheticae*
3.6   92

Eusebius, *Historia ecclesiastica*
6.2.7   92 n. 21
6.2.9   92 n. 21
6.3.7   92 n. 21
6.3.11   92 n. 21
6.3.13   92 n. 21
6.8.6   92 n. 21
6.15.11   92. n. 21
6.17   89
6.19   80
6.19.8   88
7.24.3–25.26   100

Eusebius, *Praeparatio evangelica*
5.10.8   112 n. 14
12   86 n. 5

Eusebius, *Vita Constantini*
2.27–52   55
2.48–60   47 n. 20
2.64–72   47 n. 19

Evagrius Scholasticus, *Historia ecclesiastica*
1.13   243 n. 25, 244 n. 26
7.18.2   253

Gelasius, *Historia ecclesiastica*
2.4   47 n. 19

Gregory of Nyssa, *De vita Mosis*
115   32

Irenaeus, *Adversus haeresus*
1.25.6   37

Jerome, *Adversus Jovinianum libri III*
1.3.   169 n. 9

Jerome, *Epistulae*
48.2   169 n. 9
130.2   170 n. 12

Jerome, *Vita S. Hilarionis eremitae*
2   186 n. 19

John Cassian, *De incarnation*
5.3   217 n. 63

John Chrysostom, *Contra ludos et theatra*
2   186
46   186

Lactantius, *De mortibus persecutorum*
25.1–2
49 n. 25
44.5   55

Lactantius, *Epitome divinarum institutionum*		2.1.56–57	177
		2.5.21–23	102
18.2	23	2.5.23	101 n. 47
		2.8.4	102
Life of Daniel the Stylites		2.8.17	96
36	248	3.5.16	102
59	248	4.2.4	97 n. 36
Life of Simeon Stylites the Elder		Origen, *Commentarii in evangelium Joannis*	
79	255		
		6.85	101
Life of Simeon the Younger			
118	253	Origen, *Contra Celsum*	
158	248	1.5	88
231	256	1.16.17	94
		1.24–25	82
Martyrdom of Perpetua		1.49–60	81
2.1	25 n. 38	1.66.11	94
18.4	23 n. 29	2.36.6	94
		2.76.57	94 n. 28
Minucius Felix, *Octavius*		2.76.61	94 n. 28
10	58 n. 41	4.21.16–39	94
30.5	23 n. 19	4.22	81
		4.36.32	93
Miracles of Artemios		4.38	99
16	256	4.39	97, 98, 99
		4.40	99
Miracles of Cosmas and Damian		4.51	88, 99
1.16	251	4.91.5	94
1.24	249	4.91.8	93
30	249	4.94.1–14	94
		5.38	88
Miracles of Thecla		5.45	82
13	250	5.57	88
		6.7.2	94
Origen, *Commentarius in Canticum*		6.42.35–65	94
prol. 1–7	97 n. 36	6.43	81, 104
prol. 2.1	98 n. 39	6.43.4	94
1.1.3	175	7.6.28–37	93
1.1.4	176	7.28.8	94 n. 28
1.1.7	176	7.36.30	94
1.1.9	176	7.41.12	94
1.4	176 n. 27	7.54.16	93
1.5	177 n. 29	8.17–20	58 n. 41
1.5.6	176	8.68.32	93

Origen, *De principiis*
 prol. 7 — 99
 1 preface 5 — 101
 2.4.3 — 102
 2.9.1 — 102
 2.11.2–3 — 100
 3.6.5 — 101
 4.2.5 — 96
 4.2.9 — 96
 4.3.1 — 96, 100
 4.3.1–4 — 96
 4.3.14 — 99

Origen, *Epistula ad Gregiorum Thaumaturgum*
 2–3 — 32

Origen, *Fragmenta in Genesim*
 236 — 100 n. 43

Origen, *Homiliae in Ezechielem*
 6.8 — 103

Origen, *Homiliae in Genesim*
 2.4 — 100 n. 43
 14.3 — 102

Origen, *Homiliae in Jeremiam*
 1.2 — 96 n. 32

Origen, *Homiliae in Psalmos*
 1.36 — 100
 5.36.5 — 103

Origen, *Selecta in Numeros*
 12.581B — 100 n. 43

Pamphilus, *Apology*
 88 — 99
 123 — 96
 125 — 96
 157 — 102

Paulinus of Nola, *Carmina*
 30 — 215 n. 55

Photius, *Biblioteca*
 214 — 86
 214.172a — 86
 214.173a — 86
 249 — 86
 251 — 86
 251.464B — 86

Socrates, *Historia ecclesiastica*
 1.7 — 47 n. 19
 6.13 — 92 n. 19

Sophronius, *Miracles of Cyrus and John*
 28 — 249

The Syriac Life of Simeon
 26 — 243
 28 — 239
 29 — 237
 33 — 236, 239, 239 nn. 18–19
 34 — 236
 35 — 236
 36 — 236, 241
 38 — 236, 243
 39 — 236, 239
 51–52 — 239
 54 — 239
 56 — 236
 61 — 236, 239
 62 — 240
 63 — 236, 240
 64 — 236, 237, 241
 71 — 236, 241
 72 — 236
 76 — 239
 79 — 236
 80 — 237
 81 — 236
 82 — 236
 83 — 236
 84 — 236
 86 — 237
 87 — 236
 88 — 236, 237
 89 — 236

91	236	4.10.3	18
93	236	6.1.3	23
97	236		
98	239	Tertullian, *De spectaculis*	
99	239	1	187
112	239	3	191
113	239	13.1	190
125	242, 243, 244	30	194
126	244		

Tertullian, *De virginibus velandis*
1.1   25 n. 37

Tatian, *Oratio ad Graecos*
1   183
23   182
24   183

Theodoret, *Hellenikon therapeutike pathematon*
8   250

Tertullian, *Ad nations*
10   58 n. 41

Theodoret, *Philotheos historia*
26.21   239 n. 19
26.28   233

Tertullian, *Apologeticus*
9.2–4   22, 23
9.10   23
29.16–19   25

Theodosian Code
15.1.19   68

Theophilus, *Ad Autolycum*
3.15   182 n. 8

Tertullian, *De corona militis*
1.4   20
10.5   19–20

Zosimus, *Historia Nova*
4.36.4   59 n. 43

Tertullian, *De cultu feminarum*
1.1.2   20–21
2.3.2   21
2.11.1–3   21
2.13.3   23

Greco-Roman Literature

Aelius Aristides, *Hieroi logoi*
48.18   255

Ammianus Marcellinus, *Res gestae*
22.5.1–2   124 n. 13
22.12.6   84 n. 7
25.4.17   84 n. 7

Tertullian, *De idolatria*
1.1   15
2.1–5   15
11.3–5   186
17.3   19
18.4   19

Aristotle, *Eudemus*
Frag. 10   158

Tertullian, *De pallio*
1.2.1   18
3.7.2   30
4.8.1   19
4.10.1–2   22

Artemidorus Daldianus, *Onirocritica*
2.35   255

Cassius Dio, *Historia Romana*
78.16.5   43 n. 5

Cicero, *De oratore*
1.206   158

Damascius, *De principiis*
3.159.6–3.167.25   115

Diogenes Laertius, *Vitae philosophorum*
1   157 n. 8
5.2   157 n. 8
7   157 n. 8
8   157 n. 8

Dionysius of Halicarnassus, *De compositione verborum*
25.5–6   158

Epictetus, *Diatribai (Dissertationes)*
3.3.3   43 n. 5
4.15.5–17   43 n. 5

Hermias, *Scholion on Phaedrus*
241E   87
241E8   87

Hierocles, *De providentia*
6–7   86

Iamblichus, *De mysteriis*
1.3–2.3   111
1.11.38   126 n. 19
1.11.40   126 n. 20
2.11.96–99   126 n. 19
3.20.148–149   126 n. 20
4.3.184–186   126 n. 20
7.5.259   82
7.11–12   110 n. 8
8.1   110 n. 7
8.1–5   110 n. 7
8.6.269   126 n. 20
9.8–10   110 n. 7
10.5.290–10.6.292   126 n. 18
23.9–13   108

28.6–11   108–9
165.13–14   110 n. 10
179.10–180.3   115
254.11–12   112 n. 14
255.5–11   113
255.14–256.2   113
256.4   112–13
257.3–8   112
258.7–10   112
259.4–10   109

Julian, *Epistulae*
8.415C–D   124 n. 13

Julian, *Orationes*
4.146A   119 n. 1
4.150D   119 n. 1
4.157C–158A   119 n. 1
5   83
5.161B   127 n. 22
5.161C   124 n. 14
5.166A–B   83
5.168–169D   126
5.169C   124–25
5.170B   127 n. 22
5.172D–173A   127 n. 22
5.173D–174A   124
5.174A–B   124
5.174D   124
5.175B   124–25
5.175B–C   125
5.175D–176A   125 n. 15
5.176A–B   125 n. 16
5.177A–D   125
5.177C–D   127 n. 22
5.178B   83
5.178B–C   124–25
5.178D   124 n. 14
5.180A–B   127
9   30

Libanius, *Orationes*
18.121   124 n. 13
18.125–129   124 n. 13

ANCIENT SOURCES INDEX

Livy, *Ab urbe condita*		28F	91
22.10	57 n. 38		
		Pliny the Younger, *Epistulae*	
Lucian, *Fugitivi*		10.35–36, 101–102	57 n. 38
8	159 n. 15		
		Pliny the Younger, *Panegyricus*	
Lucian, *Nigrinus*		31.1	182
30		34.4	182
		46.2	182
Plato, *Cratylus*			
408C1–4	111 n. 12	Plotinus, *Enneades*	
411E	110 n. 7	1.6.7.2–3	110
		4.4.43.16	116
Plato, *Epistulae*		5.3.17.15–21	111 n. 13
7.341C–D	111 n. 13		
		Plutarch, *De Iside et Osiride*	
Plato, *Gorgias*		2.351F–2.352A	163
525C2	101	2.352A	162 n. 29
497C	114 n. 16	3.352C	162 n. 28
		11.355C–D	162 n. 29
Plato, *Phaedo*		45.369A–B	163
69C	158	45.369B–C	159 n. 15
69D	158	64.377A–B	163
79B–D	110	67–68.378A–B	162
113E2	101	77.382DE	158
Plato, *Phaedrus*		Plutarch, *De Stoicorum repugnantiis*	
249C	158 n. 12	1035AB	158
250BC	158 n. 12		
		Plutarch, *De superstitione*	
Plato, *Respublica*		14.171F	161 n. 25
8.546A	90		
10.607E	93	Plutarch, *De tranquillitate animi*	
10. 615E3	101	77C–E	161 n. 26
		Plutarch, *Quomodo quis suos in virtute*	
Plato, *Symposium*		*sentiat profectus*	
203B–E	97–98	81D–E	161 n. 26
209E–210A	158 n. 12		
		Porphyry, *Fragmenta*	
Plato, *Theaetetus*		39	104, 105
156A	158 n. 12		
		Porphyry, *Vita Plotini*	
Plato, *Timaeus*		14	20
19D–E	92	20	89
21C	91		

Proclus, *In Platonis Alcibiadem*
149.17–150.22	115
150.4–23	115–16

Proclus, *In Platonis Timaeus commentaria*
1.31	89
1.60	91
1.63–64	92
1.68	91
1.76–77	89
1.83	92
1.86	92
1.93	91
1.162	90

Proclus, *Theologia Platonica*
1.3.22–24	110
1.5.16–1.6.3	111 n. 13

Quintillian, *Institutio oratoria*
5.13.5–60	158

Tacitus, *Agricolae*
21	57 n. 38

Tacitus, *Historiae*
1.76	57 n. 38

Vergil, *Aeneid*
1.229–296	19

Modern Authors Index

'Abd al-Razzāq b. Hammām al-Ṣan'ānī 219–20
Adkins, Arthur H. W. 6
Adluri, Vishwa 87
Allen, Pauline 234, 244
Alvar, Jaime 126
Ashley, Kathleen M. 33, 34
Assemani, Stephano Evodio 235
Astell, Ann 168
Athanassiadi, Polymnia 114, 119, 120, 125
Attridge, Harold, W. 147, 157
Austin, J. L. 64
Azmeh, Aziz al- 227
Bagnoli, Martina 235
Baldovin, John F. 207, 212, 216
Barfield, Raymond 85
Barnes, Timothy D. 48, 52, 53, 180, 186
Barrett, Justin L. 142
Barthes, Roland 17, 29, 30, 31, 33
Barton, Carlin 16
Bartsch, Shadi 16
Batten, Alicia 21
Bauer, Franz Alto 242
Baynes, Norman Hepburn 234, 248
Beacham, Richard C. 179
Beard, Mary 57, 127
Bell, Catherine 236, 238, 244
Berkowitz, Beth A. 183, 184, 189
Berthelot, Katell 95
Bidez, Joseph 243
Birk, Stine 29
Bisconti, Fabrizio 27, 28
Biscop, Jean-Luc 234, 239, 243
Boero, Dina 5, 200, 202, 235

Bornkamm, Günter 158
Borret, Marcel 175
Bourdieu, Pierre 6, 29, 30, 44, 144–46, 147, 148, 150, 156
Bovini, Giuseppe 36
Bowersock, Glen W. 120
Bowes, Kim 120, 127, 148, 150, 207, 208
Boys-Stones, George 97
Bradshaw, Paul F. 209, 211, 213
Brandenburg, Hugo 36, 205, 208, 212, 213, 252
Bremmer, Jan N. 158
Brenk, Beat 68, 208, 252
Brent, Allen 25
Brésard, Luc 175
Brown, Peter 31, 109, 139, 167–68, 169, 172, 210, 216, 220, 221, 225, 234
Brubaker, Rogers 17, 26
Bruun, Patrick 42–43, 44, 49, 57, 60
Bukhārī, Muḥammad b. Ismā'īl al- 223, 224, 225, 229
Burns, J. Patout 24
Bursi, Adam 5, 200, 202, 219
Butler, Judith 64
Butler, Shane 201, 202
Bynum, Caroline Walker 201, 220, 221
Cairns, Douglas L. 6
Cameron, Averil 32, 33, 40, 96
Caner, Daniel 236
Canivet, Pierre 233
Capra, Andrea 93
Carp, Richard M. 11
Chin, Catherine M. 3, 13, 73
Chlup, Radek 114
Clark, Elizabeth 227

Clarke, Emma C.	82, 108	Finamore, John F.	107
Clements, Ashley	202	Finney, Paul Corby	32
Cohen, Naomi G.	159, 161	Firenze, Paul	145
Colish, Maria	170	Fishwick, Duncan	126
Collins, John J.	159	Flood, Finbarr Barry	222
Collobert, Catherine	87	Foerster, Werner	159
Comte, Marie-Christine	234, 237	Foletti, Ivan	212
Connor, Carolyn L.	216–17	Fowden, Elizabeth Key	243
Cooper, Frederick	17, 26	Fowden, Garth	111
Costambeys, Marios	210, 212	Fowler, Bridget	145
Courcelle, Pierre	170	Fox, Robin Lane	255
Crawford, M. H.	42	Fraenkel, Carlos	87
Crisafulli, Virgil S.	256	Frakes, Robert	48
Crook, John	209	Frank, Georgia	215
Croom, Alexandra T.	18	Frankfurter, David	64, 148, 220
Crouzel, Henri	175	Friedman, Shamma	188
Dagron, Gilbert	250	Futrell, Alison	179, 180
Daniel-Hughes, Carly	3, 12–13, 16, 17, 20, 21, 169	Gaddis, Michael	72
		Gardner, Gregg E.	12, 181
Davies, Glenys	20	Gawlinski, Laura	18, 19, 22
Davis, Stephen J.	235, 237	Giuliano, Fabio Massimo	85
Dawes, Elizabeth A. S.	234, 248	Gleason, Maud	16
Dawson, David	159, 161	Glover, T. R.	182
Deichmann, Friedrich Wilhelm	36	Goldberg, Abraham	188
Delehaye, Hippolyte	234	Goldziher, Ignaz	221, 222
Demura, Miyako	91	González Francisco J.,	87
DesRosiers, Nathaniel	2, 3, 13	Goodson, Caroline J.	208, 209
Destrée, Pierre	85, 87	Gori, Franco	172
Dey, Hendrik W.	206, 209, 212	Gotter, Ulrich	65
Dillon, John M.	82, 107, 108	Gouldner, Arthur W.,	2
Dingeldein, Laura	4, 83–84	Grabar, André	253–54
d'Izarny, Raymond	169	Gregory, Timothy E.	253
Donner, Fred	226, 227, 228	Guidobaldi, F.	207
Doran, Robert	235, 239, 242, 255	Gunderson, Erik	16
Dossey, Leslie	25, 171	Hadas-Lebel, Mireille	186
Drake, Hal A.	45, 47, 56, 65, 71	Hadot, Pierre	170
Elm, Susanna	124, 125	Hahn, Cynthia	214, 215, 216, 235, 237
Elsner Jás	48	Hall, Stuart G.	47
Emerson, Ralph Waldo	117	Hallaq, Wael	228
Engler, Stephen	147	Hansen, Maria Fabricius	68
Ewald, Björn Christian	34, 35	Harlow, Mary	18
Eyl, Jennifer	144	Harrill, J. Albert	25
Fagan, Garrett G.	180	Harvey, Susan Ashbrook	201, 202, 234, 243
Festugière, André-Jean	109, 249		
Février, Paul-Albert	150	Henig, Martin	58

Henry, Nathalie	170	Kaestli, Jean-Daniel	253
Hernández, Pura Nieto	95	Kalleres, Dayna	63
Herrmann, Fritz-Gregor	85	Karris, Robert J.	164
Hershbell, Jackson P.	82, 108	Keane, Webb	12
Hezser, Catherine	194	Keil, Frank C.	142
Hijmans, Steven E.	52, 53, 54	Kelly, J. F. T.	100
Hilgers, Mathieu	144	Kennedy, J. B.	85
Hillner, Julia	207	Khalek, Nancy	221, 227
Himmelmann, Nikolaus	28	Kinney, Dale	68
Hodder, Ian	64	Kinzig, Wolfram	94
Hoklotubbe, T. Christopher	4, 137, 156–57, 158	Kirchner, Roderich	158
		Klein, Holger A.	235, 237
Holloway, R Ross	207	Kramer, Nobert	241
Hölscher, Tonio	32	Kraus, Samuel	188, 189
Hopkins, Keith	179	Krautheimer, Richard	68, 210, 213
Horst, Steven	142	Kretschmar, Georg	212
Hoyland, Robert	228	Krug, Antje	252
Hübner, Adelheid	243	Krulak, Todd	84
Humphries, Mark	48, 50	Kuefler, Mathew	20
Hunter, David, G.	168, 169	Landsberg, Mitchell	134
Hunter-Crawley, Heather	237	Larson, Steven J.	45
Huskinson, Janet	18	Lash, Scott	144
Ibn Abī Shayba, ʿAbd Allāh b. Muḥammad	220, 225	Latham, Jacob	126
		Latour, Bruno	136
Ibn Hishām, Abū Muḥammad "Abd al-Malek	219	Lawson, R. P.	175
		Lee, A. D.	45, 59
Ibn Rusta, Abū ʿAlī Aḥmad Ibn-ʿUmar	229	Leith, Mary Joan Winn	5, 200, 202, 216
		Lemerle, Paul	249
Ibn Saʿd, Abū ʿAbd Allāh Muḥammad	223, 229, 230	Lenski, Noel	53
		Leroy-Molinghen, Alice	233
Ibn Shabba, ʿUmar	224, 230	Leszl, Walter G.	85
Ingold, Tim	64	Levick, Barbara	42, 43
Jacobs, Martin	180, 188, 189	Lewis, Suzanne	69
Jackson, Ralph	251, 252	Leyerle, Blake	181, 186, 187
Jastrow, Marcus	188	Leyser, Conrad	208
Jefferson, Lee M.	40	Lieberman, Saul	189
Jensen, Robin M.	24, 32–33, 39, 40	Liebert, Rana, S.	93
Johns, Jeremy	228	Liebeschuetz, J. H. W. G.	65
Johnson, Lawrence J.	207, 211	Lincoln, Bruce	135–36
Johnson-Hodge, Caroline	148	Lipps, Johannes	210
Jones, A. H. M.	42	Liverani, Paolo	213
Jullien, Christelle	220, 238–39	Lizzi, Rita	139
Jullien, Florence	220, 238–39	Löhr, Winrich	143
Junod, E.	253	MacCormack, Sabine	242
Juynboll, G. H. A.	228	Machado, Carlos	210

MODERN AUTHORS INDEX

Mackie, Jillian 207, 208, 209
MacMullen, Ramsay 136, 143, 148, 149, 150, 171, 206–7
Madec, Goulven 170–71
Magee, Gregory S. 156
Majercik, Ruth 116
Malherbe, Abraham J. 143, 164
Malina, Bruce J. 6
Mandel, Paul 188
Mangez, Éric 144
Mango, Marlia M. 250
Maraval, Pierre 220
Markus, R. A. 209
Marrou, Henri Irénée 31
Martindale, J. R. 242
Marwazī, Isḥāq b. Ibrāhīm b. Makhlad al-Ḥanẓalī al- 224
Matthews, John 168
Matter, E. Ann 168
Mayer, Wendy 233, 244
McCulloh, John M. 209
McGinn, Bernard 170, 171
McGowan, Andrew 216
McGuckin, John 91
McHugh, Michael P. 173, 174
McLynn, Neil B. 63, 65, 72
Meadows, Andrew 43
Meri, Josef W. 221–22, 223, 224, 229
Metcalf, William E. 43, 44
Metzler, Karin 100
Mihai, Adrian 115
Millar, Fergus 25
Miller, Patricia Cox 201, 202, 214–15, 220, 222, 225
Mills, Harrianne 22
Montserrat, Dominic 247–48
Morgan, David 11
Moss, Candida 217
Mott, Stephen C. 164
Mounce, William D. 164
Munt, Harry 228
Muranyi, Miklos 228
Muslim, Ibn al-Hajjāj 223
Musurillo, Herbert 23
Nelson, Robert 33, 39, 214
Nesbitt, John W. 256
Neusner, Jacob 189
Newman, Hillel, I. 192
Neyrey, Jerome H. 6
Nie, Giselle de 222
Niehoff, Maren R. 95
Nock, Arthur Darby 108
Noll, Rudolf 252
North, John 57, 127
Obbink, Dirk 157
Olson, Kelly 22
Papaconstantinou, Arietta 220, 229
Parmentier, Léon 243
Parthey, Gustav 108
Pentcheva, Bissera 214
Pergola, Agnese 28
Petraki, Zacharoula A. 85
Pharr, Clyde 68
Plesch, Véronique 33, 34
Poe, Alison Crystal 27, 28
Pratt, Mary Louise 33, 34, 40
Price, R. M. 233
Price, Simon 57, 74, 127
Promey, Sally M. 201
Prothero, Stephen R. 134, 135
Pülz, Andreas 237
Purves, Alex 201, 202
Pyysiäinen, Ilkka 142
Quasten, Johannes 212
Ramelli, Ilaria 4, 80–81, 86, 87–88, 89, 90, 92, 93, 94, 95, 96, 97, 100, 102, 103, 104
Ramsey, Boniface 172
Rapp, Claudia 139
Rappe, Sara 111
Rebillard, Éric 15, 20, 24, 25, 26, 149, 150
Reznick, Ron 205
Richter, Daniel S. 161
Ridings, Riding 32
Rives, James B. 23, 25, 199
Robert, Louis 180
Robinson, Chase 227
Rosenblum, Jordan D. 2
Roskam, Geert 161

MODERN AUTHORS INDEX

Ross, William David 158
Rüpke, Jörg 99
Russell, Ben 39
Rüttiman, René Josef 251–52, 254
Ryland, J. E. 182
Sahmī, Ḥamza b. Yūsuf al- 228
Salzman, Michele 139, 205, 206
Satlow, Michael 199
Schott, Jeremy M. 64, 80, 86
Schwartz, Seth 12
Segal, Arthur 180
Shaw, Gregory 4, 81–82, 117, 126
Sheckler, Allyson Everingham 5, 200, 202, 216
Shepardson, Christine C. 63, 236, 244
Shlezinger-Katzman, Dafna 18
Shoemaker, Stephen, J. 228
Shuve, Karl 4, 96, 137, 167, 170
Sider, Robert 193
Sizgorich, Thomas 220, 226
Smith, Andrew 91
Smith, Jonathan Z. 155
Smith, Julia 237
Smith, Rowland 119–20, 125, 127
Sodini, Jean-Pierre 234, 239, 243
Solaro, Giuseppe 93
Sotinel, Claire 140
Spielman, Loren 4, 137–38, 181, 190, 195
Spieser, Jean-Michel 211, 213
Stavrakopoulou, Francesca 140
Steel, Carlos 110, 117
Stephenson, Paul 43, 49, 53
Sterling, Gregory, E. 159, 161
Stern, Sacha 186, 193
Stowers, Stanley K. 4, 46, 83, 121–24, 127, 134–37, 140, 141, 142, 143, 146, 168, 171
Stroumsa, Guy G. 15–16
Struck, Peter, T. 84
Sutherland, Carol Humphrey Vivian 42
Swartz, David 30
Ṭabarī, Abū Jaʿfar Muḥammad b. Jarīr al- 225
Taft, Robert 212, 216
Talmon-Heller, Daniella 221
Tanaseanu-Döbler, Ilinca 83, 114, 119–20, 125, 126, 127
Taormina, Lorenzo 171
Tarrant, Harold 85
Taylor, Christopher S. 222
Tchalenko, Georges 233
Teiser, Stephen 140
Thacker, Alan 205–6, 207, 208, 209, 210
Thornton, James 212
Thunø, Erik 214
Towner, Philip H. 155, 156
Trainor, Kevin 230
Tremlin, Scott 141
Trouillard, Jean 117
Trout, Dennis 205, 215, 216
Turner, Denys 168
Tzamalikos, Panayiotis 100
Ullucci, Daniel 148–49, 157
Upson-Saia, Kristi 16, 169
Urbano, Arthur P. 3, 6, 11–12, 13, 18, 30, 44
Van Dam, Raymond 48, 220
Van Nuffelen, Peter 157, 158–59, 161
Van Winden, J. C. M. 15
Ven, Paul van den 225, 248
Veltri, G. 188
Veneskey, Laura 237
Vikan, Gary 5, 200, 201, 202, 237, 238, 247, 248, 249
Villani, Andrea 93
Vrijhof, Pieter A. 140
von Rummel, Philipp 210
Vuong, Lily C. 2
Vout, Caroline 18
Waardenberg, Jacques 140
Wainwright, John J. 155
Walker, Paul E. 222
Wallace-Hadrill, Andrew 42
Wāqidī, Muḥammad b. ʿUmar al- 223, 226
Webb, Ruth 182, 187, 193
Weiss, Zeev 180, 181, 188
Weitzmann, Kurt 256
Wendt, Heidi 143

Werner, Daniel S.	87
Wharton, Annabel	64
Wheeler, Brannon, M.	222, 223
Whitby, Michael	243
White, John F.	53
White, L. Michael	25
Whitehouse, Harvey	149
Wilhite, David E.	16, 25
Wilkinson, Kate	169
Williams, Jonathan	43
Williams, Megan H.	192
Wilson, Walter, T.	160
Wimbush, Vincent	134
Winston, Diane	133
Wistrand, Magnus	179, 182
Woolf, Greg	179
Wortley, John	250
Wright, Wilmer C.	83
Wyke, Maria	21
Young, Francis	183
Zanker, Paul	31, 34, 37, 54
Zelzer, Michaela	65
Zwemer, Samuel M.	221

Subject Index

'Abbāsids, 222, 222 n. 11
Abraham, 173
Abū Bakr al-Ṣiddīq, 226
Acts of John, 253
Adam (of Genesis), 99, 160
Alcibiades, 115, 116, 117. *See also* Proclus's *Commentary on the First Alcibiades*
Aleppo, 239, 240, 241
Alexander of Alexandria, 47
allegoresis. *See* allegorical exegesis
allegorical exegesis
  biblical/scriptural, 89, 94, 96, 97, 99, 103, 105
  of Celsus, 94, 99
  of Hierocles, 86
  of Homer, 92, 95
  of Numenius, 88–89
  of Origen, 31–33, 88–89, 91, 94, 96, 97, 98, 99, 100, 103
  of Philo, 103
  of Plato, 89, 96, 97
  of Porphyry, 88
  Stoic, 88, 94, 96
altar(s), 57, 58, 69, 150, 190, 208, 209, 214, 247, 248, 254. *See also* shrine(s)
  as symbol, 58
  and martyr remains, 208, 209. *See also* relic(s); martyr(s)
  Christian, 58
  church, 57, 208
  non-Christian, 58
  on coins, 57–59, 60
  Roman style, 58
  votive type, 58, 59
  with crosses, 57
  with snakes, 60
Ambrose (bishop of Milan), 13, 14, 64, 65, 66, 67, 68, 69, 70, 71, 75, 137, 168, 169, 170–72, 173, 174, 175, 176, 177, 209, 211, 212
  and language, 64–65, 64 n. 3, 72 n. 21, 74, 75
  and the palace/*regia*, 63, 66, 67, 70, 71, 72, 73, 74, 75
  and the soul, 63, 64, 170, 172–73, 174, 175, 176, 177
  and the synagogue/*synagoga* controversy, 65, 66, 67, 68, 69, 70, 71, 72, 73, 74, 75. *See also* Callinicum
  building(s)/structure(s) of, 63, 64, 65, 66, 68, 69, 70, 72, 74, 75
  church/*ecclesia* of, 63, 66, 67, 68, 69–70, 71, 72, 73, 75
  Isaac, or The Soul, 170, 170 n. 15, 173, 174
  On Abraham, 173
  on invisible beings, 63, 64 n. 3, 74, 75
  On virginity, 172, 173
  On virgins, 172, 174
Ammonius (Origen's teacher), 86, 87, 88, 89, 90, 93
amphitheater. *See* theater.
ampulla, 237
angels, 57, 63, 99, 142, 143, 144, 150, 155, 172, 173, 174, 234
Antioch, 234, 235, 236, 238, 242, 243, 244, 245, 248
  Great church, 199–200, 234, n. 2, 236, 238, 244, 245
Apion (Alexandrian grammarian), 160

Apocalypse of John, 81
Apolophanes, 88
apostles, 146, 147, 150, 213
architecture, 3, 11, 13, 27, 30, 206, 215
Ardabur (son of Aspar), 242
Aristobulus of Alexandria, 99
Aristotle, 86, 87, 95, 158
Arius of Alexandria, 47
ascetic(ism), 137, 146, 162, 167, 169, 170, 170 n. 15, 171, 172, 173, 174, 176, 186
Asclepius, 199, 251, 252, 253, 254, 255
   priest(s) of, 18, 19, 22. *See also* priest(s)/priestess(es); priesthood
Asklepieion, 252, 254, 255
Asklepios, Palestine, 199. *See also* Ascelpius
Aspar (commander of the East), 242
astragalomacy. *See* knuckle bones (ancient)
astrology/astrologers, 122, 144
Athanasius of Alexandria, 92
Athenegoras of Athens, 139, 143, 186
Attis (consort of Magna Marta), 124. *See also* Magna Marta
Augustine of Hippo, 169, 186, 211
Aurelian, 53, 53 n. 32, 54 n. 36
   walls, 205, 206
avodah zarah, 190
baptism(al), 36, 187, 212, 213
   candidates, 187, 194
   ceremonies, 213
   rites, 187
   vows, 187, 194
"barbarian(s)," 3, 80, 81, 94, 105, 111, 160, 182, 183, 185
Bardaisan of Edessa, 89, 102
Bar-Ḥaṭar and Simeon bar-Eupolemos, 235, 236, 237, 238, 239, 240, 241, 242, 244
   The Syriac Life of Symeon the Stylite the Elder, 235, 235 n. 6, 236, 238, 239, 239 n. 19, 241, 244–45
Basil of Caesarea, 128
basilica(s), 69, 206, 207, 208, 213, 215, 239 n. 19. *See also* church(es)

Ambrosiana, 72
Apostolorum, 69, 72. *See also* basilica, Romana
   cruciform, 234 n. 2, 239 n. 19
   funerary, 206, 207, 210, 211
   Milanese, 68
   of San Giovanni e Paolo, 207–8, 208 n. 18
   Portiana, 68
   Romana, 69, 72
   Santa Sabina, 205, 210, 212, 213, 216, 217
beard(s), 27, 29, 35, 37. *See also* hair
bedchamber, 173, 176. *See also* Christ
Bethlehem, 213
bishop(s), 6, 63, 72, 73, 120, 123, 128, 129, 137, 139, 140, 147, 148, 149, 150, 151, 152, 153, 167, 171, 172, 174, 212, 214, 244
   of Antioch, 244
   of Callinicum, 13, 65, 67, 71, 72, 73
   of Eclanum, 169
   of Milan, 71, 170, 172, 174, 175
   of Rome, 207, 212
   powers of, 63, 139, 139 n. 1, 140, 143, 146, 147, 148, 149, 150, 151, 152–53, 171
boundary stone, 240, 243
Bourdieu, Pierre
   and disinterestedness, 145, 146, 150
   theory of fields, 144, 144 nn. 16; 18, 146, 147, 148
   theory of symbolic capital, 6, 44, 145 n. 21. *See also* capital
brandea, 200, 209, 217. *See also* relic(s)
brides, 173, 175, 176, 177, 212. *See also* Christ, brides of
Byzantine
   army, 244
   art, 253, 256
   artisans, 229
   crosses, 257
   healing shrines, 247, 254. *See also* shrine(s)
   icons, 214 n. 50, 253. *See also* icon(s)

SUBJECT INDEX

pilgrim shrines, 247, 254. *See also* shrine(s)
votives, 247–51
Callinicum (Syria), 13, 65, 66–75
  bishop of. *See* bishop(s)
  riot at, 65, 65 n. 4, 66, 70, 71, 72
  synagogue. *See* Ambrose's synagogue controversy
cannibalism, 182
capital
  cultural, 6, 12, 29, 35, 39, 54, 145 n. 21, 146
  human, 152, 153
  social, 137, 144 n. 16;18, 145, 145 n. 21, 149, 150
  symbolic, 6, 44, 144 nn. 16 and 18, 145, 145 n. 21, 147, 150, 156, 156 n. 5, 157, 158, 160, 163, 165
Carpocratians, 37
Carthage, 12, 15, 18, 22, 23, 23 n. 29, 24, 25, 187, 192
Celestine I (bishop of Rome), 205
Celsus, 94. *See also* Origen of Alexandria; *Against Celsus*
chastity, 168, 172
church(es), 5, 57, 63, 66, 67, 68, 69, 70, 71, 72, 73, 99, 148, 150, 152, 153, 174, 175, 176, 186, 187, 193, 200, 205, 206, 207, 207 n. 11, 208, 208 n. 18, 209, 210, 211, 212, 215, 216, 217, 241, 249, 251, 252, 253. *See also* basilica(s); altar(s)
  altar(s). *See* altar(s)
  councils, 148
  fathers, 1, 180, 181, 187
  funerary, 209, 211
  healing, 200, 211, 212, 215, 216, 217
  of Ambrose. *See* Ambrose (bishop of Milan)
  of Saint Demetrios (Thessalonike), 249
  of San Pietro in Vincoli, 209
  of Santa Croce, 209
  of Santa Maria Antiqua, 36, 38, 39
  of Sant'Ambrogio, 209
  of Santa Sabina. *See* basilica(s).

  of the Great, 234 n. 2, 236. *See also* Antioch church
  of the Monastery of the Syrians (Wādi Natrūn), 249
  Roman, 206, 208, 209, 211, 215, 216
  titular. *See* titular
Christ, 27, 37, 38, 67, 68, 69, 72, 81, 155, 156, 169, 173, 174, 176, 187 n. 19, 210, 213, 215, 216, 217, 233, 249, 253, 255, 257. *See also* Jesus
  brides of, 29, 169, 173, 175, 176
  -logos, 101
Christian,
  apologists, 181, 182, 186, 194
  art, 11, 28, 32, 33, 38, 40, 208
  assembly, 21, 24, 26, 155, 163, 164
  community, 12, 15, 17, 21, 22, 24, 29, 32, 40, 69, 170 n. 15, 172, 193, 194, 220, 222
  identity. *See* identity
  martyrdom. *See* martyrdom
Chrysippus, 158
Cicero, 158
circus. *See* spectacle (Roman)
civic power, 137, 139, 139 n. 1, 152–53, 149
  and bishops, 152–53. *See also* bishop(s)
  religion, 46 n. 17, 121, 122, 123, 128, 140, 148, 149, 152
Clement of Alexandria, 37, 88, 143
clothing, 3, 12, 14, 16, 17, 18, 19, 21, 22, 23, 29, 34, 37, 174. *See also* dress
codex calendar, 206
coin(s), 11, 13, 14, 41, 42, 43, 44, 45, 46, 228
  and iconography, 44, 47, 48, 49, 55, 56, 57
  and symbols, 47, 56, 57, 58, 60
  military themed, 44, 48, 51, 54, 56
  of Constantine, 13, 14, 41–61
  tetrarchic style, 48, 49, 50, 52
  with altars. *See* altar(s)
  with crosses, 56, 57
  with snakes, 59, 60, n. 44
  with Sol, 53, 54–56, 57, 59. *See also* Sol

Constantine (emperor), 13, 14, 41–61, 244
  as Christian, 41, 44, 45, 46, 47, 55, 57, 60
  as Pontifex Maximus, 59, 59 n. 43
  coinage of, 41, 42, 44, 46, 47, 48–49, 50–60. See also coin(s)
  edicts of, 44, 45, 55
cosmos, 79, 81, 90, 102, 108, 113, 114, 115, 117, 146, 163
costume, 17, 18, 19, 34, 35
  priestly, 19
Council of Nicaea, 59
Cronius (the Pythagorean), 88
cross(es), 56, 57, 209, 240, 241, 248, 256, 257, 258. See also altar(s); votive(s)
crown(s), 18, 19, 20, 22, 29, 59. See also wreath(s)
  laurel, 20, 22, 24
cult(s), 17, 23, 24, 59, 83, 126, 143, 150, 208 n. 18, 235, 236, 242
  Carthaginian, 22, 23 n. 29
  civic, 127, 128
  Egyptian, 162
  Ephesian, 157
  Greek, 143
  imperial, 19, 190, 234
  Milanese, 71, 72
  of Bellona, 22
  of John the Baptist. See John the Baptist
  of Magna Mater. See Magna Mater
  of martyrs, 72, 143, 149, 206, 210, 211
  of Metroac. See Metroac
  of Muhammad. See Muhammad
  of Paul. See Paul
  of Peter. See Peter
  of saints, 149, 167
  of Saturn, 23
  of Sol, 54, 54 n. 36
  of Symeon. See Symeon the Stylite the Elder
  of Telneshe. See Telneshe
  of the dead, 207
  practices, 126, 127
  relic. See relic(s)
  Roman, 22, 60, 127
cult sites (pilgrimage sites), 234, 235, 236, 237, 238, 239, 239 nn. 18–19, 240, 241, 242, 243, 244, 245
  of Abu Menas in Egypt, 237, 247
  of Saint John in Asia Minor, 237
  of Symeon the Stylite the Elder in Syria (Qal'at Sem'an), 234, 235, 236, 238, 251. See also Telneshe
  of Thekla in Silifke (Aya Tekla; Meriamlik), 235. See also Thecla of Iconium
  tomb of Symeon the Stylite at Great Church in Antioch, 234, 234 n. 2, 236, 238, 242, 244, 245
cultural
  appropriation, 28, 29, 34, 38, 39, 40
  capital. See capital
  competition, 12, 29, 40, 44
  producers/elites, 1, 3, 4, 6, 12, 16, 30, 45, 46, 56, 79, 121, 122, 128, 137. See also religious elites
  production, 6, 14, 29, 40, 79, 123, 137
Damascius (the Neoplatonist), 109, 115 n. 19
Demetrius (bishop of Alexandria), 147
demon(s), 15, 20–21, 22, 63, 65, 93, 143, 150, 151, 192, 193, 256. See also spirit(s)
Deuteronomy (book of) 183, 183 n. 13
dice (ancient), 144. See also knuckle bones
Diogenes of Sinope, 146
Dionysius of Alexandria, 100
Dionysius of Halicarnassus, 158
divination/divinatory, 122, 124, 126, 143, 144, 148, 183
dreams, 144, 151, 255, 256
dress, 11, 12, 13, 15, 16, 17, 18, 20, 21, 22, 27, 29, 34, 35, 36, 37, 38, 185, 206
  for women, 21, 23, 169 n. 11
  idolatrous, 17, 20, 23, 26
  modest/virtuous, 12, 21, 22
Easter, 211

SUBJECT INDEX

Egypt(ian), 32, 99, 109 n. 6, 112, 152, 183, 184, 230, 237
  cult, 162. *See also* cult(s)
  Hermes, 111 n. 12,
  pharaoh, 69
  priest, 83 n. 5, 91, 152. *See also* priest(s)/priestess(es); priesthood
  monk, 187
  mysteries, 156, 158. *See* mystery
  wisdom. *See* wisdom
elite religion. *See* religious elite
elite(s)/specialist(s), 1, 4, 6, 7, 12, 16, 26, 39, 40, 41, 44, 46, 56, 83, 122, 123, 124, 127, 128, 136, 137, 138, 139, 140, 141, 143, 146, 147, 148, 150, 151, 152, 165, 167, 168, 171, 172, 177, 179, 181, 186, 207, 212, 213, 216. *See also* religious elite(s)
Epiphanius of Salamis, 103
Eucharist, 51, 207 n. 11, 211, 212–13, 216, 239
eulogia, 247, 256
εὐσέβεια. *See* piety
Eusebius of Caesarea, 44, 55, 86, 86 n. 5, 88, 92, 112 n. 14, 253
Evagrius Scholasticus, 91, 243 n. 25, 244 n. 26
fermentum, 207, 207 n. 11, 212
funerary art, 11, 13, 14, 29, 217. *See also* church(es); basilica(s)
Galerius (emperor), 48–49 nn. 24–25, 49, 50
games, 21, 24, 179, 180, 181, 183, 187, 191, 192, 195. *See also* spectacle
garb, 17, 19, 21, 22, 23, 34, 39. *See also* dress
garments, 12, 18, 19, 29, 30. *See also* dress
Genesis (book of), 81, 89, 90, 97, 97 n. 36, 98, 99, 100, 102
Gindaros, Syria, 241, 241 n. 20
gnostic(ism), 28, 97, 103, 135
Gregory of Nazianzus, 128
Gregory of Nyssa, 32, 91
Gregory of Tours, 225 n. 23
Gregory the Great, 209

hagiography, 220, 236, 236 n. 8
hair, 29, 35, 37. *See also* beard(s); Muhammad
haircuts, 184, 185
headwear, 18
healing
  hand, 247 n. 1, 256
  rituals, 224, 254–56
  shrines. *See* shrine(s)
Hebrew Bible, 80, 81, 84. *See also* Old Testament
Hercules, 49 n. 25, 54, 54 n. 33
heresy, 3, 28, 103, 141, 146
Hermes, 111, 111 n. 12, 54 n. 33
Hermias (the Neoplatonist), 86, 87
Hesiod, 93, 99, 147
  Pandora myth. *See* myth(s)
Hierocles (the Neoplatonist), 86, 87, 95, 104
ḥnānā, 236, 236 n. 8, 238, 239 n. 18, 202, 220 n. 2, 240, 241, 244. *See also* sacred substances
Homer, 27, 81, 86, 87 n. 8, 88, 91, 92, 93, 94, 95, 147
  Odyssey of, 88
Hosea (book of), 81
Hypogeum of the Aurelii, 27, 28, 31
Iamblichus of Chalcis, 81, 82, 83, 83 n. 5, 86, 108, 109, 110, 110 nn. 7–10, 111, 111 n. 12, 112, 112 n. 14, 113, 114, 114 n. 17, 115, 117, 117 n. 21, 119, 119 n. 1, 126, 126 n. 20
iconography, 2, 3, 7, 27, 28, 36, 41, 42, 43, 44, 46 n. 18, 47, 48, 49, 54 n. 33, 56, 247 n. 1, 248, 249, 251, 254, 255, 258
  Christian, 36, 39, 41, 248, 249, 251, 254
  Augustan, 49, 57
  Constantinian, 41, 47, 48, 49, 55, 56, 57
icon(s), 214, 220, 253, 255
identity
  Christian, 12, 29, 32, 39, 170 n. 14, 172, 193, 194, 220, 222
  elite, 138. *See also* religious elite

SUBJECT INDEX

identity (cont.)
    Islamic/Muslim, 221, 222–23, 225, 226, 228, 229, 230, 231
    Jewish/rabbinic, 12, 192, 193, 194, 195
    religious, 3, 5, 27, 39, 169, 195, 200
    Roman, 169, 179
idol(atry), 12, 13, 15, 16, 17, 19, 20, 22, 23, 24, 26, 67, 84, 115, 148, 181, 185, 187, 188, 189, 190, 192, 193
impiety, 13, 67, 137, 157, 229. See also piety
incense, 190, 201, 214 n. 50, 243, 244, 251, 255, 256, 257
incubation, 251, 254, 255, 256, 257
Innocent I (pope), 211
Isaac (son of Abraham) 173–74
Isis, 17, 162, 163
    and Osiris, 161, 162, 163
Islamic,
    community, 223, 227, 230
    conquest, 225–26
    conversion, 228–29
    identity. See identity
    practice, 222, 227
    texts, 219, 222, 227, 231
Jerome, 169, 192
Jerusalem, 100, 213, 247
Jesus, 36, 37, 57, 94, 133, 146, 147, 156 n. 2. See also Christ
Jewish
    identity. See identity
    practice, 191, 228
    sanctuary, 14
    scriptures, 161. See also Hebrew Bible; Jewish literature
    wisdom. See wisdom
Job (book of), 81
John the Baptist, 39, 221, 249
    cult of, 221
    mosaic of, 249
    relic of, 221. See also relic(s)
John Chrysostom, 186, 211
Jonah (book of), 36, 81
Jovinian (the monk), 168, 169

Julian (bishop of Eclanum), 169. See also bishop(s)
Julian (emperor), 30, 83, 84 n. 7, 114 n. 17, 119, 120, 124, 128
    diet, 121, 124, 125, 126, 127, 128
    making-meaning of, 120, 122, 123, 128, 129
    philosophy of, 119, 120, 121, 128, 129
    piety of, 120, 124
    reforms of, 83–84, 120, 128
    religious program of, 119, 119 n. 1, 120, 121, 124–25, 127, 128, 129
    theurgic Neoplatonism, 119, 120, 121, 124, 126, 127, 128, 129
Justina (empress; wife of Valentinian II), 68
Justinian (Byzantine emperor), 104, 105
Justin Martyr, 139, 143
Khālid b. al-Walīd, 49 n. 24, 224, 225–26
knuckle bones (ancient), 144, 146. See also dice (ancient)
Lactantius, 23, 55
Lebanon, 240, 241, 243
Lent, 239
Leviticus (book of) 183
Licinius (emperor), 41, 49 n. 25, 55, 59, 60
Life of Saint Nicholas of Sion, 236 n. 8
literate specialist(s)/expert(s). See religious elite
Longinus, 88, 89, 90, 92
Ma'art al-Nu'man Treasure, 249, 252
magic(ians), 64, 183, 188, 190, 254
Magna Marta, 83, 121, 124, 125, 127, 127 n. 22
mantles, 11, 17, 18, 21, 30, 34, 35, 36, 37, 38, 129. See also dress
Marcion(ites), 103, 139, 143
marriage, 168, 169. See also nuptial imagery
martyrdom, 71, 72, 72 n. 21, 74, 142, 208, 217
martyr(s), 71, 72, 146, 147, 149, 150, 153, 205, 206, 208, 209, 211, 215, 217, 225, 244

SUBJECT INDEX

cults of, 72, 143, 206, 210, 211. *See also* cult(s)
relics of. *See* relic(s)
remains/bodies of, 72, 206, 207, 208, 209, 244, 255
shrines/chapels of, 153, 200, 206 n. 7, 215, 216, 217, 220
tombs of, 143, 150, 208, 215
veneration of, 205, 206
worship of, 206, 211
masculinity, 20
material culture, 3, 11, 13, 32, 247
Maximian (emperor), 49 n. 25, 53
Metroac, 83, 84, 127
rites of purification, 124, 125, 126, 127
midrash, 181, 183, 184, 185
Mikilta de Arayot, 183, 184–85, 191, 194–95
Milan, 65, 66, 67, 68, 69, 70, 71, 72, 73, 74, 75, 170, 171, 172, 173, 209
miracles, 74, 96, 233, 236, 239, 239 n. 18, 243, 247, 248, 249, 250, 251, 255
Mishnah, 181
modes of religiosity, 46 nn. 17–18, 121–24, 121 nn. 5–12, 136, 141, 142. *See also* Stowers, Stanley
Moses, 32, 81, 86 n. 5, 94, 160, 234
Muhammad (the Prophet), 200, 202, 219, 221, 222, 224, 225, 227, 228, 229–31
ablution water of, 219, 224
cloak of, 225
companions of, 219, 220, 223, 224, 225, 226, 227, 229, 230
hair of, 200, 202, 219, 222, 223, 224, 225, 226, 227, 229, 230, 231
nail clippings of, 200, 225, 230
relics of, 221, 222, 223, 224, 225, 227, 228, 229, 230, 231. *See also* relic(s)
saliva/phlegm/spittle of, 219, 226
sweat of, 224–25
tomb of, 228, 229
veneration of, 228, 230
Muslim identity. *See* identity
mystery (μυστήριον), 88, 113, 114 n. 16, 127, 155, 155 n. 1, 156, 156 n. 2, 157 n. 6, 158, 159, 160, 161, 162, 163, 164, 165
of piety, 155, 156, 157 n. 6, 163, 164
mystic(al), 112, 157 n. 6, 158, 170
myth(ology), 2, 4, 31, 37, 81, 84, 87, 91, 94, 95, 96, 97, 98, 99, 100, 101, 102, 103, 104, 124, 127 n. 22, 164, 190
eschatological, 90, 95, 97, 100, 101–4
Greek, 95
-making, 33
Metroac, 83. *See also* Metroac
of Atlantis. *See* Plato(nic)
of "barbarian," 94. *See also* "barbarian"
of *Er*, 87, 88
of Poros, 97, 98, 99
of *Timaeus*. *See* Plato(nic)
Platonic. *See* Platon(ic)
protological, 90, 101–4
Neoplatonist(s)/Neoplatonism, 1, 3, 4, 79, 80, 85, 86, 86 n. 5, 87, 90, 93, 95, 97, 104, 107, 108, 110, 113, 114, 116, 119, 119 n. 1, 120, 121, 125, 126, 127, 128, 129
Neopythagorean(s), 85, 88, 95, 103
Nicomachus, 88
Nigrinus (the Neoplatonist), 30
Nomina Barbara, 111–14. *See also* theurgy
Numenius of Apamea, 88–89, 90, 92, 103
numismatics, 41, 42, 44, 47, 48, 49, 51, 55, 61. *See also* coin(s)
nuptial imagery/metaphor, 168, 170, 171. *See also* marriage
oaths, 67, 73. *See also* vows
Olympiodorus, 87
Orpheus, 86
Old Testament, 103. *See also* Hebrew Bible
Origen of Alexandria, 31, 80–81, 82, 85–105, 147, 153, 168, 170, 171, 175–76, 177
Against Celsus, 82, 93, 104
as a Christian, 80, 86, 87, 89, 90, 91, 92, 93, 95, 98, 99, 102, 103, 104, 105

Origen of Alexandria (cont.)
   as a Neoplatonist, 80, 87–95
   Commentary on Genesis, 98, 99, 102
   Commentary on John, 100, 104
   Commentary on Matthew, 100
   First Principles, 100, 104
   Homilies on Jeremiah, 100
   Homily on Genesis, 100
   Metensomatosis, 101
orthodox(y), 3, 141, 142, 145, 146, 181, 221
paideia, 12, 18, 27, 28, 29, 31, 38, 40, 146, 153
pallium, 12, 14, 17, 18, 19, 21–22, 23, 30, 34. *See also* toga
Pammachius (senator), 169
pastoral epistles/letters, 155, 164
Paul, 139, 143, 164, 176, 214, 258
   as martyr, 72
   cult of, 72
   mosaics of, 214
Paulinus, 215, 216
Peter, 210, 214, 258
   as martyr, 72
   as saint, 210
   cult of, 72
   mosaics of, 214
Pew Research Center, 133
Philo of Alexandria, 88, 89, 95, 97, 99, 102, 103, 156, 157, 159–61, 163–65
   On the Cherubim, 160
   piety of, 159–61. *See also* piety
Philodemus, 157
philosopher
   look, 30, 31, 34, 37, 40. *See also* philosopher type
   robes, 30
   type, 11, 12, 14, 28, 29, 30, 31, 34, 35–36, 37, 38, 39, 40
piety, 4, 14, 16, 19, 59, 124, 157, 158, 159, 160, 161, 163, 165, 201, 202, 212, 250
   Christian, 13, 14, 20, 22, 54, 137, 155, 156, 163–65, 182, 195, 197
   εὐσέβεια, 155, 156, 156 n. 3, 156–57 n. 6, 158, 159, 160, 161, 163, 164, 165

Muslim, 200, 221, 226, 229
relic, 200, 201, 203
pilgrim(s), 201, 215, 216, 234, 237, 247, 251, 255
pilgrimage(s) site, 200, 201, 220, 223, 224, 226, 234 n. 2, 237, 238. *See also* cult sites
Plato, 37, 81, 85, 86, 87, 88, 89, 90, 91, 92, 93, 94, 95, 96, 97, 98, 99, 100, 101, 102, 103, 104, 105, 110, 111 nn. 12–13, 114–15, 125, 157, 158
Plato(nic). *See also* Neoplatonism
   Atlantis myth, 89, 90
   creation myth, 102
   demiurge, 86
   dialogues, 85, 86, 87, 89, 91, 92, 93, 94, 95, 96, 103, 158
   Euthyphro, 157
   myths of, 4, 37, 87, 90, 95, 97, 99, 100, 101
   Phaedrus, 158, 159
   Poros myth, 97, 98, 99
   Republic, 86, 86 n. 5, 87 n. 8, 89
   Symposium, 98
   Timaeus, 87, 89, 90, 92, 97, 102, 104
Plotinus (disciple of Ammonius), 86, 87, 92, 104, 110, 110 n. 9, 116, 170
Plutarch of Chaeronea, 137, 156, 157, 158, 161–62, 163, 164
popular versus elite religion, 136, 140–41, 147, 148, 150, 151, 167, 168, 177
Porphyry (the Neoplatonist), 80, 81, 82, 83 n. 6, 86, 86 n. 5, 87, 88, 89, 90, 92, 93, 94, 95, 104, 105, 108, 109, 111, 112, 113
priest(s)/priestess(es), 15, 17, 18, 19, 22, 23 n. 29, 53 n. 32, 54, 83 n. 5, 91, 123, 128, 147, 150, 152, 153, 205, 239, 254, 256
priesthood, 54, 127, 152–53
procession, 126, 212–13, 216, 234, 242–44
Proclus (the Neoplatonist), 79, 87, 89, 90–91, 92, 93, 94, 95, 104, 105, 109, 110, 115, 116, 117, 118

prophet(s), 81, 175–76. *See also* Muhammad (the Prophet)
Psalms (book of), 191–94
purity, 32, 83, 116, 145, 169, 172, 173
Pythagoras of Samos, 37, 86, 88, 163, 193. *See also* Neopythagoreans
Qalʿat Semʿān/Qalʾat Simʾan, 200, 239 n. 19, 251, 253, 255. *See also* Symeon the Stylite the Elder; cult site(s)
Quintilian, 158
Qurʾān, 133, 228
Rabbi Meir, 184, 188, 189, 190
rabbinic
  identity. *See* identity
  literature/texts, 138, 180, 181, 183, 184, 186–90, 188 n. 21, 193, 194, 195. *See also* Jewish literature
rabbis, 138, 180, 181, 185, 187
Rebecca (wife of Isaac), 173–74
relic(s), 5, 75, 143, 150, 167, 199, 200–201, 202, 205, 206, 207, 208, 209, 210, 219, 220, 221–23, 225, 230, 231, 233
  and ritual, 229
  and cult site(s). *See* cult site(s)
  as multisensory experience, 201, 202
  body parts/corporeal, 75, 167, 200, 201, 202, 206, 208, 209, 210, 217, 219, 220, 225, 235, 237
  contact substances, 200, 201, 209, 217, 220, 237, 255. *See also* brandea
  for healing/protecting/power, 200, 202, 224, 225, 230, 231, 235, 238
  noncorporeal, 204, 210, 237
  of John the Baptist. *See* John the Baptist
  of martry(s), 150, 207, 208, 210, 216, 217, 231
  of Muhammad. *See* Muhammad
  of saints, 72, 150, 216, 217, 220, 221, 225, 231, 235
  of Symeon the Sytlites the Elder. *See* Symeon the Stylite the Elder
  piety of. *See* piety
  veneration of, 122, 202, 220, 221, 222, 225, 226, 227, 228, 229, 237

religion of everyday social exchange, 46 n. 17, 121, 122, 123, 140, 141, 142, 147, 148, 149, 150, 151. *See also* popular religion; Stowers, Stanley
religious
  expert(s)/specialist(s), 134, 135, 140, 155, 156, 163, 164, 171
  literate specialist(s)/expert(s), 46, 46 nn. 17–18, 120, 121, 122, 123, 124, 127, 128, 129, 136, 137, 139, 143, 144, 146, 147, 148, 150, 151, 152, 153, 171
  nonexpert(s)/popular, 133, 135, 140, 171
reliquary, 215, 223, 225, 234 n. 2, 237
Revelation (book of) 97, 97 n. 36, 100, 100 n. 44
Roman
  Christian(ity), 39, 40, 205, 206, 207, 210, 211, 212
  coins. *See* coin(s)
  identity. *See* identity
  sack of, 210, 210 n. 26
  spectacle. *See* spectacle
sacred substance(s), 236–38, 239 n. 18, 241
  oil, 200, 214 n. 50, 220 n. 2, 235, 236–37, 238, 239 n. 18, 244, 247
  water, 200, 220 n. 2, 235, 236–37, 238, 239 n. 18, 244, 247, 255
  dust/dirt, 200, 235, 236, 238, 239 n. 18, 244, 247
  pebbles/stones, 200, 237
sacrifice, 23, 24, 57, 59, 59 n. 43, 70, 84 n. 7, 119, 122, 124, 126, 171, 173, 188, 190
saint(s), 100, 142, 146, 149, 150, 167, 206, 221, 213, 214, 215, 216, 217, 220, 221, 222, 225, 231, 235, 237, 238, 239, 239 n. 19, 240, 241, 242, 243, 243 n. 25, 244, 245, 248, 249, 250, 251, 252, 255, 256, 257, 258
  Damianos, 257
  Demetrios, 249, 251
  Gervasius, 209

saint(s) (*cont.*)
   John, 247, 251, 253
   Kosmas, 257
   Peter. *See* Peter
   Protasius, 209
   relics. *See* relic(s)
   Sergius, 225
   shrines. *See* shrine(s)
   Stephen, 257
   Symeon/Simeon. *See* Symeon the Stylite the Elder
   Thecla. *See* Thecla of Iconium
sanctuary, 14, 245, 249, 250
Santa
   Maria Antiqua. *See* church(es)
   Prudenziana, 213
   Sabina. *See* basilica(s)
Sarah (wife of Abraham), 173
sarcophagi, 11, 12, 14, 28, 29 n. 7, 31, 34, 35, 36, 37, 38, 39, 217
   Peregrinus, L. Pullius, 34, 35, 36, 39
scroll(s), 30, 34, 36, 37, 38. *See also* philosopher type; philosopher look
semiotic(s), 4, 12, 13, 18, 23
   code, 12
   language, 12
Septimius Severus, 53
Septuagint (LXX), 159, 161
shrine(s), 199, 201, 202, 220, 221, 222, 247, 248, 249, 254. *See also* basilica(s); church(es)
   healing, 251, 252, 254, 255
   martyrs. *See* martyr(s)
   of Abu Menas (Egypt), 237, 247, 248
   of Artemios, 251
   of Asklepieia, 251, 252, 254
   of Cosmas, 251
   of Cyrus, 247, 249, 251
   of Damian, 251
   of Felix. *See* Paulinus
   of John (Asian Minor), 237, 247, 249, 251
   of Qal'at Sem'ān. *See* Qal'at Sem'ān
   of Symeon/Simeon. *See* Symeon the Stylite the Elder; Telneshe
   of Telneshe. *See* Telneshe
   saints, 214, 215, 220, 221, 222
Simeon bar-Eupolemos. *See* Bar-Ḥaṭar and Simeon bar-Eupolemos
Simeon the Elder. *See* Symeon the Stylite the Elder
Simeon the Younger. *See* Symeon the Younger
sin(ners), 15, 58, 102, 172, 177, 189, 191, 234, 248
Socrates, 89, 114 n. 16, 146, 157, 158
Sol, 53, 54, 55, 56, 57, 59. *See also* coin(s)
Song of Songs, 97, 137, 168, 169, 170, 171, 173
Sophronius (patriarch of Jerusalem), 247–48
spectacle (Roman), 137–38, 179, 180, 181, 182, 183, 184, 185, 186, 187, 188, 190, 192, 194, 195
   as entertainment, 179, 180, 181, 182, 185, 187, 188, 190, 191
   as forbidden for Christians, 180, 181–82, 183, 185, 186–87, 191, 192, 193, 194, 195
   as forbidden for Jews, 181, 185, 187–90, 193, 194, 195
spirits, 90, 93, 102, 155, 192
   evil, 90, 241. *See also* demon(s)
Stoic(ism), 88, 94, 96, 97, 158, 163
Suhayl b. 'Amr, 226
sun god. *See* Sol
superstition, 136, 148, 157, 160, 161, 162, 163, 164, 221, 226
symbolic capital. *See* capital, symbolic
Symeon the Stylite the Elder, 200, 233, 233 n. 1, 234, 234 n. 2, 238, 239, 244, 252, 254, 256
   body of, 234, 234 n. 2, 235, 236, 238, 242, 243, 244, 245
   column of, 234, 239 n. 18
   cult of, 234, 236, 238, 244–45. *See also* cult site(s)
   cult site of. *See* cult site(s)
   death of, 233 n. 1, 235, 241, 242, 244 n. 26, 245

SUBJECT INDEX 325

miracles of, 243
power/protection of, 234, 235, 238, 239, 240, 241, 242, 243, 243 n. 25, 245
relics of, 234
sanctity of, 236, 238, 240, 241, 242, 245
shrine of, 234, 245
tomb of, 234, 244
veneration of, 238, 241, 242
Symeon the Younger, 225
synagogue(s)/*synagoga*, 5, 13, 14
  at Callinicum. *See* Ambrose; Callinicum
Syrianus, 90
Tatian the Syrian, 143, 182, 183, 185, 186, 191, 194
Telneshe (Telanisso; Deir Sim'an), 234, 234 n. 2, 235, 236, 238, 239, 240, 241, 242, 243, 245. *See also* cult site(s); Symeon the Stylite the Elder
temple, 15, 19, 20, 21, 53, 67, 97 n. 36, 124, 126,
Tertullian of Carthage, 12, 13, 14, 15, 16, 17, 18, 19, 20, 21, 22, 23–24, 25, 26, 30, 138, 186, 187, 188 n. 21, 189, 191, 192, 193, 194, 195
theater, 24, 68, 138, 179, 180, 181, 182, 183, 184, 185, 186, 187, 187 n. 19, 188, 189, 190, 191, 192, 193, 194, 195
Thecla of Iconium, 235, 248, 250
Theodoret (bishop of Cyrrhus), 233, 233 n.1, 239 n. 19, 250, 252
Theodosius (emperor) 13, 40, 65, 66, 71, 72, 72 n. 21, 73, 74, 75
  code of, 68
theory,
  cultural, 28, 32
  dependency, 31, 32
  of fields, 144. *See also* Bourdieu, Pierre
  of symbolic capital. *See* capital, symbolic; Bourdieu, Pierre
  social, 28
theurgy/theurgists, 82, 83, 108, 111–16, 119, 120, 121, 125, 126, 126 n. 20

Neoplatonism. *See* Julian (emperor); Neoplatonism
titulus, 210, 211, 212, 216, 217
  church(es), 200, 207, 207 n. 11, 210, 211, 212. *See also* church(es)
toga, 12, 13, 14, 16, 17, 18, 19, 20, 21, 23, 30, 35. *See also* pallium
topography, 235, 238, 239, 240, 241, 243
torah, 185, 189, 190, 191, 193, 194
  study of, 189, 190, 191, 193, 194
Tosefta, 181, 188, 189 n. 25, 190, 191, 192, 193 n. 30, 194, 195
Trajan (emperor), 182
transculturation, 33, 38, 40
tunics, 17, 18, 19, 21, 22, 30, 34, 35, 99, 102. *See also* dress
Umayyads, 221, 222, 227, 229, 228, 230
Umm Salama (wife of the Prophet), 223–24, 229
Umm Sulaym (the Prophet's companion), 223
Valentinian II (emperor), 68
Valentinus (emperor), 139, 143
Valerian (emperor), 57
veil(ing), 18, 25 n. 37, 169, 170, 172. *See also* virgin(s)
  ceremony, 170
Vespasian (emperor), 57
Vigilantius (presbyter), 211
virgin(s)/virginity, 17, 168, 169, 172, 173, 174, 175, 177
  consecrated, 172, 174
  the Virgin and Child, 256
votive(s), 58, 59, 143, 148, 247, 248, 249, 251, 253, 254
  altars. *See* altar(s)
  and healing hand, 256–58
  and snakes, 252, 253
  body-part, 250
  coin(s), 247, 252. *See also* coin(s)
  Daniel, 250
  eyes, 249, 251, 252
  Georgian, 249, 251
  iconographic, 248, 249, 251, 254, 258
  inscriptions, 247, 248, 252

votive(s) (*cont.*)
    lamps, 201, 255
    mosaic, 249
    mural, 249
    of Asklepieion, 252, 253. *See also* Asklepieion
    pre-Christian, 247 n. 1, 251–54, 257
    Symeon/Simeon, 252. *See* Symeon the Stylite the Elder
    thank offering(s)/χαριστήρια, 200, 250, 251
    to Asclepius, 225. *See also* Asclepius
vows, 57, 57 n. 38, 70, 73, 187, 194, 249
"ways of the Amorites," 184
wisdom
    ancient, 4, 80, 81, 107, 108, 109, 110 nn. 9–10, 111, 114, 115, 117, 158, 160, 162
    Christian, 39
    Egyptian, 90
    Greek, 39, 40, 81, 107, 110, 114, 115
    Jewish, 18, 22, 23, 24, 39, 57, 81, 84, 94, 99, 159
wreaths, 16, 18, 19, 22, 23, 24, 57. *See also* crowns
Zeus, 94, 98

www.ingramcontent.com/pod-product-compliance
Lightning Source LLC
Chambersburg PA
CBHW021117300426
44113CB00006B/179